Between Bonn and Berlin

Between Bonn and Berlin

German Politics Adrift?

edited by
Mary N. Hampton and Christian Søe

ROWMAN & LITTLEFIELD PUBLISHERS, INC.
Lanham • Boulder • New York • Oxford

ROWMAN & LITTLEFIELD PUBLISHERS, INC.

Published in the United States of America
by Rowman & Littlefield Publishers, Inc.
4720 Boston Way, Lanham, Maryland 20706
http://www.rowmanlittlefield.com

12 Hid's Copse Road
Cumnor Hill, Oxford OX2 9JJ, England

British Library Cataloguing in Publication Information Available

Library of Congress Cataloging-in-Publication Data

Between Bonn and Berlin : German politics adrift? / edited by Mary N.
  Hampton and Christian Søe.
    p. cm.
   Includes bibliographical references and index.
   ISBN 0–8476–9008–3 (alk. paper). — ISBN 0–8476–9009–1 (pbk. :ak.
paper)
    1. Germany—Politics and government—1990– 2. Political parties—
Germany. 3. Germany—Economic conditions—1990– 4. European
Union—Germany. I. Hampton, Mary N. II. Søe, Christian.
JN3971.A91B42 1999
320.943'09'049—dc21   99–15377
                                           CIP

Printed in the United States of America

♾™ The paper used in this publication meets the minimum requirements of American
National Standard for Information Sciences—Permanence of Paper for Printed Library
Materials, ANSI Z39.48–1992.

Contents

Preface

This multi-author book examines politics in Germany at a time when the major central European power is returning its government center from Bonn to Berlin. The move coincides with a more profound transition in German politics. Governed since October 1998 by a new center-left coalition that is led by members of the first postwar generation in power, reunited Germany is in the process of adjusting politically to a greatly altered domestic and international context. It is hardly surprising that this adjustment shows no clear overall direction yet, but rather takes the form of a meandering interplay of continuity, change and drift.

Change has come rapidly to Germany during the last decade, to a polity that has long been regarded as unusually cautious and wary of political experimentation. But all along there has been a considerable element of continuity and sometimes rigidity as well. The authors seek to untangle important parts of the complicated web of current German politics by examining public opinion and the political parties in addition to several important domestic and international policy areas.

The pace and degree of political change in Germany have quickened since the watershed election of September 1998. All of the chapters include critical post-election data and analyses that are relevant to an understanding of the power shift and its policy implications. They seek to shed light on the new balance in Germany's party system as well as on possible shifts or continuities in its governing style and direction, while recognizing the futility of any attempt to anticipate the array of specific events or decisions in German politics.

Chancellor Gerhard Schröder's "red-green" government seems vulnerable to cleavages both between and within the two coalition parties. The Greens have not fully overcome the old fissures between their more idealistic and more pragmatic wings—sometimes simplified as *Fundis* (fundamentalists) and *Realos* (realists). Nor have the Social Democrats fully resolved the intra-party differences that have long divided their party. Such internal cleavages will potentially have an impact on the direction and stability of the new German government. Meanwhile the opposition parties will have to deal with their own challenges, while they seek a return to power or struggle for political space on an increasingly crowded parliamentary stage.

The sudden resignation from government and party office by Finance Minister and SPD leader Oskar Lafontaine in March 1999 took everyone by surprise. Yet this signal change has an explanation anticipated by the chapters that deal with the Social Democratic Party's internal divisions and with the economic or social policy challenges confronting the new government. Lafontaine was not only a major political rival to the center-oriented chancellor. He also represented an important traditional left tendency within the party that in no way disappeared from the political arena with its outspoken and preferred leader. Although Lafontaine's resignation may make Schröder's role as head of government less overtly contested, it leaves an important segment of the SPD dissatisfied, disgruntled, and potentially uncooperative regarding some of the chancellor's tentative policy moves toward what he calls "the new middle." Schröder has great political skills and enjoys widespread popular support. He moved quickly to take over the post of party leader left vacant by Lafontaine's departure, thereby putting a formal end to the problematic division in leadership that had dogged the new government during its first few months in power. One need only recall the political fate of the last SPD chancellor, Helmut Schmidt, to be reminded of the problems that could await a government leader faced with a disunited party.

The new government's support for NATO's military actions against Serbia is another recent event that reflects the complexities of the current transition in German politics. Both the chancellor and his foreign minister, Joschka Fischer (Greens), have been outspoken advocates of NATO, and both have based their support largely on the established precedent of Germany acting in solidarity with its democratic allies. In that sense, their policy represents an important element of continuity with past German policy. But it also reflects tremendous change, in that a center-left government now supports German combat participation in NATO's military intervention. The full challenge of this decision only becomes apparent in light of its potentially volatile impact on each of the two governing parties. Both the SPD, but especially the Greens, have strong pacifist and anti-militarist traditions. The official Green position until the spring of 1998 was that NATO would and should be disbanded in the near future. Initially, at least, the government's NATO policy therefore widened the fissures inside both coalition parties on military and defense policy.

In yet another early and major political test, the coalition modified a hotly contested first draft of its new citizenship bill that sought to liberalize the naturalization requirements for long-time foreign residents and automatically grant dual citizenship to their children born in Germany. In its revised form, the bill gained the support of the small Free Democratic Party by including an age limit of 23 years for dual citizenship. This compromise secured passage of the milestone legislation in the federal upper house (Bundesrat), where the coalition had lost its majority after the Hesse state election in February 1999.

Such signal events also contribute to the frequently raised question of whether the current coalition government will be able to hold together. While it is not the purpose of this volume to issue predictions on such matters, many chapters illuminate significant issues and considerations that will help assess the stability and direction of the new German government.

The editors wish to thank all the authors for their contributions, not least for their willingness to complete and revise them in light of the 1998 election outcome. Their cooperation in this matter has made the volume more useful in anticipating or explaining recent and emerging trends in German politics.

The editors are grateful to Dr. Louise L. Soe and Dr. Christoph Hanterman for their generous and indispensable professional contributions to the task of turning a collection of chapter manuscripts into camera readiness.

The project commenced in the spring of 1997, when both editors were doing political research in Germany. Mary Hampton was greatly helped in bringing the project to fruition by a Research Fellowship from NATO. Christian Søe was able to draw on the research benefits of a sabbatical semester granted by his university.

1

Introduction:
Toward a Berlin Republic

Mary N. Hampton and Christian Søe

The collapse of the Cold War order has spawned a great deal of speculation about political developments in Germany. When this central European power was reunified in 1990, after more than forty years of division during the Cold War, it was alone among the major powers on the continent to emerge larger and stronger from the long East-West confrontation. The move of Germany's government and parliament from Bonn several hundred miles eastward to Berlin is a direct consequence of national reunification. The geopolitical transfer remains controversial in Germany, but it was already approved by the Bundestag in 1991, with a narrow parliamentary majority—and then delayed until 1999.

As a result of the Bundestag election in September 1998, the emergence of the Berlin Republic has come to coincide with a complete change in government leadership. In the federal chancellery, Social Democrat Gerhard Schröder, born in 1944, has replaced Christian Democrat Helmut Kohl, born in 1930. Similar political *and* generational replacements took place elsewhere in the top level of German government shortly in advance of its transfer to Berlin. The new leaders have grown up in postwar Germany. In many cases they had their initial political experiences in youthful opposition to the societal establishment of the late 1960s. By now the "68ers" are themselves well into middle age, but they have ascended to power as successors to Kohl's generation, whose politically formative years coincided with the founding period of the Federal Republic of Germany. Unlike the latter, the new German leaders have no youthful memories of the Third Reich, World War II, or, in many cases, the immediate postwar years of military occupation. In that sense, they are the first postwar generation in power.

These confluent developments give new urgency to a host of questions about the reunited country—questions that concern both the Germans and their neighbors. Is a "new" Germany emerging as the political system extends eastward under a new generation of leaders, or is it basically the "old" Federal Republic writ larger? If it is something of both, as seems more likely, what is the nature of the "new/old" mix? And what directions will this reunited Germany pursue in domestic and foreign policy? What will change; what will continue? Also, what will result from conscious political choice and direction, and what will be the role of sheer inertia and drift? The questions are many, and it is only possible to offer tentative answers based on a careful assessment of the present situation.

A Tale of Three Republics

As always when discussing German politics, questions posed in the present and future are informed through shadows cast by the past. Thus in the early postwar years, the Swiss observer Fritz René Allemann was one of many who interpreted the new West German democracy by making comparisons with its predecessor, the Weimar Republic of the 1920s and early 1930s. His pithy conclusion, that "Bonn is not Weimar" *(Bonn ist nicht Weimar)*, expressed both the early hopes and later consensus of more than one generation of Germany watchers.[1] It needs to be remembered that Allemann in no way concluded that the young West German democracy was a wholly new or unproblematic political order. He (and many others) would later find much evidence for a growing affectual identification with the pluralist democracy that at first had been passively accepted *(hingenommen)* by a politically exhausted postwar citizenry.[2] But these early observers and their successors generally held that the Federal Republic could not be regarded as having arrived at full "normality" as a political system while memories of the Third Reich remained vivid and Germany stayed divided into two rival states. Bonn was surely not Weimar, but what had followed the Weimar Republic continued to weigh traumatically upon the present, both within Germany and among its many neighbors. As a result, West Germany could be regarded as being in some ways an "exceptional" political system—even after it had become firmly established as a pluralist democracy.

After half a century's record of solid performance by the Federal Republic, comprising about four decades before and one decade after the beginning of German reunification, there is no need for a sustained exploration of the thesis that Berlin, too, will not be Weimar. To be sure, there will always be some observers for whom the Weimar metaphor comes easily to mind when discussing political and social problems that affect contemporary Germany. But there is no reason to view Germany's current problems, including those discussed in this book, as having reached catastrophic proportions. Even more important, there is no significant evidence that contemporary Germans would be prone to embrace anti-democratic politics in dealing with any crisis that might result from such problems.

For example, in recent years German unemployment rates have reached levels that in some regions of the country are comparable with those of the great depression in the early 1930s. It is clearly a very serious problem that demands vigorous political attention. So far, the strategies of neither the Kohl nor the Schröder governments have made much of a dent, while the political parties are divided (sometimes internally) over whether to promote more demand- or more supply-side reforms. Yet, although there is no solution in sight, an informed observer would have to reject as groundless any fear that Germany could be in danger of scuttling its system of democratic politics in the search for a radical alternative remedy. Instead, German voters used their ballots in 1998 to carry through the first complete replacement of democratically elected power holders since the formation of the Federal Republic in 1949. The election turned out to be a fiasco for several rival far-right parties, which *together* received less than 4 percent of the vote. The contrast to the electoral polarization in the last years of the Weimar Republic, when much of the political center collapsed, could hardly be more pronounced.

The Backlog of Reforms

In the last years of the Bonn Republic, a recurrent theme in Germany's public debate concerned the widely presumed emergence of a civic "disenchantment with politics" (*Politikverdrossenheit*) or with parties (*Parteienverdrossenheit*) and their leaders (*Politikerverdrossenheit*). Although it showed some special German characteristics, the discussion bore a basic resemblance to similar ones about the decline of trust in politics and political leaders that have cropped up in other Western democracies.[3] By 1997, however, the German discussion had come to incorporate a new subordinate theme, the existence of a "reform blockage" or "reform backlog" (*Reformstau*) that supposedly was threatening the vitality of German society.

Two successive federal presidents, Richard von Weizsäcker and Roman Herzog, chose to take prominent roles in these public discussions. The former created a considerable stir in 1992, two years before his term of office ran out, when he reflected critically on the condition of a reunited Germany in a series of published interviews. The president's remarks covered a broad spectrum of problems, but public attention soon focused almost exclusively on his severe critique of the established German political parties as having grown too self-serving and distant from the citizenry.[4] Clearly Weizsäcker had hit a sensitive nerve.

Five years later, his successor managed to create a similar public echo with his reflections on the need for a new beginning (*Aufbruch*) in Germany. Herzog has mentioned the general topic on several occasions, but he captured national attention when he expanded on the theme in a major speech given in Berlin, in April

1997.[5] Unlike his predecessor, Herzog did not single out the political parties as a major problem. Rather, he spoke about societal malaise, general attitudes and structural conditions that had left Germany in a condition of inertia, pessimism, and aversion to risk-taking or the facing of challenges. In a memorable phrase, he called for a "jolt" (*Ruck durch Deutschland*) to shake Germany out of its anxiety and torpor, without specifying exactly how he conceived that the country might be galvanized. His critique was so general that it was possible for different political parties to appropriate Herzog's wake-up call, as several of the chapters in this book show.

It is noteworthy that the Society for the German Language chose the term "reform blockage" or "gridlock" (*Reformstau*) as its "word of the year" in 1997, and included Herzog's call for a societal "jolt" among the runners-up. The annual selection is intended to highlight an expression that has captured the spirit of the time or the state of the German public debate during the past year. The choice itself came as no surprise. Hardly a day goes by in contemporary Germany without some news bearing on old-age reform, health insurance reform, tax reform or labor market reform, not to speak of educational reform or the never-ending drama of spelling reform. In one important sense the image of a state of "blockage" or "gridlock" is misleading: while traffic jams on highways and gridlock within cities depend upon *both* the density of traffic and the capacity of the road system, the policy gridlock in today's Germany has been *not* so much the result of particularly heavy reform traffic. Rather, it is best understood as the consequences of an extremely limited capacity for structural change throughout the economy, the polity as well as society.[6]

It also came as no surprise at the end of 1998, when the Society chose as new word of the year a more directly political term, namely "red-green" (*Rot-Grün*). Its choice acknowledged the central political event of the year, the election of a wholly new government coalition of Social Democrats and environmentalist Greens. The unanswered question is whether and how the new leaders will be able to address the genuine domestic problems that are reflected in the seemingly endless discussion of *Reformstau* in Germany. Meaningful reform will involve the strain of hard thought and even harder choices, not all of which are likely to be popular in a society that places a premium on stability. The stakes are far more important than a high ranking as future "word of the year." They involve the contours of the Berlin Republic.

Bonn and Berlin

The mounting German reform discussion and the recent election of leaders promising to deliver *Reformen* suggest that the country has arrived at a crossroads of sorts. That juncture gives added relevance to the initial set of questions: how will the Berlin Republic resemble and how will it differ from its immediate predecessor? At a time when the Bonn Republic is becoming history, this book seeks to take inventory of some of its major political features and raise questions about their continued relevance for Germany's future political path.

In their individual chapters, the authors seek to address the confluence of change, continuity, and drift in contemporary German politics by examining important aspects of public opinion, the party system, and the policy arena. Their studies focus on recent and current developments. They also suggest the need for adjustments in our cognitive maps in order to capture better the shifts that are taking place or that may be expected as the country relocates its political center under the first postwar generation in power.

Recently some informed journalists have reported that the new German leadership appears to feel "rather less cramped by the past" than its predecessors.[7] No reasonable observer would allege that the new generation of leaders suffers from historical amnesia. Yet it is hardly surprising that they should have a different, less personal or immediate, and therefore also less inhibited relationship to the Nazi period in Germany's collective memory. On the other hand, they do have direct personal memories of the long East-West division of the country. But here there is also a generational difference at work. The new leaders seem inclined to regard the primary legacy of the Cold War as a complex bundle of "uneven development" problems that demand practical policy responses. In dealing with the reconstruction of eastern Germany, many of them seem to find it easier and more useful to cooperate with the far-left PDS descendants of the former ruling communist party than to engage in a political pillorying of the "red socks" as ideological opponents and eventual losers in the Cold War.[8]

The Bundestag Election of 1998

The book is not an electoral study, but each of its chapters was either completed or considerably revised after the Bundestag contest of September 1998. This critical election was an important landmark in the political transition from Bonn to Berlin. The individual chapters consider the electoral outcome where it touches importantly on their respective subject—public opinion, political parties, or public policy choices. The authors are primarily interested in the trends that have emerged in German politics since 1990, that were reflected or deflected in the recent transfer of government power, and that are likely to be important in the coming years. The election of 1998 triggered important changes in German government, but it can also be seen as giving expression to broader trends that have shaped German society since national reunification.

In 1998 the new German government was, like all its predecessors, produced by the vagaries of coalition politics in a representative system based on the country's modified form of proportional representation. In advance of the September election, it had been widely expected that the outcome would be only a partial shift in power, resulting from a grand ("red-black") coalition of Social Democrats (SPD) and Christian Democrats (CDU/CSU), with the chancellorship going to the front-running party—most likely the SPD. The result would have been a considerable element of continuity and, as interpreted by rival scenarios, either considerable inertia or a newfound strength in dealing concertedly with the country's backlog of reforms. Instead, the election made possible a "red-green" coalition by giving the Social Democrats a sufficient margin (almost 6 percent) over the Christian Democrats to form a majority coalition with the small party of Greens (table 1.1). The Schröder government enjoys a parliamentary margin of twenty-one seats over the combined opposition—or eleven more than its predecessor (table 1.2). The resulting "clean break" with the previous "black-yellow" (CDU/CSU-FDP) government coalition is the first of its kind in the Federal Republic's history, and it adds new weight to the questions regarding continuity and change in German politics.

The Two Parts of the Book

The book is divided into two parts, each consisting of multiple chapters. Part One deals with developments in German public opinion and political parties as key elements in Germany's pluralist democracy. There has been much stability and continuity in the German party system, but the individual chapters point to some recent major shifts and even discontinuities in outlooks and strategies as well as in the balance of power among the parties. These developments have already had a major impact on the formation of government and the tentative direction of policy in the Berlin Republic.

Part Two addresses important areas of German domestic and foreign policy. Two of the chapters deal with socioeconomic policy matters within Germany, and three are concerned with transnational or international issues. In each of the policy chapters, too, the themes of continuity, uncertainty, and drift crop up. Not surprisingly, each author looks for indications of where Schröder's red-green government may be headed. It is worth noting that two authors see a strong need but little likelihood for more fundamental change in domestic socioeconomic policy, while the three authors who deal with Germany's international relations give more emphasis to the need for continuity in foreign policy. The rest of this chapter will briefly introduce the two parts and their individual chapters.

German Public Opinion in West and East

Since the end of World War II, Germany has been one of the countries most extensively studied in public opinion surveys and analyses. In their chapter, Dieter

Table 1.1. Bundestag Elections of the Kohl Era, 1983 to 1998
Party Percentages of the Second Vote

Year	CDU/ CSU	SPD	Greens[a] A.90/Gr.	FDP	PDS	Other[b]
1983	48.8	38.2	5.6	7.0	-	0.5
1987	44.3	37.0	8.3	9.1	-	1.4
1990	43.8	33.5	3.8	11.0	2.4	5.4
West	44.3	35.7	4.8	10.6	0.3	4.4
East	41.8	24.3	6.2	12.9	11.1	3.8
1994	41.4	36.4	7.3	6.9	4.4	3.6
West	42.1	37.5	7.9	7.7	1.0	3.9
East	38.5	31.5	4.3	3.5	19.8	2.4
1998	35.1	40.9	6.7	6.2	5.1	5.9
West	37.0	42.3	7.3	7.0	1.2	5.2
East	27.3	35.1	4.1	3.3	21.6	8.6

[a] In 1990, the Greens won 4.8 percent of the vote in the West, amounting to 3.8 percent in the enlarged Federal Republic. The separate Alliance 90 won 6.2 percent in the East, which amounted to 1.2 percent in the entire Federal Republic. Under the special arrangement for 1990, which divided the Federal Republic into two electoral areas (West and East), the eastern Alliance 90 won parliamentary representation by passing the 5 percent minimum, but the western Greens did not. By 1994, the two had merged as an all-German party with the name Alliance 90/Greens.
[b] The all-German total for 1990 includes 1.2 percent for the eastern Alliance 90.

Table 1.2. Bundestag Elections of the Kohl Era
Distribution of the Bundestag Seats, Elections from 1983 to 1998

Year	Total No. of Seats	CDU/ CSU	SPD	Greens A. 90/Gr.	FDP	PDS
1983	498	244	193	27	34	-
1987	497	223	186	42	46	-
1990	662	319	239	8	79	17
1994	672	294	252	49	47	30
1998	669	245	298	47	43	36

Source for both tables: Data from *Wahlergebnisse in Deutschland 1946-1998* (Mannheim: Forschungsgruppe Wahlen, 1998).

Roth and Andreas Wüst draw upon the rich resources of their Mannheim Electoral Research Group and its *Politbarometer* to document and examine opinion trends in Germany after unification. They present a varied portrait of German public opinion between 1990 and 1998, giving considerable attention to both some persistent differences and some elements of convergence between Germans living in the "new" eastern and the "old" western states of the Federal Republic. The German public emerges from the study as a relatively well-informed, moderate, and pragmatically output-oriented one. It is noteworthy that while clear majorities have favored neither the government transfer to Berlin nor (at least until the beginning of 1999) the introduction of a new European currency (the Euro), these issues were widely regarded as having been settled and therefore did not come to dominate the German electoral agenda in 1998. The poll series also establishes important differences in public support for the incumbent government in the election years of 1994 and 1998, with their respective narrow victory and major defeat for the Kohl coalition.

A More Complex Party System

German party politics form the subject of the rest of Part One, with separate chapters devoted to each of the parties in the Bundestag. There are good reasons for giving such weight to the German parties, also for observers who do not identify with the sweeping *Parteienkritik* mentioned earlier. The parties are quite simply key elements in the pluralist form of representative government established in West Germany after World War II and extended to the new eastern states in the course of reunification in 1990. They both register and contribute to major continuities and shifts in the political landscape.

When the West German party system was consolidated during the economic boom years of the 1950s, the outcome was a relatively simple, centrist and stable system that was often contrasted with its fragmented, polarized and volatile Weimar predecessor. It was widely referred to as a "two and one-half" party system, because it consisted of the two large parties or *Volksparteien* of the moderate center-right Christian Democrats (CDU/CSU) and the moderate center-left Social Democrats (SPD), along with the small liberal coalition party of Free Democrats (FDP). That changed in the early 1980s, when the new party of Greens was able to capitalize on some post-material issues long ignored by the mainstream parties. Its arrival in the Bundestag in 1983 somewhat complicated both the rival agendas and the balance of power in the West German party system, which now consisted of a more intricate set of "two and two-halves." In 1990, Germany's unification brought an additional and quite different newcomer to the system, the post-communist party of Democratic Socialists (PDS). This is a far-left party with a strong regional identity, whose relative success in the East reflects the very uneven political integration of the once communist-ruled area of Germany.

Compared to the 1960s and 1970s, the German party system has become somewhat more fragmented and slightly polarized. In its adaptation to societal change, however, it has maintained the overall moderate and consolidated format that was achieved already in the late 1950s. At the end of the century, the German party system could be said to consist of "two and three-halves," at least in the Bundestag. However, the weakness of both the Greens and the FDP in the East, where the PDS is concentrated, has produced what is more like two regionally defined party systems in Germany—a set of "two and two-halves" in the West and another set of "two and one-half" in the East. Moreover, in some parts of the West, such as Bavaria and the Saar, the FDP has by now become so weak that it can practically be left out of the political equation.

It is hardly surprising that German coalition arithmetic has become more complex as the party system includes more components than previously. There are also signs of an increased political rivalry and ideological distance, not least among the three smaller Bundestag parties that are regularly engaged in a struggle for survival—an increasingly neoliberal FDP, a highly diverse grouping of Greens, and a heterogeneous eastern-anchored PDS. All this gives promise of greater uncertainties in the party politics of the Berlin Republic.

The Individual Parties

In the first of six chapters dealing with political parties, Clay Clemens examines the present condition of the long-governing Christian Democrats who were ousted from power in 1998. He also provides an illuminating commentary on the politics of Bonn—the "comfortable, cozy 'federal village' on the Rhine"—with its "broad, consensual socioeconomic policies at home and ... tendency to conduct foreign policy 'in Europe's name.'" The Christian Democrats have been remarkably successful as a moderately conservative, catch-all party that has guided Germany's domestic and foreign policy direction in most of the postwar years. In a historic moment, Chancellor Helmut Kohl grasped the opportunity for national reunification in 1990 and earned a major place in German history. Yet the decade of unification became one of accumulating challenges for the CDU/CSU and its vulnerable but sometimes assertive cabinet partner, the FDP.

Clemens includes a discussion of the policy stalemate of the 1990s and argues that Kohl's form of leadership died with the 1998 debacle. "Fjr many Jhristiaj Democrjts, the future of their country and party alike lies in thinking beyond Bonn, to Berlin." For them, it is now time to concentrate on the needs of Germany as a country that should be economically more fit, less burdened by needless regulation or entitlements, but also "less bound by its darker past chapters, equipped with a strong state, unapologetic about assuring social order, confident in asserting its interest in Europe or further afield." A new generation of leaders will seek to adapt the Union, both CDU and CSU, to a German political environment that increasingly diverges from the familiar pattern of Bonn. In his conclusion, Clemens suggests that beyond both Bonn and Berlin there is also new CDU thinking that is perhaps best associated with Frankfurt, a metropolis representing a dynamic, cosmopolitan, multicultural Germany. His reflections on the present political transition also provide a valuable background for the party and policy chapters that follow.

The Social Democrats are examined at length by Andrew Denison, who includes a considerable section on their "rocky" start as chancellor party. He emphasizes that the SPD is not nearly as united as it appeared during the 1998 Bundestag campaign, when it was returned to office after sixteen years in the parliamentary opposition. The SPD's self-presentation as a force of the "new center" or "new middle" (*neue Mitte*) does not really indicate a clear direction for the new government of Chancellor Gerhard Schröder. There seem to be significant political differences between him and the party leader and new Finance Minister Oskar Lafontaine, which lie rooted in an ideological divergence that goes beyond personal rivalry. Denison gives a sympathetic portrait of the SPD as a broadly based party (*Volkspartei*) comprising some very diverse tendencies and interests. From his presentation it becomes clear that the SPD has a long way to go before it resolves the conflict between its traditionalists and modernizers—a conflict that in some ways resembles the one that Britain's Labour decided in favor of its more market-oriented proponents of a "third way." Moreover, and unlike its Westminster counterpart, the SPD must also govern with an assertive junior party. And the Greens harbor alternative policy ideas which may not always be easily accommodated.

Gene Frankland explains how the Greens have become part of the political order and a member of the new government without losing their special identity as a party committed to basic ecological and social reforms. He shows that the Greens, like their Social Democratic partners, have some important internal differences, which he assesses in terms of their likely political impact. The Greens have "come a long way," Frankland observes, and they are already now beginning to set a distinctive mark on some federal policy areas that will differentiate the emerging Berlin Republic from its Bonn predecessor. He not only anticipates some strains between the coalition partners, but also cautions that factional differences among the Greens on foreign and security policy, along with a conflictual image of coalition behavior and weak party organization, could make them vulnerable to media criticism.

The Free Democrats (FDP) have been the traditional junior coalition party in the Bonn Republic, and in this role they have been more successful than any other small party in West European politics since World War II. In view of their electoral decline and loss of government position, however, one must ask whether they really matter very much any more. Christoph Hanterman shows that the FDP mattered very much in the foreign policy area until 1998. He also suggests that the centrist and pragmatic tradition of Germany's Liberals will continue to be a major political resource for the Federal Republic, if they should be given the opportunity to join a future coalition government. Christian Søe examines the small party's turn toward a neoliberal reform agenda in the late 1990s. He suggests that this orientation may need to be counterbalanced by an emphasis on the FDP's "functional" attributes as a moderating and pragmatic coalition party of the center, even though such a combination of the roles of "reformer" and "balancer" may encounter credibility problems. Above all, the party must seek to gain a new electoral base in state and local politics. And it must do much more to restore itself in the East, where its neoliberal reform agenda turns off voters who are far more attuned to a politics that emphasizes the provision of public services.

Gerald Kleinfeld places the newest and most controversial small party in the Bundestag under the microscope. The Party of Democratic Socialism (PDS), which descended from the former ruling communists in East Germany, is unique among German parties by its simultaneous attempt to promote a regional (eastern) and a socialist (post-communist) agenda. At the same time, as Kleinfeld emphasizes, the party membership is internally divided. It encompasses at least three major orientations or tendencies, including many (often older) members who maintain a selective nostalgia for communism, some very pragmatic socialists (well represented in the leadership), and some more ideological (and often younger) neosocialists. The supporters are even more varied, but they amount to approximately 20 percent of the voters in the East and about 1 percent in the West—enough to pass the 5 percent hurdle in 1998, but not enough for future electoral security in federal politics. At the local level of government, the PDS already plays an important role in practical governance. At the state level, it has also established itself in SPD-led governments, first as a silent partner (in Saxony-Anhalt, since 1994) and then as a full cabinet partner (in Mecklenburg-West Pomerania, since 1998). It remains to be seen how this still very incomplete "normalization" of the PDS will affect its program and strategy as well as its membership and supporters. If the PDS becomes a fully established party, the left in Germany will be further divided than was true even in the last decade of the Bonn Republic. That would in turn increase the coalition vagaries in Berlin.

In a final chapter of the party section, Gerard Braunthal looks at the various expressions of right-wing politics in the Federal Republic. He points out that the fractious right-wing parties have performed relatively poorly in federal electoral politics, despite occasional Land-level breakthroughs, as recently in Saxony-Anhalt in April 1998. But his account shows that there have been waves of right-wing and neo-Nazi activity, also in the Kohl era. He also discusses the easily overlooked intellectual penetration of some of the media by New Right academics and journalists. There is a small hard core of right-wing ideologues in the country, estimated to comprise at least 5 percent of the population, and a larger pool of sympathizers, perhaps 13 percent altogether—a situation comparable to that of some neighboring countries. In the German setting, such right-wing manifestations are more disquieting, but Braunthal concludes on a positive note. Despite the current socioeconomic problems in Germany and some past irresoluteness by the government on the right-wing issue, the country's democratic institutions, liberties, and political culture—now fifty years old—have a firm grounding.

German Domestic and Foreign Policy

The policy section of the book explores more fully some themes raised in the party section. Once again, the symbolic importance of moving the German capital from Bonn to Berlin hovers over the discussion. The historic transition raises a plethora of questions regarding "what is past, or passing, or to come."[9] "What is past" is the division of Germany. As shown in all the chapters, this fact has had tremendous consequences for the formulation and articulation of German domestic and foreign policy. "What is passing" is the initial adjustment phase of German policy to the ongoing unification process, a process that is taking much longer and costing more than people initially anticipated. During this transition, the resilience of the German political system has been tested, as it has had to cope with a veritable avalanche of political and economic problems. The policy chapters examine the responses to such challenges as the demands of unification and reconstruction, augmented by the simultaneous pressures of globalization, the breakdown of the continental Cold War order, and European integration. The cumulative effect for the Berlin Republic, as it attempts to address "what is to come," appears likely to be a significantly changed and in many ways more challenging policy environment than was true for the Bonn Republic, at least until 1990.

Two chapters deal primarily with domestic policy. Irwin Collier and David Keithly examine recent and current German economic, social, and fiscal policy. They also tackle the critical issue of structural reform—recognizing both the need for it and the difficulty of achieving it. Three chapters address foreign policy and united Germany's place in Europe. Michael Huelshoff assesses German economic and political relations with the European Union (EU), while Mary Hampton examines the relationship to NATO. Finally, James Sperling provides a critical analysis of the current literature that seeks to identify the new Germany as a regional hegemon in Europe.

Domestic Policy: Between Reform and Drift

The two domestic policy chapters deal with social and economic problems that have been intensified by the dual shocks of national unification and market global-ization. The inadequacies of the "German model" (*Modell Deutschland*) figure prominently in both chapters. This concept was first advanced by the governing Social Democrats in the 1970s to herald the successful German welfare state system combined with that period's macro-economic coordination efforts, as described at length by Keithly. Beginning before unification, but accelerated by it, some of the cracks in the model turned into crevices. Collier highlights what he calls the "gridlock of social entitlements" in current German welfare state policy, while Keithly focuses on the need for "overdue reform" in a number of economic policy areas.

Collier's chapter addresses the multifaceted problems that now burden German welfare state policy. The confluence of high unemployment, a rapidly aging population, and the continuing costs of unification—with its disproportionate expansion of social entitlements relative to economic potential—all conspire to undermine the capacity of the safety net that has provided a vast array of benefits over the last half century. As Collier points out, unemployment has reached "genuinely pathological levels in the new states of Germany." Yet despite this and other unresolved problems, such as in pension and health insurance reform, the German government, first under Kohl and now under Schröder, has been slow to innovate or reform its social spending policies. The failure to do so is largely the result of politicians' lack of will to attack "the sacred cows" of entitlements in German society.

Collier details the ambitious reform course that the red-green coalition set for itself on taking office. He shows that while the coalition agreement attacked the *Reformstau* on a number of social and labor policy fronts, fundamental reforms have so far not materialized. Collier finds the basic problem to be Germany's interlocking system of social entitlements that hampers the transfer of resources (both human and nonhuman ones) from relatively low productivity uses to relatively high productivity uses. He concludes that the cumulative effect of the current system is a weakening of the capacity of the economy to innovate, which itself is the mainspring of sustained economic growth.

David Keithly's chapter addresses the dual shocks of globalization and reunification as they have affected the German economy. In the first part of his chapter, he explains the German model and emphasizes that its adaptation to new competitive challenges has been at best inadequate until now. Keithly lists a series of problems that need attention if the German economy is to compete well. They include the continued practice of giving subsidies to declining industries and especially to vulnerable ones in the eastern states; the failure to promote sufficient liberalization in some overly regulated and inefficient economic sectors; the provision of increasingly generous social insurance programs that cannot possibly be sustained in a near future where "as much as 40 percent of the population will be over sixty"; delays in an overdue reform of the burdensome tax system; and tardy privatization. These problems all contribute to a continued sluggishness in German productivity rates.

In the second half of his chapter, Keithly addresses an unprecedented economic challenge that confronts post-unification Germany. Other European countries face difficulties in the global economy, although some of them appear to be more flexible and ready for economic reform. None of them share Germany's additional task of reconstructing a large area that has suddenly moved from a centrally planned economy to capitalism. The early optimism about a relatively rapid and painless integration of eastern Germany, when Chancellor Kohl spoke for many with his vision of "blooming landscapes," has long since given way to a more realistic awareness of the enormous costs and difficulties of this process.

The slow domestic policy adaptation to these challenges raises a serious question: can institutional incremental adjustment be an adequate response to the severe problems that beset the German social and economic system? It is a question that goes to the heart of the Bonn/Berlin equation. If incrementalism can meet the needs of the Berlin Republic, then it will in many ways continue to resemble its predecessor. If not, if more determined reform measures are required to address the myriad of domestic problems that have arisen, or if the incrementalist approach continues to be pursued and simply fails, then Berlin will increasingly be forced to look for other solutions that bear less resemblance to the familiar *Modell Deutschland* and therefore *Modell Bonn*.

Foreign Policy Issues: Between Euroland and Deutschland

Starting with West Germany's first Chancellor, Konrad Adenauer, every postwar German administration has emphasized its commitment to continuity in foreign policy. Rehabilitation after World War II was seen as best served by embedding West Germany into a dense network of multilateral, crosscutting international institutions, which at the same time served to enhance German influence and maneuverability in the world. Above all, Bonn tied itself to other Western countries through European integration and the trans-Atlantic security relationship. In doing so, it successfully dampened remaining fears about German power and ambition. That line of continuity has served German foreign policy well and was on particularly prominent display during the sixteen years of leadership by Chancellor Kohl. It is noteworthy that the mantra of continuity in foreign policy continued to play a key role in the election rhetoric of 1998 and in the immediate post-election visits by Schröder as victorious chancellor candidate to Paris, London, and Washington.

The chapters dealing with German foreign policy emphasize the importance of the active commitment to continuity. However, each chapter also assesses evidence of some drift and change. Germany has indeed been a crucial motor of European integration, but how committed is united Germany to further advancement of the project? NATO has clearly been the mainstay of Bonn's postwar security policy, but are German security interests changing? Finally, how powerful is unified Germany, and what does that mean for future continuity in its foreign policy?

Michael Huelshoff specifically addresses German policy toward the EU and European integration, where he finds a great deal of continuity. He explains that for

historical, political and economic reasons, European integration has become institutionalized into the fabric of the German domestic political system, and that German political identity has become inextricably tied to Europe. Insofar, Huelshoff
argues that Germans are indeed "good Europeans," and that continuity in the
Federal Republic's integration policy should therefore be anticipated. On the other
hand, he points to the fact that Germany at times has acted as a brake on moves
toward further integration, both in the past and currently. When it seemed to be in
German interests, the Bonn Republic tended to hedge.

German hesitance appears to have grown since unification in particular issue
areas, such as in social and internal market policies. Huelshoff affirms the findings
of the domestic policy chapters, that unification has presented Germany with some
unique needs and concomitant responses. Accordingly, the Kohl and Schröder
governments have resisted the creation of a European-wide unemployment policy,
where this was seen to adversely affect specific German needs. Further indications
that the Germans have become more willing to act in the name and interests of
Deutschland rather than *Euroland* include the determination to subsidize vulnerable eastern German industries despite protests from and conflict with Brussels,
and an increased German resistance to filling the costly role of "paymaster"
(*Zahlmeister*) of the EU. In sum, Huelshoff argues that continuity now coexists
with some elements of drift and change in German policy toward the EU.

In a similar fashion, Mary Hampton explains German security policy toward
NATO in terms of both continuity and drift. Over the entire postwar period, membership in NATO has granted Germany the nuclear protection of the United States
and served to free the Bonn Republic from suspicions about its power intentions. It
has also allowed Germany and several of its neighbors to move toward the development of a European security identity alongside the trans-Atlantic relationship. For
these and other reasons, there has been a line of continuity in security policy that
has served Bonn's interests well. Hampton argues that despite a brief post-unification flirtation by some elements of the German political class with a form of disen-
gagement of the Federal Republic from the alliance, a widespread elite consensus
supportive of maintaining the NATO relationship had reemerged by 1995. Thus the
promise of continuity toward the alliance was maintained despite changes in the
German landscape, while there has been an unintended consequence of drift in the
pursuit of a European security identity.

But Hampton also unearths evidence that suggests some possibly emerging
trends toward drift or change in German policy toward NATO. For example, almost
immediately upon taking office, the SPD-Green government challenged NATO's
core nuclear policy regarding first use. This incident was indicative of a history of
resistance to NATO by key elements of the left-of-center coalition. Therefore, the
potential for subtle shifts in German security policy toward NATO would appear to
have increased under the first government of the Berlin Republic, and the policy of
developing a European security identity remains uncertain.

Finally, the question of reconfigured German power on the European continent has become far more central since the breakup of the Soviet Union and the unification of Germany. James Sperling critically examines the widespread claim that post-unification Germany is emerging as the regional European hegemon. Were this the case, then German claims about continuity in foreign policy would be suspect. Through meticulous measurement of real German power capabilities vis-à-vis west and east European states, however, Sperling rejects the proposition that Germany is or will be hegemonic. He argues rather that the Berlin Republic will be marginally more powerful than the Bonn Republic, but that German power has been and increasingly will be subsumed in the integrating European institutional framework. For Sperling, then, the pull of *Euroland* will outweigh any potential push toward *Deutschland* and a newly emerging German phoenix.

To summarize, the policy chapters examine the changes brought to bear on German domestic and foreign policy since reunification and the breakdown of the Cold War system. These shifting sands of change coexist with the rockbed elements of continuity in German politics. Change to date has occurred through the sound institutions that evolved and matured during the half-century existence of the Bonn Republic. As Bonn gives way to Berlin, the political and economic institutions appear to be resilient although they have come under increasing strain.

Will incremental institutional adaptation on the domestic front, the response until now, be adequate to deal with the myriad of problems begging for reform? Will incremental adjustment on the foreign ledger satisfy Berlin's new role in Europe? In addressing these quandaries, the policy chapters confirm that Berlin will not be Weimar; but they cast some doubt on how closely Berlin will resemble Bonn.

Notes

1. Fritz René Allemann, *Bonn ist nicht Weimar* (Cologne and Berlin: Kiepenheuer and Witsch, 1956).

2. The changes in West Germany's political culture have been well recorded and studied. See Gabriel A. Almond and Sidney Verba, *The Civic Culture* (Princeton: Princeton University Press, 1963), and David Conradt's chapter, "Changing German Political Culture," in the follow-up study, edited by Almond and Verba, *The Civic Culture Revisited* (Boston: Little, Brown, 1980), 212-72. See also Kendall Baker, Russell J. Dalton, and K. Hildebrandt, *Germany Transformed* (Cambridge: Harvard University Press, 1981).

3. See Joseph S. Nye, Jr., Philip Zelikow, and David King, eds., *Why People Don't Trust Government* (Cambridge: Harvard University Press, 1997). See also the earlier European study, Hans-Dieter Klingemann and Dieter Fuchs, eds., *Citizens and the State* (New York: Oxford University Press, 1995). For a perspective that emphasizes special German conditions for a decline in civic trust, see the work of

Hans Herbert von Arnim, who indefatigably criticizes the privileges of Germany's political class. A good example is his recent book, *Fetter Bauch regiert nicht gern. Die politische Klasse—selbstbezogen und abgehoben* (Munich: Kindler, 1997).

4. Gunter Hoffmann and Werner A. Perger, eds., *Richard von Weizsäcker im Gespräch* (Frankfurt: Eichborn Verlag, 1992). For the ensuing critical discussion, see the book, also edited by Hoffmann and Perger, *Die Kontroverse. Weizsäckers Parteienkritik in der Diskussion* (Frankfurt: Eichborn, 1992).

5. The speech was delivered at Berlin's newly rebuilt Hotel Adlon, near the Brandenburg Gate and the Reichstag, 26 April 1997. It has been widely published and commented upon. Good reports are found in *This Week in Germany* and *Deutschland Nachrichten* (New York: German Information Center), both 2 May 1997.

6. This point was made by Irwin L. Collier in an early draft of his chapter on welfare state reform.

7. Anne McElvoy, "Clashing Centres," *Prospect* (January 1999): 38-41. See also the report by Roger Cohen, "Germany Searches for Normality," *New York Times*, 29 November 1998.

8. On the CDU's 1994 and 1998 campaign slogans against "red socks" and "red handshakes," see Gerald Kleinfeld's chapter on the PDS. Clay Clemens also makes this point in his chapter on the CDU/CSU.

9. William Butler Yeats, "Sailing to Byzantium," in Richard J. Finneran and George Mills Harper, eds., *The Collected Works of W. B. Yeats*, vol. one (New York: Scribner, 1997), 197.

Part One

Public Opinion and
Political Parties

2

Where Is Germany Heading?
A Public Opinion Perspective, 1990-1998

Dieter Roth and Andreas M. Wüst

In 1990, after thirteen years of recording public opinion developments in western Germany, our institute extended its polling into eastern Germany as well. In what follows, we present and briefly analyze some of our data that show both convergences and differences between and within these two parts of Germany since unification. The data show some shifts in public opinion that suggest that many Germans have had second thoughts on such symbolically and practically important issues as the transfer of the national seat of government and parliament from Bonn back to Berlin. Further, they indicate some trends in public views concerning the present state of German society. They include polling data that measure the level of satisfaction with Germany's democracy and its German leaders as well as public perceptions of the major items on the country's political agenda, the relative competence of the political parties in government and opposition, and the country's relationship to Europe. Overall it is quite a varied and shifting picture that emerges, one in which east-west differences sometimes continue to be marked. Some findings seem to point in the direction of a political dissatisfaction or malaise that may arouse concern. The overall impression, however, is one of a German public that expresses the kind of concerns and misgivings about government performance that are frequently found in mature democracies.

Three years ago, the second German television channel (ZDF) decided on a change, that seemed to suggest that the process of national unification had been more or less completed. Starting in 1996, the ZDF's monthly *Politbarometer*, a widely watched and cited political information program prepared by our research institute, would record public opinion developments in Germany *as a whole* rather than provide separate figures for eastern and western Germany. For more than five years previously, the *Politbarometer* had been based on two independent samples for the East and West. In addition to the regular program, which showed both growing convergence and continuing differences in attitudes between the two parts of Germany, there had been a special *East-Barometer*. This latter program, which henceforth would be discontinued, had shown the development of public opinion in the eastern states (Länder) on such issues as people's concern for their economic and social situation, or their judgments about politics, parties and politicians. Officially, it was decided that there was no longer a need for the *East-Barometer* with its separate opinion sample.

The reasons for this policy decision by the ZDF were threefold and of varying importance. They included a methodological, a financial, and a political consideration. A precondition for the change was the fact that the rapid spread of telephone coverage in the East (by now to around 90 percent of the population) finally made it possible to shift from face-to-face interviewing to the kind of telephone interviews that have long been used in the western part of Germany. This meant that the time span for collecting the data (field time) would become identical in the West and East. And that was an important methodological advance.

The financial reason for the change was that the relatively high field costs for the *Politbarometer* could be reduced by close to one-half by using a sample of respondents that would number 1,000 in the West and only 250 in the East (reflecting the population ratio between the two parts of Germany), rather than the former formula of using two separate samples of 1,000 respondents in the West and 1,000 in the East.

But one should not overlook an important political reason for the change. It was rooted in some complaints heard from the German public and its politicians about having *Politbarometer* regularly report on differences in the political and social development of the eastern and western parts of Germany: After all, "we are one country now," such critics liked to suggest. They had an ideological motive for presenting an image of greater national unity and harmony, and this concern supported the decision finally to discontinue the separate samplings of the political mood in Germany's East and West.

Despite this change in our polling procedure, the data still make it possible to compare public opinion developments in the eastern and western parts of Germany. There are some pronounced differences that are hardly surprising after forty-five years of political separation followed by a difficult process of reconstruction in the former communist-ruled East. They show up in public views on the symbolically important eastward shift of the nation's government from Bonn to Berlin as well as on some less symbolic issues. But our data also show some interesting convergences when it comes to some political priorities on the nation's agenda.

From Bonn to Berlin

Responses to the question of where the German government and parliament should be seated—in Bonn or in Berlin?—indicate that there have been some second thoughts about the political implications of national unification.

The future location of the government and parliament was the subject of a major debate held in the Bundestag in June 1991, which ended with a very narrow majority decision (51.4 percent) in favor of Berlin. This parliamentary decision was based on a free vote by individual representatives, without the imposition of a binding position or "party line" by any of the Bundestag parties, with the possible exception of the post-communist PDS. Parliamentary members of the old western Länder voted with a majority for Bonn (57.6 percent), while those from the new eastern Länder overwhelmingly chose Berlin (81.1 percent). In the words of one analyst, the Bundestag vote "was a defeat of the West by the East, of the South by the North, of the Catholics by the Protestants, and of younger people by their elders. This will be of some importance for the way Germany sees itself."[1]

At the time, public opinion on the question differed considerably from that of the parliamentary majority. When asked the simple question, "Where should the government be seated, in Berlin or in Bonn?" the majority of all Germans favored Bonn (56 percent) over Berlin (40 percent). But here too, the east-west difference was a pronounced one. Sixty-nine percent of the eastern repondents "voted" for Berlin, while 63 percent of the westerners wanted to retain Bonn as the location of government (figure 2.1).

There were some differences when we asked where the government should be seated "in the long run," but here the east-west pattern was discernible as well. For the unspecified "long run," a majority (55 percent) did choose Berlin over Bonn (39 percent). However, while 81 percent of the eastern respondents voted for Berlin (figure 2.2), westerners opted for it as government center of Germany with only a small plurality (48 percent) over Bonn (45 percent).

There were no major differences in public opinion along party lines, except that PDS supporters in eastern Germany showed an overwhelming preference for Berlin. There also were no big differences among demographic groups in the East or the West, but there was a noticeably stronger preference for Berlin by people over fifty years of age. There were also some regional differences. In general, one could find the same general trend within the population as among the parliamentary delegates. There was never a majority in the public for a compromise position, such as leaving the government and some ministries in Bonn and moving the parliament to Berlin. Seventy percent opposed such an alternative.

Already one year after the Bundestag vote in favor of Berlin, the adult population appeared to have some second thoughts on the issue. Since then, with the exception of the year 1995, there has been a growing tendency to regard the parliamentary decision in favor of Berlin as a mistake (figure 2.3). By June 1997, three out of four people in western Germany thought that the decision taken six years earlier

Figure 2.1. Should the German government be seated in Berlin or Bonn?

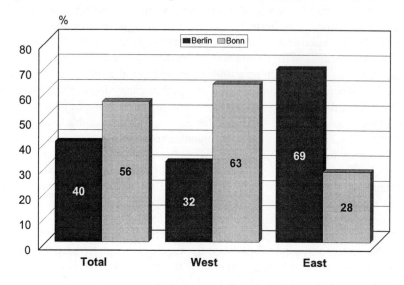

Figure 2.2. Berlin or Bonn as long-run location of German government?

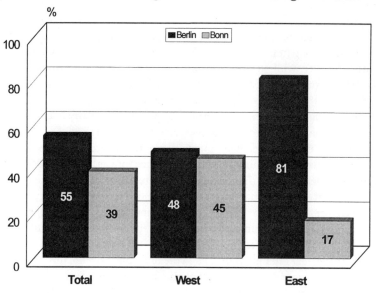

Source for both figures: Forschungsgruppe Wahlen, Politbarometer June 1991.

in favor of Berlin was mistaken, and there was even a slight majority among eastern respondents against Berlin as well. There were north-south and east-west differences in the answers, but nowhere was there a majority in support of the 1991 decision except for respondents in Berlin and the surrounding Land of Brandenburg (59 percent). The shift in opinion reflected a clear public disapproval of a parliamentary decision that had been presented officially and in the media as an important step towards defining the role of a larger Germany in Europe.

It could be argued that this trend against Berlin as the seat of the German government and parliament reflects a very specific concern and does not by itself signify any general state of uncertainty in Germany. The redesign and renovation of Berlin, especially of some of the city's run-down eastern areas, have turned out to be very complicated and expensive. There has been much negative reporting on the city's economic and political situation, with special attention to the frequent time delays and unforeseen price increases. The labor market situation in Berlin has been nothing less than bizarre, with a high unemployment recorded among construction workers in the middle of a building boom. Simultaneously, the presence of many foreign laborers without work permits gives rise to some other contentious problems. As a result, Berlin often does not receive very good press. Given the important role of economic considerations in public opinion formation, the negative trend in assessing the city as the seat of national government is really not very surprising.

The State of German Society

To get a better grasp of the development of German public opinion, we now turn to some more general assessments of the state of the country. In late April 1997, Federal President Roman Herzog gave a widely discussed speech in Berlin, in which he spoke of Germany as suffering from a pervasive discouragement, paralysis, mental depression, and a sense of doom or crisis. He also warned his fellow citizens: "The world is ready for new departures and will not wait for Germany."[2]

It was one of Herzog's typically "wise man" speeches. He carefully refrained from attacking anybody in particular, but his general analysis gave a lot of food for thought. The independent liberal press praised his frankness. The governing parties were pleased because the speech could be interpreted as a critique of the social democratic opposition for having brought political "gridlock" to the policy process. In turn, the opposition liked Herzog's statements about political paralysis, which could also be seen as referring to Kohl's conservative-liberal government.

Our data back Roman Herzog's general analysis at least with regard to the public perception of the state of affairs in Germany. Three times a year, we give German respondents a chance to assess the situation in their country by choosing among four general descriptive categories:

    1. on the whole, things are going all right;

Figure 2.3. The 1991 German parliament decision to move to Berlin was wrong: Percentage who agree with this statement.

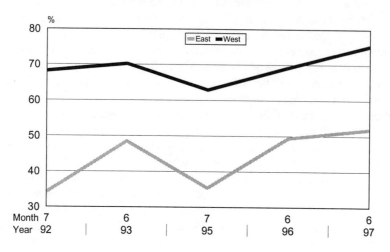

Figure 2.4. The state of German society

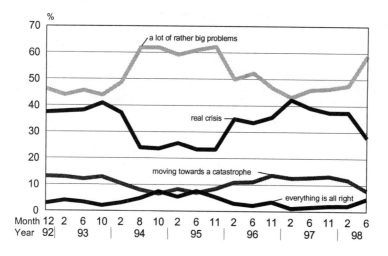

Source for both figures: Forschungsgruppe Wahlen, Politbarometer.

2. we have a whole lot of rather big problems;
3. our society is in a real crisis;
4. we are moving towards a catastrophe.

Figure 2.4 shows that the highest level of "crisis" and "catastrophe" perceptions occurred in the fall of 1996 and in the spring of 1997. A similar situation had prevailed earlier, during most of the year 1993. Thereafter there had followed a period of relative calm, where the dominant perception was that the country faced only "big problems." Here too, there were no major differences along party lines. Christian Democratic voters usually were somewhat less pessimistic than Social Democratic voters, but the differences were not great. Again there was an exception to be made for the small group of PDS voters, who overwhelmingly viewed the situation more negatively. In June 1997, 63 percent of the PDS voters perceived "a real crisis," while 17 percent thought the country was moving toward "a catastrophe."

But the situation looked different in a comparative perspective. When we asked our respondents to compare the state of German society to that of its West European neighbors, the result was always a clear majority who said that we Germans were "better off than our neighbors."

On one hand, then, it seemed that Germans had a tendency to see their country as a vale of tears, while on the other they behaved like many self-employed for whom "complaining is simply a part of business." In light of the generally pessimistic assessment of the country's condition, it was remarkable that 70 percent of the German population also believed that "there is too much yammering about the situation." The apparent contradiction suggests a need to probe further.

Our time series for the question about the general situation in Germany indicated not only that there were fluctuations in the negative assessments but also that there had been a rise of misgivings and second thoughts about the country's development. Indeed, it was possible to discern a pattern that showed some similarities to the shift in opinion regarding the "move to Berlin."

Satisfaction with Democracy

For many years we have measured "satisfaction with democracy" with a very simple question: "What would you say about democracy in Germany? Are you content with it, or are you not content with it?" Answers to this question reflect several aspects of system contentment. They include satisfaction with the pragmatic functioning of the system in terms of its output or effectiveness. But they also reflect satisfaction with the ideal aspects of the democratic system, as compared to other political systems, in terms of such matters as popular participation and sovereignty.

These practical and ideal aspects may vary in importance from time to time and from group to group. Thus satisfaction with democracy was very high in West

Germany in the spring and fall of 1990, when people realized what kind of freedom the Federal Republic offered in contrast to the dissolving system in East Germany about which they were receiving a flood of new and authentic information via the media as well as through direct contacts. At that time, the ideological system aspects clearly dominated in the widespread satisfaction with democracy. It was always possible to find some differences among groups based on differences in age, education, political interest, or political information level. Older people have tended on the whole to be more satisfied with democracy than younger people, and the higher educated have been more satisfied than people with low education. But at an extremely high point of satisfaction, as in the fall months of 1990, these group differences diminished significantly.

The situation has been quite different when the satisfaction level was much lower, as in the fall of 1993. In such a period, a more pragmatic view or output orientation tends to dominate among Germans. Then we find much greater diversity, especially among the different groups of party supporters and also among sociodemographic groups. In addition, there have been considerable differences between eastern and western Germany that are rooted in their very different political traditions before 1990. Already in advance of unification, East Germans expressed very high expectations for the system output of a Western-style democracy. These expectations were raised enormously during the whole year of 1990, when there seemed to be no end to competitive political campaigns, with which most East Germans had no previous experience. There were successive sets of elections in March, May, October, and December of 1990 for the East German People's Chamber (*Volkskammer*), the local councils, the new Land parliaments, and the Bundestag respectively. After the enthusiasm generated by the many campaigns in the year of unification, disappointments were bound to follow. That has to be kept in mind when one follows the time series of responses to the question regarding satisfaction with democracy (figure 2.5).

Immediately after the unification of East and West Germany had been officially sealed and the election campaigns of 1990 had come to an end, the expression of satisfaction with democracy in Germany dropped sharply and continuously from an overwhelming majority of 80 percent to less than 50 percent in the second half of 1993. The development over time was similar in East and West Germany but at different levels. System satisfaction was always much higher in western than in eastern Germany, and that has continued to be the case.

During the campaign year of 1994, satisfaction with democracy rose again as it always does during election years. During most of 1995, those satisfied with democracy continued to be a small majority of the whole population, but the numbers declined once again in 1996. The movement was similar in the different party groups, but the differences were a little more distinct in eastern Germany, and we found higher deviations between supporters of the government and opposition parties respectively.

Figure 2.5. Satisfaction with democracy

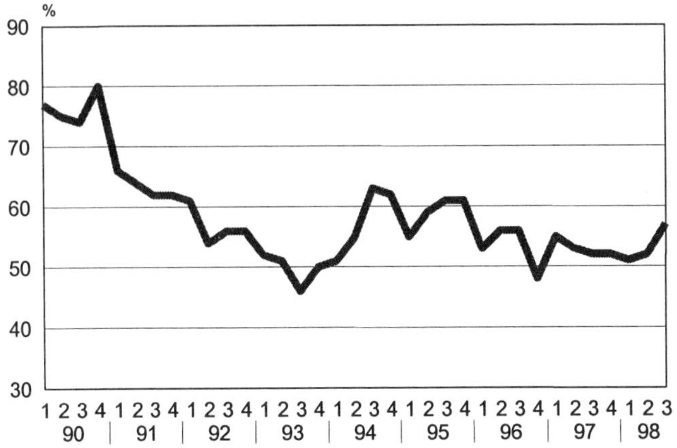

Source: Forschungsgruppe Wahlen, Politbarometer.   Shown are quarter years (1990 only West Germany).

The highest dissatisfaction with the system was found among people close to the PDS and among those who did not want to participate in elections. Between 70 and 80 percent of the people in these groups expressed dissatisfaction with democracy. Together, those two groups made up more than one-third of the eligible voters in eastern Germany. That reflected a weak integration into the political system of a segment of East Germans, resulting in a much lower level of satisfaction with democracy in the East than in the West.

However, it cannot be concluded from these figures that East Germans rejected pluralist democracy. More than 70 percent of them still thought that it had been the right decision to vote for a Western model of democracy during the first free election of the East German Volkskammer in March 1990 (widely perceived as the decisive "unification election"). That view was held by a majority even among those who expressed dissatisfaction with democracy. This fact suggests that dissatisfaction with democracy is more the result of the difficult process of change in the new eastern Länder, with its accompanying social and economic dislocations, than a general rejection of democratic values.

Satisfaction with Germany's Leaders

Another aspect of system contentment is the degree of satisfaction with decision makers. We measure this aspect with the following general question: "Are the

Figure 2.6. Are the leading positions filled by the right people?

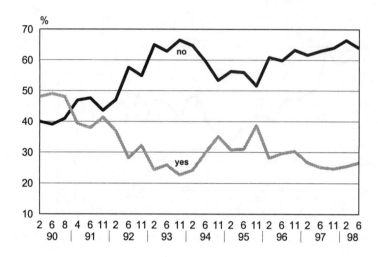

Source: Forschungsgruppe Wahlen, Politbarometer; 1990 only West Germany.

Figure 2.7. Mean evaluation of the most important German politicians.

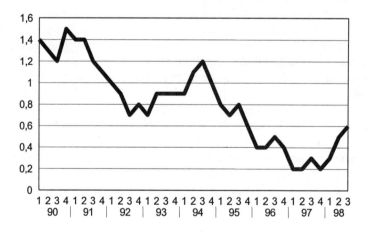

Note: Means of scale values: from +5 most positive to -5 most negative evaluation.

Source: Forschungsgruppe Wahlen, Politbarometer; 1/90 - 3/90 only West Germany; shown are quarter years.

leading positions filled with the right people?" From methodological experiments we know that people mainly associate politicians with this question, although the wording is more general. Again we have recorded clear differences in the answers to this question between respondents who support the government parties and those who support the opposition parties. The latter have been much more critical. Nevertheless changes over time have followed the same pattern as in the measurement of satisfaction with democracy. If politicians have not been doing a good job from the public's point of view, then their ratings have gone down in both groups.

Figure 2.6 shows the development of these judgments. When about two out of three respondents say that the leading positions are poorly filled, we are dealing with more than just a critical point of view. This was the case during 1993, and it was again the case between the beginning of 1996 and up until 1998. The negative judgments dropped somewhat only during the second half of the so-called "super election year" of 1994, when politicians demonstrated much greater concern for their clientele because of an unprecedented number of important and overlapping campaigns at the local, Länder, and national levels. This countertrend lasted for about a year, after which the political elite regained its poor reputation.

It is possible to make this assessment more concrete by considering the public's evaluation of the most important German politicians over time. The result is a similar picture, as figure 2.7 shows. The highest grades for politicians were recorded right after Germany's unification. From then on, the evaluations dropped to a new low in the fall of 1992, where they stayed until the beginning of the election campaigns of 1994. The federal election in that year again coincided with better ratings for the politicians, but after that the downward movement set in again. It reached a new and, so far, absolute low point in 1997. The most recent polls suggest that the downward movement may have come to an end. However, the picture will become clearer, once some of the veterans of the Kohl government drop out of the list of "the top ten" politicians—people like Helmut Kohl himself as well as Klaus Kinkel, Norbert Blüm, Rita Süssmuth and Theo Waigel.

Non-Voting

Non-voting can be seen as another indicator of a political system's performance. It was long a neglected field of research in Germany. The reason was very simple. With voter turnouts of more than 85 percent from 1953 to 1983, there seemed to be little reason, at least for the general public and most politicians, to ask about the relatively few non-voters. In 1987, however, the turnout dropped considerably from 89.1 percent four years previously to 84.3 percent. In the following Bundestag election of 1990, it sank considerably further to 77.8 percent. A similar development took place in the Land elections.

There were good reasons for explaining what happened as a kind of "normaliza-tion."[3] This hypothesis rests on the assumption that in stable political situations, where over a longer period of time there has developed widespread trust in the political system and satisfaction with its general functioning, the people will tend toward a lower electoral turnout. This tendency is exemplified by some of the older democracies, such as Switzerland or the United States. Only in a perceived crisis would there be a significant increase in the number of people who show up at the polls to decide who should be elected to solve the problems. In the case of the Federal Republic of Germany, people tended to become more relaxed about voting after 40 years of democracy. The system was not seen to be at stake in every election. Although the 1990 Bundestag election was designated as a historic con-test, especially by the government parties, the potential electorate did not share this judgment. The big decisions regarding unification had already been made beforehand. The future direction of the nation was uncertain, but the election campaign provided no clarification. With the winner (Chancellor Kohl and his gov-ernment coalition) being clear in advance, many citizens apparently saw no urgent need for going to the polls.

After 1990, the tendency to lower voter turnout continued in Land and local elections. Even in representative opinion polls, people identified themselves as non-voters in unprecedented numbers. Polls are not the best instrument for mea-suring non-voting, because they might stimulate respondents to align themselves with prevailing social norms. The norms in this case would be a willingness to participate in the democratic process by casting one's vote. Therefore the growing number of self-confessing non-voters discovered in our polls represents a note-worthy phenomenon. This does not mean that these respondents will really behave as they say they would at election time, but the probability is high and their behav-ior at the level of Landtag contests supports the hypothesis that many of them will abstain from voting. We also have noticed a higher level of personal reflection on non-voting along with new justifications given for staying away from the ballot box. Comparisons to other times of high dissatisfaction with democracy[4] show that confessing to non-voting after 1990 and up to the end of 1993 indicated an attitude of political dissatisfaction with or protest against what was perceived as a low or unsatisfactory performance or output of the political system (figure 2.8).

Changes in the number of self-confessing and non-confessing non-voters must be interpreted in the same manner, as we did in a cross-sectional analysis of these two groups in 1993.[5] Figure 2.8 shows the changes in the sum of these two groups until the fall of 1998. And once again: only in election years were parties and politicians successful in mobilizing their clientele during the campaign. In western Germany, turnout was up two percentage points to 80.6 percent in 1994 and in-creased again to 82.8 percent in 1998. In eastern Germany, turnout dropped 1.6 percentage points to 72.9 in 1994, but it substantially rose to 80.3 percent in 1998.

Figure 2.8. Non-voters in Germany

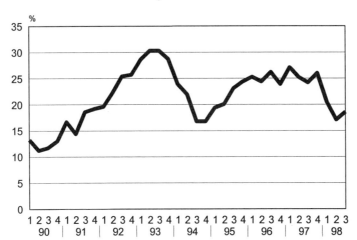

Source: Forschungsgruppe Wahlen, Politbarometer; 1/90 - 3/90 only West Germany; shown are quarter years

Non-voting and intended non-voting gives a specific group of eligible voters a chance to signal dissatisfaction with the system's political output without taking the big step of supporting one of the anti-system parties. Therefore the non-voting figures have to be watched carefully.

Top Items on the Political Agenda

We now turn to some specific issues that have concerned the public since unification. Issues are subject to change, and what is considered important from the viewpoint of the public depends in large part on its presentation in the media. There are continuing structural changes in the media, especially in the electronic outlets, which are the main source of political information for the vast majority of the people. The competition between the TV networks leads to an increase in the number of political topics they try to cover and a decrease of detailed information about single problems.

Nevertheless, from the public opinion perspective there has been one dominant problem in Germany since unification, namely unemployment. It was considered the most urgent problem in eastern Germany from the start, and it continues to rank at the top there. It became the most important issue in western Germany only after

the end of a temporary economic boom, during the first two years following unification, which had been caused by market responses to the sudden surge of demand
from the East.

For the first three years after unification, the political agenda in West and East
Germany was rather different. Thereafter the western and eastern perception of
political problems increasingly converged. Already in 1995, five years after unification, the development made it possible to speak of a shared all-German issue agenda
(figures 2.9 and 2.10).

Until the summer of 1991, the biggest problem in western Germany was seen as
"German unity," in the sense of the difficulties and the costs connected with unification. From then on, asylum-seekers and foreigners were perceived as the dominant problem, until the time of the inter-party compromise which resulted in more
restrictive asylum legislation in the summer of 1993. Unemployment became more
and more of an urgent problem in the West during the same year. By the fall of 1993,
it outranked all other problems in western Germany as had been true in eastern
Germany already three years earlier (figure 2.11).

**Figure 2.9. The most important problems in East Germany, May 1990 until
December 1993**

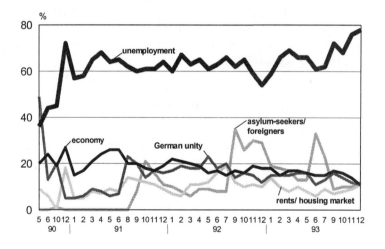

Note: Two problems could be named.

Source: Forschungsgruppe Wahlen, Politbarometer.

Figure 2.10. The most important problems in West Germany, January 1990 until December 1993

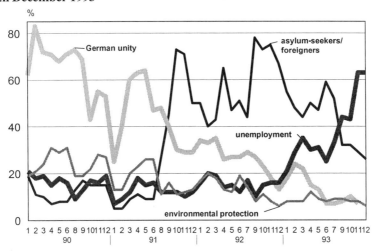

Note: Two problems could be named.

Figure 2.11. The most important problems in Germany, April 1993 until September 1998

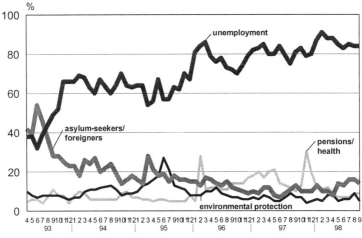

Note: Two problems could be named.

Source for both figures: Forschungsgruppe Wahlen, Politbarometer.

The Relative Competence of the Political Parties

There have been some other problems named by the respondents in our polls, such as pensions and health care, rents and housing, social security problems and education. But all of these problems—and this is even true for such issues as environmental protection and asylum seekers—have a strong economic component and can be looked at as different aspects of the dominant economic performance or output orientation that prevails among Germans. Therefore, it should be possible to find a key to the relative strength of the political parties by looking at the degree of competence the public attributes to each of them in solving these economically perceived problems.

It is too simple to try to establish a front-runner among the political parties by asking only what is the most important problem and who can best solve it. For example, many people will name unemployment as an important problem even though it does not directly affect them personally and may have no effect on their political behavior. Instead, one can look at the more general indicator of the relative problem-solving competence that respondents attribute to alternative party constellations in government (figures 2.12 and 2.13).

Because of disappointments with their economic situation and slowness in catching up to Western standards, the majority of eastern Germans soon after unification stated that the CDU/CSU-FDP government in Bonn could not solve their problems. Instead many eastern respondents believed that a government led by the Social Democrats would show greater economic competence. At the same time, however, a growing number held that neither of these alternative party governments would be able to manage the economic problems. A drastic change started in the spring of 1994, when Kohl's coalition government recaptured the competence lead and increased it until the time of the October election in that year. A similar development took place in western Germany during the spring of 1994, when the alternative SPD government lost its poll lead and fell behind the Bonn government in perceived economic competence, as measured by the polls, and stayed there until the election.

Thereafter, the development is very interesting. Since the beginning of 1996 we measure the perceived economic competence of alternative governments for the whole of Germany. The most frequent answer from the summer of 1996 until the spring of 1998 has been "none of the above can solve the economic problems." The Kohl government lost steadily in economic competence ratings after the spring of 1996, whereas an alternative SPD-led government gained, reaching the level of the CDU/CSU-FDP coalition in the spring of 1997, and soon moving ahead. Up until July 1998, there was a preference for the alternative of an SPD-led government. In August 1998, much later than in 1994, the CDU/CSU-FDP government managed to catch up. This proved to be too late to win the election. There was a perceived economic upswing, but the Kohl government was not able to earn credit for it in time (figure 2.14).

Figure 2.12. Competence in solving economic problems – East Germany

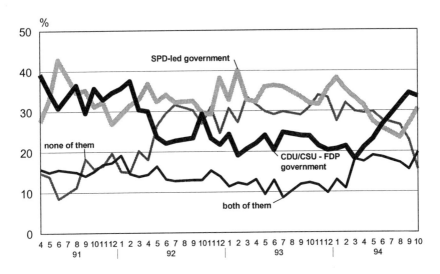

Source: Forschungsgruppe Wahlen, Politbarometer East. "Blitz" survey before the 1994 election.

Figure 2.13. Competence in solving economic problems – West Germany

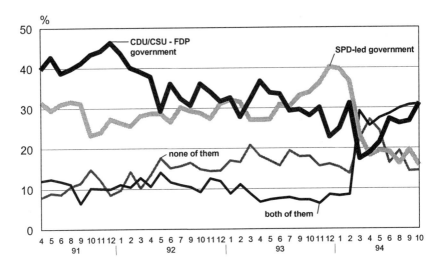

Source: Forschungsgruppe Wahlen, Politbarometer West. "Blitz" survey before the 1994 election.

Relative Satisfaction with Government and Opposition

Another general indicator of party strength lies in the public's judgments of the performance of the government and the opposition. During the first year after unification, voters expressed disappointment with policy decisions by Kohl's Union-FDP government, and the SPD opposition won more support. Such a post-election development is quite normal in a democracy. From 1992 on, however, there was an absolutely new development, which had no precedent during the two decades of our institute's recording and analysis of German voting behavior. It was characterized by a simultaneous decline in satisfaction with both the government and the opposition. In other words, the opposition was widely regarded as a nonviable alternative to the government (figure 2.15).

At that time, Germans spoke of a widespread disaffection from the established parties and politicians. Many people expressed a lack of interest in electoral participation and increasingly distanced themselves from the parties. *Politbarometer* figures from this time showed that more than 30 percent did not want to vote, and this sign of political alienation was confirmed by several state elections in 1992 and 1993 (in Baden-Württemberg, Schleswig-Holstein, and Hamburg). In this period the far-right political parties, the Republikaner and the German People's Union (DVU), achieved their best results. From the summer of 1993 on, however, the earlier political patterns returned. The opposition once again gained from the weakness of the governing parties, and the number of potential non-voters decreased.

In the state election of Lower Saxony in March 1994, this pattern continued. The big parties together garnered a much higher share of the vote than in the previous state elections, and electoral turnout stopped its decline. Polls showed that people again associated the big parties with competence to solve the predominant problems.

This political turn began a tremendous upswing movement for the government that lasted through the Bundestag election of October 1994. There were several reasons for this development. One was the general campaign atmosphere of that major election year, in which the parties once again paid close attention to their clientele. A more important reason was that the Bundestag parties were finally able to work out compromise solutions for two major policy issues that had preoccupied them for years. As already mentioned, they agreed on restrictive legislation to reduce the flow of asylum-seekers into Germany. They also worked out an insurance program for a costly system of long-term medical care. Neither solution was considered ideal by the public, but they did put an end to a long period of acrimonious dispute and political inaction in these policy issue areas.

After the Bundestag election of 1994, there followed a public opinion development that was similar to that of 1991 and 1992, although somewhat more condensed. In the beginning of 1995, the opposition gained public support, but lost much of it again later in the year primarily because of leadership problems in the SPD. The downward trend for the opposition was stopped and reversed from late 1995 on,

Figure 2.14. Competence in solving economic problems - Germany

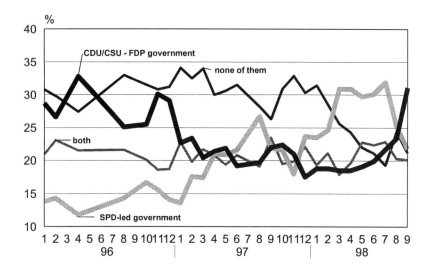

Figure 2.15. Satisfaction with the government and the opposition

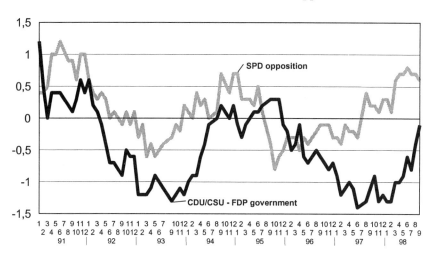

Note: Means of scale values: from +5 most positive to -5 most negative evaluation.

Source for both figures: Forschungsgruppe Wahlen, Politbarometer.

after which the SPD's ratings improved steadily. In 1998, its mean of scale values was slightly better than in 1994. Meanwhile, support for the government coalition moved downward in 1996 and by early 1997 had reached public evaluation figures that were even lower than in 1993. A new upward trend, starting in March 1998, was not strong enough to leave the "below zero" zone, as had been the case in late 1994. This is a noteworthy difference between the two election years.

These sinus curve movements of satisfaction with the government are not a new phenomenon. Such swings could always be noticed in former legislative periods, and one finds them in other Western democracies as well. The most interesting features of the development from 1990 on were, first, that the amplitudes got bigger in comparison with previous legislative periods and, second, that the government did not reach the same level of public satisfaction at election time as it had in the previous election. In 1998, this resulted in the biggest losses the CDU/CSU had to face in its party history. Most voters were no longer satisfied with the output of the sixteen-year-old government and its chancellor. Therefore, the opposition parties' victory has been primarily the result of the CDU/CSU being voted out of office.

Attitudes Toward Europe

There has been a remarkably rapid and long-term change in the German public's attitudes toward the European Community (now European Union) since late 1991. During the 1970s and 1980s, the dominant view held that there was a balance of advantages and disadvantages to membership in the Community. In 1997 this was still the view of a plurality of somewhat more than 40 percent of Germans. What changed was the relative strength of those who saw more advantages than disadvantages in membership. They outnumbered those who saw more disadvantages than advantages until December 1991, but thereafter the situation was markedly reversed, as shown in figure 2.16. From the spring of 1997 on, Germans once again became more optimistic about EU membership, but the more pessimistic view prevailed.

On the question of a European currency, German public opinion has never been in favor of replacing the familiar deutsche mark (DM) with a European unit such as the Euro (figure 2.17). Six out of every ten respondents still opposed giving up the DM in December 1997. Eighty-seven percent nevertheless took the position that the replacement would eventually occur, but only 37 percent believed it would happen according to the official schedule. The negative view of the Euro was linked to its perceived lower stability in relation to the DM: 75 percent of Germans believed that the Euro would be less stable. More than 45 percent saw more disadvantages for Germany in a currency change, whereas only 14 percent saw more advantages.

This rather unfavorable constellation of attitudes toward Europe is only half the truth. A closer look at different groups defined by their party orientation, age, or

Figure 2.16. Germany's membership in the European Union

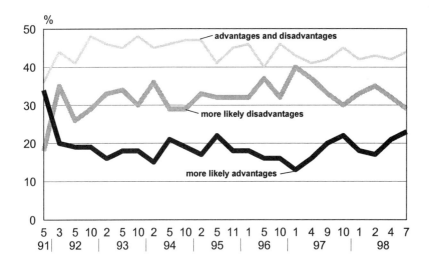

Figure 2.17. Replacement of the D-Mark with the Euro

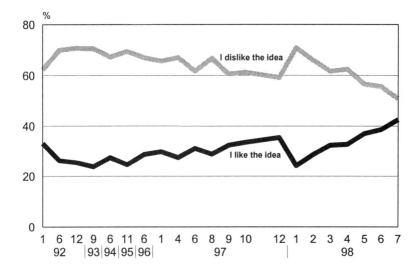

Source for both figures: Forschungsgruppe Wahlen, Politbarometer.

educational status tells us more about public willingness to accept further steps in European integration. The supporters of the Greens and the Liberals (FDP) are more favorably inclined than others towards Europe and the European currency, while the supporters of the small right-wing parties take diametrically opposed positions on these matters. The reservations about Europe and the Euro tend to diminish with higher educational status, and there is majority acceptance of the Euro among young people with advanced education.

Because they include many highly educated people in multiplicator positions, supporters of further steps in European integration appear to have a strategic advantage in the process of opinion formation. The two major parties have managed to avoid making the Euro into an electoral issue, because that would risk losing some of their own supporters to political opponents of the currency change. The schedule for the major Euro decisions, completed by the early summer of 1998, avoided a conflict with the Bundestag election campaign three months later. Partly as a result of such factors, only a small segment of the German population—9 percent in May 1998—felt that the Euro decision was a very important issue for themselves.

Conclusions

All these public opinion data show that there have been more than random second thoughts about political developments in Germany since unification. In light of the weakening economic situation in Germany and the unexpectedly high costs of unification, the public has reacted with considerable skepticism to the idea, propagated by all the democratic parties, of a faster political and economic integration of the bigger Germany into a dynamically developing Europe. In eastern Germany there were originally high hopes about a fairly rapid convergence of the social and economic conditions between East and West. These unrealistic expectations were fueled by the campaign promises of the governing parties, symbolized by Chancellor Kohl's famous vision of "blooming landscapes" in the East. There is little of that original optimism left (figures 2.18 and 2.19).

From 1990 on, there has been a growing number of Germans in the East who assume it will take more than ten years before they will be doing as well as West Germans. The only interruption in this pessimistic trend occurred in the election year of 1994. By the latter half of 1997, this group had become an absolute majority of more than 50 percent of the respondents—up from only 6 percent in 1990. During the same time period, the number of easterners who believe in the imminence of "blooming landscapes" for their region has plummeted. By 1998, fewer than 10 percent expressed the view that eastern Germans would catch up to their western counterparts within five years.

By contrast, Germans in the West have been much more realistic on this question from the time of unification onward. Except for a period in 1994 and 1995, when

Figure 2.18. How many years will it take until east Germans are doing as well as West Germans?

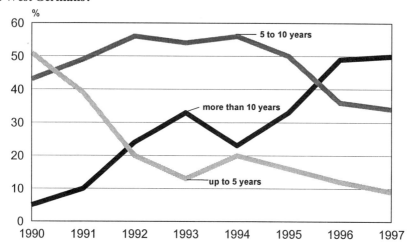

Note: East Germany 1990 until 1997.

Figure 2.19. How many years will it take until east Germans are doing as well as West Germans?

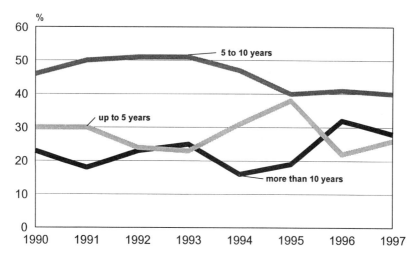

Note: West Germany 1990 until 1997.

Source for both figures: Forschungsgruppe Wahlen, Politbarometer.

there was somewhat greater optimism about the time span needed to complete the convergence process, the balance of assessments has changed relatively little in the West: Approximately as many believe that it will take "up to 5 years," "between 5 and 10 years," or "more than 10 years" as was the case in 1990. In view of the passage of eight years since unification, however, this can also be interpreted as a growing pessimism about the time needed for eventual convergence between East and West.

There have been some political consequences of the attitudinal change in Germany. The decline in support for the governing parties of the Kohl administration between the Bundestag elections helped the SPD and the Greens win votes at the state level. The Social Democrats became the governing party in several states, and this in turn gave them a blocking majority in the Bundesrat, or federal chamber, in Bonn. Although the Bonn coalition parties (CDU/CSU and FDP) were successful in their campaign of 1994, their victory over the opposition parties in the Bundestag was razor-thin. Only 0.3 percent of the popular vote separated them from their rivals. There has been a growing distance between the voters and the democratic parties in state elections. In most cases, there has been a decline in voter turnout. Right-wing parties have produced some fairly strong showings in recent state elections, including a successful return to the Landtag in Baden-Württemberg (1996), a very close call with 4.97 percent of the vote in Hamburg (1997), and a widely noticed 12.9 percent in Saxony-Anhalt (1998). On the left, the PDS has made its way from a marginal party to a third force in eastern Germany. For the first time after unification, the PDS has been accepted by the SPD as coalition partner in one of the eastern Länder, Mecklenburg-Vorpommern, after the state election in September 1998. On the same day, the PDS managed to pass the 5 percent threshold on the federal level. As a result, the post-communist party has acquired the important status of a full parliamentary group (*Fraktion*) in the new Bundestag.

Party identification has declined remarkably during the 1990s, except for a short recovery in the Bundestag election year of 1994. The group of non-identifiers, previously a minority, has grown and become the largest group. The weak identifiers hover between 30 and 40 percent, while the group of strong identifiers has declined to 30 percent or less (figures 2.20 and 2.21). The two large parties (*Volksparteien*) have suffered from this electoral development, which has both structural and political reasons.[6]

What does all that mean for the stability of the German political system? To gain some insight, we can draw on additional data. One set shows a declining satisfaction with the societal conditions in West Germany and an even lower level of satisfaction in East Germany. There are other data, however, which show rather stable value orientations within West German society and a strong tendency in the East to adopt these same values (tables 2.1 and 2.2). Such a value alignment would be a significant development, given the manner in which individual values tend to reflect personal living conditions.[7]

Figure 2.20. Party identification

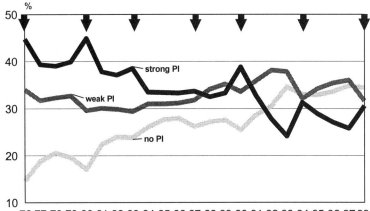

Notes: 1998 until September only.   ▼ = Federal Election Years
        West Germany only.

Figure 2.21. Strong party identification

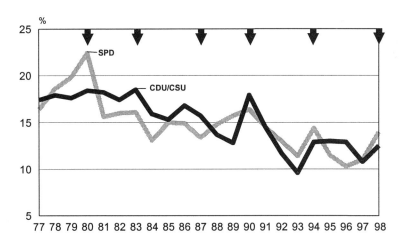

Notes: 1998 until September only.   ▼ = Federal Election Years
        West Germany only.

Source for both figures: Forschungsgruppe Wahlen, Politbarometer West.

In West Germany there was a high continuity of values over time from 1984 to 1990 and again after the unification with East Germany. It is not surprising that there are more value changes in the East, given its different starting position in 1990. But there is a similar tendency over time in the two parts of Germany, resulting in a stabilizing and converging set of value orientations. Right after their first free election, in March 1990, East Germans stressed the promotion of such values as economic growth, technical progress and meritocratic rewards even more than West Germans. In the meantime, their experiences in a competitive market society have somewhat dampened their initial enthusiasm in these matters. In the first years of freedom, eastern support for a strong police increased markedly. There has been little or no change over time with respect to wishes for formal democratic participation or the general attitude toward a state versus a private provision of health care. Even in such matters, however, there are no big difference in value orientation between East and West.

There has always been a high correlation between satisfaction with the political system and economic well-being, and this appears to hold true for eastern Germany as well. In the early 1960s, Gabriel Almond and Sidney Verba concluded in their famous study, *The Civic Culture*, that West Germans of that time were strongly output oriented, that they accepted and understood the value of having democratic institutions, but that they had not yet developed strongly affective attitudes towards the democratic system.[8]

Our polls thus show that there has been a decline of expressed satisfaction with democracy in Germany, in both east and west. However, this decline seems primarily to be rooted in dissatisfaction with the system's performance or policy output. It co-exists with a long-term identification among respondents with the political system, especially in the West. The result is a difficult one for political leaders. Voters react critically if they feel misled or cheated by the politicians and the parties. They scorn a politics that seems to take the form of tactical prevarication. If the parties do not address the widely perceived problems, voters will eventually make themselves felt by seeking a change of government, as they do in other democracies. The 1998 Bundestag election has shown that the German voters are both willing and able to vote a federal government out of office. It was the first such complete change of their national government brought on by voters in the Federal Republic, but it will hardly be the last.

Thus, an electorally determined shift in power took place in advance of the federal government's return to the capital city of Berlin. Although the political transfer from Bonn to Berlin is itself not very popular, as shown earlier, it is unlikely to become a major issue for the next few years. People will realistically view the move as irrevocable. But German attitudes towards the transfer will probably continue to reflect the degree of public satisfaction with the political system's overall performance.

Table 2.1. "Ideal Society" for east Germans

	1990	1991	1992	1993	1995	1997
Promotion of economic growth	6.3	6.0	5.8	6.0	5.9	5.8
Promotion of technical progress	5.8	5.5	5.4	5.4	5.3	5.2
Income based on individual performance	5.6	5.2	5.0	5.1	4.9	5.0
Strong police (to ensure law and order)	4.0	5.0	5.1	5.3	4.9	4.9
Stratified reward system (based on ability, education, performance)	5.7	4.9	4.7	4.7	4.5	4.7
Market Economy (instead of a more centrally planned economy)	5.8	5.4	5.0	4.9	4.7	4.6
Growth ahead of environment	2.8	2.9	3.0	3.0	3.3	3.4
Representative democracy (instead of a more direct form of democracy)	2.4	2.5	2.5	2.4	2.4	2.5
Private health care/pension provisions	2.6	2.1	2.2	2.2	2.1	2.3

Note: Means of scale values ranging from 1 to 7.

Table 2.2. "Ideal Society" for west Germans

	1990	1991	1992	1993	1995	1997
Promotion of economic growth	5.3	5.2	5.3	5.2	5.4	5.4
Promotion of technical progress	5.5	5.4	5.3	5.1	5.2	5.0
Income based on individual performance	5.2	5.2	5.1	5.0	5.0	5.0
Strong police (to ensure law and order)	4.4	4.4	4.4	4.4	4.6	4.6
Stratified reward system (based on ability, education, performance)	5.0	5.0	4.9	4.8	4.7	4.5
Market economy (instead of a more centrally planned economy)	3.7	3.9	4.2	4.1	4.3	4.2
Growth ahead of environment	3.0	3.0	3.0	3.2	3.3	3.4
Representative democracy (instead of a more direct form of democracy)	2.9	3.1	3.0	3.0	3.1	3.1
Private health care/pension provisions	3.1	3.1	3.1	3.2	3.2	2.9

Note: Means of scale values ranging from 1 to 7.

Sources for tables 2.1 and 2.2: IPOS, yearly representative polls in May or June.

Notes

This chapter was originally written in December 1997, with the text and figures updated in October 1998.

1. Udo Wengst, "Wer stimmte für Bonn, wer für Berlin?" *Zeitschrift für Parlamentsfragen* 22, no. 3 (1991): 339-43.

2. Roman Herzog, "Aufbruch ins 21. Jahrhundert," address at the Hotel Adlon on April 26, 1997.

3. Dieter Roth, "Sinkende Wahlbeteiligung—eher Normalisierung als Krisensymptom," in Karl Starzacher et al., eds., *Protestwähler und Wahlverweigerer* (Cologne: Bund-Verlag, 1992), 58-68.

4. Birgit Hoffmann-Jaberg and Dieter Roth, "Die Nichtwähler," in Wilhelm Bürklin and Dieter Roth, eds., *Das Superwahljahr* (Bonn: Bund-Verlag, 1994), 145.

5. Hoffmann-Jaberg and Roth, "Die Nichtwähler," 150 ff.

6. Dieter Roth, "Stabilität der Demokratie—Die Lehren der Bundestagswahl 1994," in Heinrich Oberreuter, ed., *Parteiensystem am Wendepunkt?* (Munich: Olzog, 1996), 24-35.

7. Ronald Inglehart, *Modernization and Postmodernization* (Princeton: Princeton University Press, 1997).

8. The latter observation may no longer be correct for western Germans, but it still seems to be appropriate for eastern Germans.

Appendix

Figure 2.22. Party Preferences in Germany, 1994-1998

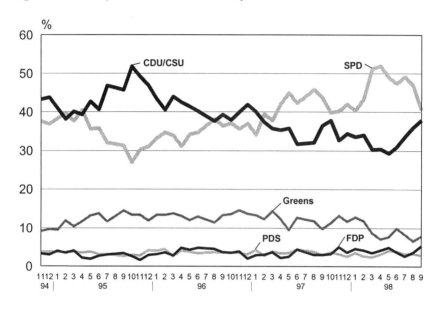

Source: Forschungsgruppe Wahlen, Politbarometer.

Figure 2.23. The political mood in West Germany, 1991-1994

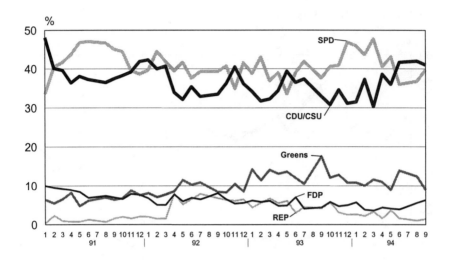

Source: Forschungsgruppe Wahlen, Politbarometer West.

Figure 2.24. The political mood in East Germany, 1991-1994

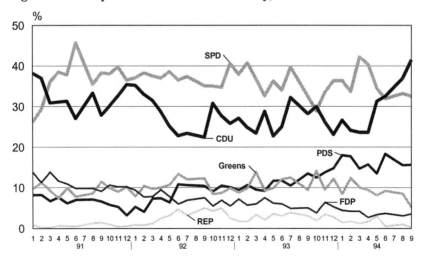

Source: Forschungsgruppe Wahlen, Politbarometer.

3

The CDU/CSU:
Undercurrents in an Ebb Tide

Clay Clemens

The Christian Democratic Union/Christian Social Union (CDU/CSU) presents a double paradox. On one hand, this most successful of all democratic parties in the history of Germany, perhaps even Europe as a whole, enjoyed its greatest triumph in 1990 by helping to reunify a divided nation under Helmut Kohl's guidance. Yet at no time did the CDU/CSU seem more adrift than in the ensuing decade. Moreover, success appeared to be a major cause of this disorientation: sixteen years in office, and a quarter century under one leader, had complicated the task of addressing policy challenges, old or new, and questions about its own future. Partly for this reason, in 1998 German voters sent the party to its worst defeat in decades, and thereby also removed a sitting chancellor for the first time ever.

To be sure, it was not the first time that a long period of success eventually came at a price for the Union.[1] The postwar CDU arose from remnants of former Catholic and middle-class Protestant parties in most West German Länder; Bavaria's Christian Social Union retained a separate organization, reflecting the distinct identity of its conservative, agrarian region. Together these Union "sisters" formed the core of CDU chancellor Konrad Adenauer's governing alliance that presided over an economic boom, close integration into the west during the 1950s and huge electoral success. Even after their small coalition ally, the Free Democratic Party (FDP), or Liberals, briefly defected, the CDU/CSU remained West Germany's premier political force, despite its chancellor's slumping appeal and a sense that the party had grown too wedded to power. In 1963 the Union-FDP alliance clung on under his heir, Ludwig Erhard; three years later the CDU/CSU settled for becoming senior partner in a Grand Coalition with its larger, center-left rival, the Social Democratic Party (SPD). But then, in 1969, both former governing partners ganged up to oust the Union from power. It fell into bitter disarray, unable to forge a coherent, common front in response to SPD chancellor Willy Brandt's popular detente policies. After becoming the CDU's federal chair in 1973, Kohl led his party into a phase of reconstruction, helping to create a programmatic identity and structures that would make it more self-sufficient and reduce its image as the mere vehicle of Bonn's governing clique. He and CSU leader Franz Josef Strauss tried rallying their Union in the 1970s, but hampered by their own rivalry and conflicts over strategy, they struggled for nearly another decade to oust Helmut Schmidt's SPD-FDP government.[2]

In 1982 the Union could finally renew its old coalition with the Liberals, a partnership that proved durable, if fractious. As chancellor, Kohl insisted on holding out until his team—amid long quarrels—reached policy compromises, often tacitly granting the FDP or CSU a veto over decisions. Such bickering indecisiveness often drew criticism, though so long as its policies—improved relations with Bonn's Western allies, fiscal restraint to dampen inflation, law and order—enjoyed what Kohl deemed a "politically sustainable consensus," his coalition clung to power. Despite criticism and challenges, he too hung on as CDU chairman and chancellor. Then, amid an apparent crisis in 1989, Communism collapsed in East Germany, providing a dramatic chance for action. With solid CDU/CSU and FDP backing, Kohl in 1990 helped attain national unity, in the process reviving his party's long-lost wing in the GDR. This "East-CDU"—for decades a puppet of the Communist regime—became Bonn's ready ally, and then merged with its western namesake. Triumph for this newly enlarged CDU/CSU in the 1990 federal election rejuvenated Kohl's government. But reunification's mounting socioeconomic cost strained its credibility and cohesion, dispelling any euphoria. Kohl's coalition seemed certain to lose power in 1994, until a brief economic boom, his energetic campaigning and—as always—discord among its left-wing rivals came to the rescue.[3] After eking out a slim victory in 1994, however, the Union-led government still faced pressing unity-related problems in the East, compounded by structural decline of the western economy and record unemployment. Bickering over a response to these tests eroded public approval of Kohl's coalition and the CDU/CSU. As it faced the 1998 campaign, his party struggled to deal with accumulated deficits in several different areas: programs and policies; structure and personnel; and electoral and coalition strategy.

Program and Policies

Despite growing emphasis on its programmatic statements from the 1970s on, Kohl's CDU still long pursued a fundamentally pragmatic approach to policy, guided by broad principles, but focused primarily on devising practical compromises that would command a sufficiently broad base of support in a party composed of many often conflicting interest groups and tendencies.

Under pressure from its trade union-oriented progressive wing, the party partly formally embraced "Christian-social" doctrine, yet also tried to balance that vaguely leftist (if devoutly non-Marxist) concern for society's neglected with strong support for private property, market mechanisms and free enterprise. As a result, the CDU became closely identified with Germany's social-market economics—a "consensus, compassionate capitalism" that relies on public sector action to protect key groups from the effects of competition, but eschews state control or ownership. While more vocal in condemning socialism, the CSU also adopted this approach, which helped it to modernize once-agrarian Bavaria. Espousing these broad principles on socioeconomic policy, without really trying to reconcile their contradictions, long served party unity. Each part of the Union—trade unionists, farmers, small business people, professionals, corporate managers—could appeal to a different dimension of "consensus capitalism." It also sold well to a public wary of both pure socialism and "brutal" laissez-faire.

At times, however, this pragmatism on socioeconomic policy led to quarrels and gridlock. Efforts by the CDU workers' group (CDA) to bolster party support for labor's right to "co-determine" management decisions ran afoul of conservative forces in the 1970s. Pledges in the early 1980s to slash regulations and subsidies faced resistance—including from within CDU ranks: the CDA and business groups had *both* grown wedded to state support or protection. Farm subsidies became vital to CDU/CSU agrarian constituents.[4] Reunification added to the breadth, and incoherence, of its socioeconomic policy preferences. Much divided them, yet easterners—accustomed to the broad if flimsy protection of "real existing socialism"—viewed capitalism ambivalently: though eager for a Western standard of living, most feared losing out in a pitiless competition.

In a sense, Kohl's Union thus proved no more able than its left-wing rivals to resolve the socioeconomic policy dilemmas thrust upon Germany by reunification and "globalization." High deficits and joblessness resulted. Partly, but not solely, due to pressure from their more market-oriented Liberal partners, CDU leaders from Kohl down *did* begin to call for enhancing German competitiveness in the early 1990s, and several initiatives received party support. But most lost momentum during intra-party consultations, before then petering out in broader deliberations that included SPD, Land and labor leaders. Western CDU progressives, and their Eastern colleagues, resisted slashing labor costs, corporate tax rates or social programs; Kohl's longtime labor minister Norbert Blüm, icon of their party's CDA, threatened to quit and spark a major crisis unless the government scaled back its reform plans. Easterners resisted trimming or reversing the so-called "solidarity tax," imposed to help fund their region's reconstruction. Farm, corporate and regional subsidies found protectors as well. CSU chair and finance minister Theo Waigel seemed unable to produce credible budget figures that satisfied the entire Union, let alone its FDP ally or SPD Bundesrat leaders. Never a specialist on socioeconomic affairs, Kohl coaxed and chided colleagues in a quest for compromise, but without clear success (especially in tacking unemployment, which reached postwar highs in the 1990s).

If the CDU ever truly espoused a programmatic goal, it was creation of a (more) united Europe—one that pools sovereignty and dilutes nationalism. Not coincidentally, the Germans most closely associated with this vision were Adenauer and his self-designated "political grandson," Kohl. The latter cajoled and pressured fellow European Union (EU) leaders to move forward. Depicting it as "a matter of war and peace," he helped shape, then sell, the convoluted agenda for political union (EPU) and monetary union (EMU) that emerged at 1991's Maastricht Conference. Kohl initially did little to mobilize CDU/CSU support for either, banking on what seemed to be solid, traditional, reflexive party commitment to Europe. Integration had indeed long enjoyed broad backing, especially from Catholic westerners, small and large business, most agrarian interests, professionals, and others tied to the CDU. "Europe" also enjoyed a positive image across broad segments of public opinion as well, in part reflecting German reluctance to sound nationalistic themes.

On the other hand, some conservatives had long resisted giving integration priority over national unity, and—even *after* reunification—questioned the party mainstream's commitment to Europe: they implicitly spurned Kohl's contention that Bonn's EC *bona fides* had helped make it possible for nervous neighbors to acquiesce in German unity, let alone his candid concession that partner states should help tie his own nation (down) into their evolving union. Yet by the 1990s this "Euro-skeptical" fringe included others in the CDU who began to worry that meeting strict fiscal prerequisites for EMU could further erode Germany's "social state." Land leaders complained about an alleged tendency toward centralizing authority in Brussels. And public uneasiness about trading in the D-mark for a "Euro" of uncertain stability struck a chord in Kohl's party too. Blunter CSU skeptics, led by Bavarian Minister President Edmund Stoiber, began finding sympathy among northern colleagues. Facing pressure, and fearing that public support for Europe might prove shallow—exposing their Union to risk from any backlash—even many integration advocates began pressing for either a slower pace or, at least, assurances that EMU would not sacrifice Germany's tradition of solid finances and stable prices (even as Bonn's own debt seemed to leave their country short of the criteria for monetary union).

In a long debate over ratifying the Maastricht accords, Kohl held firm. He and other Union leaders, like CSU chief Theodor Waigel, fell back on traditional arguments: that Germany had gained from integration and would, as Europe's top exporter, profit even more from EMU; that moving forward was vital to avert reverse momentum toward national animosity; that "multilateralizing" the D-mark would prod neighboring states to accept more "supranational" decision making on all issues. Such points carried the day, but drawing so heavily on the capital of their party's pro-Europe sentiment risked emptying the account. By the mid-1990s, Kohl and others found it increasingly difficult to mobilize CDU supporters, let alone CSU politicians, behind old slogans. Euro-skeptics could cite concrete risks from EMU (and even EPU): after stripping the social state, they warned, Germans would end up with a Euro subject to Italian profligacy. In response, Bonn pressed a macro-economic "stability pact" upon EU partners, evoking more grumbling—and suspicion that Germany would use its economic weight to dominate structures that Kohl long claimed would *overcome* national power (critics like Stoiber in fact seemingly wanted as strict a reading of EMU criteria as possible in part to rouse such international counter-pressure). Union politicians began promising to curb Bonn's EU budget contribution as well.

To be sure, Kohl's CDU remained home to more influential Europhiles than any mainstream party. Yet it also encompassed the broadest, influential array of doubters, and with him no longer around to blunt it, skepticism seemed likely to grow. At the very least, Union consensus on integration had peaked: preserving it would become an ever greater challenge for his successors.

A traditional CDU/CSU consensus on "domestic security" issues also held, while fraying at the edges. Most party leaders, for example, pressed to limit alleged abuse of German asylum laws, claiming that a flood of illegal immigrants had fed street crime, as well as radical right-wing violence. But progressives and younger, liberally minded CDU spokesmen, resisted. Proposals to ease naturalization for resident aliens have widened this rift. And Union calls to combat common or organized crime have prompted quick "copycatting" by SPD pragmatists anxious to avoid being accused of softness on law and order.

In sum, the Union—Bonn's quintessential party of government for decades—remained closely identified with traditional policies that had made the Federal Republic successful. Yet this very record also gave key elements in Kohl's party a stake in the status quo of Germany—above all its Western Länder—and Europe. Moreover, the Union's preference for pragmatic consensus that endangered no one sub-group's vital interests could also often stalemate a quest for coherent, innovative responses to new challenges or opportunities. After 1998, the party would thus have to show that it could offer successful policy formulas for governing what many were calling the "Berlin republic" in a new century.

Structures and Personnel

The CDU began as a broad, loosely structured party, with quasi-autonomous branches in each Land; affiliated interest groups exerting pressure on specific policies; a Bundestag caucus resistant to guidance from elsewhere; and functionaries also jealously protective of their room for maneuver. With only a vague, diverse program, the CDU held together primarily for the purpose of electing a chancellor, but otherwise had little presence in federal politics.

As a reformist chair in the 1970s, Kohl pledged to give his party more cohesion and a life of its own, even when *not* in control of Bonn's chancellory. Extra-parliamentary bodies like its annual congress of activists, executive committee and elite presidium gained more say over party policy positions. CDU federal headquarters prepared programmatic statements and guided lower-level branches in marketing them. But even then, Kohl saw energizing the party apparatus as valuable mainly as a way of mobilizing it behind his effort to help regain power in Bonn. Wherever this "modernization" risked *another* element of his strategy—rebuilding a broad CDU/CSU-FDP coalition—the former took lower priority. Aside from successful recruitment of more dues-paying members, which also helped out the treasury, reform did not fundamentally alter the party's original structure as a broad, loose chancellorial alliance.

After the Union regained power in 1982, modernization slowed further, for Kohl had no desire to see his party become an independent force, influencing government decisions in ways that might weaken coalition unity. He thus counted on continuing to manage it in his own way, through a network of loyal clients promoted for or named to key slots, even in Land branches; his balancing role among internal groups that required never identifying with *or* entirely alienating any single one; and continual, confidential contact with ordinary functionaries in every district-level CDU organization, usually by telephone.[5]

Structures of the federal-level party atrophied after 1982. Its loosely linked elements retained their autonomy but, never having been welded together, gained little combined leverage over government decisions. Congresses still debated resolutions, but few would seriously affect decisions of Kohl's coalition. As chair, he could not ignore the executive committee and presidium, where top colleagues might criticize his government—indeed, sharply—but these bodies could rarely overrule its actions. After putting up with an independent-minded CDU general-secretary, progressive Heiner Geissler, Kohl ousted his old friend, along with aides who had indiscreetly deplored the stagnation of party reform. This 1989 purge reconverted party headquarters into a machine focused mainly on electioneering. Even before reunification boosted the chancellor's image, he had thus deprived critics of a national platform for challenging his governance. In the 1990s, general-secretary Peter Hintze's party headquarters never amounted to an independent power base, but also often proved lackluster or ineffective.

Each Land branch *did* retain some autonomy and provided a base from which to criticize Bonn for policies or image problems that cost it support. Kohl faced sniping from provincial "barons," often old rivals, in the 1980s and their younger heirs, the "wild things," in the 1990s. But his network and contact with functionaries kept the malcontents from coalescing into a viable counterforce. As chancellor and chair, he could also often preoccupy or weaken them by backing his own candidates for top Land posts. In any case, such critics could only really hamper his governance in Bonn if they held power as minister president and sat in the Bundesrat; by the 1990s few did. Their own problems also limited the ability of Land branches to steer the party as a whole. Lack of internal democracy and campaign irregularities split Hamburg's CDU in two. An old scandal and bland leadership afflicted Schleswig-Holstein's branch, while—despite progress—Bremen's remained the weakest in West Germany. Elsewhere, power struggles and generational succession battles raged.

Nowhere, however, did Land branches face more difficulty than in the East. To avoid controversy, Kohl had given up the old, pro-regime East-CDU's buildings and bank accounts. Yet members in the GDR often could not afford normal dues, creating financial constraints and dependence on Western support. Party function-aries were new to democracy and administration, even to Land (the five regions having been created in 1990). Worse, bitter debate raged between the predominant "old-guard"—that roughly three-quarters of members who had loyally supported their Communist-era leaders—and newcomers who had joined as the Berlin Wall fell and sought a renewal that would ban collaborators with Honecker's dictator-ship from high party office. This breech persisted into mid-decade, hurting all Land branches and crippling some, like Brandenburg's.[6]

Western CDU colleagues who intervened in this squabble invited angry attack, as then general-secretary Volker Rühe discovered. Despite a gradual thinning of their ranks, the old-guard remained vocal, even resisting efforts to woo away former anti-regime dissidents from the Greens who swelled the ranks of newcomers. Kohl characteristically sought to moderate, pleading for renewal in the abstract, but avoiding overt involvement in rooting-out old-guard leaders or functionaries with murky pasts. Instead, he preferred to let others create the openings and fill them—where possible with local talent, where not with "imports," that is, politicians from the "old Länder." Indeed, from 1990 on, western "tutelage" of the eastern branches expanded. While needing financial, logistical and even strategic help, while aware of their own inexperience with democratic partisan politics, the "old-guard" and even renewal advocates often came to resent "remote control." Especially when it came in smug or superior tones and reflected lack of familiarity with their region's unique past or problems, such help evoked bitterness. Eastern CDU branches might themselves be riven, but the gap between them and the wealthy West loomed larger.

Each of the Union's various problems surfaced in its Bundestag caucus. After weak leadership in the 1980s, when government leaders often presented it with *faits accomplis*—coalition compromises that could only be rejected at risk of undermin-ing the CDU/CSU-FDP alliance—parliamentarians welcomed their new chief, Wolfgang Schäuble, in 1991. Kohl did indeed entrust this protégé with more re-sponsibility for working out legislative deals, including those that would require SPD support (so as to pass the Bundesrat). Yet that authority did little to empower or rally Bundestag backbenchers. A stern taskmaster, Schäuble demanded clarity and quiescence. In the long 1996-97 slog over reform proposals on taxes and pen-sions, morale among Bundestag members plummeted.

Fissures old and new surfaced. Emulating CSU parliamentarians, who had long used their number and unity to pressure the government, CDA trade union deputies (over eighty, more than the FDP) tried acting as a bloc. So too did the roughly sixty CDU Eastern caucus members—led first by Gunther Krause, later by Paul Krüger (both unhappy ex-ministers). They pressed Union colleagues to avoid canceling the solidarity tax that helped fund Eastern reconstruction, and sought more regional input. Liberally minded, youthful deputies formed the Young Group: though too diverse to function as a bloc, its members raised issues that could irk party or government leaders. These varied rumblings testified to the caucus members' frustration at their own impotence.

With the party again overshadowed by the government, as in the 1950s, membership stagnated. It peaked in 1984 at about 730,000 and slumped by some 20 percent over the next decade in Western Germany to under 600,000. Nor did the qualitative picture look better. The share of dues-paying women did not rise and the average member's age climbed from an already high 50 to 53 years. Older, male functionaries still dominated at the lower levels, at congresses, and in the activist corps. Despite renewal efforts, and *because* of them, the Eastern branches lost about half of their original 130,000 members. Some old guard Christian Democrats left, deploring their loss of influence or charging persecution, but—more disturbingly—some people who had joined *after* Communism collapsed also defected, having lost their earlier ardor.[7] In 1997, the party had approximately 636,000 dues-paying members nationwide.

While slumping membership plagues all European parties, CDU leaders saw it as a problem, recognition signaled by periodic efforts at a face-lift, but halfheartedness or resistance left the old profile largely intact. Unity did bring in new working class members and credible spokesmen from among the East's leftish, yet anti-regime leaders, boosting the 24,000-member CDA's hopes of attracting still more support from labor. But amid the 1990s slump, its chief Rainer Eppelmann—who had won Kohl's respect as a dissident—was compelled to defend coalition compromises, aimed at creating jobs by cutting wage costs. His CDA grumbled that becoming "a larger FDP" would not win over workers. In hopes of making their party more appealing to women, aides persuaded even Kohl to endorse a proposal requiring that any delegate's ballot in elections to the executive committee or presidium be invalid unless it endorsed female candidates for at least one-third of the open spots. To their surprise, this measure lost at the 1995 congress in Karlsruhe. Kohl's general-secretary Hintze devised a weaker alternative that would invalidate any first round of balloting in which women did not win at least one-third of all open seats for both bodies and requiring a second vote, results of which would stand. Some argued that any candidate slate would now have to reserve at least one in three spaces for women and that fear of an embarrassing second round would lead delegates to elect them—a claim at which some scoffed. This version passed, helping win a presidium seat for families, seniors, women and youth affairs minister

Claudia Nolte—a young, conservative easterner and Kohl protégé who had ironically opposed any quota system.

Nor did efforts at recruiting teens (only one in five backed the Union), students and "yuppies" succeed. Pop music in campaign spots and forming a "future ministry" had no effect. Taking up a challenge from Young Union chief Klaus Escher, the chancellor invited him and other youthful critics to help plan the 1997 congress and form an advisory commission on attracting more members under forty, but it had little impact on party decisions let alone coalition policy. As for those few ethnic Turks with citizenship, Berlin's CDU did launch an effort to woo them, but federal party leaders refused to follow suit (polls showed that, despite a basic conservatism and family-orientation, only 6 percent of German Turks favored the Union). Thus in the end, hopes of making CDU members and activists look more like a cross section of society that went nowhere.

Under Kohl's long tenure, the CDU also gained little fresh blood at higher levels. Those who might challenge him outright or resist his government's policies faced a major obstacle to advancement. Though fond of his role as patron for many CDU leaders, he discouraged any who seemed too independent. Maverick intellectuals with broad public appeal, like Kurt Biedenkopf, or even a party base, like progressive Heiner Geissler, often aroused wariness among conventionally minded functionaries, who suspected that "modernization" concealed efforts to purge them. Kohl stoked the flame of such fears as a way of further isolating men whom, despite long personal association, he also increasingly came to distrust. When several of them hesitantly moved to oust him at a famous 1989 party congress, he crushed their half-hearted coup.[8] Younger aspirants *could* build a base in certain Land-level branches, useful as protection from retaliation for sniping at Bonn's government. Yet the general decline in CDU electoral fortunes made it harder for such "princes" to depict themselves as national leaders, and any who *did* seek such prominence still had to reckon with their federal chairman.

To be sure, Kohl's tenure did ensure two generations of CDU parliamentarians cabinet experience. Yet these ministers also found it difficult to develop an independent profile: Kohl restricted all but a few to narrowly defined policy responsibilities, reserving for himself alone the role of generalist. Even his cabinet's most prominent members—finance minister Waigel and labor colleague Blüm—were politically crippled, having borne primary responsibility for complicated, often unpopular socioeconomic reforms that often ran aground.

After more than fifteen years in power, then, the "backup crew" to Kohl in his own party consisted mainly of trusted protégé Schäuble, once chancellory director, later interior minister and Union caucus chief. Already respected for his pragmatic mastery of detail, serious substantiveness, and sharp polemical skills, he won further admiration for helping negotiate German unity and then overcoming a near-fatal assassination attempt. Yet while his grit in handling arduous political work from a wheelchair impressed colleagues, some doubted his capacity to master either of Kohl's jobs. Others also came to tire of Schäuble's taskmaster style and nationally oriented conservatism. CSU leaders suspected him of wanting to govern with the SPD, which would diminish their own influence.

Another Kohl protégé, Volker Rühe, rode a political rollercoaster. After a steady climb in his parliamentary career during the 1980s, he won the chairman's nod as CDU general-secretary, only to plunge sharply after alienating East German colleagues and others put off by his bald ambition, yet then recovered by mastering a portfolio that had crushed most predecessors. Indeed, many suspected that Kohl had named him defense minister partly to clip his wings, an impression bolstered by the chancellor's periodic rejection of military budget requests. But Rühe not only dealt well with logistical limits on the post-reunification, post-Cold War Bundeswehr, but helped generate political acceptance of its deployment abroad, even in crises—long considered impossible.

Yet beyond Schäuble and Rühe, CDU reserves remained surprisingly thin for a party its size, in power for fifteen years. A few younger ministers like Matthias Wissmann showed promise, though most others once touted as potential heirs—Klaus Töpfer, Jürgen Rüttgers, Manfred Kanther—fell victim to policy problems, a bad press or mere blandness. As for the often more dynamic young CDU Land leaders who attracted media attention for modernizing their branches *and* often criticizing Kohl—Lower Saxony's Christian Wulff, Rhineland-Palatinate's Christoph Böhr, North-Rhine Westphalia's Helmut Linssen, Hesse's Roland Koch, Saarland's Peter Müller—none had an election victory as of 1998.

Future CDU leaders plainly faced a quandary: they could get ahead in their party only with Kohl's blessing, which bound them to him, or by seeking an independent power base in the Länder, which risked arousing his wariness. It would thus in effect take the chancellor's departure as chair for a full-scale regeneration of leadership to take place within his own party's ranks. And yet Kohl compounded this problem by never specifying when he might step down, in part for fear of seeing his power slipping away prematurely to an heir, and in part because of a desire to ensure that any transition took place on his terms. Confusion on that timing issue would haunt the Union in 1998.

Kohl also played a role, albeit more indirectly, within the CSU. For years, Strauss had given his party charismatic leadership, while it backed his ambition to represent conservatism nationwide and steer the Union, even Germany, from Munich. Only when this effort risked an even higher priority—the CSU's bond with and predominance in Bavaria—would colleagues rein him in. As heir to Strauss's post as party chair, Waigel opted for harmony with Kohl's CDU, accepting his role as junior partner—albeit one with considerable say. CSU officials back in Munich grumbled at this seeming surrender of their pretensions to a major, independent national role, and worried that accommodating Kohl's coalition could irk conservative Bavarians, who demanded curbs on crime and foreigners. Initially these dissidents could not mount a challenge, given Waigel's prominence as negotiator of German unity in 1990 and the weakness of his main CSU rival, Minister President Max Streibl. But Bavarian discontent over asylum and Maastricht grew in the early 1990s, as did criticism of Waigel's budget policy. Moreover, a party finance scandal rocked the CSU apparatus in Munich, paving the path for a new leader. Minister President Edmund Stoiber distanced himself from radical right-wingers—proposing to ban splinter parties, chastising maverick Peter Gauweiler—yet stole their themes. At the same time, his austere, diligent, clean image won respect. Seeing Stoiber as a rival for control of the CSU, Waigel ran against him for the Bavarian premiership, and lost. Friction between them grew, fed by charges that Waigel was "Kohl's man." Though the CSU chair did have backers in Munich, Stoiber became de facto party leader. He briefly buried the hatchet with Kohl for the 1994 campaign, given the chancellor's revived popularity, while his own image and superior CSU organization helped retain a majority in Bavaria. Stoiber's star kept rising as he sniped at the Bonn coalition's slipshod reforms and Kohl's support for EMU. As Waigel's reputation waned, federal CDU leaders felt obliged to shore him up against Stoiber—who some young Land politicians in the chancellor's own party praised and called a possible future chancellor. Despite claiming to be burdened by its association with Kohl's government in Bonn, the CSU even slightly increased its absolute majority in Bavaria at 1998's Land election, enhancing the minister president's claims on higher office in the party and, many argued, eventually national politics as well.

Electoral and Coalition Strategy

For sixteen years, Kohl's CDU/CSU served as a fulcrum of his coalition, in which he functioned as mediator-in-chief. Even when unhappy at having to compromise on their own preferences, colleagues in the party went along. Many did dream instead of an absolute Union majority, but that alternative rarely seemed plausible, a fact the chancellor emphasized. Others might have preferred a Grand Coalition, but Kohl—and most party conservatives—argued that this option, while clearly attainable, entailed its own costs: however irksome concessions to the little FDP could be, their Union would have to give even *more* ground if in harness with the SPD, and the 1966-69 precedent suggested that any such oversized, centrist government might so alienate right-wing Union voters as to make them ripe recruits for small, radical parties. As he reiterated, a healthy FDP lay in the Union's interest, as Germans wanted a moderate, center-right coalition: it was not a blissful marriage, Kohl added, but so long as his Union enjoyed a "strategic majority"—enough seats to block formation of any likely alliance that *excluded* it—the party could govern. In any case, events made his case for him: often after trailing, the CDU/CSU-FDP team rallied for four federal election victories, wooing swing voters by hyping the specter of a left-wing government, as well as by exploiting divisions within the SPD-Green opposition. And however demanding at times, the FDP remained on board.

But being wedded to this coalition for so long posed problems that Kohl or any successor would have to face. While ultimately the three partners often managed to agree on policy, continual wrangling damaged each party's image, while watery compromises diluted its own identity and widened internal rifts. Deferring contentious issues likewise also exacted a price. By the mid-1990s, the CDU, CSU and FDP seemed to have run out of common ground on policy.

Union politicians felt that depending on the Liberals cost their party heavily. When feeling bold *or* panicky, the FDP flaunted its independence, advancing or blocking policy initiatives, such as—in the 1990s—tax cuts and scaling back the solidarity surcharge. Accommodating such pressures sacrificed the priorities of CDU Easterners, CDA spokesmen, or even CSU leaders. Discord among the Liberals—on asylum, for example, or crime—could also delay coalition action and prevent the Union from capitalizing on issues vital to its own base, as well as to undecided voters. Even when the FDP gave in, too divided and weak to press its point, CDU/CSU fortunes could suffer. For *lack* of a distinct Liberal impact on policy threatened to drive key swing or centrist supporters away from the junior ally, driving it closer to the 5 percent minimum for Bundestag representation (by the mid-1990s it had already vanished from all but a few Land assemblies). Unless the Union attracted these voters, FDP setbacks risked bringing down the entire coalition. In 1983, and again in 1994, voters who preferred Kohl's CDU/CSU had to vote for the struggling Liberals and keep them above the 5 percent-threshold so that he had a viable partner. CDU leaders also waited anxiously, for instance, to see if their partner would cling on in several key Land elections in early 1996; thanks to "loaned" votes, it did.[9] Such assistance, however, not only drew down the Union's *own* electoral capital, but bailed out an ally who would then resume its self-promotion by sniping at the chancellor's party. To some analysts, this mutual dependence indicated that the Liberals could not regain meaningful independence: bound tightly to Kohl's government in Bonn, the FDP seemed at most an appendage that might cause a distracting commotion, but could rarely help his coalition or the body politics move forward.

CDU politicians also at times came to resent the key role Kohl accorded their Bavarian sister. Fearful of losing clout in a Germany that had grown more northern, more eastern and less Catholic, while uneasy that adding five new Länder diluted their own region's weight, the CSU remained anxious to preserve a distinct profile in Bonn. When unified in defense of Land interests or conservative positions, it irked many northern colleagues, who often feared that a "rightward lurch" would alienate their *own* voters. Kohl tried to woo moderate Bavarian leaders like Waigel, give them a stake in his coalition's success, and thus get them to win over—or simply subdue—hardliners. He succeeded, but only for a time—and at a cost. Binding the CSU chair into his coalition and cabinet by making him finance minister briefly produced harmony, as Waigel's role in reunification won kudos. His cheerfulness and camaraderie with Kohl even sparked talk that "Theo is a CDU man." Just such closeness, however, irritated CSU rivals. Soon they were joined by CDU Land leaders who challenged Waigel's budget figures or finance ministry efforts to balance the books with indirect taxes. Some CSU colleagues did rally to their chief, as did some members of Kohl's own party, who feared that a rival like Stoiber might prove too conservative or anti-EU. Such splits within each Union sister, along with latent differences between those in Bonn and colleagues "in the provinces," only widened *further* when the Liberals got involved in any such fray. To keep its absolute majority in Bavaria, the CSU campaigned hard against the FDP in 1998.

Such problems seemed to hasten erosion of the coalition's electoral foundations, a process already under way. Most analysts agreed that prosperity and secularization in western Germany had long been eroding the share and loyalty of traditional middle class voters, as well as church-going Catholics, who once reflexively backed the CDU/CSU.[10] Concessions to the Liberals seemed certain to disenchant even more core supporters, while coalition infighting and a stalemate on reform would also make it hard to attract the growing share of uncommitted "new middle class" voters, who prized competence and clarity. Squabbles having already weakened its always-small core constituency as well, the FDP rarely benefited from Union losses, but seemed in even *more* serious jeopardy: turned-off by the Liberal party's image problems, many undecided or swing voters saw it as too weak or too beholden to Kohl's coalition to continue serving as an independent corrective on *either* large party. Annoyance and resignation thus appeared to be driving the FDP below the 5 percent, further weakening the viability of a strategy on which Kohl's Union depended. Indeed, the Union-FDP *combined* drew a lower share of West German voters in 1994's election than had Kohl's CDU/CSU *alone* in 1983. To be sure, given the general tendency of incumbents to lose support, 47 percent after a decade in office was no disaster. But slipping down into this range raised doubts about their partnership's longevity. Panicky efforts by all three partners to seek "profile" only further dampened voter enthusiasm. Nowhere did this appear clearer than in Land elections. Once the dominant constellation throughout West Germany, the CDU and FDP combined could muster a majority only in Baden-Württemberg by mid-decade. The Union could no longer count on even its "strategic majority": during most of the 1990s, had the SPD, Greens and FDP been able to bury their differences, they could have governed in Bonn in a "stoplight coalition."

Developments in eastern Germany further fed concern about the long-term viability of a center-right coalition. Reunification euphoria had swept Christian Democrats into office during the GDR's last months, despite their often dubious pasts or bland ineptness, and also boosted the newly merged, nationwide CDU at united Germany's first federal election, while signs of recovery helped it cling to a respectable vote share four years later (FDP fortunes in the new Länder followed a similar pattern at first, though its slide in the early 1990s proved irreversible). Yet to the extent social structure undergirds voting, the center-right had no obvious base among largely secular, working-class easterners. Having opted for Kohl's CDU or the FDP mainly as a protest against the old system, a show of support for unity and—in 1994—a demonstration of optimism, they had at best a fragile affinity for either party. Disappointed expectations, let alone angry resentment, began to cost both in the new Länder. While *no* Bonn-based political party prospered there, the risks for Kohl—and for his strategy—seemed especially grave. After all, no one embodied the distant, disdained Bonn establishment more completely. By mid-decade, the CDU-FDP tandem thus enjoyed too little support to govern in any eastern Land except Saxony (where an anomalous absolute majority for Biedenkopf's branch made *any* coalition a moot issue). Even where still level with its SPD rival beyond the Elbe, Kohl's party increasingly faced only two options there: join the former in a Grand Coalition, or be relegated to perhaps permanent opposition. Yet flirting with *either* such course in turn risked further straining the CDU/CSU-FDP alliance in Bonn. Already, collapse at the Land-level had reduced its seats in the influential Bundesrat, compelling Kohl's government to attain SPD support there for most bills, which meant either stalemate, or—if Liberal preferences were ignored—still more strains. Governing against *or* with a strong opposition in the Länder threatened to continue corroding his coalition.

To be sure, the Union could still try proven or potential tactics for safeguarding at least a strategic majority. Where SPD resistance could be credibly blamed for thwarting policy compromise, as with efforts at tax or pension reform, Kohl's party could blame it for "blockading" tactics. Yet given public coolness toward many government proposals, this charge did not seem necessarily so damaging for the opposition (and to Kohl's surprise, the SPD in 1998 did not nominate its chair Oskar Lafontaine, the "chief blockader," as chancellor candidate). Another option lay in scaring undecided voters by evoking the specter of an SPD-Green government. But by 1998, this tactic also seemed less promising: growing moderation in the SPD under its charismatic chancellor candidate Gerhard Schröder and even in the "ecological party" (despite its almost suicidal call for huge gas tax hikes and withdrawal from NATO in 1998) meant that a "red-green coalition" worried fewer Germans. Finally, as in 1994, the Union would try to mobilize western voters by accusing both mainstream left-wing parties of tacitly relying on the ex-Communist PDS to form governing majorities in some eastern Länder—and perhaps even Bonn. CDU general-secretary Hintze continued this "red socks" campaign, emboldened when several former dissidents left the Greens in disgust over that party's flirtation with the PDS and joined Kohl's Union. But old-guard CDU easterners found this tactic awkward, in part given their own pasts. They and others also worried that Cold War rhetoric depicting PDS leaders as closet Stalinists could backfire by striking voters in the new Länder as yet another case of Bonn's smug establishment using the past to humiliate them. Even Kohl loyalists like Angela Merkel felt that CDU branches in the East, their support already ebbing, could ill-afford to anger more people: they operated in a very different political landscape than their western counterparts, and thus needed to compete with this ex-Communist rival, not merely denounce it. Their chair did agree to drop the provocative "red socks" symbol, but not the anti-PDS theme, and tried pounding away at it in the 1998 campaign as well (this time with a controversial poster depicting a "red handshake" between the two leftist parties).

During his long tenure, advancing alternatives to Kohl's strategic preference for a Christian-Liberal coalition proved difficult, especially when his grip was at its strongest. Moreover, an option with great appeal, especially among conservatives, aiming for an absolute CDU/CSU majority, usually seemed unfeasible. Still, some other scenarios did periodically come under discussion, prompting debate that revealed—and partly further exacerbated—uncertainty about the future.

Most practical was the alternative of aiming, or at least settling, for a Grand Coalition. Indeed, developments often seemed to make it all but inevitable: waning voter support for Kohl's Union and its FDP ally; a partly related revival of SPD fortunes, including the party's expanded Bundesrat power and the consequent necessity for accommodating it on most bills; and a sense among CDU progressives and left-leaning easterners, that post-unity socioeconomic challenges require a broad, consensus-oriented government, not one in which laissez-faire Liberals sought unpopular policies. By the mid-1990s, these trends had produced Grand Coalitions in more western Länder than at any point in decades, and in half the East's regions—where common desire to avoid relying on PDS support provided an added incentive. As a result, Kohl's government grew dependent on—and susceptible to—its main opposition when making policy (even Länder where the CDU remained senior partner in a Grand Coalition could not back government bills that did not satisfy the SPD). Moreover, this alliance-of-necessity accustomed many Union leaders—progressives, but also moderates and conservatives—in Bonn and the Länder to dealing with Social Democrats as counterparts, or partners. Ever fewer still feared (as in the 1960s) that a Grand Coalition in Bonn might undercut the democratic idea of alternation in government and pit the establishment against anti-system forces, as there could still be a healthy Bundestag opposition led by the FDP and Greens. Results-oriented leaders like Schäuble and Rühe among others began to view an alliance of the larger parties as the most sensible way to get things done. Even Kohl and Union conservatives, albeit for more tactical reasons, would not rule out a Grand Coalition. First, if electoral mathematics were to make allying with the SPD the only way of retaining power and thereby blocking a left-wing government, they did not want their own past rhetoric to be a major barrier. Second, the Union had long dangled prospects of cooperation before moderate Social Democrats to discourage them from embracing the alternative of a "red-green" coalition, thus fueling friction among an already-divided opposition.

Still, the CSU in particular and many CDU colleagues, led by Kohl, long viewed a federal Grand Coalition as, at best, an undesirable, last resort in case no other way of remaining in office seemed available. Along with requiring major policy concessions, formal partnership with the SPD would still risk burnishing the latter's own credentials as a senior governing party and—as a result of both drawbacks— bolster the appeal of right-wing protest parties for conservative voters (as it did during 1966-69). Moreover, skeptics saw this option as no more likely to avert policy gridlock than the post-1990 status quo, with Kohl's Union-FDP team intact yet forced to seek compromises that the opposition-dominated Bundesrat would accept (indeed, a stalemate on issues like tax or pension reform could be seen as proof that having the SPD in government might become inevitable, but also foreshadowed more gridlock if that happened). The CSU feared that it would have less power to stop a leftward drift as it would not be critical to the parliamentary majority in an oversized Grand Coalition. Opting for this alternative thus seemed likely to divide the Union severely.

Partly as a result, some young CDU leaders began to warn against excluding another scenario once dismissed as unthinkable: a "black-green" coalition. More attuned to a younger generation's environmental concerns and liberal social views than their elders, they claimed not to be far apart from the ecological party's "realistic" elements. Black-green coalitions also cropped up in some local councils; leaders in Saxony, Baden-Württemberg and Saarland flirted with such deals at the regional level. Again, for tactical reasons—to keep the SPD and Greens apart— Schäuble, and even Kohl, approved practical collaboration with the latter. Yet they still saw this option as inconceivable in federal politics for at least a decade given major differences on policy between the two parties' leaders and their constituents, while Union conservatives rejected the idea out of hand.

One other strategic alternative, for the new Länder alone, also drew debate. Some Union easterners feared that their party risked becoming a permanent opposition in the region's politics if it came to be seen strictly as an advocate of unpopular, market-oriented coalition programs made in idyllic, but distant Bonn. Instead, they argued, CDU branches in the new Länder should not merely jettison their weak Liberal ally, but identify much more fully with the former GDR, advocating its unique interests and becoming, in effect, an "eastern CSU." Especially if coupled with less emphasis on rooting out Communist collaborators (in party ranks or elsewhere), this tactic could, they held, help steal major issues, as well as voters, from the PDS. Such a proposal earned Mecklenburg-Vorpommern party official Eckhardt Rehberg and one-time federal cabinet minister Paul Krüger some quiet assent among colleagues. But others charged them with fostering "separatism" and tacitly favoring cooperation with the PDS in order to block the SPD from local or Land governments; even fellow CDU easterners, especially those favorable to renewal, could see little prospect of an absolute majority in the region by accommodating PDS voters. Western colleagues denounced any such tactic as sure to undermine the party nationwide.

Conclusion

In 1994, despite trailing in the polls, Kohl—aided by an economic boomlet— had helped his Union to eke out a slim victory, and well before 1998 even many of his critical colleagues had urged that he lead their party into battle once again. But as the government floundered over socioeconomic reform, dissidents began to assail its ministers and policy processes. A minor uptick in the economy seemed to make no dent in unemployment or speed rebuilding of the new Länder. Kohl's own preoccupation with diplomacy at the expense of domestic affairs also came under fire. As his public approval dropped, rumors spread that a new chancellor candidate would be needed sooner rather than later.[11] Kohl deepened his own difficulties by counting on the SPD to nominate its left-wing chair Lafontaine as chancellor candidate. For insurance, the CDU chair involved himself deeply in Lower Saxony's spring 1998 Landtag election, predicting that Christian Wulff would win and thus deal a death blow to the national aspirations of popular moderate Social Democratic incumbent Schröder. Instead the latter pulled off a major victory and an unusually united SPD rallied behind him, not Lafontaine, as its chancellor candidate. Initial polls gave Schröder three times the support Kohl enjoyed. Calls for the chancellor to make way for his heir mounted. But Kohl still regarded himself as essential to a united, robust coalition campaign, and could count on his own loyalists, as well as those (in the CSU, for example), unready to see Schäuble move in unchallenged. The caucus chief did himself no favor by presenting a "future manifesto" calling for measures, like energy tax increases, that further divided his Union. In any case, having entrusted Kohl with power for so long, most CDU/CSU leaders knew that trying to wrest this title from his hands would amount to collective suicide. Still, to hold out the promise of change, some Union and above all Liberal leaders demanded that he set a clear date for a transition of leadership to his protégé, again in vain. Moreover, the chancellory, CDU headquarters, Schäuble's caucus, and CSU leaders all vied for control of Union campaign strategy, divided over whether to build it around Kohl and traditional themes like "security instead of risk," or to try something new, and uncertain how hard to attack SPD cooperation with the PDS. Despite a strong CSU showing at Bavaria's Land election, a mild improvement in the economy and other late-summer hints of a rally, their Union never got off of the defensive.

In September 1998, Germany's electorate paradoxically made the Union's various difficulties both more dire and somewhat less urgent. In the party's worst showing since 1949, it did not merely fall far short of a majority, but finished well behind the SPD, garnering just 35 percent of the nationwide vote (and barely over a quarter in the new Länder). Some 1.6 million former CDU/CSU supporters defected straight to Schröder's camp, and more than one hundred single-seat Bundestag districts changed hands, going from Kohl's party directly to its main rival (in Eastern Germany, the CDU won just three outside the Land of Saxony). Not only did the Christian-Liberal team lose its majority, but a Grand Coalition became superfluous: the SPD and Greens would possess a comfortable governing majority on their own. Thus the Union would go into opposition for only the second time ever, for the first time since 1969. Taking full responsibility, Kohl and Waigel stepped down as chairmen of the CDU and CSU respectively.[12]

While this debacle meant that the Union was no longer Germany's strongest party and premier player in coalition politics, it also finally paved the way for

changes on every front. There would now at least be a chance to clarify the CDU/
CSU's programmatic position and stance on policies, free from pressures of day-
to-day governance and coalition compromise. Within weeks, the CDU had confirmed Schäuble as its new federal chair; he in turn named Merkel as their party's
first female general-secretary. Other women won spots on the presidium (which
would now enjoy greater clout), as did younger leaders like Wulff, Koch and Müller,
along with easterner Arnold Vaatz. As for a new strategy, almost all parts of the
CDU agreed on the need to regain its strength at the Land level and somehow win
back eastern support (though Schäuble's talk of allowing former Communists into
the ranks proved more divisive). Despite their long coalition with the Liberals,
moreover, many Union leaders spoke against maintaining an alliance while in opposition: some seemed grateful at being able to attack the FDP and hinted at a longer-
term preference for working with the SPD or even the Greens. But all also agreed
that it was not the time for thinking about coalitions: the Union needed to focus on
resolving its own internal difficulties first.

Lurking behind these more immediate problems were deeper-lying questions.
For decades, this party more than any other had come to embody and shape the
postwar status quo in a West Germany it long governed. The CDU/CSU stood for
Bonn's broad, consensual socioeconomic policies at home and a tendency to conduct foreign policy "in Europe's name." Its loose, federal, "polyarchical" structure, "catch-all" appeal, and professional campaigns were likewise reflections of
the political system and, at the same time, standards for success. So too was the
focus on a coalition strategy that allowed the CDU/CSU to govern, yet only with
partners and in a consensual way, evoking no fear of a power monopoly.[13]

But just as it was a key to success for decades, such close identification with
postwar West Germany's status quo had become a challenge—even a threat—for
the party once every familiar political landmark underwent change. Even *before*
reunification, a breakdown in the conditions allowing for consensus on socioeconomic issues, a decline in group membership, erosion of older social milieus, and
emergence of new parties all rattled the comfortable assumptions on which Kohl's
Union operated. Though the chairman resisted adapting to these new circumstances,
his skill at the political game as played by traditional rules helped his party to cling
on; indeed, the zenith of his career, if not his party's acme, still lay ahead, in the
annus mirabilis—1989-90. Yet unity *also* accelerated and added to the changes
rattling Germany's political landscape, all the more so as equally dramatic, broader
transformations accompanied it: the end of Cold War tension, unexpectedly rapid
progress toward European integration, rapid economic globalization, an erosion of
borders worldwide.

Since these developments spawned fundamentally new conditions for Germany—and thus questions about its very identity in a new century—they challenged the CDU in similar ways. Helmut Kohl long faced this test by downplaying
its difficulty. For him, united Germany was a larger, freer version of the Federal
Republic, and all other major changes were mainly chances to succeed by following

proven formulas: consensual social-market economics, European integration, personalized party management, the Christian-Liberal partnership. Few could deny that he made these approaches work longer than expected: by most accounts, he *and* they both should have failed to survive the first half of this decade. Yet his form of leadership died with the 1998 debacle. Moreover, Kohl was plainly the last politician with the generational experience and credibility needed to convince others—and himself—that many of the old approaches could still work. Like some surviving dinosaur, he had dominated even an already-changing environment, yet could not do so forever—and those who followed would inevitably be creatures of a new era, their own era.[14]

For many Christian Democrats, the future of their country and party alike lies in thinking beyond Bonn, to Berlin. By this, they mean not only taking the different nature of the East and the special problems of CDU branches there into account. They also mean growing beyond the modest expectations and limited horizons of their comfortable, cozy "federal village" on the Rhine. For them, unity in many ways ended the Federal Republic and revived Germany—a larger country that should be more economically fit, unburdened by the weight of needless regulation or entitlements, less bound by its darker past chapters, equipped with a strong state, unapologetic about ensuring social order, confident in asserting its interest in Europe or further afield. Such is the vision of Germany often articulated by, or attributed to, Schäuble and Rühe. Just as Kohl's two chief protégés may want the CDU to hold out a bolder vision, both will approach its structures and strategy differently than their patron. Though anything but unfamiliar with party politics, they represent a generation impatient with managing personnel or factional affairs in endless chats or smoke-filled rooms with functionaries. More at home in defining or mediating pragmatic, detailed substantive policy compromises, they count mainly on success in this area to keep party regulars in line. Nor will this first successor generation remain wedded to coalition with the FDP. While not counting on an absolute majority, they note—in Schäuble's unsubtle words—that the CDU/CSU needs a "strategic potential" independent of *any* partner. The longtime caucus chief even seems to prefer, at least tacitly, a cohesive, disciplined if smaller Union, to the broader, looser party of old. He worked for years patching together deals on policy with the Liberals, yet that very experience if anything seemed to exhaust his patience with them. Moreover, both Schäuble and Rühe have seemed willing to work with the SPD in seeking accords that could help Germany move beyond the confines of Bonn's traditional, self-contained, self-confining policies— on asylum, for example, deployment of the Bundeswehr beyond NATO territory, taxes and pensions. Though the 1998 result made a Grand Coalition unnecessary for the immediate future, that option is thus by no means dead for all time in their eyes.

A slightly different vision of the CDU's future had also begun to emerge in the 1990s, especially among younger, up-and-coming westerner leaders. If Kohl's traditional ideas were rooted in Bonn, and Schäuble's sights are set on Berlin, their thinking is perhaps best associated with Frankfurt. The Bundestag's "Young Group" and its counterparts in Land branches, "the wild things," see a Germany neither bound to its comfortable postwar past nor aiming for an intangible "greatness," but evolving—much like the Main river metropolis itself—into a bustling, economically dynamic, ecologically conscious high-tech oriented, internationally focused and multicultural society. Some advocate dual citizenship for foreigners born in Germany, minimizing subsidies designed to placate interest groups, policies to spark innovation by reducing labor costs, and a normal foreign policy. Beyond programmatic matters, they urge their party to regenerate itself, to permit less decision-making from the top-down and create a functionary corps that looks more like German society—with younger faces, more women, even minorities. They also feel that, should the FDP continue fading, their CDU—with a bit more openness, innovation and imagination—could win over what remains of the Liberal agenda and electorate, making dependence on coalition compromises less vital. While not hostile to a Grand Coalition, some also look beyond it to potential partnership with the Greens. And ultimately few see much reason why a regenerated Union could not aspire once again to an absolute majority.

Kohl's approach succeeded for decades, and Schäuble can expect his own to supplant it. But whereas in earlier decades, generational turnover within their party had brought few changes largely because of a broader stasis in German society, by the 1990s the clamor of younger Union politicians seeking a say coincided with a comprehensive, sweeping transformation of the overall political environment. While the CDU thus remains a center-right catch-all party focused on government, its profile seems certain to evolve in the new millennium.

Notes

The author would like to thank Professor Dr. Wolfgang-Uwe Friedrich of the University of Hildesheim: his annual German-American Research Group (*Deutsch-Amerikanischer Arbeitskreis*) has offered an invaluable opportunity to keep abreast of issues covered in this chapter.

1. For a good recent introduction to German party politics generally, see Gerard Braunthal, *Parties and Politics in Modern Germany* (Boulder, Colo.: Westview, 1998). For the early decades of the CDU (pre-1982) in particular see Geoffrey Pridham, *Christian Democracy in Western Germany* (New York: St. Martin's, 1977) and Hans-Otto Kleinmann, *Geschichte der CDU* (Stuttgart: Deutsche Verlags-Anstalt, 1993).

2. Wulf Schönbohm, *Die CDU wird moderne Volkspartei: Selbstverständnis, Mitglieder, Organisation und Apparat 1950-1980* (Stuttgart: Klett-Cotta, 1985); Carlos Huneeus, "How to Build a Modern Party: Helmut Kohl's Leadership and the Transformation of the CDU," *German Politics* 5, no. 3 (December 1996): 432-59.

3. See Christopher Anderson and Carsten Zelle, "Helmut Kohl and the CDU

Victory," *German Politics and Society* 13, no. 1 (Spring 1995); and Clay Clemens, "Second Wind or Last Gasp? The CDU/CSU and the Elections of 1994," in *Germany's New Politics: Parties and Issues in the 1990s*, David Conradt, Gerald R. Kleinfeld, George K. Romoser and Christian Søe, eds. (Oxford: Berghahn, 1995), 131-49.

4. For an interesting account of economic policy-making after 1982 see Douglas Webber, "Kohl's *Wendepolitik* After a Decade," *German Politics* 1, no. 2 (August 1992): 149-80.

5. See Pridham, *Christian Democracy*; Clay Clemens, "The Chancellor as Manager: Helmut Kohl, the CDU and Governance in Germany," *West European Politics* 17, no. 4 (October 1994): 28-51.

6. Clay Clemens, "Disquiet on the Eastern Front," *German Politics* 2, no. 2 (August 1993): 200-223: see also the detailed analysis in Ute Schmidt, "Von der Blockpartei zur Volkspartei? Die Ost-CDU im Umbruch 1989-1994," *German Studies Review* 20, no. 1 (February 1997): 105-37.

7. Figures from party reports cited in *Focus*, 26 June 1995, 46-49 and *Süddeutsche Zeitung*, 9 September 1997.

8. A satirical novel based on the Kohl era and in particular this 1989 episode, written by one of Geissler's top aides, provides perhaps the most vivid, readable account available of CDU internal politics. Wülf Schonbohm, *Parteifreunde: Ein Roman aus der Provinz* (Düsseldorf: Econ Verlag, 1990).

9. David Broughton and Neil Bentley, "The 1996 Länder Elections in Baden-Württemberg, Rhineland-Palatinate and Schleswig-Holstein: The Ebbing of the Tides of March?" *German Politics* 5, no. 3 (December 1996): 503-23.

10. For a recent analysis of the significance of these trends see Kai Arzheimer and Cornelia Weins, "Zerfallen die sozialstrukturellen Bindungen an die Union—zum Beispiel in Rheinland-Pfalz?" *Zeitschrift für Parlamentsfragen* 28, no. 2 (May 1997): 203-16.

11. One charged him with living in the "cloud-cuckoo-land" of a world statesman. *Die Welt*, 12 July 1997.

12. For a detailed if early analysis of the election results see *Der Spiegel: Wahlsonderheft 98*, 29 September 1998.

13. Josef Schmid, *Die CDU: Organisationsstrukturen, Politiken und Funktionsweisen einer Partei im Föderalismus* (Opladen: Leske, 1990), 256-84.

14. For various assessments of the Kohl era, see Warnfried Dettling, *Das Erbe Kohls* (Frankfurt: Eichborn, 1994); William Paterson and Clay Clemens, eds., *The Kohl Chancellorship* (London: Frank Cass, 1998).

4

The SPD:
Between Political Drift and Direction

Andrew B. Denison

The general sense of uncertainty that prevails in Germany at the end of the 1990s also affects the Social Democrats, who now head the national government and preside over its move to Berlin. The Social Democratic Party (SPD), with Gerhard Schröder as chancellor candidate, won a solid first place in the Bundestag election of 1998, in part by identifying themselves with what he called a "new middle" (*neue Mitte*) in German politics. This vaguely defined centrist position bears at least some rhetorical resemblance to the one claimed by Tony Blair's "new Labour" in Britain or Bill Clinton's "new Democrats" in the United States. Germany's Social Democrats also reminded voters that it was time for a change after sixteen years of government under Chancellor Helmut Kohl, and their main slogan confidently proclaimed that "we are ready" (*wir sind bereit*).

However, the SPD's impressive appearance of unity and direction during the election campaign barely papered over a number of internal problems that again surfaced in the early months of power. The Social Democrats had not really resolved the issue of ultimate policy priorities, of how to balance the various currents and constituencies within the party while also governing the country. These difficulties are likely to trouble the party's efforts to govern successfully in the coming years of change. They can be attributed to a number of factors, many with roots predating the fall of the Berlin Wall. This chapter looks at the SPD's history, its principles, its organization and its constituents in order to show how each has contributed to the party's present dilemmas.

These internal conflicts also show themselves in clashing personalities, in the contending visions of Gerhard Schröder, chancellor, and Oskar Lafontaine, finance minister and party chairman. Going into the campaign, the Social Democrats had settled on a form of dual leadership, choosing Schröder as a centrist candidate who enjoyed greater popular support, while keeping Lafontaine as party chairman, who was much more popular within the SPD, particularly on the left. A clever compromise before the election, the strategy of dual leadership nevertheless threatened policy deadlock or worse. During the first months of SPD-led government, the German press often focused more attention on an alleged power struggle between the two leaders than on the policies they were trying to implement.

As head of Germany's first "red-green" government, Chancellor Schröder now faces the formidable challenge of giving more substance to the notion of governing from the "new middle," and, more importantly, of mobilizing support for his policies, both among Social Democrats and from the public at large. Lafontaine's pivotal cabinet position, as head of an expanded finance ministry, will be a major additional power factor with which the new chancellor must reckon. Nor can he afford to ignore the junior coalition partner, Alliance 90/Greens, who also want to set their marks on the government agenda. Schröder will be governing all of Germany, but his most important source of support and influence will be his party. The challenge of getting an old and established party, riven by competing interests and outlooks, to govern from a "new middle" proved gravely difficult in the first months of the new government. The contrast between political drift and direction grew particularly pronounced in the fall of 1998: Direction led the SPD to a stunning election victory over Helmut Kohl. Drift followed, as competing constituencies pulled the party first one way, then another, leading to one of the bumpiest starts any new German government had seen.

An Old Party in a New Germany

The SPD is Germany's oldest and biggest party. Yet age is not always an advantage, and large membership does not guarantee electoral victory. In the almost five decades between 1949 and 1998, the Social Democrats had a first short experience in the federal cabinet as members of the grand coalition with the Christian Democrats under Chancellor Kurt-Georg Kiesinger (CDU) from 1966 to 1969. Thereafter they governed the Federal Republic for thirteen years under Chancellors Willy Brandt (1969-1974) and Helmut Schmidt (1974-1982). The SPD then was forced to return to the parliamentary opposition when its junior partner, Hans-Dietrich Genscher's Free Democrats, abandoned the SPD-FDP coalition to form a new government with Helmut Kohl and his Christian Democrats.

The SPD's long period in opposition—and some of its problems—thus predated the fall of the Berlin Wall. Nevertheless, the challenges of unification, compounded by a widening Europe and an opening global economy, confronted the SPD with an even greater need to modernize—and condemned the party to further electoral defeats in 1990 and 1994. In advance of the 1998 Bundestag contest, the

SPD made some very important changes—on party program and party unity—that helped improve its electoral prospects significantly, but the party remains hobbled by a series of structural problems.

The first of these problems lies in the SPD's own traditions of socialism and solidarity, and in its long history of opposition to the German establishment. This legacy goes back to the party's formation in 1863, as a self-declared representative of the growing industrial working class in Germany.[1] The next seventy years saw the SPD become the largest party by 1912 (38.5 percent of the vote), leave the parliamentary opposition to join other parties in patriotic support of the war effort in 1914, split over the issue of support for German war aims, and then play a key role in ending the war and founding the Weimar Republic. The tradition as an anti-capitalist and anti-military party made it difficult for the SPD to bend to the requirements of governing, but it served in several coalition governments before Hitler's rise to power in 1933. The SPD was outlawed that same year. Many leading Social Democrats went into exile, others ended up in concentration camps.

The historical legacy is an honorable mix of idealism and realism, but it has not always been favorable to the formulation of practical political goals. Thus, the SPD had difficulty finding a successful strategy for itself in the new West German democracy after World War II. The first postwar leader, Kurt Schumacher, had come out of a Nazi concentration camp with serious physical injuries but undaunted in spirit. He channeled his energies into rebuilding the party and brought it to within a hair of victory in the Federal Republic's first elections in 1949 (SPD 29.2 percent, CDU/CSU 31.0 percent). Having lost, he defined the party's role as one of "constructive opposition." To him that meant political resistance to what he saw as an emerging "conservative, clerical, capitalistic, cartel-ridden" Germany and Europe.[2] Schumacher died in 1952, but the party continued to oppose the westward orientation of Adenauer's Germany, particularly in regard to NATO membership and German rearmament.

Only in the late 1950s did a new leadership emerge that slowly moved the party toward the middle of the West German political spectrum. The SPD accepted social market economics and German rearmament in 1959 in its landmark Godesberg program. Soon thereafter, in 1960, chief strategist Herbert Wehner announced the SPD's support for NATO membership in a watershed speech to parliament. During 1962, Wehner followed an "embracement strategy" in trying to lead the Social Democrats into government as partners of the Christian Democrats. Yet it was not until a year after the 1965 Bundestag election (SPD 39.3 percent) that the SPD finally joined such a grand coalition under Chancellor Kiesinger (CDU). The SPD leader and reformer Willy Brandt took on the post of foreign minister, and his party used the opportunity to acquire for itself a public image of competence in governing. The grand coalition lasted until 1969, when the SPD's further electoral advance (to 42.7 percent) and the FDP's availability as a reform-oriented junior coalition partner made it possible for Brandt to form the first SPD-led government in Bonn.

Spearheading a new Ostpolitik of reconciliation and normalization with the communist states to West Germany's east,[3] Brandt also tried to channel and tame the radicalism of the "68er" youth movements, the so-called APO or extra-parliamentary opposition. Appealing to all Germans to "dare more democracy," he encouraged the 68ers to join the Social Democrats. They did, and in droves. Membership in the SPD went from 820,000 in 1970 to an all-time high of 1,022,000 in 1976.[4] Germany's APO began its "long march through the institutions." Brandt's chancellorship came to an end in 1974 when, already weakened by a fight with unions and some leading members of his own party, he decided to resign after one of his close advisors, Günter Guillaume, was revealed to be an East German spy.

Helmut Schmidt, former defense and finance minister, stepped in to replace Brandt. Less the visionary, more the technocratic manager, Schmidt focused on financial austerity and military security to a greater degree than many new, young and idealistic party members thought necessary. He was able to consolidate ties with the West and give Germany a more significant international role, for example, by playing a key part in initiating what are now the so-called G-7 summits among the world's seven largest market economies.

Germany had weathered the economic turbulence of the early 1970s relatively well in comparison to other Western democracies, and Schmidt campaigned successfully for reelection in 1976 on a slogan of "Model Germany" (Modell Deutschland). This second SPD chancellor established a public image of authority and competence, but he was far less effective than Brandt at winning the hearts and minds of his own party's rank-and-file. He was further weakened by their opposition to his support for new NATO missiles, and increasingly also by his inability to end deficit spending in the face of an economic slowdown. Schmidt's chancellorship finally ended in October 1982, when the FDP abandoned the thirteen-year-old coalition and joined a new government led by Helmut Kohl (CDU).

Back in opposition, the SPD sought to block Euromissile deployment during the early 1980s, soften NATO's confrontational policies toward the Warsaw Pact, and assert Europe's interests more strongly in the Atlantic partnership. Domestically, the SPD developed a post-materialist[5] tilt in its attempt to compete with the emerging challenge from the Greens, who had entered the Bundestag in 1983. The Social Democrats sought to revive their own image as reformers by taking up issues like environmental protection, women's rights, participatory democracy and post-national European integration. They also set out to replace the old 1959 Godesberg program with a new basic statement reflecting these new post-materialist priorities.[6]

Ironically, the Berlin Wall fell less than two months before the adoption of the program in 1989. Germany was left to face the decidedly materialist issues of national unification and reconstruction at the very same time that the end of the Cold War robbed the peace issue of its salience. The SPD was poorly prepared for the rapid move toward national unification. Oskar Lafontaine's severe electoral defeat (SPD 33.5 percent) in December 1990 drove home the problems of his party's post-materialist shift. In that first all-German Bundestag election, the western Greens lost enough voters to the SPD to fall below the 5 percent threshold for parliamentary representation, but even more right-leaning SPD voters defected to support the FDP or CDU/CSU.

The SPD in post-wall Germany has reason to be proud of its political traditions, of its opposition to Germany's darker sides, of its solidarity with Germany's downtrodden. But the party is torn by inner divisions over a lingering socialist utopianism and anti-militarism as well as a commitment to a working class that has become an ever smaller part of German society.[7] The old leftist principles often clash with the new Federal Republic's political reality. Holding labor and public sector workers as core constituencies has made it difficult to capture new constituencies among both market and high-tech oriented, middle-class professionals and green-tinted environmentalists. The SPD is torn between support for workers' rights and solidarity with the down-trodden on the one hand, and commitment to economic efficiency and environmental issues, unshackled from an inflexible labor force and an overgrown public sector, on the other. Indeed, some even have argued that "solidarity" has become little more than a slogan designed to keep the party's various constituencies from open clashes over the party's priorities.[8] The mantra may have muted some of the intraparty disagreements, but it provides no real consensus on political direction and strategy for the post-Cold War era. In sum, the SPD's rich historical legacy has complicated its adjustment to the new political realities created by a united Germany, a widening Europe, and an expanding global economy.

The SPD's Structural Quandaries

The difficulties posed by SPD's historical legacy have been compounded by a number of deep-seated structural problems relating to the SPD as a program and membership party, as a party with a fragmented organization, and as a party with a highly diverse set of constituencies. Each of these topics will be briefly examined, before turning to the party's most recent political record.

Between Conscience and Responsibility

As a program and membership party, with an activist and principled base, the SPD has often tended toward idealistic solutions to many of Germany's problems. Shaped by more than a century of theorizing about socialism and democracy, about capital and labor, and about war and peace, and having an identity rooted more in opposition than in government, the Social Democrats have placed greater emphasis on programmatic principles than Germany's other established parties. The SPD is, as such, less pragmatic than the CDU/CSU and the FDP.[9] Both the ponderous process of program writing and the constraints such programs then place on SPD politicians create a certain rigidity that has undermined the party's ability to respond quickly to changing domestic and international circumstances.

This condition has been exacerbated by the relatively strong role played by many 68ers who joined the party in the early 1970s under Brandt. By the 1990s, they belonged among the party's senior activists and functionaries, and as such they came to have considerable influence in shaping the SPD's programmatic direction. Oriented by an eco-pacifist, post-materialist mind-set, they expected the same orientation in the SPD's programs and leadership. Their numbers, positions, and seniority gave them considerable influence at party conferences, and as a result SPD programs often ended up sounding more radical than the leadership wanted or many German voters would support. The party was thus continually torn between what Max Weber called an "ethic of conscience and moral conviction" (*Gesinnungsethik*) and an "ethic of responsibility" (*Verantwortungsethik*), between those striving for an ideal order based on high principle and those attempting pragmatically to reform the existing order.[10]

The relative influence of the 68er generation has also grown because the SPD—like Germany's other major parties—has had great difficulty attracting new members in the 1990s, especially among the young. As a self-proclaimed *Volkspartei* that places great emphasis on maintaining a large membership base, the SPD had 778,000 members at the end of 1997, almost 20 percent more than the CDU. Yet membership continued to drop, from the all-time high of 1,022,00 in 1976, and also from 949,000 at the end of 1990.[11]

Fragmented Organization

The SPD also was plagued by a lack of organizational coherence. German political scientist and leading expert on the SPD, Peter Lösche, has spoken of the party as a "loosely coupled anarchy."[12] First of all, there was a divide at the federal level between the party headquarters, headed by the party chairman, Oskar Lafontaine, and the parliamentary caucus, led by Rudolf Scharping, and after the September 1998 election, Peter Struck. The party headquarters is very much dominated by the SPD's activist functionaries, giving it a decidedly more idealistic orientation than the parliamentary caucus that deals with day-to-day issues of legislation.

There is yet another intraparty cleavage that stems from the fact that the SPD state (Land) governments frequently have different priorities than the federal party organization. This becomes particularly troublesome when the SPD tries to coordinate the policies of its delegations in the Bundestag and the Bundesrat (Germany's upper house, made up of representatives of the various Land governments). Finally, the SPD values its pluralistic participatory tradition. It contains a profusion of working groups, commissions, and other loose affiliations of members and non-

members. Even as they variously help to shape the party's programmatic development, they add to the impression that the SPD is a hydra-headed political animal.

Contradictory Constituencies

The SPD is the most heterogeneous of Germany's political parties, and this
makes it difficult for the party to portray a clear, coherent and unified theme. Peter
Lösche has captured some of the diversity to be found under the SPD's roof:
"Traditionalists and modernists, materialists and post-materialists, work council
members and yuppies, social service recipients and millionaires, petty bourgeoisie
and effervescent bohemians, Ossis and Wessis, micro-chip euphoric engineers and
technophobic eco-pacifists."[13] While cleavages run in a variety of directions, the
deepest remains the one between many post-materialist, post-national SPD functionaries or activists and a German public that is preoccupied with consolidating
national unification and overcoming Germany's economic malaise. Compounding
this diversity problem was the SPD's 1998 campaign strategy of claiming to represent Germany's "new middle."[14] Having won over many former CDU and FDP
voters, it will not be easy to pursue a government policy that also satisfies the
demands of the SPD's left for a "totally new politics."[15]
    This divide also complicates the SPD's coalition politics. While many of the
party's functionaries may tend toward green policies, winning elections calls for
appealing to the middle and drawing swing voters away from the CDU and the FDP
instead of the Greens. Governing in coalition with either the Greens or the CDU—
whether at the Land or the federal level—risks alienating SPD voters on one end of
the spectrum or the other. While the negotiations over a coalition agreement for the
new Red-Green government in Bonn showed the Greens to be very pragmatic and
accommodating in their willingness to accept SPD positions, experience at the Land
level in Hessen and North Rhine-Westphalia prove that coalitions with the Greens
can be troublesome and divisive for the SPD.

Failure and Success in United Germany

The SPD's historical ballast and its structural quandaries aggravated its adaptation
to the new post-1989 realities. In the first democratic elections after the fall of the
wall, the Social Democrats performed weakly in the new states of eastern Germany.
They lost both the 1990 and the 1994 all-German Bundestag elections; and they
suffered a crisis of leadership, changing their party chair three times between 1989
and 1995. Yet the SPD's long difficulties at the federal level should not conceal a
strong performance at the state level since the early 1990s, especially in the "old"
western region of the Federal Republic. Here their electoral success has ensured
the Social Democrats a majority in the Federal Republic's upper house, the Bundesrat,

since 1991. With its success in the 1998 Bundestag election, the party will now enjoy the advantageous position of controlling both houses of German parliament. Examining these failures and successes in greater detail can provide a better idea of how the SPD's divisions and dilemmas have manifested themselves.

Moving East

At the time of national unification, the SPD lagged behind both the CDU and the FDP in establishing itself organizationally in the East. Its rivals gained a significant head start by inheriting the infrastructures of their related bloc parties in the German Democratic Republic, whereas the SPD had to build its party organization from scratch. In 1946, the post-war East German SPD had been forced to merge—in what was really a purge—with the East German communist party to form the ruling Socialist Unity Party (SED). When the GDR began to collapse in October 1989, a number of clergy members, teachers and other citizen activists founded a new Social Democratic Party, and underlined its independence from the SPD by calling it the SDP. The following year, this fledgling party merged with its much larger West German counterpart. But western money and other support could not make up for the SPD's very low organizational presence in the new eastern states.[16]

This is in striking contrast with the SPD's position in the West, where the ratio of SPD members to registered voters is much higher. Here there were 150 SPD members for every 10,000 registered voters in 1996, while there were only 24 members for every 10,000 voters in the East. The western ratio of SPD members to registered voters ranged from a high of 4.42 percent in the Saar to a low of 0.75 percent in Baden-Württemberg. In the East, this ratio reached from a high of only 0.35 percent in Brandenburg to a low of 0.14 percent in Saxony.[17]

In part, this regional difference is due to the difficulties of building up a new political organization in the East. But the SPD's efforts to increase its eastern membership were initially made more difficult by the need to draw a sharp contrast between the SPD and the post-communist Party of Democratic Socialism (PDS). The eastern Social Democrats were at first determined to keep former SED members from joining their party. Later, when this opposition abated, former Communists showed some reluctance to become involved in the SPD. The different role of labor unions in the East and West also helps to explain the regional disparity in the SPD's organizational density. In the old western states, the SPD and the unions work together much more closely. In some cases, membership in a union goes almost hand-in-hand with membership in the SPD. In the East, by contrast, there is a relatively high level of union involvement, but this leads much less frequently to membership in the SPD.

Finally, it is important to underline a different understanding that prevails with regard to the implications of party membership. In the West, only about 10 percent of the membership is active in meetings and other party activities. Most are content to pay their dues and leave it at that. In the East, activism by dues-paying members is at a much higher level. And indeed, with far fewer members, a much higher percentage of eastern members holds some kind of political position at the local or district level. As such, the eastern party organization is based more on paid office holders than unpaid volunteers. The SPD's members in the East also come from different milieus than those in the West, with both the clergy and white collar professionals playing a much larger role. These circumstances are unique to eastern Germany. Some observers, however, believe that the low-membership, paid-professional party is on the way to establishing itself throughout Western Europe.[18] The SPD resists this trend, wishing to maintain its character as a *Volkspartei*. Indeed, the SPD appears to be the only party that is gaining eastern members, having gone from 26,846 members at the end of 1996 to 27,441 at the end of 1997, a modest increase of just over 2 percent that contrasts with the drastic membership losses in the East of both the CDU and, especially, the FDP.[19]

There are other signs that the party's position in the East has improved. Despite its relatively weak organizational presence, the SPD made significant electoral breakthroughs in the second cycle of Landtag elections that took place in 1994. Thereafter, it served as a cabinet member in four of the five new states, as discussed below. Manfred Stolpe, formerly a high-level church official in the German Democratic Republic, and then premier of Brandenburg, has long been the SPD's most noted personality in eastern state politics, but there are several prominent Social Democrats from the East in the Bundestag, such as Wolfgang Thierse of Berlin. The East remains an important factor in the SPD's electoral strategy. It is a far more difficult political terrain, also because the eastern voters show less party loyalty than their western counterparts. But that is also an opportunity, for swing votes can determine election outcomes.

The Bundestag Elections of 1990, 1994 and 1998

There were many reasons why the SPD fared poorly in unified Germany's first two federal elections, where Helmut Kohl defeated Oskar Lafontaine in 1990 and Rudolf Scharping in 1994. Kohl was certainly a strong candidate, and he profited from an incumbency bonus, but the campaigns of both Lafontaine and Scharping showed serious flaws that helped the chancellor in his efforts to retain office. Lafontaine displayed an openly skeptical attitude towards rapid unification, and this along with his association with greenish post-materialist positions did not reflect the Zeitgeist of 1990. Four years later, the SPD had a more centrist chancellor candidate, but Scharping also failed to lead his party to victory. Kohl was fortunate to benefit from a timely upswing in the economy in 1994. The overall strength of the government and opposition parties did, however, end up much closer than in 1990, with the Union-FDP parliamentary majority dropping from 144 seats to 10. But the close balance between the "ins" and "outs" in the Bundestag was primarily due to the return of the Greens. The PDS also increased its parliamentary presence in 1994, primarily by garnering almost a fifth of the votes in the East. The SPD's share of the entire popular vote was only 36.4 percent, up from 33.5 percent in 1990—but still its second lowest result in a Bundestag election since 1961.[20]

The upward trend for the Social Democrats continued. At the beginning of 1997, the SPD surpassed the CDU in opinion polls, and it stayed ahead through the September 1998 election. Schröder, telegenic and ostensibly pro-business, together with Lafontaine, capable of enforcing party discipline without alienating traditional party constituencies, proved a winning combination. The SPD took 40.9 percent of the vote, up 4.5 percent from 1994.

This strong showing, combined with a Green party that pulled 6.7 percent, dashed any thought of a grand coalition and set the stage for the first red-green coalition government at the federal level. One month later, after negotiating a comprehensive coalition agreement with the Greens, Gerhard Schröder became the Federal Republic's seventh chancellor. Representing the Greens, Joschka Fischer became vice chancellor and foreign minister. The troubles this new government encountered and the underlying structural dilemmas they reflected will be addressed later, after a brief discussion of SPD leadership challenges in the 1990s and the notable successes at the Länder level.

Changing Leaders

While Helmut Kohl had been the head of the CDU since 1973, the SPD has had trouble finding a long-term replacement for its veteran leader, Willy Brandt, who was the party chair from 1964 to 1987. Brandt was followed by Hans-Jochen Vogel, who served until 1990, when he was replaced by Björn Engholm, then a highly regarded premier of Schleswig-Holstein. Caught up in political scandal, Engholm resigned as party chair and premier in 1993. Thereupon Rudolf Scharping, who had won the election for premier in the old CDU stronghold of Rhineland-Palatinate two years earlier, became the SPD's youngest postwar chair. Politically, he was chosen as the result of a rank-and-file membership vote, in which Scharping ran ahead of both Gerhard Schröder, the popular premier of Lower Saxony, and Heidemarie Wieczorek-Zeul, member of parliament, European policy expert, and very much on the left of the party. Yet Scharping's experience at the national level was limited, and neither Schröder nor Lafontaine willingly accepted his leadership. Scharping, failing to defeat Kohl in 1994 and unable to unify and motivate an increasingly frustrated party, was toppled in a dramatic coup orchestrated by Lafontaine at the party congress in Mannheim in November 1995. Lafontaine had been premier of the Saar since 1985, but he had a checkered political record in addition to his unsuccessful bid for the chancellorship in the year of unification. Much earlier, in the late 1970s and early 1980s, he had led party opposition to Helmut Schmidt and NATO's double-track decision. None of this seemed to have detracted from his popularity among many of the SPD's activists and functionaries: He was clearly their preferred choice for party leader.

The SPD's apparent leadership crisis, reflected in the high turnover of party chairs, arose from a number of factors. The 1990s "grandchildren generation" (a term given to Brandt's successors in leading party positions) was excessively large. Those who had been stars in the SPD youth organization, the Young Socialists, in the 1970s still competed with one another for power—only in the 1990s they vied for leadership of the party. The roster included Gerhard Schröder, Oskar Lafontaine, Rudolf Scharping, Björn Engholm, Heidemarie Wieczorek-Zeul, Heide Simonis, Renate Schmidt, Herta Däubler-Gmelin, and a number of others. Simonis, herself premier of Schleswig-Holstein, judged that, "We are too many, too ambitious, too much of the same age, and too good."[21] Over the years, the grandchildren built up different power bases that they tended to play off against one another, often at the expense of party unity. They had trouble projecting both authority and unity. As a result, many German voters appeared not to take them seriously.

It is possible to put a better light on the leadership constellation that emerged after Lafontaine's coup. The new SPD chair succeeded remarkably quickly in pulling the party together, in improving its morale. There were signs of approval from a broader German public, with support for the SPD moving from a low 33 percent in the summer of 1995 to a high of over 40 percent by the spring and summer of 1998,[22] or very close to the party's result in the September Bundestag election.

Lafontaine clearly spoke for the 68er generation of party activists and functionaries. Yet this was only part of the broader SPD constituency. Rudolf Scharping, who remained parliamentary floor leader through the election, was less popular among the party activists, but he found support among traditional blue collar SPD voters. The final figure in the SPD's leadership troika of the late 1990s, Gerhard Schröder, then premier of Lower Saxony, was clearly the SPD's most popular politician. Telegenic and authoritative, he was also the only SPD leader who consistently did better in the polls than Helmut Kohl.

Schröder spoke for business and high-tech in Germany, and he cultivated close relations with Germany's corporate leaders. Of the three, he was also the strongest advocate of a more flexible labor market in Germany. While Schröder was popular among Germany's voters, many SPD members and functionaries found him self-serving and opportunistic. Still, they could not ignore his electoral magnetism, especially after his conclusive victory in the March 1998 state election in Lower Saxony.

The day after his party won an absolute parliamentary majority in the Landtag, Gerhard Schröder was named to be the SPD's chancellor candidate for the Bundestag election in September. Schröder, Lafontaine, and Scharping could hardly be more disparate as political leaders, but this triangle had the potential of holding together the SPD's traditional (and tempestuous) constituencies, while reaching out to new ones. The Bundestag election of September 1998 demonstrated the success of this electoral strategy, though differences between the three leading Social Democrats surfaced soon thereafter. The tenuous nature of the arrangement quickly showed itself. After losing his leadership post in parliament to become minister of defense, Scharping had clearly lost rank within the party. This left Lafontaine and Schröder jockeying for advantage, causing many to ask who was really in charge.

Governing the Länder

In contrast to its various difficulties at the federal level, the SPD could point to remarkable political success in Germany's sixteen states—success that gave the SPD a majority in the Bundesrat after 1991. By 1998, the party participated in all but three of the Land governments. Several factors may help to explain this. First, the CDU's state leaders were generally less impressive personalities than Helmut Kohl at the federal level. Second, there has been a tendency in the Federal Republic toward a German form of "cohabitation," with a federal government of one party balanced by the other party holding a majority of the Land governments: Thus, the CDU had controlled a similar majority in the Bundesrat in the years of the SPD-FDP coalition (1969-1982).[23] Finally, with Landtag elections occurring intermittently between federal elections, the SPD has often profited from periods when the Kohl government was relatively unpopular.

By the fall of 1998, the SPD held an absolute Landtag majority in three states, namely Lower Saxony (Gerhard Schröder), the Saar (Oskar Lafontaine), and Brandenburg (Manfred Stolpe). In four states, the SPD governed in coalition with the Alliance 90/Greens: Schleswig-Holstein, Hamburg, North Rhine-Westphalia and Hesse. In three states, the SPD had formed a grand coalition with the CDU: Bremen, Berlin, and Thuringia. (In the latter two states, however, the SPD was the CDU's junior coalition partner.) In the single case of the Rhineland-Palatinate, the SPD had built a coalition with the liberal FDP. These various governing coalitions offered a test-bed for possible national configurations. A different and controversial arrangement had been reached in the eastern state of Saxony-Anhalt, where the SPD avoided a grand coalition with the CDU by forming a minority government that was dependent on the parliamentary toleration of the PDS. Following the September 1998 elections, the SPD in Mecklenburg-West Pomerania went one step further to form a state government that included the PDS as full coalition partners, creating Germany's first "red-red" coalition.

The strong position in many German Länder gave the SPD a solid majority in the Bundesrat. This provided a powerful tool to block many types of legislation proposed by the Kohl government—at least, when the SPD-led state governments played along. As a result, the SPD could drive a hard bargain with the Kohl government on a number of reform proposals, while remaining aware that the appearance of an obstructionist strategy carried its own risks. Kohl's inability to push through different types of legislation, above all his government's major proposal for tax reform in 1997, hurt his own and his government's standing in the polls. But it did not necessarily improve the SPD's position.

Taking the Reins of Government

Moving into government after sixteen years in opposition would be difficult for any party, but the SPD's persisting inner divisions and structural dilemmas compounded the problem significantly. From the onset of the coalition talks in early October, observers noted that two sets of negotiations were taking place, those between Schröder and Fischer and those between Schröder and Lafontaine.[24] Nor was lack of unity the only problem for the SPD. Schröder made a timid start, cautious to exert the authority of his office, reluctant to propose dramatic new initiatives—leading a *Spiegel* title page to ask: "Where is Schröder?"[25]

The jockeying for position in the initial weeks after election victory took place over cabinet posts and policy issues. In regard to cabinet posts, the German press put Lafontaine at the center of the various controversies, describing him as having elbowed his way into a new position of power, taking over as minister of the powerful finance ministry, and then drawing significant responsibilities from the economics ministry—Europe and government cost control—into his own portfolio. This, combined with Lafontaine's neo-Keynesian focus on fiscal demand stimulus,[26] incensed Schröder's hand-picked candidate for economics minister, Jost Stollmann. In the end, this "modernizer," software entrepreneur and party outsider threw in his hat, refusing to take the post. Nor was Stollmann the only victim of Lafontaine's ambitions.

As parliamentary floor leader, Rudolf Scharping was too much of a potential competitor for Lafontaine, who wanted his own candidate, then-party executive director, Franz Müntefering, to be in this key position. One of the results of the settlement brokered by Schröder was Scharping's reluctant transfer to the difficult post of defense minister. At the same time, however, Schröder clipped Lafontaine's wings, by choosing deputy floor leader Peter Struck, rather than Müntefering, to replace Scharping as head of the SPD parliamentary group.

On policy questions, the image quickly took hold of an SPD divided into two camps: the "traditionalists" led by Lafontaine at finance, and the "modernizers" holed up in the chancellery, led by Schröder and his influential chancellery minister, Bodo Hombach. The conceptual differences between the two positions found clear delineation in books written respectively by Lafontaine and Hombach. In the summer before the election, Lafontaine and his wife, economist Christa Müller, called for governments to do more to dampen the downside of globalization and rein in the excesses of "casino capitalism" in their book, *Fear Not Globalization*.[27] Bodo Hombach, speaking for the modernizers, put forward an alternative vision of reform in his book, *Politics of the New Middle*. He basically called for what could be termed a social democratic form of supply-side economics.[28]

At one level, this was a theoretical struggle between a neo-Keynesian demand-side approach and a pro-investment, pro-flexibility (i.e., more supply side) approach to Germany's economic and employment problems. At another level, it was about clientele and constituencies. Traditional party interests would presumably gain from Lafontaine's approach of putting more money in the pockets of Germany's consumers, particularly those of the lower and middle classes,[29] whereas potential new constituencies in the business community complained about a betrayal of the new middle. But the divisions were also very much about personal ambitions and the tentative balance of power between Lafontaine and Schröder as they adjusted to the new political playing field.

There were additional sources of tension stemming from success in the Bundestag election of 1998. During the long years in opposition, the SPD had developed a practice of party coordination that continually sought a balance between the parliamentary group, the party headquarters, and the SPD-governed Länder. Into this equation now came the federal government, with the chancellery as the predominant new power center. A back and forth on various proposals, particularly in regard to taxation and energy policy, reflected the challenge of getting the cabinet members to work together. In an early turnaround, leaders from both coalition parties decided that a regular "coalition round" was necessary to promote mutual coordination. Länder governments also attempted to reassert their own authority against Bonn and party headquarters. Wolfgang Clement, successor to Johannes Rau in North Rhine-Westphalia, the SPD's most important stronghold, even hooked up with Bavarian minister president and CSU head Edmund Stoiber to oppose new tax plans coming from Bonn.

Failure and success in united Germany thus came together in a dramatic way for the SPD in the fall of 1998. After winning an impressive election victory, the SPD turned around and, in the words of *The Economist*, made "one of the worst starts to running any top European government since the second world war."[30] The party's structural dilemmas have certainly made the move into government responsibility a difficult one, but the nature of Germany's challenges, both at home and abroad, makes easy and quick solutions impossible. The approach taken by the SPD to Germany's challenges is at once a reflection of the party's internal dilemmas and an indication of where the first government of the Berlin Republic will go.

The Struggle to Reform

The SPD's structural problems have been compounded by the changing nature of Germany's society and economy in a widening Europe and a more global market. *Modell Deutschland*, as developed in the 1970s, and still viewed nostalgically by many in the SPD in the 1990s, has long since run into trouble.[31] Policy dilemmas have arisen that are of particular salience to the SPD: Social services vs. competitiveness; worker's rights vs. labor market flexibility; ecology vs. growth;

cosmopolitanism vs. immigration limits; national reticence vs. greater international responsibility; Germany as a civilian power vs. NATO out-of-area responsibilities. This variety of challenges does not permit easy and coherent policy choices. It does make the notion of a "new middle" very attractive, to the extent that such a "third way" claims to be able to reconcile many of these competing objectives.[32] Yet doing so in principle is easier than in practice. Vested interests quickly strained the unity of the "new middle" once the SPD actually began to govern. A review of various domestic and international choices by the SPD will demonstrate the deep-rooted dilemmas the SPD will continue to face in trying to maintain party unity while seeking to govern Germany from the "new middle."

Domestic Policy: Retooling the German Model

In preparing for the 1998 Bundestag election, the SPD presented itself as the party of "innovation and fairness" (*Innovation und Gerechtigkeit*). It made every effort to portray itself not only as the party that would look after Germany's less fortunate, but also the party that would be capable of preparing Germany for the twenty-first century. Many party taboos fell by the wayside as the SPD sought to strike a more even balance between social justice and economic growth. Nevertheless, the two principles are inherently in tension with one another, party programs notwithstanding.

Gerhard Schröder was the figurehead, if not spearhead of the party's new push for flexibility on economic matters. In advance of the big pre-election party congress in Hanover, in December 1997, Schröder put forward "Twelve Theses" on economic reform that emphasized not only traditional SPD ideas like solidarity, but also the positive role of stiff competition in the creation of wealth. This marked a clear departure from the SPD's frequently jaundiced view of competition as the downside of market economics. As was to be expected, Schröder's theses created a considerable stir and received wide press coverage. Nevertheless, at Hanover, those who saw globalization as an opportunity prevailed over those who defined it as a threat. Even the party's social welfare wing, led by Rudolf Dreßler, largely adopted this new approach. [33]

Notably, Schröder's theses did not arise in a political vacuum. Much of their substantive contents built on the work of the SPD's Economic Forum, an entity made up of some thirty business leaders—many of whom were not members of the SPD. In a similar move, the SPD's Friedrich Ebert Foundation (FES) had asked its Manager Circle consisting of close to 1,500 business executives—again including many who were not SPD members—to develop new economic ideas. Schröder also drew upon this relatively independent group's ideas in formulating his theses. During the campaign, this novel approach to programmatic innovation largely succeeded in winning the SPD public confidence on economic matters without entirely alienating the party traditionalists.[34] Later, however, the new government's early difficulties winning support among Germany's business leaders and economists, including many from the Economic Forum and the Manager Circle, reflected the continued strength of more traditional leftist notions, as propounded most powerfully by Oskar Lafontaine.[35]

Schröder's Twelve Theses, which at the time also found the support of Lafontaine, were largely adopted as one of the four main planks of the SPD's Hanover party congress platform. Two of these planks, entitled "Innovation for Germany" and "From Utopia to Reality: Entering the Information Age," dealt with broad economic themes. The other two addressed foreign and European policy.[36] As their titles indicate, the domestic policy planks were very much intended to leave the impression of an SPD that had shifted its focus to competitiveness and modern market economics, and (by implication) somewhat away from distributive and interventionist government policies. Innovation in Germany's labor market was given particular priority. The platform supported, for example, the creation of a (partially subsidized) low-wage labor sector in Germany—a reform that would weaken the unions by undermining universal wage settlements. The Hanover congress also pushed educational reform—of the type that supports programs for the best and the brightest, as opposed to simply expanding access to higher education across the board. Finally, the SPD emphasized its desire to help small business by improving the availability of financing for new "innovative" ventures. Hanover gave the SPD the modern, pro-business veneer it needed to the win the election. It could not guarantee that the party would not try to back away from some of the proposed changes.

Catering to the "new middle" proved extremely difficult in the early months of the new government. Tax relief for small firms, greater labor market flexibility and lower non-wage labor costs all clashed with the desire to ease the tax burden on the poor and increase state support for families. Ambitious plans for an energy were reduced to nothing as they ran the gauntlet of special interests.

Tax reform has become the central arena for retooling the German model, dominating both pre-election politics and the first months of the new government. The plan advanced by Helmut Kohl's government in the spring of 1997, died in October of that year. In a German version of legislative gridlock, the SPD in the Bundesrat refused to go along with the plan or the subsequent compromises the CDU/CSU and FDP were willing to offer. While some Social Democrats were initially sympathetic to parts of the Kohl government's proposal, the SPD, under the influence of Lafontaine, decided to either significantly change or block the project, by using the power of the SPD's Bundesrat majority. The Social Democrats basically argued that the plan's tax cuts were overly generous to big earners and unaffordable in a period of unprecedented budget deficits. More importantly, in an election year the SPD could hardly have been expected to give Kohl a tax reform that would have disproportionately hurt some traditional SPD constituencies. Lafontaine proved himself an effective tactician in this conflict, thereby also strengthening his influence in the party.

During the campaign, the SPD argued with some justification that tax rates were not the main source of the country's economic problems. Compared to other OECD countries, German income taxes are average. But non-wage labor costs, in the form of social service contributions tied to employment, run up to twice as high as those in other OECD countries. The SPD thus insisted that lowering non-wage labor costs was a way to improve Germany's employment situation, whereas the Kohl government emphasized a reduction of taxes on investment and profit. The SPD also argued that the social costs of unification, particularly the high unemployment bill in the East, were being born disproportionately (as non-wage labor costs) by those wage earners paying into the German unemployment fund. Finally, there was the widespread belief in the SPD that easing the burden of the middle class would be better suited to create what was seen as a much-needed demand stimulus for the German economy than would reducing taxes on upper income brackets. The Social Democrats played their hand well in this debate. It had a large role in undermining Kohl and securing Schröder's victory.

Indeed, Germany's economic situation in the late 1990s brought with it a certain political irony. Despite an enduring Social Democratic predisposition to fiscal demand stimulus, the chronic budget deficits of Helmut Kohl's government provided the SPD with irresistible targets for attack. It gleefully portrayed CSU finance minister Theo Waigel as a Pinocchio for his broken promises about taxes and spending. Paradoxically, the SPD, traditionally Germany's party of big government, found itself in the position of calling for fiscal stringency and budgetary consolidation. Holding this line in government proved more difficult.

This raises a larger point. If Germany is going to reduce its tax burden (particularly its social service taxes); if Germany is going to develop a more flexible labor market; and if Germany is going to reduce the role of the public sector in the economy (now almost 50 percent), then it will need at least the acquiescence of the powerful constituencies (labor; public workers; social service advocates) that benefit from the current dispensation. And these are SPD constituencies. In opposition, the SPD had little incentive to mobilize them in the name of reform, when reform would only benefit the political position of the ruling CDU. The SPD in government faces the same general pressures for reform, but it will have less reason to obstruct. It may even have an easier time delivering the key constituencies (and their representatives in the Bundestag and Bundesrat) that oppose reform. In the same way that it took Richard Nixon to go to China and Bill Clinton to rewrite welfare, it might just take the Social Democrats to trim Germany's bloated public sector and promote measures to loosen up its inflexible economy.

Yet the first months of government showed a predilection to support old constituencies, not confront them with the need to sacrifice. The path of least resistance meant rescinding cuts made by Kohl in the areas of retirement and sick benefits, while only minimally reducing social insurance contributions from 42.3 to just under 40 percent of gross income. The idea of raising energy taxes to cut these non-wage labor costs (and help the environment), strongly supported by the

Greens and favored by many in the SPD, ran aground. The coalition agreed to raise the gasoline tax by a mere 6 pfennig—and energy-intensive industry would be spared. Top tax-rates would go down, but initially only 4 percent as compared to the 13 percent Kohl had wanted.[37]

Big business was naturally upset at the prospect of higher costs—and lower subsidies. The German Federation of Industries made its anger felt, provoking Schröder to claim they misunderstood the concept of the "new middle," which he put in a different category: "This matter of the new middle applies to a precise group of people: those who are self-employed, those in the craft industries, those in medium-sized industries, those in the leadership of the scientific and cultural communities."[38]

In some sense, of course, the "new middle" was the old middle, as German elections have long been fought over the moderate middle of the middle class. To the extent that it was new, the concept related to the way in which high technology and global markets had changed the organization of business in Germany, and thus the ways in which they could be supported. But it was also new in suggesting a moderate leftist sympathy for lean government—with the exception of education and support for families.

The struggle over taxation and economic policy also took place at the European level. On the one hand, as noted earlier, the notion of the "new middle" found its counterpart in Tony Blair's "new Labour" and his "Third Way." On the other hand, there was a sense that a European Union, where Social Democrats had become cabinet members in eleven of fifteen governments, offered new opportunities for more activist and coordinated policies on employment, taxation and political influence over the emerging European Central Bank.

Lafontaine led this charge. He made no secret of his desire to put European as well as national monetary policy at the service of job creation, by lowering interest rates and keeping the Euro from becoming overvalued—even at the expense of higher inflation. Finding support from Dominique Strauss-Kahn, personal friend and French minister of finance, Lafontaine tried to forge what the press dubbed an "axis" with the French Socialist government of Lionel Jospin. With Germany assuming the presidency of the EU in the first half of 1999 (coinciding with the introduction of the Euro), it was clear that the Schröder government's domestic politics would be very much influenced by what was happening on the European stage.

Closely related to the issue of tax and finance, indeed a main focus of tax reform, was of course the vexing problem of unemployment, which in Germany had been above 10 percent since 1996. Here, the government made a new go at a tripartite "Alliance for Jobs" that the Kohl government had attempted unsuccessfully over a year previously. Labor minister, Walter Riester, feisty former unionist with a reformist bent, was to head an effort to get national representatives of industry and labor together with government to work out a grand package on jobs, education and taxation.[39] Concerted action, as this traditional corporatist approach to economic challenges in Germany has been called, has the advantage of shaping a consensus, but often at an agonizingly slow pace. Nevertheless, there is hope that this approach, also centerpiece of the much-discussed "Dutch Model," can create a climate for change. In the Netherlands, a "continental" alternative to Thatcherism has brought unemployment dramatically down over the past decade, without high inflation or dramatic cuts in living standards. The Dutch labor market's high level of part-time and short-term job possibilities is another feature that attracts attention in Germany.

Energy and the environment have pitched one side of Schröder's government coalition against the other, and it is here that difference between the Greens and the SPD are more important than differences within the SPD. While the two parties share a programmatic commitment to end Germany's reliance on nuclear energy, the Greens are much more adamant in their insistence that this be done quickly. Schröder has kept them at bay, trying to work out a deal with industry for a long-term exit strategy, and going so far as to exclude Jürgen Trittin, Green environment minister, from some important meetings in the chancellery. Disagreement over the level of energy taxes, as mentioned above, also reflects the political difficulties of putting ideas hatched as an opposition party into practice when holding the reigns of government.

Beyond economics, the question of law-and-order has risen to the top of the German public's list of concerns in recent years. It has been difficult for the SPD to respond adequately. This became clear in the related issue of granting political asylum that deeply divided the party in 1992. Many Social Democrats had been strongly committed to a liberal asylum policy, also in reaction to the Third Reich's record of political persecution. Yet in the end, the SPD agreed to tighten the Federal Republic's generous asylum laws for fear that a continued massive influx of asylum seekers would inflame racist and neo-Nazi movements across Germany. In the late 1990s, issues of crime and anti-foreigner sentiment remained connected for many Germans. In pre-election maneuvering, Gerhard Schröder seemed to respond by taking a stand in favor of expelling foreigners who were convicted of crimes. But this hardly seemed to be an issue on which the Social Democrats could score points by appearing to be "tough." Significantly, Henning Voscherau made a surprisingly poor showing in Hamburg's 1997 election after he had chosen to make law-and-order in the city a major campaign issue for his SPD. In polls, the German public rated the SPD less competent on crime prevention than the CDU. Thus, Social Democrats had good reasons to tone down the emphasis on this question as the Bundestag election approached, recognizing that its salience could only harm the SPD.

In justice and home affairs, the SPD-led government set a new accent from the onset: modernizing Germany's antiquated immigration laws by opening up the possibility of dual citizenship for Germany's resident aliens—an approach the Kohl government had continuously rejected. As if to balance this dramatic shift, the new minister for home affairs, Otto Schily, soon made a speech proclaiming the German boat to be full. His widely reported remark was interpreted as a signal to those fearful of new immigration that limits on newcomers would be maintained.

Schily, at sixty-six the oldest cabinet member, had been a prominent early member of the Greens. He had switched in 1989 to the SPD where he quickly moved into a leading parliamentary role. His appointment in the cabinet was a sign that immigration and justice matters would receive a different accent in the new government, but his role in both parties also reflected some common currents to which all sought to appeal: the reality that the dividing line between green and red was not always entirely clear.

In sum, retooling the German model posed a profound problem for the new coalition government. It was not that ideas were lacking. Indeed, there was a plethora of reform plans for tackling Germany's labor market inertia, feeble high-tech entrepreneurialism and bloated public sector. The political problem lay in cutting through the knot of interest groups that defended the status quo. This problem was compounded by the structural and organizational challenges faced by the SPD in trying to contain all the contending currents within the party, whether in east or west, at the state or federal level of politics, or, most importantly, between party headquarters, under finance minister Oskar Lafontaine, and the chancellery under Gerhard Schröder.

Foreign Policy: Finding a New Role in Europe and the World

It was, however, foreign not domestic policy that divided the SPD most deeply during most of the 1990s. Questions about the use of force were the most divisive, but differing views on questions of internationalism and the desirability of European monetary union also led to acrimony, both within the party and vis-à-vis the Kohl government. Yet in advance of the Bundestag election of 1998, the SPD, here guided more by Rudolf Scharping than by Oskar Lafontaine or Gerhard Schröder, also moved toward a "new middle" course on foreign policy, which emphasized the importance of "continuity" with the Kohl legacy and downplayed any differences that remained.

In so doing, the SPD leadership relied on a time-tried method for delaying controversy: they defrayed all potentially controversial questions—from future combat scenarios to the fate of conscription—to a "military structure commission" that would be created soon after taking power. Defense minister Scharping has since renamed this useful political instrument the "Government Commission on the Future of the Armed Forces" and given it two years to come up with its recommendations. Big changes in the Bundeswehr will thus only be slow in coming. Containing controversy will continue to have priority. But there will now be a forum to focus discussion on how to adapt Germany's military forces to the challenges of the twenty-first century.

The significance of "continuity" serving as the primary principle of the new government's foreign policy should not be overlooked. Only a few years ago, such a focus on similarities with the Kohl government would have been highly unlikely. The fall of the Berlin Wall saw many Social Democrats wary of rapid and complete German unification, critical of NATO's continued existence, and opposed to any additional role for the Bundeswehr beyond territorial defense and UN peacekeeping. Instead, they responded favorably to ideas of a pan-European collective security system and a UN-based "world domestic policy." The ensuing years have seen moderates in the SPD leadership move a fractious membership toward mainstream positions on Germany's major foreign policy questions. The success of this endeavor was most clearly demonstrated when, only a few weeks after the election, SPD and Green members of parliament approved NATO airstrikes against Serbia— and this without the UN mandate demanded by their party programs before the use of force would be endorsed.

It was in the Scharping commission that major shifts in SPD policy came about, both on the use of force and on Europe's role in the world. The commission's draft took a significant step in stating that the SPD no longer opposes, in principle, the use of the Bundeswehr for UN-mandated "enforcement" missions. This is important as the Bundeswehr's future role has been one of the most divisive issues within the SPD since the end of the Cold War. During the Gulf War, the SPD had vociferously opposed both the military engagement in general and the sending of German combat aircraft to Turkey, a NATO ally that was threatened by attack from Iraq. In the ensuing years, many of the party's foreign policy experts argued that Germany must stay in the mainstream of other European countries when it came to supporting international actions like those in the Persian Gulf or Bosnia, but most of the party's activists remained avidly opposed. They would countenance nothing more than Bundeswehr participation in UN blue helmet operations. Indeed, even the 1991 Bremen party congress decision to endorse participation in such blue helmet operations was hotly contested, with delegates warning ominously of a creeping "militarization of German foreign policy."[40]

During the first half of the 1990s, the delicate intra-party balance on this issue also forced the leadership to argue, somewhat speciously, that the German constitution prohibited sending any German forces whatsoever outside the territory of the NATO alliance. The SPD thus took the German government to court over Chancellor Kohl's decision to send German ships into the Adriatic Sea to help monitor a weapons embargo against former Yugoslavia in 1992, German crews on AWACS to help enforce NATO's Deny Flight, and German peacekeepers to Somalia (both in 1993). In July 1994, in a landmark ruling, the Federal Constitutional Court rejected the SPD's line of argument and declared that the Basic Law did not bar such "out-of-area" operations.

Nevertheless, many Social Democrats continued to oppose any German participation in "combat" or enforcement operations. When Germany decided to tribute special Tornado aircraft to NATO's enforcement operations over Bosnia in July 1995, most of the SPD's parliamentary caucus rejected the plan. Yet continued Serbian atrocities, particularly the massacre at Srebrenicia, have slowly eroded opposition to the use of force in general, and, more importantly, to Bundeswehr participation. When NATO finally conducted a major air campaign against the Bosnian Serbs in September 1995, Social Democrats withheld criticism. With the formation of NATO's Implementation Force, the SPD was willing to countenance German logistical support, but no enforcement role. In 1996 there was a major intra-party shift on this issue as well. The change was clearly demonstrated in SPD support for full German participation in the enforcement of the Dayton accords. In the run up to the election, the Hanover congress in December 1997 provided this change of party view with a programmatic seal of approval. The SPD could thus proclaim that "continuity" would characterize the foreign policy of a Schröder government.

This new position was put to the test most dramatically in the weeks between the election and the inauguration, as NATO moved to launch massive air strikes against Serbia. The outgoing Kohl goverment, understandably, wanted no members of the German military taking part in offensive operations without the approval of the SPD and their Green coalition partners.[41] Schröder, Fischer and other members of the incoming coalition's leadership all agreed that Germany must support the operation, both politically and with Bundeswehr units, and this despite the absence of a clear UN mandate. Moreover, this decision by the leadership was backed in parliament, where a surprisingly large number of SPD and Green deputies voted in favor of force, party programs demanding a UN mandate notwithstanding.[42] Nor did Schröder and Fischer hesitate to support Anglo-American strikes against Iraq in December 1998, despite the criticism of some party members. Continuity in terms of Germany's commitment to cooperate with NATO and the United States on conflict prevention and crisis management reflected a realization that any break with the allies would quickly conjure up the specter of Germany pursuing a separate or "special" national path (*Sonderweg*).[43]

The SPD's strong anti-militarist tradition has been paralleled by a long dedication to internationalism, first of the socialist, later of the liberal variety. Strengthening international institutions (and NGOs) in order to foster international cooperation has been a centerpiece of SPD foreign policy for many years. Indeed, one could speak of many Social Democrats as "integrationist" in their view of the European Union as a peace community, as a sort of model for world order. The competitive side of international relations has rarely received the same amount of attention as the cooperative side in SPD thinking about foreign policy. Nor have Social Democrats been comfortable talking about "national" interests, especially about interests that might be uniquely German.

For this reason, the Hanover platform and the early outlines of the Schröder/ Fischer/Scharping policy are notable. The Hanover program, as drafted by the Scharping commission, did take up older SPD principles of internationalism and

Scharping commission, did take up older SPD principles of internationalism and solidarity, of the need to promote cooperation as the basis of world order. But it also brought with it a different and somewhat contradictory view. The platform simultaneously painted the picture of a competitive world order in which Europe must assert itself if its civilization and its social market economies were to survive. Similarly, a deeper and more global partnership with the United States (and the SPD did often put greater emphasis than the CDU on the global nature of the Atlantic partnership) must be accompanied by efforts to counter Washington's unilateralist inclinations. The platform struck a remarkable balance—not often seen on the part of the SPD—between the goals of international responsibility and world order (sustainable development and UN reform) and the narrower goals of Europe and Germany ("fair trade," i.e. no social or environmental dumping, and also a German seat on the UN Security Council).

The coalition agreement also reflects the policy priorities of the SPD's left and the Greens, such as insisting on support for a UN monopoly on the use of force, and calling for the Alliance to adopt a policy of no-first-use of nuclear weapons.[44] Using the cover of this agreement, foreign minister Joschka Fischer declared his intention to raise the issue of no-first-use in the context of NATO's development of a new strategic concept. This anti-nuclear salvo drew sharp criticism from the United States, France and Great Britain, where memories of Fischer's active role in opposing NATO's nuclear deployments in the early 1980s remained strong. Defense minister Scharping was left to smooth over ruffled feathers, saying that this was clearly a matter that could only be decided in consensus with the other allies. While Fischer may have won points with his own party, thus compensating for his controversial support for the use of force in Kosovo and Iraq, he also provoked the first mini-crisis between the new red-green government and its Atlantic allies.[45]

European integration also had a central place in the foreign policy of the SPD in the 1990s. Support for the project has certainly been driven by the SPD's integrationist impulse, but this support has not made choices about Europe's post-Cold War evolution any easier. The SPD has straddled the choice between deepening and widening the European Union (EU). In terms of deepening, the party wanted Europe's "democracy deficit" to be overcome by strengthening the European Parliament and expanding the range of qualified majority voting in the Council (to include the Common Foreign and Security Policy). It also wanted the EU to play a much larger role in the expensive areas of employment and social rights. At the same time, the SPD pushed for continued efforts at EU enlargement.

If forced to choose, most Social Democrats would prefer a European Union deepened both democratically and socially to one that was widened at the expense of democratic and social goals. This was reflected in the new government's reluctance to put forward a time table on enlargement, wanting to first make sure that the necessary reforms within the EU were achieved. These included better employment policy coordination, preventing "social dumping" in low-wage EU countries over EU decision-making, and last, but not least, cutting Germany's net contribution (pushed even more strongly by Schröder than by Kohl).

While the new government made every effort to underline the importance of "continuity," with extensive visits to Paris, London, Warsaw, and other European allies, Schröder also argued that Europe was for Germany a free choice, not a historical imperative.[46] A more relaxed view of national power and national interest as personified by Schröder[47] thus clashed with the idealism infused with atonement that guided the strong anti-military, pro-integration wing of the party (and its Green coalition partner).

On European Monetary Union, the Social Democrats took somewhat of a zigzag course. They were disappointed that the 1991 Maastricht Treaty did not secure a strong political union as a quid pro quo for monetary union, but generally endorsed the treaty anyway. In the ensuing years, a number of prominent SPD Land politicians voiced criticism of the monetary plan, most notable among them Gerhard Schröder. In part, this was motivated by a certain populist inclination. Large majorities of Germans continued to mistrust the Euro, thus making Kohl and the CDU vulnerable on this question. There were also those Social Democrats who were concerned that the Maastricht criteria unnecessarily circumscribed deficit spending as a means to stimulate economic growth. Despite such reservations in the SPD, the more probable monetary union became, the less Schröder and others attempted to oppose it. They refrained from making the Euro a major issue in the September election after the final decision from the European Council in May 1998. Once in government and with Germany's EU presidency looming, attention turned to a successful start for the Euro, and the need to make European monetary policy conducive to the SPD's own domestic goals.

In summing up the SPD's foreign policy, it is appropriate to recall the maxim: "You don't win elections with foreign policy, but you can certainly lose them with foreign policy." The more realistic thrust of the SPD's foreign policy manifestos went a long way toward removing foreign and security policy as a major vulnerability. But while the party's mind, calculating on a 1998 election victory, and then on the responsibilities of government, supported the new thrust of policy, the party's heart remained more internationalist and pacifist than the Hanover platform indicated. Pragmatism on foreign policy will not always be easy. Nor will the "principle" of continuity always offer complete answers to the challenges of a rapidly changing world. European integration and Atlantic partnership will remain Germany's primary foreign policy interests, but the Schröder government can be expected to bring a more dynamic style and globalist outlook to their pursuit.[48]

Conclusion

After years of drift, the SPD appeared to reestablish direction in advance of the 1998 Bundestag election. Whether the party will be able to govern effectively after its success at the polls depends on its ability to address the numerous domestic and foreign policy challenges that have emerged with German reunification, the widening of Europe, and globalization. The SPD's tenuous consensus on streamlining Germany's economy and playing a larger diplomatic and military role in the world also depends on its ability to contain intraparty dissonance. The leadership faces a host of competing interests and values in trying to remain loyal to the SPD's traditions, true to the party's program and membership, heedful of the assertive 68er-generation functionaries, and attractive to both potential SPD voters (especially swing voters from the middle) and to the party's coalition partner, the Greens. In short, the SPD's success at the polls in 1998 does not guarantee its success in governing. The evidence to date is mixed.

The SPD's cross-cutting dilemmas are most clearly exemplified in the party's long reluctance to choose between Oskar Lafontaine and Gerhard Schröder as chancellor candidate, followed by the strong impression in the early months of the new government that the tenuous balance of power between the two limited Schröder's maneuvering room. While Germany's voters preferred Schröder, SPD activists favored Lafontaine. Schröder knew he could not win the chancellorship without Lafontaine and the party behind him, and he scrupulously refrained from action that could alienate either. Schröder had already been censured by the party for his open attacks on Rudolf Scharping, which had left the latter weakened and vulnerable to Lafontaine's Mannheim coup in 1995. He could not risk the party's wrath a second time. Even as chancellor, he remains dependent on the party's base.

In Germany's type of parliamentary democracy, the party organizations normally play an important electoral role, but the significance of the SPD's party apparatus is particularly great. It is a big and powerful organization, and experience has shown that its chancellors (and chancellor candidates) are gravely weakened if they do not have a united party behind them. And here lay Schröder's campaign dilemma: his popularity in the German media and the German public had partly been won by profiling himself as an iconoclast in the SPD. Maintaining his standing in the polls while seeking peace with the party proved no easy task. In the end, his strong victory in Lower Saxony's state election (March 1998) secured him the party's nomination as chancellor candidate, but Schröder has had to continue courting both the public and his own party before and after the Bundestag election.

Lafontaine, in turn, has also had to restrain himself. Many believed that his main aim has been to secure a place in the German cabinet for the political ideas of 1968—as permutated by the peace and ecology movements of the 1970s and 1980s and tempered by the realism of long opposition and a growing taste for power. An SPD victory would further this agenda, even though Lafontaine did not head the ticket.

Despite all their philosophical differences, Lafontaine came to recognize that Schröder was too big a political asset to waste in the pursuit of his own personal ambitions.[49] At the same time, with Lafontaine heading the party and Schröder the government, the SPD returned to the uncomfortable dual leadership that prevailed when Brandt was chairman and Schmidt was chancellor. Whether a harmonious sharing of these roles can be found and maintained, with Lafontaine massaging the party with visions of social solidarity while Schröder leads a German government committed to cutting public spending, seems less than certain.

Long after the great election victory of September 1998, the SPD's commitment to "innovation and justice" will be tested repeatedly in the policymaking process of the Berlin Republic. The continuing political dilemma will be how to settle upon and implement effectively an optimum balance between these two grand and not always compatible values.

Notes

1. See Susanne Miller and Heinrich Potthoff, *Kleine Geschichte der SPD: Darstellung und Dokumentation 1848-1990*, seventh revised edition (Bonn: J.H.W. Dietz, 1991).

2. See Miller and Potthoff, *Kleine Geschichte der SPD*, 198.

3. Perhaps the best discussion of this period is Arnulf Baring, *Machtwechsel: Die Ära Brandt-Scheel* (Munich: Deutscher Taschenbuch Verlag, 1984).

4. Figures cited in Alf Mintzel and Heinrich Oberreuter, eds., *Parteien in der Bundesrepublik Deutschland* (Bonn: Bundeszentrale für politische Bildung, 1990), 432.

5. On post-materialist values in the SPD, see Thomas Leif and Joachim Raschke, *Rudolf Scharping, die SPD und die Macht* (Hamburg: Rowohlt, 1994). On the concept of post-materialist values, see Ronald Inglehart, *The Silent Revolution* (Princeton: Princeton University Press, 1977).

6. Parteivorstand der SPD, *Basic Policy Programme of the Social Democratic Party of Germany: Adopted by the Programme Conference of the Social Democratic Party of Germany at Berlin, 20 December 1989* (Bonn: SPD, 1990).

7. On the SPD's triple legacy of opposing the status quo, struggling with its own inner divisions, and governing intermittently, see Hermann Schmitt, "Die Sozialdemokratische Partei Deutschlands," in Mintzel and Oberreuter, eds., *Parteien in der Bundesrepublik Deutschland*, 129-57, here 130-35.

8. See Peter Lösche, "Die SPD nach Mannheim: Strukturprobleme und aktuelle Entwicklungen," *Aus Politik und Zeitgeschichte*, no. 6 (1996): 21.

9. Hermann Schmitt writes: "Social democratic and socialist parties are traditionally definite program parties. Every even partially far-reaching change in the official party position necessitates programmatic discussion and majority approval. Here the SPD is no exception, with the general social democratic orientation being complemented by German thoroughness." (Author's translation) Schmitt, "Die Sozialdemokratische Partei Deutschlands," 140.

10. See Max Weber's famous 1918 speech at Munich University, "Politics as a Vocation" (*Politik als Beruf*), in H. H. Gerth and C. Wright Mills, *From Max*

Weber: Essays in Sociology (New York: Oxford University Press, 1946), 120 f., where *Gesinnungsethik* is translated as "an ethic of ultimate ends."

11. Klaus von Beyme, *Das politische System der Bundesrepublik Deutschland*, 8th ed. (Munich: Pieper Verlag, 1996), Table 4.5, 161.

12. See Peter Lösche, "Lose verkoppelte Anarchie," *Aus Politik und Zeitgeschichte*, no. 43 (1993): 34-45; see also Peter Lösche and Franz Walter, *Die SPD: Klassenpartei, Volkspartei, Quotenpartei* (Darmstadt: Wissenschaftliche Buchgesellschaft, 1992).

13. See Peter Lösche, "Die SPD nach Mannheim," 23.

14. The unique importance of the "middle" in German politics is well-explained in Gunter Hofmann, "Vom Wunsch, ein Bürger zu sein," *Die Zeit*, 17 September 1998.

15. See Tobias Dürr, "Neue Mitte oder alte Fehler," *Blätter für deutsche und internationale Politik*, no. 4 (April 1998): 394-98.

16. See Heinrich Tiemann, "Die SPD in den neuen Bundesländern: Organisation und Mitglieder," *Zeitschrift für Parlamentsfragen*, no.3 (1993): 415-22.

17. The figures for registered voters (*Wahlberechtigte*) are from 1994, those for party members are from December 1996. These figures come from the SPD party headquarters in Bonn.

18. See, for example, Ralf Dahrendorf, "Die neue Parteienlandschaft," *Die Zeit*, 2 July 1998.

19. Membership figures from the SPD party headquarters in Bonn.

20. See Stephen J. Silvia, "The Social Democratic Party of Germany," in David P. Conradt, Gerald R. Kleinfeld, George K. Romoser, and Christian Søe, eds., *Germany's New Politics: Parties and Issues in the 1990s* (Providence and Oxford: Berghahn Books, 1995), 149-70.

21. *Der Spiegel*, 13 November 1995, cited in Peter Lösche, "Die SPD nach Mannheim."

22. Politbarometer, reported in *Süddeutsche Zeitung*, 19 September 1998.

23. See Kurt Sontheimer and Ludwig Beck, *Grundzüge des politischen Systems der Bundesrepublik Deutschland*, tenth revised edition (Munich: Pieper, 1998), 344.

24. See Werner A. Perger, "Der Doppelstratege: Gerhard Schröder muß mit den Grünen paktieren—und mit Oskar Lafontaine," *Die Zeit*, 1 October 1998; and Günter Bannas, "Der Sprengstoff steckt in der SPD," *Frankfurter Allgemeine Zeitung*, 21 October 1998.

25. *Der Spiegel*, 9 November 1998.

26. See Nikolaus Piper, "Die Rückkehr von Keynes," *Süddeutsche Zeitung*, 2 November 1998.

27. Oskar Lafontaine and Christa Müller, *Keine Angst vor der Globalisierung. Wohlstand und Arbeit für alle* (Bonn: Dietz-Verlag, 1998).

28. Bodo Hombach, *Aufbruch: Die Politik der Neuen Mitte* (Düsseldorf: Econ Verlag, 1998).

29. See Heike Göbel, "Lafontaines Steuerwende," *Frankfurter Allgemeine Zeitung*, 13 October 1998.

30. "Who's Running Germany?" *The Economist*, 5 December 1998, 13.

31. See the chapters by David Keithly and Irwin Collier in this volume.

32. On the similarities between the "third way" and the "new middle," see Rainer Hank, "Auf dem dritten Weg," *Frankfurter Allgemeine Zeitung*, 10 October 1998; and Gina Thomas, "Blair, Schröder, Europa," *Frankfurter Allgemeine Zeitung*, 30 October 1998.

33. Thomas Hanke, "Streben nach Markt und Macht–Gerhard Schröders zwölf Thesen zur Modernisierung von Wirtschaft und Gesellschaft," *Die Zeit*, 19 September 1997.

34. Hanke, "Streben nach Markt und Macht."

35. A disappointed Ulrich Pfeifer, head of the FES Manager's Circle, spoke of "Kastratentum und Chaos." See Thomas Hanke, "Kanzler ohne Kompetenz," *Die Zeit*, 15 October 1998.

36. "Innovation für Deutschland" and "Von der Utopie zur Wirklichkeit: Aufbruch in die Informationsgesellschaft." From the SPD Web site: www.spd.de.

37. See Thomas Hanke, "Die Steuerreform ist nicht mutig. Aber mit der Reform der Sozialversicherung kann die Regierung viel retten," *Die Zeit*, 19 November 1998. See also the coalition contract, "Aufbruch und Erneuerung-Deutschlands Weg ins 21. Jahrhundert," available from the SPD's Web site.

38. Cited in Jordan Bonfante, "Who's On Top?," *Time*, 9 November 1998.

39. See Arne Daniels, "Mehr als der Runde Tisch," *Die Zeit*, 1 October 1998.

40. See Parteivorstand der SPD, *Protokoll vom Parteitag der SPD in Bremen*, 28-31 May 1991.

41. See Udo Bergdoll, "Nichts ohne den neuen Kanzler," *Süddeutsche Zeitung*, 9 October 1998.

42. The overall vote was 500 to 80, with 21 no-votes from the SPD. See *Süddeutsche Zeitung*, 17 October 1998.

43. See Christoph Schwennicke, "Ansichten der Akrobaten: Wehrpolitiker der SPD sagen plötzlich etwas ganz anderes als bisher," *Süddeutsche Zeitung*, 17 October 1998.

44. See Chapter XI, "Europäische Einigung, internationale Partnerschaft, Sicherheit und Frieden," in the coalition agreement, *Aufbruch und Erneuerung–Deutschlands Weg ins 21. Jahrhundert*.

45. See "Bonner Haltung zur Atomwaffen-Strategie der NATO: Alleingang ausgeschlossen," *Süddeutsche Zeitung*, 3 December 1998.

46. See Christian Wernicke, "Nachsitzen für Schröder: Was weiß der Kanzlerkandidat von Europa?" *Die Zeit*, 16 July 1998.

47. See Karl-Rudolf Korte, "Unbefangen und gelassen: Über die außenpolitische Normalität der Berliner Republik," *Internationale Politik*, no. 12 (1998): 3-12.

48. See Michael Stabnow, "Es weht ein frischer Wind," *Frankfurter*

Allgemeine Zeitung, 26 October 1998.

49. For a discussion of Lafontaine's options and outlook, see Franz Walter, "Führungskrise und Strukturprobleme," *Zeitschrift für Politikwissenschaft* 7, no. 4 (1997).

5

Alliance 90/The Greens:
Party of Ecological and Social Reform

E. Gene Frankland

The Greens have come a long way since their birth eighteen years ago as an anti-establishment movement party. Their founders, ranging far left to far right, shared a deep discontent with the Bonn "party cartel." They sought to form "a party unlike the others" based on: grass roots democracy, social responsibility, ecology, and nonviolence. Programmatic strife lead to the early departure of their conservative wing. After a poor showing in the 1980 federal election, the Greens bounced back to challenge the West German established order based on representative institutions and passive citizenship, economic growth and consumptive lifestyles, and loyal membership in the Western Alliance.

The conventional wisdom was that the Greens were a protest party whose heterogeneous alliance of activists would sooner or later disintegrate. In the meantime, mainstream observers' nightmare was that they might destabilize the party system and precipitate a crisis of governance. The unruly Greens advocated "fundamental opposition": no deals, no alliances, and no coalitions with other parties. One should not forget the hostility of major party politicians. For example, after the Greens' breakthrough in the 1983 federal election as the "eco-pax" movement party, they found themselves blocked from parliamentary seats on intelligence services control panels.

Nevertheless, the Greens contributed to the democratic development of the Federal Republic during the 1980s by channeling youthful protest into the system, by forcing the major parties to take up "new politics" issues (e.g., environmental protection and women's equality), and by working toward a participatory political culture. At the federal level, they functioned as an alternative opposition while at the state level they had their first tastes of governmental power. Despite their commitment to grass roots democracy, the Greens became "semi-parliamentarized" as the new social movements waned. Although they received more votes in the 1987 federal election, bitter factionalism had largely immobilized the party by the end of the decade.

Caught off balance by German unification, the Greens were voted out of the Bundestag in December 1990. Electoral "shock therapy" led to structural reform and a more pragmatic style, which correlated with gains in state elections. The Greens participated in coalitions in four states during the early 1990s.[1] In the 1994 Bundestag election the Greens, having merged with the eastern *Bündnis 90* (Alliance 90), were returned as the third largest parliamentary group. During the mid-1990s, complex problems stemming from German unification, European unification, and economic globalization produced a condition widely known as *Reformstau* (a backlog of reforms) in Bonn. While the major parties seemed adrift, the Greens were closing ranks to present themselves as the reformist "motor" for a new federal government.

In early 1998, SPD-Green coalitions governed five states, and polls indicated that 10 percent of the national electorate supported the Greens. Following a series of tactical errors and factional quarrels during the spring of that year, the Greens suffered setbacks in the state elections in Lower Saxony and Saxony-Anhalt (where they lost their parliamentary group) and in the local elections in Schleswig-Holstein. Summer 1998 polls indicated that their national support had declined to 5-7 percent. The Greens thereupon closed ranks around a toned-down program. With a lot of effort, they held on to their parliamentary group in the Bavarian Landtag in the September 13 state election. Two weeks later, they returned to the Bundestag, with two fewer seats than in 1994. The workable red-green majority came as a surprise. Negotiations with the SPD soon produced a coalition agreement with sufficient green fingerprints to win endorsements by the Greens' federal conference. At last the Greens have an opportunity to demonstrate that they can achieve ecological and social reform at the national level after years of talking about it.

Here we argue that the Greens have indeed "grown up" since 1990, but with a weak organization, a factional cleavage on foreign and security policy, and a conflictful image of coalitional behavior that leave them vulnerable to media attacks on their competence. This chapter considers the problems of structure, program, and strategy of the small Green party during the Bonn-Berlin transition. We begin by reviewing the development of the Greens during the first half of the 1990s.

The Greens and the New Germany

During the 1980s, the Greens critiqued the set of factors—from neo-corporatist decision-making to NATO membership—that according to conventional wisdom explained the success of the Federal Republic. Yet, paradoxically, as Andrei Markovits and Philip Gorski argue, "By generation, outlook, spirit, behavior, total habitus . . . the Greens were completely *bundes-republikanisch*."[2] In 1989-90, the national unity question transformed the political landscape, leaving the Greens confused, ambivalent, and discordant. The alternative party had been many things to many people during its first decade, but it had never been nationalistic.

After the public debate had shifted to how unification should occur, Greens were still discussing the "two German states" concept.[3] It was not until September 1990 that they finalized a pact with *Bündnis 90*. The authors of their common platform saw the East German democratic revolution as having been betrayed by West German party elites determined to "annex" the GDR. The Greens ran an amateurish electoral campaign that attempted to refocus public attention on global warming. They ended up on December 2, 1990, with 4.8 percent of western votes (and no Bundestag seats); *Bündnis 90* won 6.1 percent of eastern votes (eight seats).[4]

The unexpected defeat shook the Green party from top to bottom. The Neumünster conference in April 1991 passed most of the structural changes long favored by its *Realos* (realists). Soon the last of the prominent *Fundis* (fundamentalists) exited the party.[5] A more civil, reformist image contributed to the Greens' electoral victories in western states during 1990-94.

Nevertheless, united Germany's political opportunity structure required a "marriage of convenience" with *Bündnis 90* if the Greens were to have a real chance at winning Bundestag seats in 1994. The 2,200 easterners came out ahead of the 36,320 westerners in the symbolic issue of the official name for the united party, *Bündnis 90/Die Grünen*.[6] There were a couple of organizational changes in response to eastern demands, but there is no evidence that these innovations have had any practical significance in party decision-making. Observers have seen the merger in 1993 as more important informally because of the tendency for eastern views to overlap more with the views of *Realos* than with the Left's.

Prior to December 1990, many Green activists felt that the alternative party could ignore modern campaign techniques. Following electoral "shock therapy," the party's federal executive board commissioned survey analysis, employed a professional advertising agency, and embraced informational technology. Compared to 1990, the Greens' 1994 federal campaign was professionally planned and executed. In October the Greens won 7.3 percent of the votes, becoming the first party ever to make a comeback into the Bundestag after having lost its parliamentary group (*Fraktion*).[7] The Greens won 7.8 percent of western votes, but only won 4.3 percent of eastern votes. Only five of the forty-nine Green MPs came from the former GDR (and one of them defected to the CDU in 1996). Furthermore, in the eastern state elections of 1994, only Saxony-Anhalt Greens managed to win Landtag seats.

Although there have been Green Landtag vice-presidents, the major parties had blocked Greens from this largely symbolic office in the Bundestag. In November 1994, Antje Vollmer of the Greens was elected as one of its vice-presidents with the support of the CDU/CSU leadership. Chancellor Kohl held private meetings with Green parliamentary and party leaders. Increasing contacts between the Greens and corporate executives, union leaders, and church officials provided further evidence of the party's established status. However, the Greens have long resisted the organizational model of the major parties, whose dysfunctionalities had set the stage for their founding in 1980.[8]

Party Structure and Leadership

The 1980 Federal Program of the Greens declares, "We have decided to create a new type of party structure founded upon grass roots democracy."[9] Green party organization was envisaged as the countermodel of the mass-membership, bureaucratic-oligarchical party organization. During the 1980s, the Greens' membership grew to 41,000—without an aggressive recruitment campaign. Some of the founders feared that the larger the party grew, the more difficult it would be to maintain intraparty democracy. Ironically, the lack of a large membership pool made it impossible for grass roots-democratic procedures to work as designed. Most reports indicate that between one-fifth and one-third of the members were "active" in the late 1980s. After subtracting the thousands who were local councilors and the hundreds who were parliamentarians and staff assistants at state and federal levels, one found that not many Green activists were available to oversee the work of the party's mandate-holders.

In recent years, the CDU, the SPD, the FDP, and the PDS have lost members (while the CSU has claimed incremental growth). However, the Greens have seen their membership grow: 43,899 (1994), 46,410 (1995), 48,034 (1996), and 49,215 (1997).[10] This trend is noteworthy because they managed to grow during a period marked by *Parteienverdrossenheit* (public disenchantment with parties). Since 1994 the Green western parties have reported larger memberships. Three of five eastern parties have reported incremental growth; however, the total eastern membership stood at only 2,898 in late 1997 (compared to 46,317 in the West and Berlin). The post-communist aversion to any political party and the privatistic pursuit of material security has made recruitment difficult for the Greens in the ex-GDR.[11]

Despite reports of the pernicious influence of leftist functionaries, the Greens hardly have a central party bureaucracy. Robert Leicht is on target when he observes that "there is no real national Green party, but a patchwork of independent regional parties held together by a loose holding organization at the centre."[12] In fact, there have been few functionaries at either the federal or state level. In 1997 the federal office had twenty-two full-time employees, about the same as ten years ago; in comparison, the SPD's federal campaign unit alone employed some thirty people.[13] According to Heide Rühle, the Greens' federal party manager, "We have neither the personnel nor the financial resources to do justice to our expectations."[14] Managers of entrenched Green parties in Hesse, Berlin, and Baden-Württemberg reported four to nine full-time employees while managers of struggling eastern parties reported one to three full-timers.[15] The Greens' Bundestag staff has been about ten times larger than the federal party staff, and their Landtag staffs have been (at least) three times larger than those of the state parties. Given their institutional resources, Green parliamentary groups except in questions of "high politics" (e.g., coalitions) have operated autonomously from party organizations.

Because of fears that Green parliamentarians would assimilate conventional values, the party instituted anti-elitist rules in the early 1980s. Most of these rules have fallen by the wayside. For example, midterm rotation of seats to those lower on the electoral list (*Nachrücker*) to prevent the emergence of a "political class" proved so disruptive to the work of parliamentary groups that the federal party and most state parties abandoned it in the late 1980s. However, two major rules still differentiate the Greens from the major parties. First, they forbid the simultaneous holding of a parliamentary mandate and an executive office in the party. At the 1991 Neumünster conference, the proposal to abandon the separation of mandate and office fell short of the necessary two-thirds majority. At the 1994 Cologne conference, delegates rejected a plan to allow some overlap between parliamentary and party leadership. In December 1997, a proposal surfaced to reorganize the party after the 1998 federal election by downsizing its federal executive board and creating a larger presidium including parliamentarians and ministers. *Realo* and Left prominents argued that federal governmental participation would necessitate closer coordination and quicker decision-making. There could be no certainty about its passage by federal delegates, who relish their reputation of standing up to party leaders.

Collective leadership is the second surviving anti-elitist rule of the Greens. Instead of a chairperson, as other parties have, the Greens elect federal speakers, who have little power on paper (and have been paid significantly less than Green members of the Bundestag). During the 1980s, the party had three federal speakers; since 1991 it has had two. The Greens' quota system has resulted in a male speaker and a female speaker. Since 1991, intraparty harmony has made it desirable that one speaker come from the *Realos* and the other from the Left. The merger agreement with *Bündnis 90* did not require that one speaker come from the east, but many easterners expect it. In late 1996, newcomer Gunda Röstel (realist, female, eastern) emerged as the "ideal" co-speaker to balance senior co-speaker Jürgen Trittin (leftist, male, western). A single speaker would seem likely to move to the center of the party as an integrative figure. However, the Greens have chosen a leadership structure that represents their diversity, and tends to contribute to their media image of disunity.

Likewise the Bundestag Greens have elected multiple speakers: three in the 1980s and after 1994 two. The quota system has required at least one speaker to be female. In 1994 Leftist newcomer Kerstin Müller was chosen to "balance" *Super-Realo* Joschka Fischer. Although parliamentary issue-specialists commanded their policy niches, the Greens' Bundestag parliamentary group of 1994-98, compared to its predecessors, had a "power center"—Fischer and his allies. Opinion polls have indicated that the telegenic Fischer is known by 92 percent of the public, with a more positive image than several major politicians, including Kohl.[16] Fischer's intraparty critics have seen him as being so ambitious for federal ministrial office that he would compromise everything that the Greens stand for. Nevertheless, Fischer's integrative performance at the 1997 Kassel conference earned him an unprecedented standing ovation by federal delegates.

Although the media have long treated Fischer as the de facto chairman of the party, the Greens have not become a "one man" party. Trittin (and before him Ludger Volmer) as federal co-speaker endeavored to represent the views of the Left. Despite his missteps during the 1998 campaign, with the formation of an SPD-Green federal government, Trittin's role in keeping the Left behind compromises with the SPD could be vital. Furthermore, one encounters regional "princes" (*Landprinzen*) among the Greens. Despite their early vision of high circulation of activists between the party leadership (or parliamentary group) and the grass roots (*Basis*), there has been high continuity of Green leadership in several states, most notably since the early 1980s in Baden-Württemberg with Fritz Kuhn and Rezzo Schlauch (who appeal to the moderate mainstream) and in Berlin with Hans-Christian Ströbele (who is further to the left than Trittin). In recent years Green activists have moved toward more acceptance of the role of prominent personalities (*Promis*) in simplifying policy complexities and providing emotional handles for citizens. Yet, Heide Rühle's remark captures the ambivalent feelings lingering at the party's grass roots, "We need our *Promis*, but we can't bear them."[17]

The Greens have developed as an increasingly parliamentarized party with a weak party apparatus and a highly individualistic membership. It is, however, a party with two "faces." In the western states, the Greens have entrenched themselves as the third party, with membership growth, access to institutional resources, and relevance to power equations. In the eastern states, the Greens have struggled to stay afloat as the fourth party, with sparse membership, lack of access to institutional resources, and marginal relevance to power equations. With the Greens as the SPD's federal partner, organizational reforms to increase the party's efficiency could follow, and the eastern Greens' odds of staving off the loss of activists to other parties should improve. The media frenzy over the "radical" 1998 program of an aspiring Green party of government changed the dynamics of the federal campaign, forcing its party and parliamentary leaders to work together as a crisis management team.[18]

Program and Policies

Although critics have long discounted the Greens as a "one issue" (environmental-ist) party, this charge was inaccurate even during their early years. The party articulated the demands of diverse groups disillusioned with the major parties' policies. Without a unifying ideological model, early programs simply enumerated the demands of issue specialists within the movement party. Bitter factionalism hampered programmatic integration during the mid- and late 1980s. Although the departure of dogmatic eco-socialists and radical ecologists during 1990-91 simpli-fied this process, intraparty disputes have erupted into public view on a number of occasions during the Greens' second decade.

The impetus for a more credible, problem-solving approach came in the mid-1980s from the economic policy working group of the Bundestag Greens. The first result was the 1986 reconstruction program (*Umbauprogramm*), outlining an action plan to transform the economy that did not shy away from costs, trade-offs, and timetables.[19] However, verbal radicalism prevailed in the 1987 electoral program, which took an absolutist approach to foreign, defense, energy, and women's policy issues. The authors of the 1990 electoral program reiterated the party's identity: anti-militarist, anti-capitalist, and anti-patriarchal. The 1994 election program sought to integrate economic, ecological, and social policies, and to declare the party's readiness for a reform coalition with the SPD. However, it also included foreign and defense policies, reaffirming the party's political "otherness" (*Anderssein*), which would have made a SPD-Green coalition unworkable.

In late 1995, factional conflict reignited after nearly half of the Bundestag Greens voted for *Bundeswehr* participation in the NATO-lead (IFOR) forces within the former Yugoslavia, which the 1995 Bremen conference had rejected. Fischer main-tained that military force may be necessary in places, such as Bosnia, to stop "genocide." On the Left, Trittin remained true to the Greens' principle of nonvio-lence while Ludger Volmer allowed for the possibility of a German role in UN "peace-keeping" forces, but not "peacemaking" forces. Intense debates occurred also in many state parties, but *Promis* on both sides agreed (with three Landtag elections looming) not to renew the debate at the 1996 Mainz conference. When the Bundestag voted in late 1996 on German participation in the follow-up stabilization (SFOR) forces within Bosnia, Greens abstained or voted no.

The 1998 electoral program reflected the Left's perspective by rejecting any German military participation in UN peacemaking forces. However, factional leaders agreed on the wording of a resolution that would allow the Bundestag Greens to support continuation of a German military role in Bosnia. Unexpectedly the March 1993 Magdeburg conference defeated (by a one vote margin) the com-promise, exposing the deep division of the party on an issue of foreign policy that is likely to confront the new federal government. Following three months of nega-tive editorials and the passage of a modified resolution by the Greens' *Länderrat* (the highest party body between federal conferences), 70 percent of Bundestag Greens voted to continue the Germany's SFOR role in Bosnia.

The future of NATO had revived factional quarreling in 1997 over the Greens' foreign policy. Fischer argued that NATO's eastern expansion was inevitable and the best thing for the Greens would be to accept it and get into federal government where they could influence this process. Volmer rejected NATO expansion as a provocation of Russia and favored instead strengthening the OSCE (Organization for Security and Cooperation in Europe). When the Bundestag vote came on NATO's eastern expansion, the Greens split with the plurality abstaining. The 1998 electoral program favored an evolving European security order in which the OSCE's role increases and NATO's role decreases. However, it explicitly rejected Germany's unilateral withdrawal from NATO because of the destabilizing effects on neighboring countries. Rather the 1998 electoral program favored the steady demilitarization of German foreign policy by ending military conscription and halving the *Bundeswehr*'s size in four years.

One must not overlook the consensus that has emerged among the Greens in support of European integration. In their leftist 1984 Euro-program, the Greens attacked the institutions of the European Community and embraced an "essentially utopian political strategy" to bring about change.[20] The party challenged the Maastricht Treaty in the Federal Constitutional Court in 1993. However, its 1994 Euro-program endorsed European integration as the best defense against nationalism and favored working within the EU to make it more democratic, multicultural, and ecological. The Treaty of Amsterdam signed in 1997 was critiqued by the Greens for its failure to address the EU's "democratic deficit"; the parliamentary group abstained when the ratification vote occurred in the Bundestag. The 1998 electoral program supported both the EU's eastern expansion and the introduction of the Euro single currency.

Early Green programs tended to be reflective of the anti-capitalist views of eco-socialists and radical ecologists. However, in their 1994 electoral program, the Greens outlined an "ecological offensive" to steer the economy with higher energy taxes toward eco-capitalism. The concept of ecological tax reform also enjoyed popularity in the mid-1990s within the SPD and the CDU, but these parties backed away from its political risks as unemployment figures climbed. In contrast, the Greens put ecological and social tax reform at the core of their 1998 electoral program. They proposed new energy taxes and the end of ecologically harmful subsidies. These changes would be phased and would be fine-tuned along the way to deal with unintended consequences. Revenues generated by eco-taxes would be used to lower labor costs, to cushion the negative impact on the less affluent, and to invest in renewable energy and public transportation.

Headlines and sound-bites had no room for the fine points of the Greens' controversial plan to raise the cost of gasoline to 5 DM per litre over ten years. Major parties' spokespersons jumped on it as evidence of the Greens' irresponsibility, and eastern Greens expressed their misgivings with the Saxony-Anhalt election looming. Green spokespersons pointed out that the gradual rise in gasoline taxes would be partially offset in the short run by lower auto taxes and in the long run by the development of more fuel efficient automobiles. Furthermore, there would be provisions to address the special needs groups, such as commuters without access to public transportation. Despite statements by a number of research institutes and even major party energy specialists in support of significantly higher gasoline prices, charges that the Greens would make driving the priviledge of the more wealthy individuals stung the party. The short program (*Vierjahresprogramm*) passed by the Greens' *Länderrat* in June 1998 made no mention of 5 DM gasoline, which party leaders viewed as "the false symbol for the right thing."

The Greens maintained their traditional anti-nuclear energy position in the 1998 electoral program. They argued that Germany should begin immediately the process of decommissioning its nuclear reactors. In contrast to the 1994 program, the new program mentioned no timetable for the exit from nuclear power. However, Röstel declared later that it was doable within eight years. The SPD leadership obviously had a longer time frame in mind, yet there would be room for negotiation in coalition talks after Gerhard Schröder's mid-summer pronouncements in favor of shutting down the oldest nuclear reactors.

The Greens' 1980 federal program contained commitments to socioeconomic reform, such as a guaranteed annual income. However, the "eco-pax" movement party tended to neglect programmatic development in technical policy areas, such as income taxes, pensions, and social assistance. During the mid-1990s, a small group of financially savvy parliamentarians within the Bundestag Greens emerged and generated reform ideas, which many outside experts viewed as "innovative." For example, Andrea Fischer drafted a basic federal support plan (*Grundsicherung*) that would add a further foundation stone to the current social welfare system. The 1997 Kassel conference overwhelmingly endorsed her plan, which became part of the 1998 electoral program. At its core would be a subsistence support of 800 DM per single person (with 560 DM more per additional member of the household). The price tag of 12 billion DM would be financed through inheritance taxes and property taxes. The Greens stand for the renewal of the social state, but Andrea Fischer admitted that a new federal government could not simply undo the earlier social program cuts.

Greens have moved from being a protest party to a programmatic party that endeavors to work out credible plans of action toward the resolution of societal problems. In their 1998 electoral program the Greens presented themselves as the party of comprehensive ecological-social reform with detailed plans for moving toward a sustainable, socially just, democratic, and gender equal future.[21] To the delight of partisan critics, the Greens misjudged what should go into the "external" electoral program (154 pages) of an aspiring party of government in a period of socioeconomic insecurities. Three months later, their short program (13 pages) attempted to correct the situation by focusing more sharply on the relevance of Green policies to bringing unemployment down.

Electoral and Coalitional Strategy

Between May 1995 and March 1998, the Greens enjoyed national support levels of 10-13 percent, according to the monthly surveys of the Mannheim Research Group on Elections. Rüdiger Schmitt-Beck's study, utilizing multiple indicators to analyze 1992-96 data, determined that the Greens' core electorate had grown nationally from 4 to 6 percent (and their potential electorate had grown from 8 to 12 percent).[22] The regional trends were divergent: the western core increased from 4 to 7 percent while the eastern core electorate decreased from 4 to 3 percent. On the other hand, the *Polis* 1997-98 study found that 32 percent of westerners and 38 percent of easterners had a "good" opinion of the Greens, which was higher than the CSU, PDS, and FDP in the west and higher than the CDU, CSU, and FDP in the east.[23]

The social structural profile of Green strongholds has changed little through the years: large cities (especially with a significant post-industrial sector), above average educational levels, low levels of church membership, and universities. The 1998 electoral strategy of the federal party, which had a campaign fund 22 percent less than in 1994,[24] targeted these cities. From private donors Fischer raised money to take his own campaign on the road through the countryside.

As in 1994, the federal executive board turned to a professional advertising and media agency to communicate the mature (*"volljährig"*) face of the party. Symbolically the traditional sunflower logo of the party disappeared from its public advertisements to convey the message that the Greens have become competent in more policy areas than just the environment. For the first time, the federal office produced a placard series featuring large photos of individual leaders: Fischer, Müller, Trittin, and Röstel.

Analysis of the September 1997 Hamburg election, the March 1998 Lower Saxony election, and the April 1998 Saxony-Anhalt election indicated that since the last state election there had been a decline of Green support levels of 4-8 percent among eighteen- to twenty-four-year-olds. Among twenty-five- to thirty-four-year-olds, there had been declines of 6 percent (Hamburg) and of 4.1 percent (Saxony-Anhalt) of Green support levels while there had been a 0.4 percent increase in this age group's support for Lower Saxony Greens.[25] Similar results in other elections have led observers to conclude that the party of youth is in danger of becoming the party of the 1968 generation. The electoral challenge of the Greens has been to respond to the more careerist concerns of today's youth. Against the backdrop of the university strikes of 1997, the Bundestag Greens' higher education spokesperson, twenty-seven-year-old Matthias Berninger, proposed major reforms of the universities.

In terms of 1998 strategy, there was no difference between activists of the Green-Alternative Youth Alliance (GAJB) and their seniors in the federal party and parliamentary leadership; both sought a red-green coalition in Bonn. Many Greens had tactically preferred Gerhard Schröder as SPD Chancellor candidate because his more centrist appeal (compared to Oskar Lafontaine's more leftist appeal) would mean less competition in mobilizing their potential electorate. However, the SPD with Schröder turned out to be more effective in appealing to red-green voters in the elections of spring 1998 than had been expected, with the danger that this trend might pave the way for a grand coalition with the CDU.

On the other hand, Schröder and the Greens had worked together in Lower Saxony (1990-94), which was the first red-green coalition to survive a legislative period. The *Realo*-dominated Hesse Greens' coalition with the SPD (1991-95) became the second one. The early red-green governments in Hesse during (1985-87) and in Berlin (1989-90) were turbulent affairs. Nevertheless, the Hesse Greens could point to concrete successes, such as, laws passed regarding waste disposal, energy, and computer data protection. In Berlin, "ultimately, the coalition's main impact was cognitive. . . . that it existed."[26] The Berlin Alternative List has been one of the most leftist Green parties, and most committed to grass roots-democratic procedures.

North Rhine-Westphalia Greens have also traditionally had a leftist majority at their state conferences. Their 1995-98 experience in governing with the SPD was marked by crisis. However, the first NRW coalition outlived the first Hesse coalition because of its federal relevance. It survived vocal opposition from parts of the Greens' grass roots and a minority of the Landtag Greens. Right-wing Social Democrats sought to sabotage the coalition by pushing the licensing of a massive brown-coal strip-mining project that would create thousands of jobs, but also immense amounts of pollution. In other states, where the SPD and the Greens have shared power, there have been serious disputes over infrastructural projects, such as airports (Saxony-Anhalt) and highways (Schleswig-Holstein). With the SPD rediscovering the appeal of the "old politics" of material security, the Greens found themselves under heavy pressure to compromise on developmental projects favored by the SPD (and opposed by local citizen groups) in order to make progress in other policy areas.

During the early 1990s, there were two "traffic light" coalitions or *Ampelkoalitionen* (SPD, FDP, and Greens) at the state level. Neither survived the legislative period, nor left behind any Green enthusiasm for governing with the FDP in the future. On the other hand, the left-liberal thinkers of the Greens have sought to appeal to socially liberal FDP voters. FDP leaders declared the Greens their primary target in the 1998 campaign.

Green party and parliamentary leaders have made it clear that they share the SPD leadership's view that there can be no federal deals with the PDS. The PDS toleration of a minority SPD-Green government may have worked in Saxony-Anhalt during 1994-98, but it is not transferable to Bonn. In the aftermath of his party's defeat in the April 1998 Saxony-Anhalt elections, former Green parliamentary leader Hans-Jochen Tschiche envisaged a future for a new eastern party combining the Greens, the SPD left wing, and the reform wing of the PDS. However, other eastern Greens are in favor of keeping some distance from the PDS. Since

1994, the PDS has had little success in its campaign to penetrate the alternative-left milieus of the western Greens; however, this might change if the Greens were forced into many awkward compromises as the SPD's junior partner.

The emergence of CDU-Green alliances in over twenty councils after the 1994 North Rhine-Westphalia local elections and CDU support for a Green Bundestag vice-president gave rise to speculations about the black-green alternative. Previously Baden-Württemberg Greens and Saxony Greens had debated this option, but majorities had opposed its pursuit. Even *Realos* have concluded that there is insufficient policy commonality to warrant consideration of the CDU-Green option at the federal level. At this premature stage, it would split the Greens and cause the CSU to divorce the CDU. Disappearance of the FDP and the emergence of a new generation of CDU leaders coupled with Greens' frustrations in dealing with SPD leaders could pave the way for black-green coalitions in a couple of the states. The Konrad Adenauer Foundation has found this futuristic alternative worthy of research.[27]

Conclusion

Despite numerous predictions of the Greens' imminent demise, they survived to play a disproportionate role during the mid-1980s in resetting the policy agenda in Bonn. In 1990, the small party that prided itself on its ability to outmaneuver the major party "supertankers" was left waterlogged in the wake of Kohl's rush to German unification. The electoral defeat of December 1990, however, rather than sinking the Greens, accelerated the institutional learning process that had been moving many of its politicians in a reformist direction.

After their parliamentary comeback in 1994, the Greens have become more institutionalized and more comfortable with modern campaign techniques. Their traditional adversary culture (*Streitkultur*) has reemerged at times, but factional leaders of the 1990s have been more conscious of negative media images than those of the 1980s. With the exception of foreign and security policies, the Greens have jettisoned most of their New Left ideological baggage. Since 1994, *Promis* from both wings have advocated a red-green federal government.[28] A number of Green leftists teamed up with *Realos* to keep alive the NRW coalition with the SPD.

During the 1998 campaign year, the Greens often seemed their own worst enemy. For example, the remarks of a Green Bundestag backbencher that Germans should take no more than one vacation flight every five years made the headlines on the day of the local Schleswig-Holstein elections—in which the Greens lost one-third of their votes. The Greens managed to avoid similar blunders during the final phase of the federal campaign. Following the Greens' electoral success on September 13 in returning to the Landtag in Bavaria (not one of the party's strongholds), they appeared certain to clear the 5 percent threshold and reenter the Bundestag two weeks later—as they did with 6.7 percent of the votes (47 seats). In the western states, including Berlin, the party won 5.5 to 11.3 percent of the votes; in the eastern states its support ranged from 2.9 to 4.4 percent. The Greens increased their electoral share compared to 1994 in three states (the most by 1.1 percent in Berlin), while they lost ground in thirteen states (the most by 1.9 percent in Hamburg).

The electoral outcome represented Schröder's "dream scenario": a workable majority of twenty-one seats stemming from a strong SPD performance and a relatively weak Green performance.[29] Coalition negotiations between the two parties progressed more harmoniously than has been typical at the state level. The Greens' leaders made numerous compromises on policy details and timetables in exchange for framework commitments by the SPD, for example, to begin the exit from nuclear power and the process of ecological tax reform. The Greens gained three cabinet posts, including the Foreign Ministry for Joschka Fischer, and five parliamentary state secretaries (junior ministers). The red-green coalition agreement and the personnel lineup were overwhelmingly approved by the Greens' federal conference.

Fischer, rightly, declared the Greens' decision to share responsibility in federal government as their most historic since the founding of the party in 1980. The opportunities are considerable, but so are the risks. Most visible is the party's lack of consensus in regard to foreign policy issues, such as NATO's role in Kosovo. Future crises are likely to produce strife between the moderating Fischer and the leftist-pacifist wing of the party. Sharing power nationally is also likely to challenge the party's current weak, decentralized structures. Due to the Greens' alternative identity, there are limits to the party's normalization. Green ministers will be allowed to retain their parliamentary seats for the time being, but there are activists in the party who see this as contradictory to the Greens' goal of democratization. The federal executive board favors a partial easing of the rule requiring separation of party office and parliamentary mandate, which may pass, but a majority of delegates do not seem likely to accept a total abandonment of this rule. In addition, federal delegates are used to participating in policy development, thus giving party conferences an element of unpredictability. Furthermore, how can the Greens maintain a distinctive profile after moderating their programmatic demands for major eco-social reforms? The outcome of the successful 1990-94 red-green coalition with Schröder in Lower Saxony was, after all, an absolute majority for the SPD in that state. The media will be ever alert for evidence that the "chaotic" character of the Greens is reasserting itself. Assuming that the red-green partnership survives beyond its honeymoon, the near future challenge of the Greens will be to appeal to moderate voters without becoming a "Green FDP" and losing the support of its left-alternative activists. After eighteen years of growing up, the small Green party has become an insider in federal power politics; the stakes are high both for it and for the Berlin Republic.

Notes

1. The early 1990s saw SPD-Green governments in Hesse and Lower Saxony and SPD-FDP-Green governments in Bremen and Brandenburg; however, the latter case involved a Green parliamentary group that was nonaffiliated with the national party.

2. Andrei S. Markovits and Philip S. Gorski, *The German Left: Red, Green and Beyond* (New York: Oxford University Press, 1993), 275-76.

3. Ralf Fücks, "Ökologie und Bürgerrechte: Plädoyer für eine neue Allianz," in *Sind die Grünen noch zu retten?*, Ralf Fücks, ed. (Reinbek: Rowolt, 1991), 33-43.

4. If the Greens and *Bündnis 90* had merged before December 2, 1990, through a special electoral law clause for the first all-German election, the Greens would have qualified for seats in the Bundestag.

5. Jutta Ditfurth and her radical ecologist entourage resigned from the Greens after the Neumünster conference, April 1991. Her fundamentalist allies, the Trampert-Ebermann eco-socialists, resigned from the party in early 1990 to launch a radical leftist association. Both subgroups fizzled.

6. Thomas Poguntke, "Bündnis 90/Die Grünen," in *Intermediäre Strukturen in Ostdeutschland*, Oskar Niedermayer, ed. (Opladen: Leske and Budrich, 1996), 90.

7. The eight MPs of the eastern *Bündnis 90/Grüne* parliamentary group (which included two East Greens) fell short of the number needed to qualify for *Fraktion* status (and the procedural tools and institutional resources that it provides) during 1990-94.

8. Joachim Raschke, "Political Parties in Western Democracies," *European Journal of Political Research* 11 (1983): 112-13.

9. *The Program of the Green Party* (English Translation) (Bonn: Die Grünen, 1980), 5.

10. The membership data utilized in the text were provided by Dr. Norbert Franck of the Bonn federal office of the Greens (January 1998). In August 1998, party membership reached 50,021, *Schrägstrich* (September 1998): 6.

11. Interviews by the author of state party officials in Potsdam, Magedeburg, Dresden, and Erfurt (between March 3 and April 3, 1996).

12. Robert Leicht, "Whatever Happened to the German Left?" *Prospect* (August/September 1998): 29.

13. Christiane Schlötzer-Scotland, "Arbeitsplatz vor Umwelt," *Süddeutsche Zeitung: SZonNet Aktuell*, 25 September 1997.

14. *die tageszeitung*, 2 February 1997, 11.

15. Interviews by the author of state party officials in Stuttgart, Wiesbaden, and Berlin (between February 9, 1996 and March 20, 1996) and as cited above in note 11.

16. "Die alten Dämlichkeiten," *Der Spiegel*, no. 14 (1998) On-Line, and

Forschungsgruppe Wahlen e.V., Mannheim, *Politbarometer*, 2 December 1997 and 2 June 1998.

17. *die tageszeitung*, 27 February 1997, 11.

18. The "G7" campaign committee, which operated outside the party charter and met without staff present, included: Fischer, Müller, Werner Schulz (parliamentary manager), Trittin, Röstel, Rühle, and Dietmar Strehl (party treasurer) ("Keine Eigentore mehr," *Süddeutsche Zeitung: SZonNet Aktuell*, 26 June 1998).

19. E. Gene Frankland, "Green Politics and Alternative Economics," *German Studies Review* 9, no. 2 (February 1988): 111-32.

20. Wolfgang Rüdig, "Green Parties and the European Union," in *Political Parties and the European Union*, John Gaffney, ed. (London: Routledge, 1996), 262.

21. *Grün ist der Wechsel: Programm zur Bundestagswahl 98* (Bonn: Bündnis 90/Die Grünen, 1998), 5.

22. Rüdiger Schmitt-Beck, "Vor dem Wahljahr 1998: Wählerpotentiale von Bündnis 90/Grünen und ihre Wahrnehmungen politischer Probleme," University of Mannheim, unpublished paper, September 1997.

23. Günter Schaub, "Reform macht Angst . . . Eine Umfrage über Grundwerte und politische Meinungen im Wahljahr," *Die Zeit*, 30 July 1998.

24. Christiane Schlötzer-Scotland, "Abschied von grünen Illusionen," *Süddeutsche Zeitung: SZonNet Aktuell*, 14 November 1997.

25. *Berichte der Forschungsgruppe Wahlen e. V.* (Mannheim), no. 87 (24 September 1997), 54; no. 70 (17 March 1994), 18; no. 88 (4 March 1998), 16; no. 72 (30 June 1994), 17; and no. 89 (29 April 1998), 16. The results of the Bundestag election on 27 September 1998 fit the pattern. The Greens lost most compared to 1994 among eighteen-to-twenty-four-year-olds (4.2 percent) and twenty-five to thity-four-year-olds (2.7 percent). On the other hand, Bavarian Greens two weeks earlier actually gained 2 percent among eighteen- to twenty-four-year-olds compared to the 1994 state election. See *Berichte der Forschungsgruppe Wahlen e. V.* (Mannheim), no. 76 (21 October 1994), 18; no. 91 (27 September 1998), 18; no. 75 (28 September 1994), 11, and no. 90 (16 September 1998), 16.

26. Charles Lees, "Paradise Postponed: An Assessment of Ten Years of Government Participation by the German Green Party," University of Birmingham, Institute for German Studies, Discussion Paper No. IGS95/4 (December 1995), 18.

27. See Jürgen Hoffmann, "Sowing the Seeds for Future Cooperation," *German Comments: Review of Politics and Culture*, no. 48 (October 1997): 53-61.

28. According to one "insider" estimate, 30 per cent of the Green party members have no interest in sharing power ("Die alten Dämlichkeiten," *Der Spiegel*, no. 14 (1998).

29. Ian Traynor, "Kohl's long reign comes to an end," *Manchester Guardian Weekly*, 4 October 1998, 1.

6

The FDP:
Do the Liberals Still Matter?

Christoph Hanterman and Christian Søe

One of the political uncertainties in the Berlin Republic concerns the future role of the Free Democratic Party (FDP). For five decades, this small liberal force held a unique position of influence and vulnerability on the federal political scene in Bonn. In the last few years before the move to Berlin, the FDP came very close to electoral oblivion, but it managed to hang on as crucial majority-maker in Germany's coalition politics. This special role, and the political leverage that went with it, came to an abrupt end after the Bundestag election of September 1998.

Yet the same electoral result that swept Helmut Kohl's conservative-liberal government out of office also gave the Free Democrats a new lease on life. It ensured the FDP's parliamentary survival for at least the first legislative period in Berlin—albeit in the unaccustomed role of junior opposition party. From this new and marginal position, the Liberals are now trying to establish that their continued presence in German politics makes a vital difference. That will not be an easy case to make in electoral terms, where it ultimately counts. On the other hand, the FDP does have a long record of performance as well as some distinctive policy ideas to back up its quest for parliamentary survival and eventual restoration of cabinet status in a future government. A political obituary for the Free Democrats, endangered though they are, would be premature at this point.[1]

Paradoxically, electoral decline has in some ways invigorated the small party, at least at the top. Beginning in the mid-1990s, a new generation of leaders began to shift the FDP in what amounts to a neoliberal direction. Like some other reform parties elsewhere in Europe, the Free Democrats have adopted positions that stress the need to "slim down the state," that is, to strengthen the free market and reduce the government's economic and social role. The reorientation is still in progress, and the FDP couples its renewed emphasis on market-oriented reforms with some remaining concessions to Germany's tradition of state intervention. But the programmatic shift has already modified the small party's long-established "functional" image as a moderate balancer in Germany's overwhelmingly centrist system of governance.

The reorientation involves both existential risks and opportunities for the Free Democrats. They like to emphasize that the outcome—in the form of parliamentary survival or oblivion—is likely to have an impact on the overall balance of power, style of governance, and direction of policy in German politics. "Without the Liberals," they remind whoever will listen, "Germany would be a different republic."[2]

Most FDP reformers carefully avoid any public self-identification with neoliberalism, a term that frequently is given an "uncaring" or "unsocial" connotation also in German political parlance. Yet the reformers like to present their self-styled "new" FDP as the only real alternative in German party politics to a kind of hegemonial "social democratism." They claim that this outlook, which supposedly dominates all of the other parties in the Bundestag, has become a "structurally conservative" hindrance to some overdue social and economic reforms in Germany.

From these reformers' perspective, the FDP is—or should be—a catalyst of policy innovations that would revitalize an overtaxed and overregulated Germany. They promote their own party as a "modernizing" force in a country hampered by rigidities that stem from excessively intrusive role of the state. And they argue that their "new" FDP represents values, attitudes and interests that are also crucial to the creation of a more open and dynamic information society in Germany. Their outlook has been given programmatic expression in the party's 1997 Wiesbaden Basic Principles, and their ideas and metaphors have come to dominate the FDP's self-presentation during the last few years.[3]

Not surprisingly, the neoliberal reformers have run into some inertia within their own party. There has also been some active resistance from more conventional Free Democrats, who question what they regard as too narrow an economic focus that neglects some of the FDP's other traditional concerns. One such area is civil liberties, where the Greens now lay claim to some libertarian positions that for a long time were staked out by the Free Democrats. Another is foreign policy, where statecraft still tends to prevail over markets: Here prominent Liberals long played a leading role as foreign ministers (first Walter Scheel, from 1969 to 1974; then Hans-Dietrich Genscher, from 1974 to 1992; and thereafter Klaus Kinkel until 1998). On the whole, the FDP membership has been supportive of the party's reformers, but it is by no means fully united behind them.

The rest of this chapter turns first to an assessment of the political condition of the German Liberals, with special attention to their almost total collapse in the East and their two leadership turnovers in the 1990s. It then examines the FDP's traditional "functional" role as balancer in the coalition politics of the Bonn Republic along with the recent efforts to find a niche as a more distinctive reform party. A special section assesses the party's mediating and innovating foreign policy role until the end of the Kohl era. Finally, the chapter makes some concluding observations on the Free Democratic efforts to regain political influence in the emerging Berlin Republic.

Travails of a "Political Mermaid"

As a result of the 1998 Bundestag election, the FDP was relegated from the federal government to the parliamentary opposition after twenty-nine consecutive years as junior coalition partner—first of the SPD (1969 to 1982) and then of the CDU/ CSU (after 1982). The party must consider itself fortunate to have survived at all, by winning 6.2 percent of the crucial second vote that determines parliamentary representation. This was a setback when compared to the FDP's already low result of 6.9 percent in 1994, but it was better than most pollsters had given reason to hope for a few days before the election.

The 1998 outcome opened a new chapter in the party's remarkable history. After its formation in December 1948, the FDP's perennial role as junior partner in government gave it a disproportional presence and leverage in German federal politics. As the FDP began its fiftieth year of existence, it could still claim to be the most successful small party in contemporary western Europe in terms of the length and scope of its participation in national government. It had been present in all Bonn cabinets since the beginning of the Federal Republic in 1949, except for two fairly brief intervals in the distant past (from 1956 to 1961, and from 1966 to 1969). Despite its modest and dwindling electoral base, the FDP has never been absent from the Bundestag.

However, the FDP's impressive record in Bonn has long been offset by a drastic reduction of its role in sub-federal politics. Since the end of the 1960s, the FDP has repeatedly experienced difficulty in passing the 5 percent electoral hurdle for parliamentary representation at the state (Land) level. Here periodic strings of electoral setbacks have been followed by partial recoveries, while the party's structural weaknesses remained unrepaired. Germany's reunification gave the FDP a temporary electoral boost, but a few years later the electoral disasters resumed at an alarming rate. Between 1993 and 1995, for example, the party failed to win any parliamentary representation in twelve out of thirteen Landtag races. As a result of this unprecedented series of shutouts, the FDP was present in only four of the country's sixteen state parliaments after 1995. And it was a coalition partner in only one, later two, of the sixteen state cabinets.[4] The Liberals have also been reduced to a very thin and spotty representation in local government councils throughout most of the Federal Republic. Even where it retains a presence, the FDP has often become a marginal player rather than a majority-making power broker. As a result of this atrophy below the national level, German wits never tire of referring to the FDP as their country's political mermaid—*"die Dame ohne Unterleib."*

In federal politics, the Free Democrats have managed to stay above the water line, even if at times only barely. Here the stakes can be presented to the voters as considerably higher than in local or state politics. In Germany's risk-averse political culture, Free Democrats have often issued prudential appeals for tactical voter support. But this traditional self-presentation, which essentially tries to define the FDP as a broker who delivers moderation, stability and continuity in governance, has not attracted a solid core of voters that would guarantee the party's parliamentary existence. Nor does it harmonize easily with the party's new emphasis on the need for fundamental market-oriented reforms that almost inevitably would be accompanied by dislocations.

The Liberal Collapse in the East

No discussion of the FDP's difficulties would be complete without some attention to the party's special problems in the East. For a brief period, Germany's reunification in 1990 appeared to revitalize the ailing liberal party. In the first all-German Bundestag election, in December 1990, the FDP attracted 11 percent of the decisive second or party vote—its best result in nearly three decades. In the eastern region that had been under communist rule for over forty years, the small party performed even better. Here it received 12.9 percent of the popular vote (compared to 10.6 in the western states)—a higher total than the Liberals had received in any Bundestag election held in the "old" Federal Republic. Also in 1990, the FDP was elected into each of the five new eastern state parliaments as well as the legislative assembly of united Berlin, and it became a government coalition partner in four of them. For a while, the FDP could credibly present itself as the first "truly all-German" (*gesamtdeutsche*) party. Alone among the "old" parties in the Federal Republic, the FDP had a somewhat broader electoral base and a *much* larger membership in the East than in the West.

The FDP's political windfall in the new states would soon be squandered, as first became evident in the rapid decline of its membership. At the time when several eastern parties joined the FDP in August 1990, the Free Democrats had recorded an immediate threefold boost in membership—from a little more than 66,000 to over 200,000, of whom about 136,000 were new eastern members. Even considering the fact that the first eastern figures were politically inflated, the rise was meteoric. The many new members were largely inherited from two old bloc parties (the Liberal Democrats, or LDP, and the National Democrats, or NDPD), but they also included a few hundred eastern dissidents who had founded two tiny liberal parties at the beginning of 1990.

For a short while, the FDP's center of gravity appeared to have shifted eastward. This led to some speculation about a possible return to a selective "social liberal" policy agenda in response to the problems of reconstruction in the East. But it soon became evident that the former "Ls" and "Ns" would not seriously attempt to move the FDP in a more interventionist direction. Instead, most of them simply abandoned their new and unfamiliar party home, where they missed both the clubby atmosphere and the careerist advantages that had made membership in the bloc parties worthwhile.

At the end of 1990, FDP members in the East still numbered 111,000. The initial loss of 25,000 within five months can be ascribed not only to more reliable counting procedures but also to the first ripples of what soon became a tidal wave of defections. Seven years later, the eastern membership had plummeted by another 94,000 (a loss of about 85 percent). As a result, at the beginning of 1998 there were only 17,000 easterners left in the party, while the number of westerners had declined much less dramatically in the same period from 66,000 to 52,000 (a loss of 21 percent). In other words, the East-West membership ratio in the FDP had moved from almost 2 to 1 in favor of the far less populous East, at the time of party unification, to 3 to 1 in favor of the West by the beginning of the Bundestag election year of 1998. It is possible to relativize this development by pointing out that with an West-East population ratio within Germany of about 4 to 1, the eastern states are (still) slightly better represented in the small party's membership. Yet the mass exodus has drained away any potential advantage that might have stemmed from the initial preponderance of easterners in the FDP right after German reunification.[5]

Significant developments in the party's membership, leadership, electoral base, and program served to reinforce a far more western identity for the Free Democrats. Indeed, for many eastern Germans, the FDP came to be seen as the epitome of the "better-off" and "know-it-all" westerners—the overbearing *Besserwessis*. Easterners particularly resented and seemed unable to forget the FDP's campaign gaffe of 1994, when it briefly engaged in a self-ironic flirtation with the label, "party of higher income earners" (*Partei der Besserverdienenden*). The phrase backfired and came to reinforce the widespread perception of the FDP as socially somewhat arrogant or uncaring. Nowhere is such a trait a greater political liability than in the East.

The party's electoral trend in the eastern states has been nothing short of disastrous. In the Landtag contests of 1994 and 1995, the FDP dropped *far below* the 5 percent threshold in every single one of the new Länder. As a result, the Liberals failed to retain—and have so far failed to regain—any parliamentary representation in the five eastern states or united Berlin.[6] The FDP would also have been shut out of the Bundestag on the basis of its low electoral support in the East alone. In 1994 the FDP was able to survive with 6.9 percent of the vote overall, because it retained a sufficient electoral share in the West (7.7 percent) to make up for the crumbling of its electoral position in the East (3.5 percent). Here the FDP had managed in a period of just four years to traverse an entire electoral range from a record high to a record low—a rapid electoral collapse for which there is no precedent in the West. The Bundestag election of 1998 basically reproduced this pattern, with the Free Democrats slipping by another 0.7 percent to 6.2 percent of the vote overall, based on results of 7.0 percent in the West and 3.3 percent in the East.[7]

Thus the severely weakened FDP now depends on a slim western margin of electoral support to remain a player in German parliamentary politics.

Two Leadership Changes

The party's general plight was not helped by the manner in which the Liberals seemed to bungle the first steps of their far-reaching leadership turnover in the 1990s. Long in advance there had been party discussions of the need to prepare for a "successor generation" of new leaders, but when the time came, the Free Democrats were remarkably ill prepared. The FDP has always prided itself on being the home of some outstanding personalities, but in 1992 and 1993 there were simply no strong candidates to replace veteran foreign minister Hans-Dietrich Genscher or party leader Otto von Lambsdorff when they stepped down from their respective posts. After some confusion, Klaus Kinkel, a top civil servant, ended up replacing both of them. In the foreign ministry, he showed administrative competence but seemed to lack political skill or cabinet leverage in dealing with a very changed international situation facing Germany after the end of the Cold War. As the new head of his party, Kinkel seemed to be out of touch from the beginning. He had joined the FDP only two years earlier, in early 1991, and he showed little understanding of the party's complex internal politics. Inevitably, if somewhat unfairly, he was blamed for its mounting misery at the polls, which began a few months after he became party leader.

After a concentrated series of electoral disasters, the battered Klaus Kinkel resigned as party leader in the early summer of 1995. He was replaced by Wolfgang Gerhardt, who had the distinction of leading the FDP in the state of Hesse when the Liberals returned to the Landtag there a few months earlier—the party's single success in a total of thirteen state races between 1993 and 1995.

From the start Gerhardt relied heavily in strategic matters on Guido Westerwelle, the party's new general secretary. This young Liberal soon began to set a distinctive mark on the party with his energy, flamboyance, and assertiveness—to some, also jarring—neoliberal rhetoric. A third important figure in the party has been the far less visible Hermann Otto Solms, who retained influence even after his displacement by Gerhardt as leader of the Bundestag caucus in 1998. Very soon this troika found a division of roles and public images in which Gerhardt personifies the upright and well-spoken leader of the party. Westerwelle acts as articulate and combative strategic reformer, while Solms remains a competent if thoroughly unexciting Bundestag politician. In this strongly revised second edition, then, the FDP appears to have successfully carried through its generational change at the party top. Here, at least, it can claim to have stolen a march on both the CDU and SPD with their delayed or incompletely resolved leadership issues.

From Balancer to Reformer

The new leaders immediately began to carve out a more distinctive political niche for the FDP in Germany's party system. Here they were able to take advantage of a membership referendum on a symbolically important policy issue. In the first such general membership vote taken in the FDP, it was decided in late 1995 to rescind the party conference's strong civil libertarian opposition to electronic eavesdropping by law enforcement authorities. This was an issue that had divided the small party and estranged it from the more conservative (CDU/CSU) government partner. One of many individual Free Democrats who objected to what they viewed as a regressive policy change was Justice Minister Sabine Leutheusser-Schnarrenberger, a prominent civil libertarian. In a dramatic protest, she resigned from her cabinet office and was replaced by a more compliant party member.

With this law-and-order issue apparently behind them, the new leaders were able to concentrate on developing what Westerwelle likes to call the "new" FDP. In assessing recent electoral setbacks, they concluded that the FDP had come to depend far too much on what is often called the party's "functional" identity, in the sense of its systemic role as junior coalition partner in Bonn.[8] Their solution was to give the party a much sharper reform image, embodied in a draft program prepared by a party commission directed by Westerwelle. At the regular party conferences in 1996 and 1997, Free Democrats debated, amended and finally adopted these positions as the Wiesbaden Basic Principles.

The FDP reformers were critical of what they saw as the reduction of their party's "functional" contribution to that of a pliant and convenient majority-maker. In a frequently voiced criticism of the Free Democratic 1994 campaign strategy, they asserted that it had amounted to an electoral bid to support the FDP in order to keep Helmut Kohl as chancellor. Here they exaggerated, but their charge carried the rough truth of caricature: Kinkel's FDP had indeed campaigned with the simple argument that Kohl and the CDU could "not make it on their own" and therefore needed the FDP to stay in power.

Free Democrats have always been uneasy with a "functional" appeal that does not stress their party's political autonomy but, instead, emphasizes its role as a coalition partner. Yet some modified form of this electoral approach may be unavoidable for a quintessential coalition party like the FDP. Such a strategy has repeatedly been instrumental in helping to convince a crucial portion of coalition supporters to cast their second vote for the FDP. In 1994, according to a major German electoral analysis, tactical CDU-oriented voters made up over 60 percent of the FDP supporters. The situation had not changed very much four years later, in 1998, when a pre-election poll showed that such tactical supporters continued to make up a solid majority (57 percent) of the FDP's prospective voters.[9]

There has always been a more sophisticated version of the functional argument, going back to the party's early theorist, Karl-Hermann Flach.[10] It emphasizes the FDP's role as a moderating and countervailing force in its relationship to the larger coalition partner, as in a Madisonian recipe for taming power through the process of majority-building. In addition, Flach argued that the FDP also should act as a dynamic or motive force, producing new ideas and prodding a larger and inertia-ridden chancellor party into action. In this more expansive form, the functional argument for the FDP dovetails with the small party's programmatic claim to represent an autonomous, liberal direction. In effect, both Flach and some later strategists argued that the FDP should act as *both* a prudent "brake" and a dynamic "motor" in the political system.

Thus, it was not in itself a *novum* when Westerwelle and others presented the FDP as a reform-oriented party in the late 1990s. What came as somewhat surprising to most observers was the direction taken by the innovators as they sought to differentiate the FDP from the purported "social democratism" of all other Bundestag parties. Here too, there was a tradition that could be cited for legitimation purposes. After World War II, the FDP had been by far the most market-oriented of the Bundestag parties, and some early Free Democrats had intellectual ties to Ordo-liberalism.[11] In their coalitions with both Social Democrats and Christian Democrats in Bonn, the Liberals had a long-established record of resorting to market arguments—rarely, to be sure, against the business interests of the small party's middle-class supporters.

There was an additional element of calculated self-differentiation in the FDP's new strategy. As junior government party, the FDP has often found it useful to engage in forms of limited conflict with its larger partner. There have been periods when differences became almost muted, as in the years under Kinkel's leadership. After the leadership change in 1995, Westerwelle chose once again to focus on some political disagreements between the FDP and the CDU/CSU.

The shift in the FDP's self-presentation became clear at the beginning of January 1996. With three important state elections coming up on March 24, the FDP leadership used the party's traditional new year meeting in Stuttgart (*Dreikönigstreffen*) to publicize the new direction. On this occasion, Westerwelle poured scorn on the Christian Democrats for sharing, in effect, an outdated "social democratic" orientation. By contrast, he presented the FDP as the party committed to individual freedom and initiative. In a typically less ideological stance, Gerhardt insisted that a start be made on overdue tax reforms by reducing and ending the "solidarity surcharge tax," which added 7.5 percent to income tax bills to support the restructuring of the economy in the East. The FDP leader called elimination of this tax an important signal to foster individual initiative and reduce the public sector's involvement in the German economy.

In the weeks and months that followed, leading Free Democrats kept promoting the FDP as the "tax reduction party" (*Steuersenkungspartei*), in the conviction that this issue would make it more visible and attractive to swing voters. Their strategy seemed vindicated by the surprisingly good outcome for the FDP in all the state elections of March 1996. In each of the three Länder, the Liberals cleared the 5 percent threshold without difficulty, something that no longer could be taken for granted.

These victories came at just the right time to give the reformers new momentum. Many Free Democrats had expressed reservations about becoming a kind of "single-note" party. Such warnings frequently came from the FDP's Freiburg Circle. The members of this informal center-left discussion group number perhaps a couple of hundred people. They support free market ideas, but they insist that the party not forget its civil libertarian heritage or social commitments either. Misgivings have also been vented by many centrists, including Hans-Dietrich Genscher, the former party leader and veteran foreign minister, who resent the rhetorical iconoclasm that often accompanies the reformers' promotion of a supposedly "new" FDP.[12]

A very different position has been advanced on the party's right wing. Here one finds members who propagate a stronger nation-state emphasis as well as law-and-order demands, including sharp restrictions on immigration into Germany. Its leading figure until late 1997 was Heiner Kappel, who took increasingly populist positions resembling those of the Austrian party leader Jörg Haider. While Kappel finally left the FDP, others with similar views have remained in the party. They receive considerable attention from the press, but they seem to represent a numerically weak undercurrent. So far, at least, all predictions that electoral or ideological considerations might drive the FDP to embrace a nationalist form of right-wing populism have come to naught.[13]

The Wiesbaden Basic Principles begin by lauding the achievements of liberal democratic politics and market economics in Germany, but then turn to the country's failure to reform, to remain competitive, and to prepare for the future. "We cannot continue as hitherto," the program asserts, and then targets what it calls Germany's "politics of indulgence" (Gefälligkeitspolitik). This awkward term originates from Westerwelle's program committee. As a pejorative neologism, it has utterly failed to catch on in German parlance, but it has not been for want of promotion: The term is used no less than thirteen times in the first four pages of the new FDP program.

In place of Gefälligkeitspolitik, the program calls for a reduction in entitlements, subsidies, and regulations. It argues that Germany has become entangled in a "structural conservatism" that must be replaced by more open, competitive, liberal forms of interaction. In an aside, the program admits that "we Liberals" have also contributed to the lamentable state of affairs. Now, however, Free Democrats are called upon to oppose the "social conservatives" and the "conservative socialists" of all parties, by promoting a society that emphasizes individual responsibility and reduces the role of the state. The emphasis is clearly on the need for economic reforms and less state intervention, but these demands are accompanied by a long celebration of additional traits of what the program calls a "liberal civil society" (liberale Bürgergesellschaft).[14]

If all its parts are given equal weight, the Wiesbaden program makes only a half-turn toward neoliberal rhetoric, strategies and goals. Yet it leaves no doubt that the FDP favors reforms that in some ways would "shake up" what is portrayed as a stagnant German society. Indeed, after President Roman Herzog in April 1997 issued his much-discussed call for a "jolt" to awaken Germany from its pessimism and torpor, a leading FDP strategist pointed to the Liberals' new program and claimed, "We are the jolt that goes through Germany."[15]

So far, the intended jolt has been more like a slight ruffle in political effect. The reformers like to point out that their party now sometimes draws disproportionately more support among younger people, below the age of thirty, than at any time since its distant heyday as "social liberal" reformer. Overall, however, relatively few voters have been attracted by the new and, for many, somewhat jarring image of the FDP. Despite strong efforts to promote the "new" FDP in Hamburg, the party went down to another defeat there in September 1997. The hopes for parliamentary comebacks in four other state elections in 1998 were similarly dashed.

Part of the problem lies in the inability of the FDP to deliver on its reform agenda. Some of its proposals for deregulation and broad tax reform (including tax reductions) find support among individual politicians in other parties, both CDU/CSU and SPD. But they were largely blocked by the gridlock that prevailed in German politics in advance of the 1998 Bundestag election. The SPD used its controlling majority in the federal upper chamber (the Bundesrat) to stop a tax reform advanced by the Kohl government. The FDP took credit for a relatively small tax reduction that scaled back the "solidarity surcharge" for reconstruction in the East from 7.5 to 5.5 percent. It also claimed authorship of a moderate loosening of the legislation that regulates store closing hours in Germany. But for the most part, the FDP as a government member could do little to advance the more far-reaching reforms it advocated. In the opposition after the September 1998 election, the FDP can advocate more freely but deliver even less.

The FDP's Foreign Policy Contributions

Democratic elections are rarely won on foreign policy issues, and political parties are normally identified more with their domestic than their external policy agendas. However, the small FDP has always been different in this respect, and that could have implications for a Berlin Republic in which the Liberals became a marginal factor. It is in any case remarkable that the FDP showed a distinctive foreign policy profile from the beginning of the Federal Republic, even while serving as member of the first West German government of Chancellor Konrad Adenauer after 1949. Twenty years later, the small party became closely identified with its role as Bonn's foreign minister party or *Außenministerpartei*. In almost three decades of heading this ministry, while serving in the coalition governments of Brandt and Schmidt (SPD) as well as Kohl (CDU), the FDP came to be regarded as a standard bearer in Bonn's external relations. For a long time, it was able to benefit in Bundestag elections from this prominent position within the federal government.[16]

The FDP generally earned respect for promoting continuity, balance and moderation in foreign policy under a professionally competent leadership. Not least, it established a record of firmly rejecting what it called "populist" tendencies, from both the right and left in German politics. Over the years, such "populism" has also come from vocal individuals within the chancellor party. In the early 1980s, for example, the FDP leadership backed the double track position against strong protest from the left wing of the SPD (and some individual Liberals). Likewise in the late 1990s, it supported European monetary union against such prominent Christian Democrats as Edmund Stoiber and Kurt Biedenkopf (and again a few Liberals). The FDP was successful most of the time in withstanding such pressures, but not always. The most serious exception was the quick and unilateral German recognition of Croatia and Slovenia in 1991. This decision, which was largely driven by populist impulses, had unintended but serious consequences for the deterioration of the political situation in the Balkans.[17]

The FDP's attributes of competence, moderation and continuity seemed particularly well embodied by the veteran foreign minister Hans-Dietrich Genscher during his unusually long tenure in office from 1974 to 1992. Genscher showed a unique understanding of how to maximize political opportunities and take advantage of them, even as he benefited from some peculiarities of the German domestic and international power constellation. Internationally, Germany had been a main prize of the East-West confrontation during the Cold War. With Genscher overseeing its foreign policy, the Bonn Republic gained more weight than its geopolitical position would have suggested. In advancing (West) Germany's international position, Genscher stressed his country's integrative potential in NATO and the EC as well as its special responsibilities in Central and Eastern Europe. He and his party made possible the policy of reconciliation with Eastern Europe, strongly supported the Helsinki Process, advanced and may have invented NATO's double-track strategy, opposed SDI ("starwars"), promoted the legitimacy of Poland's western border, and worked continuously toward European unification. His foreign policy style, eventually called "Genscherism," also helped legitimate the FDP as an important coalition ally of the SPD and CDU chancellor parties, before and after 1982 respectively.[18]

The FDP's specific contributions have necessarily varied both with the incumbent in office and the changing political contexts, domestic as well as foreign. At times, for example, a determined chancellor Schmidt or Kohl would reach into the foreign policy area and overshadow the FDP minister—as happened during the year of German unification. And in the setting of post-Cold War Europe, Genscher seemed to become frustrated by a reduced room for maneuver coupled with the unfamiliar demands of a new international constellation, which his own policies had played a role in bringing about. His successor, Klaus Kinkel, was a career bureaucrat, who appeared more as an administrator of foreign policy than a master of statecraft. Moreover, his persona and political style lacked some of the reassuring qualities associated with Genscher. But then again, Kinkel had to operate in a very different domestic and international setting than Genscher.

Inside the coalition government, the FDP's weight also weakened along with its standing in the polls and partly because of the newly assertive role adopted by Helmut Kohl in some major foreign policy matters. In addition, there seemed to be less electoral interest in international affairs, even as Germany had become a larger and more powerful player. Similar to the publics in some other countries, Germans seemed to be preoccupied with domestic matters in their concerns about the immediate social and economic ramifications of German unification, European integration, and market globalization. All this meant that the FDP no longer drew major electoral benefits from having one of its own leaders serve as foreign minister.

Yet there were some important continuities with the Genscher era as well. Both Kinkel and his party continued to play a corrective role and pursued a foreign policy that included a liberal emphasis on the protection of human rights. They also followed the "Genscherist" approach of seeking to weave a dense net of overlapping, complementary institutional structures to channel international relations more predictably and safely. Moreover, the FDP and its foreign minister prepared the sensitive political terrain for out-of-area deployment of German troops, insisted on opening the EU to countries in eastern Europe, and pressed for the recognition of Russian security concerns in the face of NATO expansion.

In a remarkable move in 1993, the FDP played the familiar role of power broker between the two large Bundestag parties in the question of German participation in NATO's out-of-area activities in post-Cold War Europe. The big parties appeared either politically eager (CDU/CSU) or legalistically reticent (SPD) to provide a green light for the Bundeswehr. In this situation, where a broad parliamentary consensus was politically important, the FDP resorted to what some would call a "political trick" or artifice by questioning the legal basis for German participation (of which the FDP approved politically) before the Federal Constitutional Court. The FDP "lost" its legal case, but it could claim to have helped produce a face-saving device for the reluctant SPD (and some Greens) to give support to German involvement. It was not lost on observers that the move had also improved the FDP's relations with the SPD, which thereafter seemed to become more appreciative and supportive of the small party's foreign policy moves. Some observers would even see parallels to the late 1960s, when agreement on major foreign policy matters had been a precursor to the formation of Willy Brandt's SPD-FDP coalition. In 1998, that was not to be, but the reason was *not* lack of a basic foreign policy agreement between FDP and SPD.

The FDP has also strongly supported an opening of NATO to members of the former eastern bloc, even while remaining more sensitive than its conservative coalition partner to the special security needs of Russia. The FDP rejected any linkage between NATO expansion and the ratification of the START II treaty by the Russian Duma. And it has pushed for a replacement of NATO's current doctrine (based on the Harmel formula of deterrence and détente) to reflect the post-Cold

War situation. In line with its long support of the Helsinki process, the FDP favors a stronger Organization of Security and Cooperation in Europe (OSCE), which would eventually become the continent's premier security organization (in the sense of Chapter VIII of the UN Charter).

In matters of European integration, the FDP has maintained the same openness to participation by the countries of eastern Europe. It has opposed a narrow reading of Germany's special responsibilities toward this region, which in the past has suffered so much from German politics of military conquest. The three FDP members of the Bundestag's foreign affairs committee supported the eastward extension of the EU in principle, followed up by negotiations for association and full membership of individual countries as soon as possible. Once again, the FDP showed a special sensitivity in seeking to avoid any "shock of rejection" among the prospective new member countries.[19]

In sum, the foreign policy record of the FDP is an impressive one. None of the other small Bundestag parties (CSU, Greens, or PDS) can match its contributions to the Bonn Republic's external relations. Even the two big parties, despite their considerable resources in foreign policy expertise, cannot equal the FDP's long experience at the helm of the foreign ministry. Its domestic role as pragmatic balancer and moderate mediator seems to be well suited for the area of international relations, where ideologically driven innovations are particularly out of place.

Thus, the FDP's neoliberal turn in domestic affairs cannot really have a parallel in foreign policy. Traditional statecraft may come to play a reduced role in a globalized economy, but it will not wither away soon. Whether the FDP will ever direct German foreign policy in the Berlin Republic is an open question, but its expertise in such matters remains a valuable political resource for the Federal Republic.[20] It also remains to be seen, whether the Greens will be able and willing to continue the pragmatic style and direction of foreign policy that have so long been identified with the FDP.

Conclusion

The existential task for the Free Democrats in the Berlin Republic will be to demonstrate that they continue to matter as a distinctive voice in Germany's political chorus. Parliamentary survival will remain their bare minimum goal, but the maximum goals include an eventual inclusion in a future government coalition.

In Gerhard Schröder's government, the Greens have taken over the role of junior coalition partner that the Free Democrats so long claimed for themselves. Already before the recent power shift in Germany, the FDP recognized that the Greens had become its main rival in the struggle for political survival and influence. For the first time in 1994, the Greens barely topped the FDP in a Bundestag election (by a margin of 0.4 percent of the vote). The Greens were able to consolidate the newly won position as "third force" in German politics four years later, in 1998 when, with a comparable margin (0.5 percent), they also displaced the FDP as junior government party. It is too early to tell whether the FDP can ever return to a similar position of leverage in the Berlin Republic, but at least the Liberals are able to point to their long and in many ways impressive record of performance in Bonn. They show themselves eager to capitalize on any gaffes made by the Greens, and will use them to promote the FDP as an experienced, reliable, and therefore preferable, coalition partner. Ironically, both of these small parties need to overcome a serious regional deficiency in the East, where voters so far have shown little interest in either neoliberal or postmaterial agendas.

FDP reformers understandably try to interpret the loss of cabinet position in the federal government as a golden opportunity for their party. As they see it, the FDP now has a chance to pursue a more uncompromising neoliberal orientation. In rhetorical high gear, they will even celebrate the new freedom to define what they call a "pure FDP" agenda (*FDP pur*), untrammeled by considerations for a larger coalition partner. At the same time, many Free Democrats refuse to embrace such an undiluted neoliberal message, or recognize that it may lack political credibility and practicality even in the western German setting.

There is clearly an element of incongruity in the FDP's latter-day demands for supposedly overdue legislative reforms, if one considers its long period of government responsibility until 1998. More seriously, there is at the end of the 1990s no obvious electoral group or political ally waiting to support the FDP in its specific reform orientation—although the other parliamentary parties by now all claim to stand for some (other) kind of "reform" and "innovation."

If it wishes to remain useful and acceptable as a future government partner to either the SPD or the CDU/CSU, the FDP probably cannot afford to abandon completely its traditional identity as centrist balancer in German party politics. Here it may even have a structural advantage over the Greens. Despite neoliberal displays of scorn for "social democratism" and "structural conservatism," this veteran German coalition party seems more prepared by experience and outlook to accept "pragmatic" compromises in the governing process, if given the opportunity, than some members of the Greens.

In the end, the German voters will decide whether Free Democrats have made their case well enough to merit some kind of continued role in the Berlin Republic's system of parliamentary and governing politics. Meanwhile this endangered opposition party is most likely to engage in a delicate balancing act, as it tries to be politically visible and attractive. That may require the FDP to present itself *both* as a propagator of lower taxes, deregulation or other market-oriented reforms *and* as a reminder of the moderate, centrist and often "muddling" tradition of coalition governance in Bonn.[21] "Pure" neoliberalism (*FDP pur*) is unlikely to find much support in either the German electorate or among potential coalition partners, just as the "functional" argument by itself appears to have a limited electoral appeal. But a flexible combination of the roles of innovative reformer and moderating balancer could well turn out to be the optimum survival strategy for a "new/old" FDP in a "new/old" Federal Republic of Germany. It would, then, also serve as an element of continuity and reform in Berlin.

Notes

The authors have collaborated on the format and contents of this chapter. The fourth section, dealing with the FDP's foreign policy contributions, was written by Christoph Hanterman. It draws on his doctoral dissertation as well as his later research. The rest of the chapter was written by Christian Søe, whose research has been supported by grants from California State University, Long Beach. Both authors wish to thank the many individuals in Germany who have helped them with information and insights. It is not possible to name everyone who granted interviews, but Hans-Jürgen Beerfeltz, Hans-Jürgen Beyer, Rudolf Fischer, Wulf Oehme, Wilfried Paulus, and Klaus Pfnorr have been especially helpful in responding to repeated requests for background information. Christian Søe also wishes to thank Professor Dr. Wolfgang-Uwe Friedrich of the University of Hildesheim. His annual German-American Research Group (*Deutsch-Amerikanischer Arbeitskreis*) has made it possible for a California resident to stay abreast of political developments in Germany.

1. Speculation about an impending demise of the FDP goes back at least to the late 1950s, when some observers foresaw the emergence of a two-party system in West Germany.

2. The words are those of former party leader, Klaus Kinkel, but they could have come from many other Free Democrats. See Christian Søe, "The Free Democratic Party: A Struggle for Survival, Influence, and Identity," in David Conradt et al. (eds.), *Germany's New Politics: Parties and Issues of the 1990s* (Providence, Oxford: Berghahn Books, 1995), 171-202; here 172.

3. See *Wiesbadener Grundsätze: Für die liberale Bürgergesellschaft* (Bonn: F.D.P. Die Liberalen, 1997), 1-34. See also Guido Westerwelle, ed., *Von der Gefälligkeitspolitik zur Verantwortungsgesellschaft* (Düsseldorf: Econ Verlag, 1997), which includes the text of the Wiesbaden program along with commentaries by leading Liberals who served on the party's program commission. Shortly before the Bundestag election of 1998, Westerwelle advanced his arguments for a "change of politics"—rather than a "change of government"—in his book, *Neuland. Einstieg in einen Politikwechsel* (Düssseldorf: Econ Verlag, 1998).

4. The FDP was reelected to the Landtag in 1995 in Hesse, and in 1996 in Schleswig-Holstein, the Rhineland-Palatinate, and Baden-Württemberg. It was a cabinet member in the latter two states, serving as coalition partner of the SPD and CDU respectively. In February 1999, it managed to squeak by the 5 percent clause in Hesse, in the first Landtag election after the formation of Schröder's SPD-Green government. This was a marginal result for the FDP as well as a setback from its tally

in 1995. But the 1999 outcome in Hesse nicely illustrates the vagaries of German coalition politics, with the pivotal role that can be played by small parties. In conjunction with a major electoral advance of the CDU in Hesse and a drastic setback for the Greens, the FDP's meager result (5.1 percent) was just enough to bring about the loss of a parliamentary majority by the state's incumbent "red-green" coalition government. In the aftermath, a new CDU-FDP Land government in Hesse also deprived the SPD of its majority in the federal upper chamber (Bundesrat).

5. For more background, see Søe, "The Free Democratic Party: A Struggle for Survival, Influence, and Identity," 173-76 and 183-87.

6. In eight of the ten western states, the FDP performed somewhat better in Land-level politics, but even here it was able to win enough votes to keep parliamentary representation in only four of them (see note 4). In two western states, Bavaria and the Saar, the Liberals performed at the same low level as in most of the East.

7. See *Wahlergebnisse in Deutschland 1946-1998* (Mannheim: Forschungsgruppe Wahlen e.V., 1998), 139-45.

8. Interviews by Christian Søe with leading FDP politicians and activists, June 1996, 1997, and 1998.

9. The data come from the two publications, *Die Bundestagswahl 1994* and *Die Bundestagswahl 1998* (Mannheim: Forschungsgruppe Wahlen e.V., 1994 and 1998), 65-66 and 82-83, respectively. See also Søe, "The Free Democratic Party" (1995), 193.

10. Flach's ideas on the FDP as a "third force" in German politics are discussed at greater length by Christian Søe, "The Free Democratic Party," in H. G. Peter Wallach and George K. Romoser, eds., *West German Politics in the Mid-Eighties* (New York: Praeger, 1984), 115-18.

11. See A. J. Nicholls, *Freedom with Responsibility: The Social Market Economy in Germany 1918-1963* (Oxford: Clarendon Press, 1994).

12. In December 1997, for example, Genscher chose to express his misgivings in a number of interviews timed to precede the FDP's traditional new year meeting in Stuttgart. There was an almost immediate defensive response from several reformers.

13. Experience reminds us to be careful in speculating about the political future of Germany's Liberals. The FDP's neoliberal turn, which is a main theme of this chapter, has taken many observers by surprise. It was conspicuously absent among the three scenarios that until recently dominated the discussion about the small party's future—in addition to the very real possibility of its political demise altogether.

One of these scenarios suggested that the FDP would basically continue in its role as a small coalition and clientele party, relying as heretofore on its primarily "functional" appeals to voters and potential government partners alike. An alternative scenario foresaw the possibility of the FDP taking a sharp rightward turn toward a populist orientation, in the manner of Jörg Haider's Freedom Party in

Austria. The third scenario anticipated a more inclusive and pragmatic "all-German" reorientation, reflecting the small party's remarkable (but short-lived) eastward shift in its voter and membership strength in 1990.

All three possibilities were explored with great insight by Wolfram Kaiser, "Between Haiderisation and Modernisation: The German Free Democrats since Party Unification," *German Politics* 2, no. 2 (August 1993): 224-42. Kaiser himself suggested that the third option, which he called modernisation, was the most promising one for the FDP. As late as 1996, however, Peter Lösche and Franz Walter concluded that the FDP would be likely to follow the populist path. See the final pages of their stimulating book, *Die FDP: Richtungsstreit und Zukunftszweifel* (Darmstadt: Wissenschaftliche Buchgesellschaft, 1996).

14. The Wiesbaden program has the typical "catch-all" quality of many such party documents. It includes a liberal commitment to greater devolution, gender equality, toleration of minorities, and special attention to the need for continued immigration, including a change in the immigration and citizenship laws to encourage the integration of legal newcomers. There are other pages dealing with the "social" side of the market economy, the importance of individual freedom and responsibility in the emerging information society, the danger of luddite reactions to scientific research and the new technologies, and a commitment to a liberal understanding and support of the constitutional order (*Rechtsstaat*) as well as culture, the arts, and education. After stating a commitment to the unification of Europe as a priority of the FDP's foreign policy and another to international human rights, the program returns to the theme of reducing the role of the state as an act of responsibility toward the next generation. Here it also speaks of ecological concerns, but argues that there should be a preference for using market solutions to advance environmental protection. See *Wiesbadener Grundsätze—Für die liberale Bürgergesellschaft*, 1-34.

15. See Hans-Jürgen Beerfeltz, "Wir sind der Ruck durch Deutschland," *liberal* 39, no. 3 (August 1997): 5-12. For a brief discussion of Herzog's speech, see chapter one in this book.

16. See Christoph Hanterman, *Political Innovation and Political Survival: Coalition Politics, Free Democrats, and Germany's Centrist Foreign Policy, 1969-1990* (Ph.D. dissertation, University of California at Santa Barbara, California, 1996).

17. See Beverly Crawford, "Explaining Defection from International Cooperation: Germany's Unilateral Recognition of Croatia," *World Politics* 48, no. 4 (July 1996): 482-521; esp. 502-11.

18. See Emil J. Kirchner, "Genscher and What Lies Behind Genscherism," *West European Politics* 13, no. 2 (April 1990): 159-72. Also Christian Søe, "Hans-Dietrich Genscher," in David Wilsford, ed., *Political Leaders of Contemporary Western Europe* (Westport: Greenwood Press, 1995), 155-64.

19. Interview by Christoph Hanterman with Ulrich Irmer in Bonn, 14 November 1997.

20. See also Christoph Hanterman, "Paralysis or Activism? The Impact of Coa-

lition Political Dynamics on German Foreign Policy," paper presented at the American Political Science Association, annual conference, San Francisco, September 1996.

21. For an earlier exploration of this role, see Christian Søe, "The FDP: The Politics of Hanging On and Muddling Through," *German Politics and Society*, no. 14 (June 1988): 19 ff.

7

The PDS:
Between Socialism and Regionalism

Gerald R. Kleinfeld

The Party of Democratic Socialism (PDS) is sui generis among the political parties that have won parliamentary representation in Germany after unification. It is the only party to rest on an almost exclusively eastern regional base, and it is alone in having a communist-descended far left identity. But the PDS is no longer a complete outsider, and it cannot be ignored in a discussion of the current changes and uncertainties of German party politics. Although it is of only marginal electoral importance in the populous West and therefore remains relatively small and vulnerable from a national perspective, the PDS is the third largest party in the East, and runs ahead of its most powerful rivals in central parts of eastern Berlin. Its strong presence in the new eastern states complicates the coalition arithmetic at the federal, state (Land) and local levels of politics in united Germany. In an early symbolic reminder of the special place staked out by this new party, it was the united vote of the PDS parliamentary group that in June 1991 provided the pivotal margin necessary for a narrow Bundestag majority in favor of moving the federal seat of government from Bonn to Berlin. When the transfer is completed, the national government and parliament will be located near the electoral stronghold of this unique party that critically questions some basic policy assumptions of the enlarged Federal Republic of Germany.

PDS leaders have adapted with remarkable skill to the new context of pluralist politics, in which they seek to be accepted as full players. And they have come a long way in breaking free from the initial ostracism they encountered on the political scene of united Germany. Polls show that a majority of today's Germans classify the PDS as a "normal" party.[1] It has played a supportive role in local and state governments in eastern Germany. And in November 1998, the once widely shunned PDS made a major breakthrough in its search for political respectability and influence. At that time, the erstwhile political outcast joined the Social Democrats as a full partner in a new SPD-led government coalition in the eastern state of Mecklenburg-West Pomerania. The advance of the PDS to cabinet status has raised many hackles, but the new left government in Schwerin appears determined to meet the pragmatic test of "governability," albeit with an agenda that will involve a considerable degree of neo-Keynesian state intervention.

Nevertheless, the origin in communist-ruled East Germany has some continuing significance in setting the PDS apart from the other parliamentary parties. In 1989, when popular demonstrations created a revolution that undermined the German Democratic Republic (GDR), the still ruling communists of the Socialist Unity Party (SED) struggled to survive as a separate political entity. They renamed their party in two steps, first PDS-SED, then PDS, and adopted a distinctive new program. At the time, many observers dismissed the PDS as a residual and transitional phenomenon that would fade into political insignificance after national unification. They basically expected the united country to be a West Germany writ larger, especially in the area of institutions such as political parties. Instead, the PDS has managed to survive by securing a remarkably broad eastern base.

As its name implies, the PDS defines itself ideologically as both democratic and socialist. In the traditional sense, at least, it has positioned itself clearly to the left of the SPD and today's Greens. In some ways, it can be compared to the small socialist people's parties in some Scandinavian countries, although these post-communist parties have a far longer and more pluralist democratic tradition. Yet the PDS also functions as a party that seeks to represent the special concerns of a considerable part of the population in Germany's new eastern states. Thus, the PDS is not only a left socialist party, with a recent communist past; it is also an eastern regional party. These identities overlap, but they also create some tension and ambiguity within the party and in its self-presentation to the public as well as in its relations with other political parties. On the other hand, there can be no doubt that communist traditions linger on in the PDS and that many in the party still do not endorse the democratic and socioeconomic structure of today's Germany.

In the first all-German election of December 1990, the PDS won only 2.4 percent of the party vote in the freshly united country. It was able, however, to benefit from a onetime dispensation of the electoral law requirement that only parties winning 5 percent of the total vote are given proportional representation in the Bundestag. For this first post-unification election only, it was sufficient to win such a minimum share of the party vote in either the "new" eastern or the "old" western region of the Federal Republic. The PDS easily met this requirement by garnering 11.1 percent of the party vote in the East—compared with an insignificant 0.3 percent in the West. Representation in the Bundestag helped the PDS and its leadership gain media exposure. Nevertheless, there were still grounds to believe that the PDS would not last long, at least at the federal level of politics. Here the 5 percent threshold would be national in scope for the next Bundestag election, and the structural weakness of the PDS in the populous West was widely expected to prove fatal. Once again, the skeptics were confounded.

By 1994, the party had solidified its electoral base in the new eastern states. Here over 6,000 elected local officials represent the PDS, including numerous mayors. In the 1994 Bundestag election, held in October, the PDS won a share of 4.4 percent of the party vote, largely by attracting just short of 20 percent in the new eastern states compared to less than 1 percent in the West. Although its share of the total vote had almost doubled over four years earlier, the PDS still fell below the electoral threshold. This time, however, it was able to benefit from a provision in the electoral law that suspends the 5 percent clause for any party that succeeds in winning at least three single-member districts. Here the regional concentration of the PDS turned to its advantage, and it met this requirement by scoring plurality victories in four eastern Berlin constituencies. That led in turn to proportional representation for the PDS in the Bundestag, based on its national share of the party vote (4.4 percent). As a result, the PDS ended up with thirty deputies, enough to form a recognized Bundestag group and be represented on legislative committees.

Four years later, in September 1998, the PDS again advanced in the party vote and finally passed the national electoral threshold, albeit narrowly. It won 5.1 percent of the party vote in the Federal Republic as a whole, again largely derived from the party's large share of the eastern vote (21.6 percent) but also supported by an advance in its marginal share of the western vote (1.2 percent).[2] Having met the 5 percent mark, the PDS was granted full caucus (*Fraktion*) status, entitling it to have members chair parliamentary committees and to nominate one of the vice presidents of the Bundestag. Unlike the other small parliamentary parties of Greens and Liberals (FDP), which normally win no single-member districts, the PDS again benefited from its regional concentration in 1998 by scoring plurality victories in four districts of eastern Berlin. Its Bundestag delegation rose from thirty to thirty-six members.

Far from quickly disappearing, then, the PDS has survived and added something new and different to the German party system. Its considerable strength in eastern Germany ensures it a role not only in the five eastern state legislatures, but also in the assembly of united Berlin, and in the national parliament as well. Indeed, the PDS now functions as a real or potential power broker in many local councils and some state legislatures in the East. It could one day gain a pivotal role on the left in national politics.

Membership and Structure

The PDS is a complex party, whose leaders, members and voters differ substantially from each other. In late 1989, there were some practical reasons for not dissolving the SED and founding a new party. A new set of leaders hoped to retain both the considerable economic assets of the SED and its organizational structure. The former proved mostly an illusion, but the latter became of crucial importance to the renamed party. There is a trade-off to this linkage with the recent political past. The PDS is by no means the SED in a new form, but it does have an ambivalent relationship to the former East German regime. During the 1998 election campaign for the Bundestag, PDS leaders took the unusual step of publicly acknowledging responsibility and regret for "acts of injustice" by the rulers of the GDR. This mild expression of culpability in turn triggered objections from some of the party's most stalwart defenders of the ancien regime, organized within the PDS around the so-called Communist Platform.[3] There are additional ways, as will be indicated below, in which the PDS has tried to distance itself from the political record of the SED even while stopping short of cutting all ties to the mother party.

In the fall of 1989, the SED had a membership of 2.8 million. The numbers plummeted in the months that followed. By June of 1990, the PDS counted only 350,000 members.[4] This total shrank further, so that by early 1998 there were only about 100,000 members left, or less than 5 percent of the 1989 SED membership. The fall-off is less severe if one considers that many former SED members continue actively to support the PDS. In any case, even today the PDS registers by far the largest membership in the East of any political party, larger than those of the CDU and the SPD combined. Both members and active supporters are a major asset in organizational work and election activities, where the PDS (unlike the eastern SPD) has no problem finding candidates or campaign workers.

The membership losses had many reasons, but they coincided with a purge from the leadership of some persons believed to be political liabilities for the party. Along with replacing the old SED leadership, the PDS altered the party structure. One of the important contributions of Gregor Gysi, the first party chair, was to give the PDS a new image. Gysi, a gifted public speaker and brilliant advocate, rallied members as well as supporters. Not only did he speak at numerous gatherings, but he became a sought-after participant in television talk shows. His ready wit and charm, somewhat masking a toughness and shrewdness, continue to be attractive in a German political climate more used to long-winded exhortations.

The PDS leadership is formally in the hands of a party executive consisting of the party chair and vice chairs, the party manager, and the party treasurer. In 1993, Lothar Bisky was elected party chair to succeed Gysi, who has remained parliamentary leader of the party in the Bundestag. Gysi continues to be a significant voice within the party, based on a recognition of his contributions to the formation of the PDS and his continuing popularity with many voters. He has remained for many in the West, if not in the party itself, the personification of the PDS, and the party tries to take advantage of this in its public self-promotion.

Elections to the party executive take place at the federal party convention. In addition to its Land and district organizations, the party maintains a number of associated working groups, called *Arbeitsgemeinschaften* (AGs). Each of these

AGs, which vary considerably in size, political activity and effectiveness, deals with a major policy theme or voter category. Theme groups are organized around such varied subjects as employment issues, health and social policy, media questions, sport policy, economic policy, as well as such topics as disarmament or peace and international policy. Voter groups include senior citizens, women, young people, jurists and others. There are also special advocacy or "platform" groups, such as the Communist Platform and the Ecology Platform. The system, which does not fail to include a group for "Christians in the PDS," supports the party's claim to represent a broad political diversity and bolsters its efforts to attract certain electoral target groups.

While the origins of the PDS are in a party with highly centralized and dogmatic Leninist traditions, the present system provides ample opportunity for dissent. Beyond the various factions, it is possible to recognize at least three major tendencies competing for influence on the direction of the PDS. One, concentrated among older party members, recalls a nostalgic past under the German Democratic Republic. Its traditionalists are reluctant to surrender a familiar, if often vulgarized, version of Marxist-Leninist ideology. Another group, concentrated among the leadership cadre at the federal and state levels, consists of more pragmatic socialists who link the survival of the party to its political modernity and adaptability. A third category consists of differing and more theoretically oriented outlooks. It comprises mainly somewhat younger members who seek to pressure the party into a more ideological socialist stance.

Program, Leadership, and Factions

From the beginning, the PDS has claimed not only to be the Party of Democratic Socialism but also the party of eastern Germans, in fact, the only home-grown party of significance in that region. This claim is itself an important source of voting strength, and it even earns the party sympathy among many eastern voters for the other parties. In the 1994 Bundestag election, the CDU included in its campaign strategy an effort to label the PDS as political "red socks," a sarcastic reference to the party's communist origins. This was done to mobilize voters behind the CDU and, if possible, block the post-SED party from gaining national representation. But the campaign met with only limited approval in the more populous West, and it failed utterly in the East. There, many CDU members and activists flatly refused to use the "red socks" posters provided by the party headquarters in Bonn. They realized that the polemical message would turn off some of their own potential supporters, who widely regarded the PDS as a relatively "normal" party with a respectable record of community service. In fact, the PDS responded cleverly to the intended taunt by adding to its own campaign materials a pin bearing a miniature set of red socks. Some observers even believe the well-publicized issue helped the PDS gain new support among eastern voters.

The 1994 experience did not stop the CDU from trying a different anti-red message in the Bundestag campaign of 1998. In that year, the Union's secretary general, Peter Hintze, introduced a poster that featured a "red handshake" between the SPD and PDS. The provocative image seemed designed to arouse suspicion against the front-running Social Democrats for their alleged willingness to enter into coalition deals with post-communists. The poster received considerable publicity at the outset, but it was rarely seen in the final phase of the campaign. Instead, much softer versions of the warning against "red-red" (or "red-deep red") politics prevailed. Even the liberal FDP, which enjoyed practically no support in the East, took up the fight against a "red-green-red" specter.

The dichotomy between a regional party and a socialist party with national aspirations is a constant problem for the PDS, but also an opportunity. André Brie, its elections organizer, takes that into account when outlining what he sees as the party's three most important constituencies. First, the PDS needs to recognize its distinctly regional base and promote some special eastern German concerns and interests. Second, the PDS is also the party that speaks for many of the more than two million former members of the SED, who would otherwise be politically isolated. They constitute, Brie readily admits, the "core of the activists of the PDS."[5] Third, he defines the PDS as a distinctly socialist party. Brie sees this last component as the basis for an appeal to both western and eastern voters who are politically to the left of the SPD or the Greens. While some observers view the PDS primarily as a party of people who were "losers" in Germany's unification, it is probably better understood in terms of these several faces or identities, as a party that expresses socialist critiques of the new capitalist order—and at the same time voices regionally based demands on that same order.[6]

The PDS does not hesitate to portray itself as an eastern party, claiming that the East has been badly treated by western Germans, who have invested too little, exploited too much, withdrawn profits too freely, and dumped goods to compete with local products. Moreover, the PDS complains that western traditions and practices have been imposed upon the East, resulting in a disruption of the region's social and cultural life. These charges tend to ignore or minimize the legacy of prolonged communist rule, but they make sense to many easterners who in some sense feel dislocated or "deprived" after unification, regardless of political affiliation. Thus, the PDS has consistently sought to stress its eastern identity, differentiating itself from all the other German parties with their much stronger western base and more national scope.

The relatively pragmatic "eastern" part of the program coexists uneasily with an underlying ideological commitment to a far-left socialism that raises basic reservations about contemporary German politics and society. Here the party has already gone through several stages of development since its formation. The PDS program of 1990 sought to distinguish the PDS from the SED and come to terms with the popular enthusiasm for unification. This was not the time to attack the social and economic model of West Germany. Instead, the PDS sought ways to keep a distance from some of the most objectionable aspects of life in the GDR, without rejecting the past completely, so that both former SED members and others could identify with the post-communist party. In 1990, then, the PDS accepted the social market economy, with the reservation that it needed to be made more compatible with the socialist values proclaimed by the party. The PDS proposed that while socialism might not be as efficient as capitalism, it was more humane. In what since then has become a standard gesture by the post-communists, the party also sought to demonstrate its own grassroots credentials by advocating some elements of direct democracy. In some respects, this first program embodied the party's inner contradictions. Reflecting on the collapse of the GDR, Hans Modrow, the last SED-PDS prime minister, had described socialism as "a dream."[7] The 1990 program sought to preserve elements of that dream. It affirmed socialism and also accepted a modified market economy.

The program presented a different and more attractive face of socialism than the one known from the GDR. The claim to represent a much better "third way" became an essential element in the party's struggle for survival and influence. Like Modrow, Gysi now called socialism "a vision," or "an ideal." The "real existing socialism" of the GDR was discredited, he admitted. Instead, socialism actually meant "the dream of a just, united, peaceful, humane, ecological, and democratic society without war, hunger and misery, in which every person would have the opportunity for the development of his/her capabilities and a genuine chance for the satisfaction of personal needs."[8] As German unification brought dislocations, above all a hitherto unfamiliar mass unemployment in the East, Gysi reinforced the new image of socialism as an antipode to the failures of both the GDR and the Federal Republic of Germany. Now he and other PDS leaders attacked the Bonn government for a policy they presented as "colonizing" and "deindustrializing" the East. Thus, their criticism of the new order linked the defense of regional interests with idealistic socialist alternatives.

By 1993, in a new program designed to help the party compete in the following year's general elections, the PDS no longer felt it necessary to stress its acceptance of the social market economy. It now emphasized the latter's shortcomings and posited that capitalism endangered "human civilization and culture."[9] The capitalist "Great Powers" of western Europe, the United States, and Japan were portrayed as engaged in a struggle for control of the world.[10] In the new program, the PDS identified itself as a constructive socialist opposition to this existing order. Socialism was presented as merely a practical future goal where "democratic planning" would ensure correct decisions on social and economic issues. The new program also gave a prominent place to other critical positions on current issues and, once again, emphasized some distinctive eastern concerns. At the fourth PDS convention in 1995, party chair Bisky announced that "From the Pope to the German Trade Union Federation, practically everyone knows that the development of western capitalism, which has functioned for decades since the end of the Second World

War, has reached its end. At the same time, global problems demand a fundamental and deep social change."[11]

By 1997, the party had gone further with its socialist self-definition. For one thing, the PDS began to print its own logo with the subscript, "The Socialists," much as the FDP has long presented itself as "The Liberals." The change was hardly a subtle one. By this time, it was considered desirable to stress the party's distinctive socialist reservations about the kind of market-driven economy accepted by the SPD in its Godesberg Program of 1959. As a result, the PDS now presents itself as alone among the Bundestag parties in raising fundamentally critical questions about the economic and social order of the Federal Republic.[12] Its own ultra-left envisages "overcoming capitalism" in order to solve "the world's problems."[13] The oppositional stance varies in intensity and scope, but it appears to unite the various elements within the party—traditional holdovers, pragmatic reformers of various stripes, and ideological activists of differing hues. But it is socialism with a distinctive democratic claim, as leading PDS politicians continually stress.

The leadership is clearly concerned about the party's lingering image as a GDR relic, even as they continue to push within the PDS for a democratically defined socialist orientation.[14] The attempt to discard what Brie and Gysi themselves call "post-Stalinist" manifestations is not always an easy task. The party convention in 1997 revealed continued discord among the party's factions. PDS leaders were able to block the ultra-left Communist Platform on some points, including access to a leadership post, but lost on some others. Notably, simultaneous membership in two political parties was henceforth declared to be unacceptable. This move was primarily directed against a small circle of activists who wanted double membership in the PDS and the tiny western-based DKP, the German Communist Party.

Traditionalists in the party tend to see the honorary PDS chair, Hans Modrow, as their key representative in the leadership. When he presented Modrow to the party in his new post, Gysi's announced to loud applause: "We have a new honorary chair, and he is from the GDR."[15] Modrow, who was considered a moderate during his term as the GDR's last communist head of government, had moved towards a dissolution of the East German state after the popular upheavals in late 1989. But he had also presided over the purging of the files of SED officials to remove incriminating documents in advance of possible future public scrutiny. That protective hand alone has guaranteed him a respected place in the hearts of many, and he has helped numerous old SED members who feel rootless in the new Germany see the PDS as "their" party. For them, the PDS remains a political base in the new society. Like Modrow, they are aging, but they are still the party's backbone as members or voters. Yet it cannot be overlooked that Modrow was a would-be reformer in the GDR. His present role supports the conclusion that the PDS is not a miniature version of the old SED, but a different, post-communist party. Even so, the membership remains solidly composed of individuals who were the mainstay of the SED system.[16] And, as Petra Pau, recently elected to the Bundestag from Berlin, points out, the PDS is "anti-capitalist."[17]

The party's pragmatic reformers are a diverse group. Bisky and Gysi are but two who have agreed and disagreed. Lothar Bisky, the party chair, is both a pragmatist and a convinced socialist. What he sees as socialism is not clear, but he is an open critic of the socioeconomic structure of Germany today and sees his party playing a national as well as regional role in the future. Helmut Holter, now deputy premier of Mecklenburg-West Pomerania, is young, intelligent, pragmatic, yet flirts rhetorically between communism and left socialism. Among the prominent new thinkers are the brothers Brie, André and Michael, who are determined to see the PDS survive. Silvia-Yvonne Kaufmann, a competent and agile thinker, has become deputy chair of the party. Like the leaders of any other democratic German party, they must work to persuade a diverse membership. In general, the reformers show interest in cooperation with the SPD and the Alliance 90/Greens in state governments and, if it should ever become possible, at the federal level as well. Other tendencies in the party prefer to draw the line at participation in local government, pointing to the considerable policy constraints that would be the prize of coalition membership at a higher level.

The ideological new thinkers in the party include both self-designated communists and socialists, some of whom are distinct from the reformist leadership only by their rejection of its outspoken pragmatism. Their ideological discussions seek to differentiate nicely between such phenomena as "state socialism," "modern socialism," and "social democracy," whereby "modern socialism" is perceived to have had its beginnings in the GDR. They conduct an eager debate about issues like the proper role of the state, various forms of state intervention, and effective ways to represent social groups in the economic structure and process.[18] On the ultra-left Angela Marquardt stands out as the quixotic and young leader of the self-styled Communist Platform. She has failed to win a post in the PDS leadership, and the latter clearly seeks to marginalize her militant faction. After the 1994 elections, André Brie freely expressed his concern that the western supporters of the PDS contained "too many old communists" of the DKP and, further, that some "younger members of the party" were among the most ideological.[19] But the ultra-left is tolerated within the party, albeit not without debate, and even defended.

Thus, there is discord within the PDS that pits a more pragmatic socialist tendency within the leadership against old, nostalgic traditionalists and some new ideological purists. The latter two groups are somewhat uncomfortable with efforts to cooperate with the SPD, fearing that this would lead the PDS to accept the established German political, social, and economic systems. The party's own concept of socialism remains ambiguous, but its criticism of the Federal Republic from what it considers a truly socialist perspective is quite emphatic. The leadership stresses the need to work within the system, and Lothar Bisky regards the left-socialist parties of Scandinavia as prototypes of the future development of the PDS.[20] Such an evolution will at best take time. And it will be complicated by the paradoxical situation of the PDS as a post-communist party that is rooted in eastern German concerns even as it seeks to be relevant also for voters in the West. The party's election strategy reflects some of these divergent elements, but also manages to present the PDS and "Gysi's motley crew" to their best advantage.

Strategy and Elections

Before each major election, the PDS like the other parties sets out an election program and devises a campaign strategy. For obvious reasons, the PDS does not wish to appear as a doddering remnant of the SED. Instead, the PDS portrays itself as a modern party, a clear socialist alternative, and a true representative of eastern interests as well as of pragmatic reform-oriented goals. Party leaders show a ready appreciation of effective promotional means designed to attract and hold on to new voters. It is above all André Brie who is responsible for a campaign that is glitzy, imaginative, and also tough. As a result, the PDS campaign revels in the techniques of commercial advertising, with catchy slogans and clever posters.[21]

At the same time, the PDS seeks to mobilize its special electoral base, the many former members of the once-massive SED. These are not only voters, but often also activists, who can be used to garner support among the general population in eastern Germany. Many of the state and party functionaries of the GDR remained with the PDS, and a considerable number of the intelligentsia, as well. If that presents an image problem in the West, it constitutes a major campaign asset in the East. Here many PDS organizers can draw on a long, practical experience of administrative work in their own localities. They frequently continue to show a mastery of local matters, and they have therefore been able to help fellow easterners adapt to the unfamiliar and confusing changes that have accompanied unification.[22] Theirs is essentially a form of ward politics that has consistently helped the PDS gain respect and sympathy, as even their rivals will often acknowledge.[23] Not surprisingly, PDS voters also include some former SED members who have become successful in the new Germany, often as managers, businesspeople, or carried-over members of the vast public bureaucracy.

In addition, the party seeks to attract a variety of eastern protest votes. This is not done without some nostalgic references to the past, which typically ignore the role of the SED in bankrupting the GDR economy.[24] As the only truly home-grown party, the PDS claims that it represents the region best, whether in local, state, or national representative bodies. It will refer to the GDR as having in effect been "annexed" to western Germany under conditions that were essentially exploitative. And it makes an all-German connection, by presenting the eastern region as having become an "experimental territory for the shrinking of social benefits and democracy in the entire country."[25]

On the national scene, the PDS seeks to establish itself as the only truly socialist alternative in German politics. Here the party's reach for a broader western base of supporters still exceeds its grasp. The far-left socialist message, combined with a regional identity, simply engenders much more support in eastern Germany. Still, the PDS has reason to hope that its claim to represent a democratic socialism will attract more western voters who find the SPD or Greens too moderate in their reform politics—and wish to have them "pulled to the left."

Although they failed to establish a solid national base for the party, the 1994 and 1998 Bundestag campaigns exemplified the party's ability to transcend its political origins. Both capitalized on Gysi's popular appeal, and both concentrated on such themes as the need for a truly left opposition, better representation for the East, and an end to the conservative-liberal Kohl-Kinkel government. The selection of the party's candidates was geared toward broad popular appeal, leading to the inclusion of some well-known personalities who did not belong to the party. A major goal was to present the PDS as inclusive and pluralist.

The PDS makes a strong appeal to young voters. One widely displayed 1994 poster showed a young couple kissing, and proposed that "the first time, PDS," while another proclaimed that "change begins with opposition."[26] In 1998, the party directed a similar message at young people as well as women and other target groups simply by displaying advertisements picturing representative individuals along with the slogan, "this is our country too." Roughly one-third of voters between the ages of eighteen and thirty-five in eastern Berlin supported the PDS in 1994,[27] and the proportion was similar four years later. Women and men vote for the party in approximately equal numbers, with relatively slight gender variations among age groups.[28] There is evidence that the party's oppositional stance has attracted voters of all ages who are bitter over the paucity of job opportunities in the East or unhappy in general with some developments there since unification.

Parallel with its electoral advances at the federal level, the PDS has established itself as the only significant third party in most of the eastern state legislatures and town councils, somewhat behind the CDU and the SPD but far ahead of the Greens and the Free Democrats. In some parts of the region, its relative strength has made government by a parliamentary majority increasingly difficult or impossible without the formation of a grand coalition of the CDU and SPD, as in united Berlin and two of the five new eastern states. There has also been experience with a more unusual alternative—unusual at least above the local level. It consists of a state having a minority government that stays in office by relying on the parliamentary support or "toleration" by the post-communists. Here the PDS in effect functions as a kind of "silent partner."

The SPD and the Greens formed such a minority government in Saxony-Anhalt from 1994 to 1998. Thereafter an SPD minority government continued in office when the Greens failed to win parliamentary representation. In both cases, the PDS provided the needed votes in the legislature to keep the government in office. The Saxony-Anhalt model lay behind the "red socks" campaign in 1994, but despite such attacks it has worked for longer than a full legislative period. It may well be replicated in other eastern states where new Landtag elections result in similar "hung" parliaments. For PDS pragmatists, the arrangement is attractive because it represents a major advance in political status and potential influence.

It is hardly surprising that this experience has stimulated the governmental appetite of the PDS. At its 1997 party convention, the PDS openly announced that it was ready to consider full participation in governing coalitions with the SPD— that is, membership in "red-red" coalition governments.[29] Even earlier, strategist André Brie had stated his expectation that the PDS would be included in such governments at the state level as early as 1998.[30] In that year, Saxony-Anhalt held on to the "silent partner" model, as already noted, but Brie's more ambitious scenario was followed in Mecklenburg-West Pomerania after its Landtag election in September. Here the PDS had managed to capture almost one-quarter of the popular vote (24.4 percent). Instead of renewing their previous grand coalition with the CDU in this eastern state, the Social Democrats opened negotiations with the PDS that concluded at the end of October 1998 with a coalition agreement between the two left parties. As a result, Germany for the first time came to see the full inclusion of the PDS as junior partner in a state government, another major step in its search for political recognition.

By 1998, the PDS directed much of its campaign against what the party broadly targeted as "neoliberalism."[31] By this was meant the efforts of the CDU/CSU, and especially the FDP, to reduce the state's role in the economy, to privatize publicly owned enterprises, to encourage more flexible work rules, and to reduce the non-wage benefits received by German workers. The PDS insisted that the central issue was now the preservation and continuation of the German social state (*Sozialstaat*). It spoke in favor of broad measures such as a redistribution of wealth "from the top down," a public job creation program, and an ecological restructuring of society. The party also opposed the introduction of the euro as a form of neoliberal "monetarism" rather than a "genuine" currency union that would support a strong social policy. Any new currency, the party declared with a characteristic democratic flourish, should be introduced only after approval in a popular referendum. Critics charge the PDS with promoting a populist agenda that ignores the overriding need for a more flexible labor market and more cost-effective public policies.

In defense policy, the party has a distinctive platform, to say the least. It demands the dissolution of NATO and the West European Union (WEU), and their replacement by global and all-European security organizations. It would also disallow the use of German troops for missions outside of Germany. Moreover, the PDS seeks an immediate cut of 30 percent in the German defense budget, and cuts of 10 percent in the following years. The party wants the military draft abolished in favor of an army based on voluntary service.

Such unorthodox positions in a major policy area, along with the lingering onus of its communist antecedents, would still make it difficult for the PDS to be considered as a coalition partner in a national government. However, the PDS has already shown itself ready to behave pragmatically at the level of state politics when the situation calls for it. As for coming to terms with the communist past, the PDS has also made efforts to improve its image. To be sure, it still appears to take a political position of equidistance between the West and East German states, as when it makes appeals for "a common democratic, social, and ecological renewal of Germany in which the experiences of *both* eastern and western Germans [italics mine] are equally represented."[32] On the other hand, PDS leaders have distanced themselves from some notorious actions by the SED regime. After the Bundestag election of 1998, they announced the party's determination to go further in this respect. The PDS now plans to develop a new program by the year 2000, in which it will seek to come fully and finally to terms with the GDR's form of socialism.[33]

Conclusion

The PDS remains a diverse political mixture, a party whose voters, members and leaders form anything but a coherent whole. Presenting their party as a floating critique of the new Germany, the PDS leaders are essentially pragmatic socialists. But the membership includes many nostalgic traditionalists carried over from the SED as well as some younger socialist purists. And PDS voters comprise a broad range of easterners along with a few westerners, many of them young, who over-whelmingly disapprove not only of the Federal Republic, "in its present form," but also of the recent German Democratic Republic. According to a 1998 poll, 87 percent of PDS supporters opt for a blend of the two systems.[34]

With all its internal contradictions, the PDS can be said to have performed a valuable function in the unification of Germany. It has helped to represent and even integrate, however selectively and incompletely, about one-fifth of the eastern German population, even while adding to the public debate perspectives that would otherwise have been ignored in the political process or, at best, have found extra-parliamentary expression.[35] In its own way, the PDS has provided a political home for people who would have felt utterly displaced among the established western parties that were extended into the new eastern states in 1990.

The PDS has defied early political obituaries by surviving and even becoming something of an established party itself. It has had an impact upon the political order of the East and also plays a visible opposition role on the national scene. In the short to intermediate term, the PDS is likely to continue in its present role, now importantly augmented by examples of both indirect (silent) and full partnership in a government coalition at the state level.

The nature of its long-term presence in national politics depends upon regular representation in the Bundestag. That, in turn, means breaking the 5 percent barrier or continuing to win at least three directly elected district seats. To do the former, the PDS must seek to expand in the West. To do the latter, the PDS must grow in the East. The resultant dual strategy inevitably carries with it some ambiguities. They stem less from peculiarities of the electoral law than from the unresolved dilemma of being both a party that seeks to represent special eastern interests of regional redistribution largely from the West and, as well, a party which appeals to far-left socialists everywhere in Germany. The latter role requires it to advance a socialist program that is convincingly democratic and acceptable to the German left on the national scene. Efforts in that direction, however, could lose the PDS some of its special appeal to about 20 percent of eastern voters. This dilemma hovered over the party's 1998 campaign, much as it had in the Bundestag election four years earlier, but it seemed to energize rather than inhibit the PDS. Indeed, the party improved its position in both the East and West, as it managed for the first time to pass the national 5 percent hurdle.

So far, however, the party's efforts to attract additional voters in the West have met with meager success. Here its eastern identity continues to be a major handicap. Moreover, its strongly socialist philosophy and its broadside attacks on what it portrays as a brutal "neoliberalism" do not appear to find much credibility in the more prosperous part of Germany, where even the moderately conservative CDU and CSU support a generous welfare system. Until now, efforts to attract "progressive" voters in western university towns and big cities have brought more media attention than votes. On the other hand, PDS strategists understand well that even a small increase in western support will improve the party's chances of survival at the federal level, assuming that it can continue to hold on to its eastern voters. Once again, the outcome of the 1998 Bundestag election reflected the ambiguity of such a double-pronged strategy.

Party leaders recognize that political survival also requires the PDS to overcome what has been called its "biological dilemma." In other words, it must find younger replacements for its aging supporters among former members of the SED. The party counts on modern image strategies, together with its socialist and regionalist record, to help deal with this problem. Right after the Bundestag election of 1998, party leaders also announced an organizational renovation that would include more efforts to increase its presence in the West.[36]

Even if it should stagnate in the West, the PDS could still hold on in the East. This is an option favored by some members who see the strategy of campaigning in the West as a mistake.[37] They would like to see the PDS turn into something like a socialist version of the regional Bavarian CSU. Even that scenario, however, would require attracting new members and voters in the East. They would find the PDS to be a self-consciously pluralist party, whose internal debates and decision-making structures differ markedly from those of its authoritarian predecessor.

Voting analysis gives the PDS further cause for concern. The party has advanced but still remains relatively weak among working class voters for whom it claims to speak.[38] It is strongest among former SED members, who are located in various social strata. Intellectuals, officials, and teachers in the East show a disproportional support for the PDS, and it even attracts some businesspersons. The PDS continues to garner votes among the young, but it became clear in Saxony-Anhalt that right-wing parties could become a rival vehicle of political protest, not least among younger voters. In that state's most recent Landtag election, in April 1998, the ultra-nationalist German People's Union (DVU) attracted 12.9 percent of the vote and recorded stronger support from young male voters than the PDS.[39] The result shocked the PDS as much as the other parliamentary parties, making it keenly aware of this potential competition on the far right. In that respect, the elections of September 1998 for the Bundestag and the Landtag in Mecklenburg-West Pomerania were reassuring: At both levels, the right-wing parties failed by wide margins to pass the 5 percent hurdle, whereas the PDS recorded gains.

While the long-term role of the PDS at the national level remains uncertain, even after its relative success in the 1998 Bundestag election, it appears destined to be a highly visible parliamentary presence at least during the first years of the Berlin Republic. In the eastern states, including the eastern part of Berlin, the PDS is well positioned to remain an important political player who cannot easily be isolated from the governing process. Already now, from townships and cities to districts, elected PDS representatives can and do play a role in power-sharing and decision-making. In some eastern state legislatures, governing coalitions have been built to accept, tolerate or avoid parliamentary support from the PDS. The breakthrough to full coalition status in Mecklenburg-West Pomerania could be duplicated elsewhere in the East, whenever future state elections produce similar "hung" parliaments. Recognition of its "governability" status in turn is likely to bring more respectability to the PDS. Polls already now indicate that voters may have moved ahead of the older parties in their willingness to accept the post-communists: A 1998 survey showed that a majority (54 percent) of all Germans wanted the PDS to be treated like a "normal" party, even though only 19 percent believed that it had broken with its SED legacy. In eastern Germany alone, three-quarters (74 percent) classified the PDS as a "normal" party.[40]

Thus, it seems that by now Germans widely regard the PDS as another player rather than a complete outsider in their party system. How the new experience of full membership in a state government will affect the PDS and its supporters remains an open question, but here too a kind of "normalization" seems plausible. In opposition, the PDS has advocated a fundamental "pull to the left" in German politics. As a coalition partner, it will be subject to cabinet discipline and considerations of practicability, as when trying to find effective policies to reduce unemployment or meet fiscal constraints. Even though a partial leftward shift seems likely in any state government that includes the PDS, the result is most likely to be a pragmatic defense or neo-Keynesian extension of the established social market economy—a resistance against neoliberal reforms rather than its transformation in a socialist direction. Power sharing in the pursuit of such incremental goals will probably not satisfy the party's most ideological wing, but it could advance the political integration of many PDS voters in the East. Overall, shared government responsibility also seems likely to have a tempering effect on the post-communist party itself as far as day-to-day practice is concerned. On the other hand, the PDS overall has not yet firmly accepted the social and economic order of the Federal Republic of Germany. Its understanding of socialism, vague and contradictory as it may be in a party with many wings and directions, contrasts with the social market economic philosophies of the other parties and the political underpinning of German society. And, there still lingers a communist tradition in the party.

The presence of elected PDS representatives at the federal, state and local levels inevitably complicates the balance of power in German party politics. Having opened the cabinet door to the PDS, Social Democrats can hope to become senior partners in more eastern state governments and thereby strengthen their hold on the Bundesrat. Ironically, the SPD may also have helped make the PDS a stronger rival for the left vote in the East and, to a much smaller degree, perhaps in Germany as a whole. Whether some centrist voters will react by drifting toward the moderate right, as some CDU strategists have assumed, remains to be seen. Other CDU politicians have urged the CDU to accept former SED members in its ranks. Neither of the two major parties has a clear idea on what will work to defuse the support behind the PDS, except to wait out the biological clock. In the meantime, the Berlin Republic differs from its Bonn predecessor also because of the strategic regional position held by this communist-descended party.

Notes

1. See the concluding remarks to this chapter and note 40.

2. Forschungsgruppe Wahlen e.V., *Bundestagswahl 1998* (Mannheim: Forschungsgruppe Wahlen, 1998, Report No. 91), 85-87 and A2-3.

3. In the summer of 1994, PDS leaders also expressed regret for the participation of the SED and the GDR in what they referred to as the "illegal" invasion of Czechoslovakia thirty years earlier.

4. Manfred Gerner, *Partei ohne Zukunft? Von der SED zur PDS* (Munich: Tilsner, 1994), 113.

5. André Brie, speech before a conference of the PDS, 23 August 1997, 6.

6. Gero Neugebauer, "Hat die PDS bundesweit eine Chance?," in Michael Brie, Martin Herzig, and Thomas Koch, *Die PDS. Postkommunistische Kaderorganisation, ostdeutscher Traditionsverein oder linke Volkspartei? Empirische Befunde und kontroverse Analysen* (Cologne: PapyRossa, 1995), 8.

7. Hans Modrow, *Aufbruch und Ende*, second edition (Hamburg: Konkret Literatur, 1991), 155

8. Gregor Gysi, *Wir brauchen einen dritten Weg* (Hamburg: Konkret Literatur, 1990), 9-10.

9. See Karlheinz Niclauß, *Das Parteiensystem der Bundesrepublik Deutschland* (Paderborn: Schöningh, 1995), 113.

10. See *PDS Program*, Section 1, "The Capitalistic Metropoles."

11. Cited in Brie et al., *Zur Programmatik der Partei des Demokratischen Sozialismus. Ein Kommentar* (Berlin: Dietz, 1997), 337.

12. Gregor Gysi, *Nicht nur freche Sprüche* (Berlin: Schwarzkopf and Schwarzkopf, 1998), 273.

13. Sahra Wagenknecht in Sahra Wagenknecht and Jürgen Elsässer, *Vorwärts und vergessen: Ein Streit um Marx, Lenin, Ulbricht und die verzweifelte Aktualität des Kommunismus* (Hamburg: KVV Konkret, 1996), 97.

14. See Gerhard Hirscher, *Kooperationsformen der Oppositionsparteien*, aktuelle analysen 8 (Munich: Hanns-Seidel-Stiftung/Akademie für Politik und Zeitgeschichte, 1997), 21.

15. See Patrick Moreau, *PDS—Anatomie einer postkommunistischen Partei* (Bonn: Bouvier, 1992), 97.

16. Christian von Ditfurth, *Ostalgie oder linke Alternative—Meine Reise durch die PDS* (Cologne: Kiepenheuer and Witsch, 1998), 144.

17. Petra Pau, "Die PDS auf dem Weg in die BRD," in *Die PDS—Herkunft und Selbstverständnis,* ed. by Lothar Bisky et al. (Berlin: Dietz: 1996), 123.

18. Rainer Land and Ralf Possekel, "PDS und Moderner Sozialismus," in Brie, Herzig, and Koch, *Die PDS*, 112-30.

19. Interview by the author with André Brie, Berlin, June 1996.

20. Interview by the author with Lothar Bisky, Berlin, September 1998.

21. See the description of the 1994 election campaign in Gerald R. Kleinfeld, "The Return of the PDS," in David P. Conradt, Gerald R. Kleinfeld, George K. Romoser, and Christian Søe, *Germany's New Politics* (Providence: Berghahn Books, 1995), 221-54. The author will examine the party's 1998 Bundestag campaign in a successor volume, with the same editors and publisher (1999).

22. *Frankfurter Allgemeine Zeitung,* 13 October 1997.

23. See Günter Pollach, "Die PDS auf der Kreisebene in Ostdeutschland," in *DISPUT*, no. 5 (1997): 7.

24. Eckhard Jesse, *Die Demokratie der Bundesrepublik Deutschland* (Berlin: Landeszentrale für politische Bildungsarbeit, 1997), 181.

25. See David Francis Patton, "The Party of Democratic Socialism: 'Polarized Pluralism' in the New Federal States," paper presented at the American Political Science Association Conference, Washington, D.C., 1997, 21.

26. For an analysis of the 1994 elections and the makeup of PDS voters and members, see Kleinfeld, "The Return of the PDS," 221-51.

27. See Pau, "Die PDS auf dem Weg in die BRD," 121-22.

28. Forschungsgruppe Wahlen e.V., *Bundestagswahl 1998*, 18-20, 85-87.

29. *Süddeutsche Zeitung,* 20 January 1997.

30. Author's interview with André Brie, April 1996.

31. See *PDS Pressedienst*, no. 17 (1997): 5.

32. *PDS Pressedienst,* 7.

33. *Rheinische Post,* 2 October 1998.

34. See the Emnid opinion poll in *Der Spiegel*, no. 32 (1998): 38.

35. Gero Neugebauer and Richard Stöss, *Die PDS. Geschichte, Organisation, Wähler, Konkurrenten* (Opladen: Leske and Budrich, 1996), 303.

36. See *Rheinische Post*, 2 October 1998.

37. See for example the "Brief aus Dresden," written by leaders of the PDS in

Saxony, in *Süddeutsche Zeitung*, 13 June 1996.

38. Forschungsgruppe Wahlen e.V., *Bundestagswahl 1998*, 18-20, 85-87.

39. Viola Neu and Ulrich von Wilamowitz-Moellendorff, "Die Deutsche Volks-Union (DVU) bei der Landtagswahl in Sachsen-Anhalt," *Das Parlament*, 5 June 1998, 12. One-third of the state's male voters between eighteen and twenty-four supported the DVU in April 1998, or more than twice as many as voted PDS. However, male voters over forty-five, and especially those over sixty-five, showed a marked preference for the PDS over the DVU.

40. Forschungsgruppe Wahlen e.V., *Bundestagswahl 1998*, 86. However, such public tolerance is often mingled with continuing reservations about the PDS. The same poll shows that a plurality of eastern German respondents (47 percent) would have been against the formation of a national government that rested on the parliamentary support of the PDS. Moreover, it is noteworthy that in November 1998, one-half (49 percent) of all Germans disapproved of the inclusion of the PDS in the state coalition government in Mecklenburg-West Pomerania, while 30 percent approved (but 97 percent among PDS supporters). See Forschungsgruppe Wahlen, *Politbarometer*, no11 (1998): 3.

8

The Right-Wing Scene:
A Danger to Democracy?

Gerard Braunthal

Right-wing extremism—the rejection of a pluralist society that values democracy and human rights—did not vanish in Germany with the sudden demise of the Nazi regime in 1945.[1] In postwar West Germany, as elsewhere in the industrial and postindustrial world, rightist parties and groups surfaced to challenge the mainstream parties and the status quo.[2] These parties, such as the Republikaner, have not fared well in most elections in Germany since its unification in 1990. At the regional level there have been some notable recent exceptions to their generally lackluster performance.

However, neo-Nazis and skinheads have repeatedly committed acts of violence against individuals seen as "other," primarily permanently settled foreigners and political asylum-seekers coming from the Third World or the less developed European countries, but also leftists and homosexuals. Although such violence seemed to have peaked in the early 1990s, it has risen again in the late 1990s. It produced fear among some observers at the time that the political system was being seriously undermined. While the rightist scene received media attention throughout the world, especially given Germany's past, few paid attention to the controversial writings of New Right academics and journalists who are placing new accents on the country's past and present.

This chapter examines the shifting right-wing scene in Germany in the 1990s to see whether the programmatic goals of rightist parties and the New Right affect government policies and whether the rightist discontent and protest expressed through the ballot and the bullet pose a serious threat to the democratic system as Germany prepares to move its national center of government back to Berlin.

Right-Wing Parties

In the wake of the Nazi collapse, Allied authorities prohibited the revival of Nazi parties, the use of Nazi symbols, and the utterance of racist statements. The German people became democrats perforce, although a small percentage remained unreconstructed Nazis who supported the German Reich Party (DRP) or the Socialist Reich Party (SRP).[3] In 1952, the Federal Constitutional Court declared the SRP unconstitutional because its goals were not in consonance with the country's free and democratic order. Article 21 of the Basic Law (constitution) gives the Court the right to ban a party on this basis.

In 1964, in a second cycle of right-wing politics, the National Democratic Party (NPD) was founded, absorbing the weakened DRP. It gained the support of many citizens who had been affected by the economic recession or who were dissatisfied with the government's rapprochement with the communist bloc. Between 1966 and 1969, the NPD received more than the minimum 5 percent of the total vote needed to qualify for seats in seven out of eleven Land elections, but it never was able to muster that minimum for the Bundestag. Since then, with few exceptions, such as in some city council elections, it has not fared well at the polls. In 1995, its chairman, Günter Deckert, received a two-year jail sentence for making provocative racist speeches. His replacement, the Bavarian Land chairman, Udo Voigt, appealed openly to neo-Nazis to join the party, which in 1997 had about 4,300 members, of whom 1,000 were newly enrolled in Saxony. The NPD's youth branch, the Young National Democrats, with growing strength in eastern Germany, is the most active youth chapter of any rightist party. In the 1990s, it has been led by neo-Nazis, who are demanding the rebirth of a new Germany based on a *Volksgemeinschaft* ("people's community").[4]

In 1983, in the third cycle of right-wing politics, Franz Schönhuber, a former Waffen-SS sergeant, and two dissidents of the Bavarian Christian Social Union (CSU) founded the Republikaner party. Its nationalist and antiforeigner program was aimed at citizens who were buffeted by a new downturn in the economy or by a high technology modernization process and who were concerned that foreigners, whom they blamed for a high crime rate, were going to receive jobs, housing, and social services at their expense.

The party's program pledged to preserve the state and the democratic order because the Republikaner leaders did not want their party to be identified as right-wing extremist. They feared that the Constitutional Court might declare the party unconstitutional or that the government's domestic intelligence agency—the *Bundesamt* or *Landesämter für Verfassungsschutz* (Federal or Länder Office for the Protection of the Constitution)—might label it as right-wing extremist and put it under surveillance.

Despite the Republikaner leaders' claim to support a democratic state, the *Verfassungsschutz* officials announced in the early 1990s that their commitment to democracy was insufficient. The officials said that the Republikaner brochures, campaign literature, and the leaders' public speeches and occasional contacts with neo-Nazis provided enough evidence to classify the party as right-wing extremist. To buttress their case, the officials cited the leaders' antiforeigner and anti-Semitic statements, their derogatory stereotyping of minority groups, and the veiled support of violence against foreigners by some local leaders. The authorities made it clear that the party's future was in danger unless it moderated its messages.[5]

The Republikaner formed a nationwide organization, but its strength lay primarily in Bavaria and Baden-Württemberg. The party, with a membership of 15,500 in 1997, has been beset by power struggles among its leaders, who have not refrained from intrigues, vituperative exchanges, and ousters of their opponents. Schönhuber was forced to resign as chairman in 1994; Rolf Schlierer, the deputy chairman, took over his post. The thirty-nine-year-old lawyer and physician from Stuttgart intended to make the party more moderate and attractive to the middle class by forbidding his associates to enter into any pact with ultra-rightists. Schlierer's model of a rightist leader is Jörg Haider, chairman of the Austrian right-populist Freedom Party. But Schlierer, a colorless speaker, lacks Haider's populist appeal.

The Republikaner's electoral success peaked in 1989, when they received 7.5 percent of the total vote in the West Berlin city-state election, giving them eleven seats in the Berlin assembly. In the same year they received 7.1 percent of the West German national vote in the European Parliament election. Their six deputies in this parliament allied themselves with the French National Front and other European rightist parties in a voting bloc.

This unexpected electoral strength produced alarm abroad that Germany might be on the verge of neofascism. Studies showed, however, that the Republikaner had amassed substantial support from conservative voters who were protesting the establishment parties' inability to deal with major issues, such as mass high unemployment and immigration. Their vote indicated no permanent commitment to right-wing extremism. The Republikaner received their greatest support from young men, many living in small towns and in working-class districts of large cities, especially in neighborhoods with low-cost housing projects and few social and cultural amenities. Many were workers with low incomes and minimal education; others were small shopkeepers, salaried employees, civil servants, farmers, and police agents.[6]

After 1989, the Republikaner could no longer maintain the momentum that they had gained in that year. Their poor showing in Bundestag elections and in most Landtag elections, except for those in Baden-Württemberg, suggested a declining protest vote. Their espousal of German nationalism and quest for unification years before the merger of the two German states took place robbed them of a major campaign issue once the country was unified. The Republikaner's position that Germany must restrict immigration was supported by large segments of the electorate, forcing the governing parties and the SPD to confront the issue. In 1993, the

CDU/CSU, FDP, and SPD, whose conservative wings also favored a limit on immigration, voted to amend Article 16 of the Basic Law, in effect severely limiting the constitutional right of political asylum-seekers to enter the country. Thus, the Republikaner had played a role in moving the country's political agenda to the right.

The Republikaner had to compete with another party, the German People's Union (DVU), founded in 1987 by Gerhard Frey, a Munich right-wing publisher. The DVU, with about 15,000 members and branches in all Länder, received few votes in national elections, but mustered more than 5 percent of the vote in 1991 in Bremen and in 1992 in Schleswig-Holstein, primarily because of its opposition to immigration. However, the party's Landtag (state parliament) deputies, as is true of Republikaner deputies in Baden-Württemberg, did not distinguish themselves in their parliamentary activities. Some left the party caucus, others quarreled among themselves, were uninformed about the issues, and made few contributions to the legislative debates.[7]

The DVU failed to retain its foothold in the state parliaments of Bremen and Schleswig-Holstein in the Landtag elections of 1995 and 1996 respectively, but this rightist channel of populist discontents has proven its ability to rebound. In September 1997, it narrowly missed gaining representation in the city-state of Hamburg, with 4.97 percent of the vote. Seven months later, in April 1998, the DVU scored a breakthrough in eastern Germany by winning 12.9 percent of the vote in the Landtag election of Saxony-Anhalt. Observers in Germany and abroad were shocked by the DVU electoral support, the highest that a right extremist party had received in a Land or national election in postwar Germany. Lacking an organization in Saxony-Anhalt, DVU chief Frey poured 2-3 million DM into the campaign, which paid for over 1 million direct mailings to households and for wall posters throughout the Land. Frey's efforts convinced 30 percent of youth under thirty, primarily males, to cast their vote in protest for the DVU, a higher percentage than for any other party. The angry youth had become disillusioned by the failure of the politicians to ease the prolonged economic crisis in their Land. Viewing themselves as the economic losers, they had been hit hard by unemployment or had worried about losing their precarious jobs. Thus they were also prone to accept DVU antiforeigner slogans, "Foreigner bandits get out" and "German money for German jobs."[8]

In the September 1998 national election, most of these voters abandoned the DVU, primarily because they did not want to waste their vote on a minor party. Many hoped that the establishment parties, aware of their earlier protest vote, would make a reduction of unemployment and continuing limits on immigration top legislative priorities. Throughout the Federal Republic, the fratricidal rightist parties, lacking a forceful leader, received less than 4 percent of the vote.

Dissident leaders from the Republikaner party and other rightist groups have sought to unite all rightist parties in order to increase their electoral chances. While round-table meetings took place in North Rhine-Westphalia, Rhineland Palatinate, and Schleswig-Holstein in the mid-1990s, the current Republikaner chiefs are wary of associating with the far right NPD and DVU. In addition, personal rivalries and turf wars between the parties make it unlikely that a new single rightist party will be founded in coming years, unless a talented and charismatic leader emerges, comparable to the Austrian rightist Haider or Jean-Marie Le Pen, head of the French National Front. If that were the case, then such a party could expect to gain the 5 percent minimum to enter the Bundestag.

Neo-Nazi Groups

From 1949 on, rightist leaders in West Germany capitalized on the latent neo-Nazi and ultrarightist views of a small segment of the population. Old Nazis, neo-Nazis, bored youth who knew little about the Nazi era, and those who preached violence or terrorism formed numerous small groups. In the 1970s, when the neo-Nazi scene heated up, about two dozen groups, with a total of 1,000 members, of whom 200 were fanatic racists and anti-Semites, were active. They idealized the Nazi state and Hitler, contended the Holocaust was a lie and denied the gassing of a single Jew, and said that only pure Aryans should be Germans. They did not shirk from violence or terrorism to challenge the establishment. Nearly 90 percent of the members were men, most of whom were between the ages twenty and thirty. The groups, often jointly, planned actions to harass foreigners or leftists or to march in demonstrations honoring the Nazi leader Rudolf Hess.[9]

In the late 1970s, in an isolated terrorist act, a "defense sport group," which normally practiced shooting at a weapons range, raided a military depot in northern Germany and held up two banks in order to amass weapons and money for future use. Among those arrested was Michael Kühnen, who was to become head, among others, of the Action Front of National Socialists, a revolutionary cadre organization that maintained contacts with fascist groups in other countries.

In 1979, the Free German Workers Party (FAP) was founded. Although not a party running candidates for public office, it was one of the leading West German neo-Nazi groups, having at its peak more than four-hundred members. When violence against foreigners increased in the early 1990s, the Ministry of the Interior, which in the past had a record of more vigorously pursuing extremist leftist than extremist rightist groups, outlawed over the years twelve rightist groups, including the FAP in 1995. After each ban, police agents confiscated in the homes of group members a rich assortment of rightist literature, communications equipment, and membership lists. In justification of its bans, the ministry said the groups failed to support the constitutional order, were anti-Semitic and fanatically opposed to foreigners living in Germany, honored Nazi leaders, and adopted Nazi rituals. By banning the groups, ministry officials hoped to root out neo-Nazism.[10]

The ministry's expectations were too optimistic. True, some of the less fanatic fellow-travelers quit the neo-Nazi scene and others were frightened off, but in the period from 1994 to 1997 the number of neo-Nazis hovered between 2,000 and 3,000, of whom 1,000 joined newly formed underground autonomous cells or groups (*Kameradschaften*). These were to consist, according to a plan devised by leading neo-Nazis, of ten to fifteen persons in a locality, who would be linked to other groups in the region by a modern communications network. Most groups were formed in Baden-Württemberg, Berlin, and northern Germany.[11]

In the 1990s, rightist terrorism remained a danger. For instance, in 1992, Christian Worch of the National List group and other neo-Nazis initiated an "anti-antifa (antifascist) campaign" to intimidate leftists, judges, prosecuting attorneys, publishers, and politicians, whom the neo-Nazis labeled as "enemies of the people" if they had participated, or intended to participate, in actions against rightists. Lists of such political enemies, whose lives could be endangered, were circulated on the computer "Thule network" (discussed below). In 1996, Worch received a two-year prison sentence for continuing the activities of a banned organization.[12]

In the mid-1990s, a new terrorist danger emerged when a few German rightist mercenary soldiers returned from the former Yugoslavia where they had fought alongside Croatians against Serbs. German authorities were worried that the mercenary soldiers could some day provide military training to rightist youth in Germany, especially because the soldiers may have been responsible for setting up, in late 1994, a depot near Frankfurt/Main containing smuggled weapons and dynamite from the former Yugoslavia.[13] Finally, a terrorist threat could come from neo-Nazis who have joined the German army, of whom some, in uniform, have committed violence against foreigners.

To curtail extremist organizations and violence against foreigners, a tough new crime prevention law took effect in December 1994. It expanded the definition of incitement to violence and racial hatred to include statements defaming whole groups and minorities; outlawed the use of Nazi-like flags, badges, uniforms, slogans, and gestures; increased penalties for crimes involving personal injury; established special anti-extremist police units; set up a central communications network to coordinate information of suspects' movements; and broadened legal grounds for holding suspected and repeat offenders.[14] Under the new law, many neo-Nazis have been arrested and sentenced to prison terms. Yet, in 1998, several neo-Nazi groups were still operating legally; the *Verfassungsschutz* was keeping their members under close observation.

Neo-Nazi Propaganda

Even though the number of neo-Nazis is but a tiny fraction of the German population, their propaganda reaches far and wide through flyers, newspapers, demonstrations, and meetings, and more recently through computer games and the World Wide Web network. In 1987, computer games, aimed especially at schoolchildren, featured, for instance, wars between "dictators" and "allies" or the destruction of Jews or Turks in gas chambers. A government agency put twenty-one games sold by neo-Nazis on its proscribed list for youth. The computer Thule Network, named for a mystical northern place that rightists view as the cradle of European civilization, serves about 250 activist neo-Nazis as an organizational, communications, and propaganda medium. In the ten electronic mailboxes linked to the network, the activists exchange encrypted messages, which are difficult to crack, about planned meetings and demonstrations, and publish lists of antifascists who are allegedly threatening them. The activists have also put racist messages surreptitiously in nonrightist mailboxes and have maintained contacts with foreign fascists through the Internet.[15]

Despite their high-tech approach, the neo-Nazis have not abandoned the illegal distribution of pamphlets, posters, books, films, and videos, most of which they receive from abroad. One of their key contacts had been Gary Rex Lauck, leader of the self-styled "National Socialist Party of Germany—Overseas Organization" in Nebraska, who had smuggled publications, such as *NS-Kampfruf* ("National Socialist Battle Cry"), into Germany for two decades. In 1995, the Danish government took him into custody in response to a German warrant for his arrest. He was subsequently turned over to German officials; a court sentenced him to four years, imprisonment for his conspiratorial dealings with individuals and groups in Germany.[16]

Ernst Zündel, a German émigré living in Toronto, has also mailed hundreds of thousands of neo-Nazi brochures and videocassettes to Germany and other countries each year. One of his brochures is a report by the American self-styled engineer Fred Leuchter who wrote that it was technically impossible for poison gas to have been used in Auschwitz and Maidanek concentration camps. According to the Federal Constitutional Court, Holocaust revisionism is not protected under Germany's guarantees of freedom of speech and is a punishable offense, but Zündel cannot be prosecuted in Canada, where historical revisionism is not punishable. In 1995, the German telephone company Telekom announced that it had voluntarily blocked access to Zündel's World Wide Web site for its subscribers, after state prosecutors in Mannheim warned Telekom that it was helping to incite racial hatred. Zündel, incidentally, has been the protégé of Ewald Althans, a neo-Nazi leader in Germany, who achieved notoriety in the controversial documentary, "Profession: Neo-Nazi."[17]

Neo-Nazi newspapers have been published for many decades. The most important are Gerhard Frey's two newspapers (*Deutsche National-Zeitung* and *Deutsche Wochen-Zeitung/Deutscher Anzeiger*), with a combined weekly circulation of 100,000, which are rabidly nationalist and xenophobic. They call for a "Germanization" of the Germans, warn about the "invasion" of foreigners, defame democratic institutions and leaders, minimize Nazi crimes, deny German responsibility for starting World

War II, and print anti-Semitic remarks. They have a loyal readership but an un-known effect on the broader public opinion.

Skinheads

In Germany, the skinheads, imitating their British counterparts, emerged in the late 1970s and early 1980s. Comparable to the members of rightist parties or to the neo-Nazis, most of them are young men who often come from broken families, have dropped out of school, and have little self-esteem. They bond together against a society that has provided them with no perspective and hope for the future. They treat women contemptuously. There are three groups of skinheads: (1) a small number of antifascist skins or "skinheads against racial prejudice"; (2) a greater number of "oi-skins" who, although patriotic and xenophobic, are less interested in politics than in having a good time; and (3) a still greater number of racist and anti-Semitic Nazi skins ("Hammerskins" or "White-Power-Skins"), who hate foreigners and anything non-German, use Nazi symbols as a provocation against the estab-lishment, and see themselves as members of an international neo-Nazi skinhead movement.

Since the early 1990s, the number of rightist skinheads has increased apprecia-bly, especially in eastern Germany, Berlin, and Hamburg, to a total of seven-thou-sand in 1997. As early as 1983, the GDR criminal police had reported the formation of rightist skinhead groups, which engaged in violence at soccer games, attacked foreigners, and desecrated Jewish cemeteries. When the skinheads were put on trial, the GDR authorities simply labeled them as rowdies rather than as rightists, in order to maintain the myth that all East Germans had been anti-Nazis. Many of the skinheads had fathers who served in the communist secret police, which sug-gests that joining the skinheads was their way of challenging parental authority. The chief East German skinhead and neo-Nazi leader was Ingo Hasselbach, who finally left the rightist scene in 1993 as a result of the escalating violence against foreigners throughout Germany. He achieved international notoriety when his book *Führer-Ex* appeared in nearly all European countries and the United States.

A new neo-Nazi group "Blood and Honor" was organized in all parts of Ger-many, scheduling grill picnics and rock concerts to promote rightist skinhead cul-ture among apolitical youth. More than fifty skinhead bands are active. Their sing-ers have had to moderate the racist and xenophobic content of their songs after the police and courts took action against them. Editors of skinhead fan magazines "Fanzines") and distributors of skinhead compact discs and tapes have had their wares confiscated and have been put on trial for violating existing laws against racism.[18]

Neo-Nazi and Skinhead Violence

A wave of neo-Nazi and skinhead attacks on foreigners and others who did not conform to their concept of "Germanness" erupted after unification in 1990, especially in the former GDR.[19] There, young people, some barely in their teens, who were bored and frustrated by unsatisfactory jobs or lack of employment altogether, sought a scapegoat for their problems. They attacked, often at random, foreigners, and occasionally leftists and other enemies. The East German police, at first understaffed and insufficiently armed, was not able to quell the mounting violence of rightist hooligans, who severely injured or, sometimes, killed their victims. Among the most publicized and brazen assaults, in September 1991, bands of right-wingers attacked hostels housing foreign workers and asylum-seekers in Hoyerswerda in northern Saxony. In August 1992, in Rostock, a port city on the Baltic, nearly one-thousand rightists rioted for nearly a week and set fire to a shelter, which housed about three hundred Romanian gypsies and Vietnamese workers who had to be evacuated. In both cities, the young rightists were cheered on by numerous residents, equally hostile to the foreigners.

Violence was not restricted to eastern Germany, where the economic and social consequences of unification were precipitating factors, but also was prevalent in western Germany, where rightists assaulted foreigners, many of whom had lived there for decades. In November 1992, the rightists set fire to an apartment building in Mölln, a small town in Schleswig-Holstein, killing a Turkish woman and two Turkish girls. In May 1993, five Turkish women and girls perished in a similar attack in Solingen in the Ruhr area. These were two of the most damning attacks in the early 1990s. Neo-Nazis and skinheads were involved in thousands of other incidents, such as the one near Berlin in which five skinheads beat to death an Angolan guest worker in 1992. The daily attacks caused alarm in Germany and other countries that the situation was getting out of control and that the government and the police were responding too slowly.

Fortunately, the number of incidents of right-wing violence, which includes primarily injuries to persons and damage to property, dropped off sharply from a high of 2,639 in 1992 to 790 in 1997. However, the number of other punishable right-wing offenses, which include distribution of illegal propaganda material, rose from 8,328 in 1993 to 10,929 in 1997.[20]

The decline in violence can be attributed to many factors: the spontaneous reaction of hundreds of thousands of Germans who marched in candlelight protests in numerous cities and towns, the government's belated move to pass legislation giving police and judges the power to deal more severely with the perpetrators, the dedicated social workers who worked tirelessly with rightist youth groups, and the precipitous drop in the number of asylum seekers in Germany—the primary target of the rightists—as a consequence of the 1993 change in the Basic Law restricting asylum.

The New Right

Right-wing extremist parties and the mainstream establishment have received some intellectual support since the 1960s, but particularly since the early 1980s, from neo-conservative academics and journalists, who position themselves as a bridge between the two camps.[21] Known as the New Right, they number several hundred individuals, some of whom are organized in small groups or projects. Their intellectual model is the French New Right, which surfaced in the 1960s, as a countercultural revolt against the New Left.

The German New Right adherents sparked the famous *Historikerstreit* (historians' dispute) of the mid-1980s, in which conservative historians (and some politicians) relativized the legacy of World War II and the Holocaust. Thus, the historian Erich Nolte wrote in effect that Stalin's gulags (forced labor camps) were no different from Hitler's concentration camps. In unified Germany, most New Right followers continue to distance themselves from the right-wing parties, although their views rest on the antidemocratic "conservative revolution" of the Weimar era. They call for a vibrant German nationalism, which means that the ruling political and cultural elite should sever the country's close ties to the United States and the West; for the German government to be self-assertive in a world dominated by power politics; and for a policy of "ethnopluralism" (*Ethnopluralismus*, a new expression for the separation of ethnic groups that should maintain their national identity, and a denial of multiculturalism). To publicize their ideas in what they see as a hostile media dominated by leftists, their books have appeared under the imprint of several conservative publishing houses. Some of the writers have also had articles appear in the journals *Criticón, Nation Europa,* and *Junge Freiheit* (Young Freedom). *Nation Europa* and *Junge Freiheit,* with a circulation of seventy-thousand, have carried interviews with ultraconservative CDU and FDP politicians, who are currently in a minority in their parties, and with German and foreign rightists. The *Verfassungsschutz* has placed the two journals in its right extremist category because, under the cover of supporting democracy, they have eroded the barrier between democracy and extremism.[22]

A leading member of the New Right is Rainer Zitelmann, a young historian who had held an editorial post on the conservative newspaper *Die Welt.* Dismissed from his post in 1994 for having given other ultraright intellectuals considerable space in the cultural affairs section of the paper, he still writes occasionally for the newspaper. Publisher of a dozen books on history and politics, he insists that daily politics should no longer be determined by the memory of the Nazi past. Rather, "a line has to be drawn against this permanent self-flagellation and self-hatred, which produces neo-Nazis in the end. We must become normal."[23]

In April 1995, the conservative *Frankfurter Allgemeine Zeitung* published a controversial advertisement entitled "Against Forgetting," which had been drafted by Zitelmann and two other New Rightists, Karlheinz Weissmann and Heimo

Schwilk. Signed by several hundred prominent Germans, it said that May 8, 1945, was not only the day of liberation from the Nazi dictatorship but also the "beginning of the expulsion, terror, and new oppression in the East and the division of our nation."[24] The intent of the advertisement was to relativize history by implicitly equating the terror of Nazi Germany (which led to millions of casualties during World War II) with the Red Army's expulsion of Germans from eastern territories (which resulted in the killing of thousands) and with the carving of Germany into four occupation zones.

The 1995 advertisement typifies the *Weltanschauung* of the New Right practitioners, many of them influential in the right wings of the CDU/CSU and the FDP, who are currently saying that Germany's history and its role in world politics need to be reassessed. Their goal is to counter what they see as a cultural and political hegemony of the "Left." (In reality, no faction, whether artistic or political, holds a hegemony in the Federal Republic. For instance, the media's political spectrum ranges from moderate liberal to moderate conservative.) The New Right practitioners, despite their lack of an organized movement with a common ideology, have been successful in creating a more conservative climate in which the Bonn policymakers make some decisions that are near to the right of the spectrum. Many instances can be cited: in 1990, Chancellor Kohl, worried about the rightist vote in the upcoming election and eager to please the right wing of his party and the CSU, delayed for a while Germany's formal recognition of the Polish-German border (a permanent loss of German territory to Poland), until protests became too insistent; in 1992, Kohl was one of the few foreign leaders who did not shun a meeting with Austrian president Kurt Waldheim, the former Wehrmacht officer whom the U.S. government accused of having participated in "acts of Nazi persecution" during the war; and in 1993, Kohl nominated Steffen Heitmann, a CDU right-winger, for the post of federal president. Heitmann's nomination was withdrawn after he made damaging remarks, including one that Germany was "overrun with foreigners." Kohl's actions helped to pacify the conservatives in the governing parties and to coopt former supporters of right-wing parties.

During the 1998 national election campaign, the two rival candidates for chancellor, Kohl and Gerhard Schröder (SPD), sought to attract conservative and potential rightist voters by portraying themselves as moderate centrist leaders who were capable of alleviating the highest level of unemployment since World War II, seen by citizens in public opinion polls as the top national problem. CSU leaders in Bavaria played to rightist fears by suggesting that foreigners indicted for criminal acts ought to be expelled from Germany, an idea that Schröder had voiced in fall 1997, although with the reservation that the social causes for criminality must be considered. In their campaign speeches, Kohl and Schröder failed to suggest that foreigners should be integrated more into German society. In short, the two rival candidates, in an attempt to maximize their party's votes, made no proposals, other than their support for the euro (the European currency), that might drive voters into the rightist camp. Yet when Schröder won the election and formed an SPD-Green government, he backed a proposal to liberalize the stringent citizen-ship laws, which might produce a new right-wing backlash.

Conclusion

In a country that seems uncertain about its role in the world, New Right intellectuals have backed those policies of the Kohl government that emphasize nationalism and patriotism, and that limit foreigners' rights. The stability and continuity of the mainstream parties are not reflected in the rightist scene, where political parties and neo-Nazi groups have emerged, grown, and withered frequently. However, there has always been, as in many other countries, a core of ideologues, estimated to comprise at least 5 percent of the population, who prefer a rightist authoritarian system. According to a preelection 1998 poll, 13 percent of the respondents (in western Germany 12 percent, and in eastern Germany 17 percent) have a right extremist authoritarian and antiforeigner mind-set.[25] Most of these survey respon-dents cast their votes for the establishment parties, but the hard-core ideologues voted for one of the three right extremist parties.

Thus, there is a potential threat to the country's democratic system that will not be reduced unless the government deals more resolutely with social and economic problems, especially unemployment; integrates the foreigners living permanently in Germany into the existing multicultural society; and takes the initiative to treat East Germans with respect rather than condescension. A high percentage of Ger-mans, and not just the rightists, are still prejudiced against foreigners and Jews (of whom there are relatively few—about 62,000—in the country). Despite strong statements from the former federal president Richard von Weizsäcker that right-wing violence was unacceptable, the Bonn government dragged its feet for too many years. It took resolute action only when it was worried about its image abroad and the possibility that foreign investments in Germany might decline. Yet, despite such past irresoluteness on the right-wing issue and despite Germany's many current problems, paralleling those of other countries, the democratic insti-tutions, liberties, and political culture—one-half century old in West Germany—have a firm grounding. Unless there are catastrophic economic developments, their future in united Germany seems assured.

Notes

The author thanks Stephen Kelberg, Hannelore Koehler, Gero Neugebauer, Klaus-Henning Rosen, and Jacob Suhl for comments and suggestions on an earlier draft of this chapter.

    1. For definitions, see Richard Stöss, *Politics Against Democracy: Right-wing*

Extremism in West Germany (New York and Oxford: Berg, 1991), 14-37.

2. For comparisons with right-wing movements in other states, see Herbert Kitschelt, *The Radical Right in Western Europe: A Comparative Analysis* (Ann Arbor: University of Michigan Press, 1995).

3. See Ekkart Zimmermann and Thomas Saalfeld, "The Three Waves of West German Right-Wing Extremism," in Peter H. Merkl and Leonard Weinberg, eds., *Encounters with the Contemporary Radical Right* (Boulder: Westview Press, 1993), 50-74.

4. Bundesminister des Innern, "Verfassungsschutzbericht 1996" (mimeographed, n.d.), 130-32; *Süddeutsche Zeitung*, 30 April/1 May, 1998.

5. "Verfassungsschutzbericht 1997" (mimeographed), 92-96.

6. Hans-Joachim Veen, Norbert Lepszy, and Peter Mnich, *The Republikaner Party in Germany: Right-Wing Menace or Protest Catchall?* (Westport and London: Praeger, 1993), 29-40.

7. *Blick nach Rechts* (Bonn), 24 January 1996, 3-4.

8. *Süddeutsche Zeitung*, 28 and 29 April 1998; Viola Neu and Ulrich von Wilamowitz-Moellendorff, "Die DVU bei der Landtagswahl in Sachsen-Anhalt vom 26.04.1998," *Konrad-Adenauer-Stiftung Arbeitspapier* (April 1998).

9. Bundesminister des Innern, *betrifft: verfassungsschutz '78* (Bonn, 1979), 31-35.

10. *dpa press release*, 24 February 1995.

11. In comparison, neo-Nazi groups had about 1,000 members in 1978 (Bundesminister des Innern, *betrifft: verfassungsschutz '78*, 18; "Verfassungsschutzbericht 1996," 85, 105-6; "Verfassungsschutzbericht 1997," 86; letter from Klaus-Henning Rosen, Ministry of the Interior, November 27, 1997).

12. Bundesminister des Innern, "Verfassungsschutzbericht 1996," 107-8, 114.

13. *Die Woche*, 3 March 1995.

14. German Information Center (GIC), New York, "Spotlight on ... Right-Wing Violence and Hate Crimes in Germany," January 1997.

15. *Freitag*, 6 January 1995; *New York Times*, 22 October 1995.

16. GIC, *The Week in Germany*, 7 April 1995; 6 September 1996.

17. *New York Times*, 22 January 1995; 22 October 1995; *Blick nach Rechts*, 21 August 1996. For details on Althans, see Marc Fisher, *After the Wall: Germany, the Germans and the Burdens of History* (New York: Simon & Schuster, 1995), 225-37.

18. *Blick nach rechts*, 13 July 1993, 2-3; Verfassungsschutz Rheinland-Pfalz, "Skinheads" (mimeographed, n.d.); *New York Times,* 8 February 1994; Bundesminister des Innern, "Verfassungsschutzbericht 1996," 100-4.

19. See Ruud Koopmans, *A Burning Question: Explaining the Rise of Racist and Extreme Right Violence in Western Europe* (Wissenschaftszentrum Berlin für Sozialforschung, paper no. FS III 95-101, 1995).

20. Bundesamt für Verfassungsschutz, "Verfassungsschutzbericht 1997," 71.

21. For details, see Michael Venner, *Nationale Identität: Die neue Rechte und die Grauzone zwischen Konservatismus und Rechtsextremismus* (Cologne:

PapyRossa, 1994); Diethelm Prowe, "National Identity and Racial Nationalism in the New Germany: Nazism versus the Contemporary Radical Right," *German Politics and Society* 15, no. 1 (Spring 1997): 1-21. For a discussion of the New Right, see Jacob Heilbrunn, Robert Lieber, Hans-Georg Betz, and Peter Schneider, *Germany's New Right: Revival of Nationalism or Call for Normalcy?* (Washington, D.C.: Friedrich Ebert Foundation, 1997).

22. Bundesamt für Verfassungsschutz, "Rechtsextremismus in der Bundesrepublik Deutschland: Ein Lagebild" (mimeographed, Cologne, 1997), 25-26.

23. Cited by Jacob Heilbrunn, "Germany's New Right," *Foreign Affairs* 75, no. 6 (Nov.-Dec. 1996): 88. For critical responses by Josef Joffe et al. and a rebuttal by Heilbrunn, see *Foreign Affairs* 76, no. 2 (Mar.-Apr. 1997): 152-61.

24. Cited by Heilbrunn, "Germany's New Right," 91. See also *The Week in Germany*, 12 May 1995.

25. Richard Stöss and Oskar Niedermayer, "Rechtsextremismus, politische Unzufriedenheit und das Wählerpotential rechtsextremer Parteien in der Bundesrepublik im Frühsommer 1998," *Arbeitspapiere des Otto-Stammer-Zentrums* (Freie Universität Berlin), no. 1 (1998): 2-4, 15.

Part Two

Public Policy Quandaries

9

The German Economy:
Shocks to the System

David M. Keithly

During the four decades of Germany's division, the Federal Republic (FRG or West Germany) grew comfortable and prosperous, becoming a largely contented and secure state as well as an integral part of Western Europe. Following the years of the "economic miracle" of the 1950s and 1960s, the social market economy, as the Germans refer to their system, continued to perform reasonably well. It held up during the economic turmoil of the 1970s; consistently exhibited an acceptable "misery index," reflecting low rates of inflation and unemployment; and provided West Germans with a standard of living that was the envy of Europe. Moreover, it became the foundation for a bountiful welfare state. Such was German economic success that the system was heralded in the 1970s by the then governing Social Democrats as *Modell Deutschland*, or, the "German model" of a modern industrial society. Part and parcel of this model, one extolled at home and abroad over the years, were economic prosperity, administrative competence, political dexterity, and social stability.

In the late 1990s, as Germany's Social Democrats readied themselves to return to power and lead the governmental transition to the Berlin Republic, they indicated their awareness that *Modell Deutschland* had lost much of its luster. Before his party's victory in the 1998 Bundestag election, chancellor candidate Gerhard Schröder spoke about providing "a new beginning" for the German model.[1] Both he and other leading Social Democrats, including Oskar Lafontaine, acknowledged that this would involve much more than a facelift. Meanwhile the parties of Chancellor Kohl's conservative-liberal coalition tried to present themselves as the real modernizers, who had been held back by a legislative gridlock brought on by the SPD with its majority control of the federal upper house or Bundesrat. The ubiquitous presence of a German *Reformstau* or "reform tie-up" had become conventional wisdom even if there was no agreement about the diagnosis or remedy of the ailment. The term itself had already been dubbed the "word of the year" by the Society for the German Language in 1997, when Federal President Roman Herzog gave his widely echoed trumpet call for a "jolt" through German society.

What was the renowned German model and what had happened to make it appear outdated and unsustainable? Changes in the international economic environment beginning in the 1980s confronted the Federal Republic, like other West European countries, with fresh and momentous challenges. Then came the shock of German unification. For Germany, these two developments became inextricably linked, compounding the problems of high taxation, excessive regulation and overbureaucratization that characterize it along with many other European welfare states. They all face the competitive rigors of an expanded global marketplace, but Germany's situation is in some ways more complicated precisely because of the need to transform the economy of its new eastern states. Quite apart from the attendant social problems, national unification exacerbated lingering economic difficulties in Germany by the imposition of new and heavy public expenditures. By 1995, public spending's share of Gross National Product (GNP) approached 52 percent, up from around 45 percent in 1989. In effect, unification had engendered one of the largest Keynesian demand stimulation programs ever carried out in a major advanced economy. Now, durable fiscal adjustment is required to get a handle on financial circumstances.

This chapter will first examine the western German model or "social market economy" with its mounting structural problems that are increasingly underscored by economic globalization. Then it will turn to the severe strains that have been added as national unification brought a sudden extension of this challenged system into eastern Germany to replace the latter's dysfunctional planned economy.

Modell Deutschland

The social market economy is based upon a distinctive and now time-honored system of democratic and liberal corporatism. In the German context, corporatism involves institutionalized arrangements whereby employer associations, labor unions, and government officials participate in the formulation of economic and social policies. The central aim of German democratic corporatism has been to balance various societal interests, thereby fostering a climate of cooperation and sense of community. Close elite collaboration has been among its hallmarks. Wage demands and social conflict were kept under control, subordinated to a broadly defined national interest. The state has regulated markets with an eye to promoting favorable conditions for competition and business enterprise, above all, by controlling cartels and monopolies.

The domestic institutional and legal arrangements within which markets operate are customarily referred to in Germany as *Ordnungspolitik*. Academic economists have described these distinctive features as "measures and institutions which impart to competition the framework, rules, and machinery of impartial supervision which a competitive system needs as much as any game or match if it is not to degenerate into a vulgar brawl."[2] The founders of the social market economy, adherents in the main of the "Freiburg School" of market economics, identified the key facets of the *Ordnungspolitik* as open markets, free prices, the right to property, and currency stability. Yet, the state has come to oversee and administer a massive social welfare system designed to assist the disadvantaged and those unduly affected by market forces. This dual state role, providing a framework for enterprise while according extensive social guarantees, leads some to characterize the social market as slightly incongruous, a not altogether unfair observation given the amount of public sector growth in the last decades.

The centerpiece of democratic corporatism is codetermination (*Mitbestimmung*), an institution designed to provide workers with broad representation in the workplace and to facilitate labor-management consultation. Codetermination in its present form emerged over a period of two decades through a series of laws, the first of which was passed in 1951. The roots of codetermination actually extend back into the nineteenth century when liberal, socialist, and Catholic groups began institutionalizing labor-management consultation. After World War II unions argued that with more say in enterprise management they would be in a position to deter big business from colluding with antidemocratic political organizations.[3] Allied occupation authorities, eager to strengthen German trade unionism, undertook measures that stimulated the process.

In large firms, at least one-third of the seats on the supervisory board (*Aufsichtsrat*), and all those on the workers' council, are reserved for unions. In smaller firms with only a factory council (*Betriebsrat*), a certain percentage of seats are slotted for labor representatives. In companies large enough to have both a supervisory board and a firm council, labor is represented twice. More than in any other developed country, German firms bear some resemblance to representative systems of governance, composed of company boards, specialist members of those boards, and trade unions.

After the founding of West Germany, codetermination helped integrate the labor movement in the political process, anchoring it subsequently into the socioeconomic order. Labor and management assimilated each other's interests in many respects, subordinated their own preoccupations to broader national concerns, and, as a rule, alleviated industrial strife through negotiation. In consequence, strike action was rare. Directly, through union representation and codetermination, and indirectly, in the political process through union coordination activities, labor made its voice heard. The perennially low West German "misery index" was largely a function of sustained consultation and mutual restraint in income demands by economic actors. The results were impressive. Prior to the energy crisis of the early 1970s, the unemployment rate was less than 1 percent, while annual inflation remained at around 3 percent.

The Call for Reform

What has gone wrong? To say it all at once: the economy has been long headed for trouble. Not only did the strong, impartial state managing the *Ordnungspolitik* expand persistently beginning in the 1970s, but it exhibited an increasing propensity to intervene in the economy. In the process came a change in focus. Instead of the emphasis on maintaining open markets and providing tax advantages to the small and medium-sized businesses that form the backbone of the German economy in many areas, attention was now shifted toward broader fiscal policies. Keynesian measures of fiscal stimulus at times supplanted more market-oriented policies premised on hard money. Interventionist macroeconomic policies became widely regarded as indispensable to sustaining high growth and employment rates. Successive German administrations seemed less resolved to assign priority to enhancing market efficiency. Recession in the 1970s, oscillating exchange rates, and soaring energy costs promoted state intervention and subsequently contributed to public sector expansion. Instead of concentrating on structural policies designed to reinforce an environment conducive to market operation, state and federal administration increasingly exerted regulatory authority. Bureaucratization grew; regulation increased by leaps and bounds. Perhaps most far-reaching in potential consequence, the welfare state was set on a course that, given current demographics, will jeopardize the country's prosperity.

In the 1950s and 1960s, no serious observer would have depicted Germany's economy as unregulated or laissez-faire. But its contours changed following the two decades of the economic miracle. With copious welfare benefits, a plethora of regulatory agencies, growing bureaucratization, and rising taxation to finance it all, Germany's economy, though still widely esteemed, increasingly came to be regarded by observers as fettered in the face of intensifying global competition. Some economists suggest that lack of innovation and sluggish growth were the long-term offshoot of democratic corporatism: unions exerted substantial influence as the reward for social partnership; people condoned rising taxes in the belief government would sustain high employment levels; welfare benefits became the corollary of social responsibility; and business accepted the burgeoning public sector in return for governmental restriction of competition.[4] From this perspective, the cost of cozy corporatism in efficiency and dynamism is substantial. Corporatism tends to produce government intervention on behalf of established companies, and job creation is thwarted by a lack of innovation and want of new firms. It is somewhat paradoxical that two pillars of systemic strength, stability and order have ended up contributing to the system's weakening. Democratic corporatism, predicated as it is upon consultation and cooperation, fostered complacency about

economic developments, something hardly conducive to innovation and entrepreneurship. True, consensus politics, collective wage bargaining and customarily
cooperative relationships among economic players have engendered stability and
continuity over the years. But the very stability that was a source of Germany's
economic strength contributed in no small way to the present rigidities economists
find so worrisome.

Large banks with close ties to established industries have continued to dominate capital markets, for example, and they have far more clout than is the case in
most other developed economies. Venture capital, a primary vehicle for development of high technology firms, remains relatively scarce given the society's afflu-
ence, and financiers shy away from ambitious "small-cap" firms. Stock markets still
have a secondary function in the financial system, and firms, especially smaller
ones, remain largely unaccustomed to raising capital through equity shares. The
relatively minor role of the stock market in the German financial system reflects the
twofold legacy of powerful large banks with extensive corporate holdings, and of
the Nazi dictatorship that disbanded the stock exchange.

Citing Asia's financial difficulties, German bankers are quick to point out that
Germany's economic reliability ultimately carries more weight with international
investors than dazzling and largely deceptive growth figures. Nevertheless, structural rigidities and the natural cautiousness of the banking community throttle the
flow of investment funds into start-up companies and to entrepreneurs. "Banks
invest in security," is now a customary complaint among the ambitious and
high-flying; "they first ask you about assets and real estate, not about your business plans or your product."[5] Many businesspeople deplore the conservatism and
inflexibility they see as intrinsic to bank ownership. A frequent allegation in political
and journalistic circles is that banks wield excessive influence and authority through
equity share-holding and representation on company boards. Financial data attest
to the extent of bank ownership of companies. Of the "big three" German banks,
Deutsche Bank owns shares in over eighty major firms; Dresdner Bank in fifty-five,
Commerzbank in fifty.[6] And these numbers reflect merely ownership, indicating
little about other financial holdings and the exercise of corporate supervisory functions. In short, banks have substantial clout in the domestic economy and exercise
considerable influence abroad through their holdings of companies operating internationally.[7]

In labor markets, rigid laws and regulations are designed to accommodate
trade unions concerned about their diminishing societal roles, but their effect is
to elevate wage levels, hinder workplace flexibility, and render layoffs and firings
difficult. The workforce has been accorded sweeping legal protection, designed
to prevent what is perceived as "antisocial" employment reduction. Sustained layoffs are in fact sometimes feasible only through bankruptcy. Such labor market
interference produces significant, albeit "invisible" contingent wage costs, amplifying company expenses. In consequence, firms frequently prefer paying overtime to hiring additional workers. Part-time and temporary employment opportuni-

ties are infrequent by developed country standards. True, stable relationships between labor and management have contributed to labor peace and a general willingness on the part of firms to invest extensively in worker training and skill improvement. Workers, for their part, have displayed considerable commitment to their employers. Organized labor has carried the banner for the social partnership.

But the cost of such affinities can be considerable; in terms of labor market rigidities it can be steep indeed. Some liken Germany's labor market to a medieval guild system in which craftsmen run closed shops that fix wages and discourage outside competition.[8] Industrial associations negotiate wages with trade unions that, as a rule, determine the price of labor across entire sectors, not just at the company level. Negotiations about wages and working conditions take place on a regional or even national basis.

Beyond this, but connected to it, the German economy has encountered more difficulties adjusting to the expanding demand for services than other economies have. Excessive regulation and trade union inflexibility are in part to blame. Nonetheless, negative attitudes toward parttime work and flexible work schemes are widespread. Indeed, employers' associations and union officials fundamentally agree that a principal reason for the reluctance of companies to hire parttime are the entrenched prejudices of lower and middle management.[9] Blame there is enough to go around: employers cite excessive regulation; unions refer to management prejudice; economists point to union inflexibility.

Traditional work schedules and arrangements are often incompatible with a service economy. Yet, government regulation has increased over the last years, and trade unions remain substantially bluecollar and are still largely organized around manufacturing and heavy industry. Such is the economic drag of these factors on the service sector alone that the annual growth rate in the last fifteen years is at least one full percentage point lower than it otherwise would have been.[10] According to a 1997 study, services play an increasingly important part in the economic life of developed countries, with the exception of Germany.[11] Service sector expansion has helped generate economic growth and increase employment levels in many countries. Germany, by contrast, "is an outright service desert." Warning that Germany risks falling further behind its economic competitors, the study underscored the tight correlation between service sector development and overall economic growth. OECD (developed country) studies indicate that the German economy is also a laggard with respect to parttime work.[12] Parttime employment represents less than a 15 percent share of overall employment in Germany, whereas in the Netherlands it is over 35 percent. Norway and Sweden have similar large percentages of their labor force engaged parttime. The United States and Japan, for their part, have around 20 percent. Recognizing this aspect of labor market rigidity, Chancellor Kohl in January 1998 urged an increase in parttime positions to boost the economy and spur job creation.[13]

Compounding economic alignment difficulties has been governmental unwillingness to resist demands for subsidization of declining industries such as steel, coal and shipbuilding. Much of the traditional coal and steel complex is wholly dependent upon subsidies, and could not survive without them. Subsidization of European agriculture by national governments as well as by the European Union (EU) has been effectively out of control for decades. The EU's Common Agricultural Policy (CAP), the European farm support program, regularly consumes more than 60 percent of the EU's budget.[14] Seldom has Germany advocated CAP reform. Unification, with the subsequent addition of large agricultural tracts in the East, has provided it with no incentive to do so. Subsidies, by their nature not market-driven investments, invariably result in inefficiencies. They increase the size of the public sector and tend to divert funding from more lucrative areas, in particular, high-tech "sunrise" enterprises.

Inflexibility and overregulation have become prominent attributes of the social market economy, say self-reproaching Germans in increasing numbers. Building and construction industries must abide by a surfeit of stringent codes; transportation markets remain heavily regulated with respect to market access, fares, capacities, and types of service; telecommunications, a major growth area in the United States in the last decade, remained a government monopoly until 1998. By contrast, American telecommunications monopolies were dismantled years ago, giving rise to the creation of smaller, entrepreneurial service providers in local, long distance and wireless sectors. Such is the uneasiness about slow-gaited reform in Germany that seldom does a day go by without some media examination of the subject. Tax reform, pension reform, spelling reform and university reform have been among the chief issues of recent public discourse. According to the German Press Agency (*dpa*), 11,500 of the 185,000 domestic news stories it carried in 1997 had the word "reform" in the headline.[15]

In its annual report for 1997, the politically independent Council of Economic Advisors urged the political establishment, labor and management to take comprehensive action to reform the economy in order to overcome the chief problems besetting the country.[16] The report concurs in the main with Germany's leading economic research institutes regarding the salience of certain issues. Economic growth is not having much impact on employment, the report specified, and if the German economy is to create jobs, the *Ordnungspolitik* must create more favorable investment conditions. Growth will begin translating into greater employment only in the wake of deep-reaching adjustment. In a follow-on statement, one Council member underscored the importance for the German economy of persistently meeting strict deficit reduction criteria.

The Reform Agenda

For years, the leading German economic research institutes have identified areas requiring sweeping reform. They have repeatedly called for alterations of the complex social, financial and legal arrangements, mandated by government and having micro- and macroeconomic effects. That is, Germany's economic vitality compels substantial adjustments to the *Ordnungspolitik*. Most German economists have long championed more market-oriented policies; greater flexibility, particularly in the labor market; and dynamic deregulation. Germany must come to grips with economic difficulties that are chiefly on the supply side, they argue. In this context, a supply-side agenda involves improving incentives by reducing burdens on income, opening markets, and eliminating protection accorded incumbent suppliers. In all its annual reports to the government in recent years, the Council of Economic Advisors has advocated cost-cutting measures and moderate wage agreements to boost productivity growth. It has urged Germans to adjust better to changes in the global trade structure. In addition, the Council has expressed its considerable disappointment that the attempt to reduce taxes and nonwage labor costs was unsuccessful in 1997.[17] The Council operates on the premise that people will invariably move in a direction promising higher rewards and away from activities with lower potential rewards. Put less prosaically: demand curves slope negatively and supply curves slope positively.

Germany began to pay a price some time ago for its procrastination in addressing a number of crucial issues. Most of Germany's elite, and much of the general public, now agree upon the areas of primary focus. As so often, though, the devil lies in the details. Moreover, sound economic advice is one thing; political courage to implement it quite another. A brief discussion of the areas most stubbornly resistant to reform will illuminate the political difficulties.

Subsidies

Subsidies to a number of declining industries such as steel and coal remain large, notwithstanding government promises over the years to reduce them. Continued subsidization of coal has boosted electricity costs to an international high. Electricity costs in Germany are among the highest in Europe, half again as high as they are in France, for example. Natural gas prices in the Netherlands are less than half those in Germany. Energy costs have a significant impact upon competitiveness. Some of the Länder make a practice of attracting direct investment through subsidization. Agriculture in certain areas continues to receive large federal subsidies. Agricultural regions are frequently Christian Democratic bastions, while areas with heavy industry tend to support the Social Democrats, affording both major political parties incentives to maintain subsidies. Unification added to political pressures for subsidies, and subsidization bills reached the 10 percent mark of annual GNP in the 1990s. Among EU countries, Germany is now the leading subsidizer in absolute terms. According to some studies, elimination of subsidies would boost employment by as much as 9 percent.[18]

Deregulation

Germany's economy would benefit substantially from deregulation. More than half the economic activity in Germany occurs in sectors where competition is restrained or stifled. Extensive market interference means that producers continually must use factor markets that are heavily regulated. The labor and energy markets are salient examples. Transport markets are another; regulation here results in considerable inefficiencies. Typically, only those carriers not competing with the Federal Railway have been exempted from regulation. Operating losses of the Federal Railway often entail several billion marks annually, and economists estimate that "regulatory distortions" in the transport sector cost taxpayers more than DM 5 billion a year.[19] Retail trade continues to be burdened with almost guild-like regulation. Individual stores are seldom allowed to offer discounts and rebates on merchandise. Clearance sales can be held only at certain times of the year. Strict zoning laws control the establishment of large retail stores and supermarkets. The Store Closing Law (*Ladenschlußgesetz*) was liberalized only in 1996, and opening hours for stores are still limited by law, a measure that places many firms at a comparative disadvantage.

Regulation inherently protects established producers and closes markets for newcomers. The upshot is less dynamism and efficiency in the economy. Studies conducted by the Kiel Institute for World Economics have repeatedly found little or no evidence justifying heavy regulation in such areas as transportation, banking and insurance, telecommunications, retail trade and energy. Distortions in the labor market, according to some economists, have contributed hugely to the decline in yields on fixed productive assets, a matter of concern for a country with such a large manufacturing base. Whereas production accounted for over two-thirds of total company profits in the 1960s, the profit figure declined to around one-quarter in the 1980s.

Social Security

Germany has more than 1,500 social insurance funds managing its social welfare system. Although nominally independent, most are closely supervised by public authorities. Skyrocketing expenditure, which ratchets up contribution levels, and exorbitant nonwage labor costs, would in themselves be sufficient reasons for a fundamental overhaul. Germany's nonwage labor costs, now the highest in the world, rose from around 40 percent of wage costs in the 1960s to over 80 percent in the 1980s. But beyond this, demographics will force change. The German population is rapidly aging. By the year 2030, as much as 40 percent of the population will be over sixty. Short of radical system reform, and with fewer and fewer employed persons to support pensioners, the share of GNP earmarked for social spending alone could exceed 50 percent.[20] Unification has placed fresh strains upon the system and resulted in a society that is far less affluent overall, with the subsequent need to adjust to the new situation. In a report issued in October 1997, the German Institute for Economic Research asserted that unification is the main cause of the financial difficulties afflicting the country's social welfare programs.[21] It argues that action is needed to correct the imbalances that have arisen since unification. In short, the country can no longer afford its level of entitlements.

Taxation

Taxes, particularly corporate taxes, in Germany are high, even by European standards. The marginal burden of income tax and social security contributions for the individual is over 60 percent, and the combined tax rate on net corporate profits can exceed this figure. Tax reductions would afford greater economic incentives. Continued high levels provide significant performance disincentives and, moreover, nurture an already substantial shadow economy. The "unofficial sector" (read: underground economy) generates at least 15 percent of GNP, and some estimates cite a considerably higher figure. Europe-wide, around 28 million people work in the shadow economy, which produces between 16 and 20 percent of total GNP, according to EU reports.[22] Few suggest the size of the domestic shadow economy will decrease anytime soon. In Western Europe, the number of people working in the underground economy tripled between the mid-1970s and mid-1980s; German figures are comparable.

Unification added to the tax burden in the 1990s, but the marginal rate of tax on income lessened only slightly in the 1980s, before the enormous costs of unification rolled in. Soaring public debt in recent years has thwarted efforts to reduce tax burdens. Recent efforts to reduce budget deficits have been carried out primarily by means of tax increases, not spending cuts. Germany's reputation as a high-tax, high-regulation country significantly contributes to the somewhat tarnished image of *Standort Deutschland*—the German production site. Economic experts concur that Germany is losing appeal as a business location, especially as a hub for transnational corporate operations. Of the approximately 300,000 new jobs the German economy is projected to create in 1998 and 1999, most will be in adjacent East-Central European countries, virtually none in Germany proper.

Privatization

Although slow in coming, progress has been made in this area. State holdings in companies such as Viag (metals and chemicals), Veba (energy) and Salzgitter (steel and engineering) have been eliminated. German flag-carrier Lufthansa, completely privatized as of October 1997, made record profits in 1997 and 1998, and the value of its stock shot up accordingly. The state ownership share of the Düsseldorf airport was sold in 1997, with the Cologne-Bonn airport scheduled to follow. Legislation in 1997 eliminated the monopoly position of Germany's electricity producers, partially opening energy markets to Europe-wide competition and requiring Germany's electricity grids to be made available to firms in adjacent countries. The initial step in the privatization of the postal service, a hitherto immense state telephone, bank, and mail service monopoly, involved subdivision into *Deutsche Post*, *Postbank*, and *Deutsche Telekom*. The latter was officially privatized in 1998, as telecommunications were thrown open to competition in a dozen European countries. Germany has more than thirty companies now offering telephone service. As a result of reorganization, *Deutsche Post* has become a government-owned corporation scheduled to be floated on the stock market in the year 2000. In 1998, the postal service lost its exclusive right to deliver letters weighing more than 100 grams, packages, and mass mailings.[23] It will have to face only limited competition for five years after deregulation procedures take effect, but its chief executive insists that it is capable of competing in open markets. Unification helped catalyze privatization nationwide, above all, by amplifying budgetary pressures that, in turn, accelerated the tempo of privatization.

Productivity

Even prior to unification, productivity was increasing more slowly than in many other countries. Labor productivity in Germany grew by less than 2 percent a year in 1980-90. This decline stands in contrast to the prior two decades when German productivity growth was among the world's highest, far exceeding the OECD average. Contributing to the productivity slowdown are relatively short working hours with long holidays, and generous social benefits anchored in law or guaranteed through labor-management contracts. Germans work on average 1,700 hours a year, as opposed to 1,900 in the United States, and nearly 2,200 in Japan.[24] Social benefits and other nonwage labor costs have resulted in staggering production expenditure increases. Exacerbating difficulties is the conspicuous lack of much correlation between wage and productivity levels. Between 1990 and 1993, wages in Germany increased by nearly a quarter, whereas productivity per hour of work increased by 8.5 percent.[25]

Yet, some trade unions continue to advocate combating unemployment through job-sharing and reduced worktime schemes, measures many economists regard as having deplorable effects upon productivity and growth. In April 1997, Germany's largest union, IG Metall, proposed a shorter thity-two-hour workweek to boost employment.[26] The principal employers' organization, the Federation of German Industry or BDI, rejected the proposal out-of-hand, insisting that hundreds of thousands of jobs would be lost by additional worktime reductions, above all, because companies would be compelled to bear the additional nonwage and tax costs of hiring new workers. The BDI added that additional labor costs provide firms with more incentives to relocate plant and equipment outside Germany.

In February 1998, in the wake of demonstrations by public-sector employees, the chairman of the public employee's union came out in favor of a thirty-hour workweek to reduce unemployment. "Purely mathematically," he argued, without much elaboration of methodology, a reduction in the workweek by a few hours would translate into as many as 150,000 new jobs.[27] Public officials were quick to dismiss the proposal as unrealistic, with many asserting that work reduction schemes would create no new jobs at all.

External Shocks

Although some of Germany's long-term economic problems are inherent in the system itself, including a weighty public sector, bountiful social benefits and a lavish welfare state, the principal and compelling challenges have come in the form of external shocks. Foremost was unification, with the attendant integration of seventeen million people and a decrepit economy into the Federal Republic. The process entailed one of the greatest strains a Western democracy has ever had to withstand.

Unification was traumatic, but it also represented an opportunity. With hindsight, Germany let the occasion go by. When German policymakers transferred their overtaxed and overregulated social market economy lock, stock, and barrel to the new states, they failed to take advantage of the window of opportunity for introducing a needed structural reform of *Modell Deutschland*. The dizzying tempo of unification, the strain upon leaders, and the urgency of decision and improvisation all contributed to the omission. The unification process would have allowed deregulation, debureaucratization, a more flexible labor market, at least in the eastern states, and a gradual reduction in the prim management-labor relationships that were yesteryear's socioeconomic points of character. Hence, the first year or two of unification was the time to introduce broader structural reforms.

The reconstituted Länder once forming the German Democratic Republic (GDR) seemed a prime candidate for a low-tax, low-regulation, lower-wage experiment that might have served as a model of economic development for other parts of Germany, and, indeed, elsewhere. Some areas of Europe that suffered decades of communist mismanagement pursued just such a course with reasonable degrees of success. The Czech Republic, for example, has managed to maintain unemployment levels at below 6 percent since 1994. The new eastern Länder might well have been spared high unemployment had serious efforts been made during the unification process to deregulate, and to keep down wage costs, above all, nonwage labor costs. It was then, many observers now wistfully admit, that the window of opportunity for Germany was wide open. During the unification process, proposals to debureaucratize through national reform were on offer. One outspoken proponent of such measures was the former Economics Minister and Chairman of the Free Democratic Party, Otto von Lambsdorff. The pressure of events in part precluded the necessary actions, even if the political will had been extant, which it was not.

Another determinant was the resistance to change engendered by a system dependent on consensus politics, where vested interests often exercise what amounts to a suspensive veto. Opponents of a low-tax and lower-wage area in the former GDR advanced two arguments: first, that considerable divergences in wage rates would result in an exodus of labor from eastern Germany that was needed for the reconstruction of the economy, and, second, that a large, low-wage area would drag west German levels down and reduce the pace of innovation throughout Germany. Although both represented potential problems, even taken together, these pale beside a devastated export sector and double-digit unemployment, which were the direct consequence of the effort to equalize eastern and western wages. Establishing wage parity between East and West rendered industrial assets valued at tens of millions of marks virtually worthless. Wage differentials within individual countries are not unusual; indeed, wage differentials within the EU are substantial. The German system's ability to withstand the shock testifies to its underlying strengths, but its inherent rigidities manifested themselves as well.

The second external shock sorely testing the system took the form of the transformation of the world economy and the longer-term trends involving changes in international trade and competitiveness. Shifting trade patterns must be a prime concern to a country with a large trading sector, and changes in international trade will invariably affect the country with the world's largest share of manufactured exports.

Rapid technological development and keener competition from areas with lower wage scales began adversely to affect the West German economy in the 1980s. Exporters started to lose markets, an alarming trend for a manufacturing economy, where more than one job in three is generated in the export sector. Japan acquired a large portion of foreign markets for passenger and utility vehicles in the 1980s. West Germany lost over half of its machine-tool business in the United States from 1974 and 1985, and machine-tool production declined by over 10 percent in the 1990s.[28] As will be discussed below, industry in the former GDR confronted similar problems beginning in the late 1970s. Productivity in West Germany lagged behind that of most of its international competitors as well as of many European countries already in the 1980s.

Global trade expansion and heightened international competitiveness have had a substantial impact on the German economy. New markets have also brought keen competitors. The last two decades have witnessed developments that Germany will ignore to its peril: declining market share in the United States and limited market share in Asia. Germany still sells only 7 percent of its total exports in Asia. The determinants of West Germany's emergence as an export powerhouse, including education, a highly skilled workforce, suitable infrastructure and technological superiority have been matched by potential competitors, or undermined by the country's apparent difficulties in changing and adapting. The initial challenge came from Asia, in particular from Japan, Taiwan and South Korea. With the collapse of the Soviet Empire and the ensuing liberalization of East-Central Europe, there arose fledgling market economies that present Germany with both challenges and opportunities. Two decades ago, Asian economies with substantial cost production advantages and skilled workers were still far from Europe. Now, these very attributes are to be found in Europe's new democracies and would-be members of the European Union. Germany is the largest single investor in East-Central Europe, and its economic involvement there is growing with rapid strides. With an 18.5 percent export increase to the region in 1997, East-Central Europe began that year to receive more German exports than the United States.[29]

From Central Planning to the Social Market

The transition from command economies to market economies in the Central and East European Countries (CEECs) and the Soviet Union should be included among the most profound economic and institutional changes to be effected in the twentieth century. Such a transformation is without precedent, and the principal actors are unable to avail themselves of prior experience. The road from centrally planned to market economies has been a rocky one; the journey longer and more difficult than most envisioned. In some cases, lack of understanding about the character of Soviet-style command economies, with the attendant difficulty of properly measuring the starting place in centrally planned systems when transition commenced, represented an obstacle on this road. Many misjudged or underrated the changes that were necessary, and hence the distance to be traveled between one economic system and another. In the German context, the social and economic disparities between the GDR and the Federal Republic were startlingly deep. Moreover, observers and public officials were given to underestimating these, if not suppressing them outright. Germany is politically one, but it encounters economic stumbling blocks that are producing East-West social faultlines.

The economic quandaries of German unification can be considered under three headings: the legacy, the price and wage adjustment, and the loss of export markets. Each represents a severe problem. Taken together, their impact is compounded.

The Legacy

Characterized by a predominance of large industrial enterprises, insufficient light industry and manufacturing, and a lack of small and medium-sized firms, the GDR's economy was in many ways typical of communist central planning. Prices did not reflect scarcities. They were set arbitrarily, manipulated by state planning authorities to subsidize agriculture and heavy industry, and designed to discourage consumer spending. Production in the GDR seldom correlated with demand; costs had little bearing upon input or output decisions. Despite unremitting SED (Communist Party) efforts to raise living standards, priority continued to be accorded to heavy industry and defense, to the detriment of consumer goods and the service sector. The low percentage of employment in the service sector, measured against the total labor force, indicated its small importance in the overall economy. At below 20 percent, this figure can be compared with the average in OECD countries, which is between 55-70 percent.[30]

Consumer production in the GDR was "socially determined," meaning that product availability reflected decisions on the part of the central planners about what people should have. The salient example of such state paternalism was "Main Task," the much-heralded program begun in the early 1970s to improve living conditions, "to further enhance the material and cultural living standard of the people on the basis of a rapidly accelerating tempo of socialist production, increased efficiency, increased scientific technological progress, and the growth of labor productivity."[31] For the better part of two decades, monumental investment was made in the housing sector in accordance with the dictates of "Main Task," resulting in the construction of the multistory apartment blocks that ring virtually every eastern German city.

In the hope of eventually overcoming a lingering "legitimacy gap," the result of precarious popular support for the regime, the SED endeavored to lift its standing through domestic policies. Living standards in the GDR, as the SED saw it, correlated tightly with popular contentment. "Main Task" thus manifested the tacit arrangement between rulers and ruled: in return for acquiescence, basic necessities would be readily, and inexpensively, available.

The abiding legacy of "Main Task" is palpable. City centers were allowed to deteriorate as housing block settlements were erected in outlying areas. Rampant neglect of existing structures left buildings unrenovated, and medieval towns in ruins. Low or even nominal rents were the norm, reflecting high levels of housing subsidization in the former GDR. Following the regime's collapse, higher, market-oriented, housing costs were widely viewed as "unfair" and became a major source of social grievance. Perhaps most anguishing of all, unpretentious apartments packed into block settlements, often built at break-neck speed and in slipshod fashion, have themselves badly deteriorated over the last years. Many are dreary, sordid places where few people with a choice elect to reside. It is not for nothing that the apartment blocks are popularly derided as *Arbeiterschließfächer* (working class lockers). Some apartment blocks have become vast slums, costlier to maintain than to tear down and rebuild. Attendant social dilemmas are enormous.

In the GDR, the agricultural sector generated over 8 percent of GNP, a notable anomaly in such a highly industrialized society. Largely self-sufficient in the production of eggs, dairy products, meat and potatoes, and more than 80 percent self-sufficient in agriculture overall, the GDR was a net exporter of farm produce.[32] Such autonomy came at a steep cost: according to some estimates, nearly 32 billion East

German marks (12 percent of the GDR's annual budget) was spent on agricultural subsidies every year.[33]

Despite the extensive investment in agriculture, exceeding that of Western European countries by a factor of two as a percentage of national income, and notwithstanding the conspicuously high percentage of population employed in the agricultural sector, farm productivity lagged far behind that of Western European agriculture. Although crop yields usually surpassed those of other Soviet bloc states, these seldom approached West European production levels. Moreover, agriculture in the GDR had its share of "value-subtracting" enterprises, in which resource wastage was so prevalent that production procedures cost more than could be obtained in revenue from output. Once world price levels for inputs and outputs asserted themselves, value-added was negative.

In centrally planned economies, industry and agriculture were broadly earmarked by the phenomenon of "value-subtraction." By some estimates, the figure on "negative value-added" in Polish, Hungarian and GDR industries was at least 25 percent.[34] In the GDR's agricultural sector, it likely exceeded 20 percent.[35] And these figures do not reflect the cost of environmental degradation, precipitated by an obsolete plant and equipment, mechanized agribusiness, profligate energy use, and, particularly in the GDR's case, heavy reliance upon lignite (brown coal) as an energy source. The price of a ravaged environment, one paid primarily by the local populace, adds hugely to the tab, but is, in the main, immeasurable.

On July 1, 1990, the agreement on Monetary, Economic, and Social Union (MESU) between the GDR and the FRG came into force, marking the irreversible step toward the complete unification of Germany on October 3 of that year. A market economy and a command economy were thereby abruptly and immutably merged. The essential feature of MESU was the disbursal of West German deutsche marks in the GDR at the politically determined, but financially unsound, exchange rate of 1:1 or 2:1, depending on the transaction.

By this time, the GDR's economy was in dire straits, and in far worse condition than public discourse imparted. Why, though, were so many people caught unawares? Several SED party reports from the autumn of 1989 attested to looming economic disaster. The most candid was delivered to the Politburo by senior economic officials at the end of October.[36] Among its findings:

- foreign debt to the West was out of control, and the ability of the GDR to service the debt was increasingly doubtful.
- merely halting the increase in foreign debt would necessitate a decline in living standards of between 25-30 percent.
- domestic consumption was not covered by indigenous production, ratcheting foreign debt higher as promised living standards were maintained.
- GDR work productivity was less than 40 percent that of the FRG.
- the country's capital stock was being rapidly depleted, and required enormous investment to repair and replenish.

- the rate of investment in industrial sector production had fallen continuously since 1970, precipitating a decline in national income growth.
- the GDR would become internationally insolvent sometime in 1990.

In spite of such alarming reports, the severity of the economic crisis in the GDR was underestimated in the West, and, not surprisingly, soft-pedaled in the East. Years of SED coverup and deception contributed to misreckoning. And complicating a sober appraisal of the country's problems were the rising popular expectations beginning in late 1989. They were by no means discouraged by politicians who preferred to offer visions of a bright future rather than pleas for moderation and patience.

The *Treuhand*

Be that as it may, estimations bordered on the fanciful. The last SED-led administration of the GDR officially assessed the net capital worth of the country's industrial plant at DM 15 trillion.[37] The first freely elected government, headed by Christian Democrat Lothar de Maizière, arrived at a figure of around half this. July 1990 saw the establishment of the *Treuhandanstalt,* or *Treuhand,* the Trust Agency for Privatization, the organization set up to privatize the GDR's economy. This agency used the capital worth figure of DM 750 billion as a point of departure. It then lowered the number to DM 400 billion at the time of the signing of the Unification Treaty. A year later, the *Treuhand* reduced its estimate to zero; that is, assets would merely equal liabilities.

For its part, the *Treuhand* was entrusted with every major decision about the property it administered, including which firms would be sold, which would be temporarily assisted or subsidized, which would be liquidated, whether land would be leased or sold, and what the duration of respective leases would be.[38] Founded as a public holding company, this trust agency became the world's largest single enterprise in terms of the amount of property administered, assets managed, and the number of employees supervised. In effect, the *Treuhand* was tasked with reorganizing the entire centrally planned economy of the GDR.

The *Treuhand* was empowered to execute comprehensive modernization of plant and equipment as it deemed necessary; to implement measures, however draconian, in an effort to confer viability upon enterprises; and even to close firms when circumstances dictated. Often operating under stringent time constraints, its officials had to balance competing economic and social interests. The *Treuhand* faced agonizing tradeoffs between the short term and the long term, having to weigh, for example, the objectives of rapid privatization against the need for economic restructuring. Forced to navigate between the scylla of economic realities and the charybdis of political expediency, officials would repeatedly encounter mutually exclusive policy goals. There were ceaseless charges of eliminating jobs and selling property far below real value. The *Treuhand* had the thankless task of contradicting popular wisdom: it is far easier to take from one and give to all, than to take from all and give back to one. The people experiencing upheaval tended to forget, though, that the collective property regime under communism—public ownership and state resource allocation—proved ineffective and was largely responsible for the economic muddle.

When the *Treuhand* wound up its operations at the end of 1994, it was running a deficit of nearly DM 300 billion.[39] Negative equity, ensuing from the deplorable condition of eastern capital assets, left the *Treuhand*, and ultimately the German Federal Government, to pick up the bill. Dilapidated industry, ecological degradation, deteriorated infrastructure, and decaying cities were the cardinal bequests of the SED.

The New Economic Order

With political unification in October 1990, the five newly emerged eastern states embraced the social system of the FRG. For the people of the new eastern states, unification marked the beginning of a transformation that would radically alter their lives. As workers and firms were subjected to the rigors of market forces, the situation that had created the ironic GDR quip, according to which "they pretend to pay us, and we pretend to work," also passed into history. Many of the jobs people assumed to be guaranteed for life began to disappear. Professional qualifications were downgraded, and much of the work experience acquired under "real existing socialism," counted for little.

Inadequacies in the personnel sphere have considerably hampered enterprise development in eastern Germany. Market economies generally have two critical components: functional institutions and a state of mind.[40] Economic agents operating within the institutions of a market economy must demonstrate certain qualities and be able to perform in accordance with market forces. After forty years of central planning, the GDR's workforce had little understanding of the operation of markets. Sheltered and subsidized producers had little incentive to develop the personnel that are instrumental to making markets function. Economic competition, especially when global markets are involved, requires a range of specific skills that were for the most part lacking in the GDR. The thousands of supervisory board members the *Treuhand* required for new or reorganized firms largely had to be brought in from the West. In a 1990 poll, three-quarters of the West German firms with operations in the eastern states indicated that indigenous management lacked qualifications, was unmotivated, and performed poorly.[41] This was the legacy of a society that did not encourage individual initiative or nurture self-employed businesspeople, much less entrepreneurship. If it had a number equivalent to those self-employed in the FRG in 1989, the GDR would have had over 900,000.[42] It had but several thousand, in fact.

Shortage of management and entrepreneurial skills should be viewed against the backdrop of enterprise organization in the former GDR. Even by Soviet bloc standards, decision-making was highly centralized. Lacking real financial objectives, and for the most part directly responsible to East Berlin ministries, large industrial enterprises resembled government departments more than they did business firms. Business skills in the Western sense were a rare commodity, and, furthermore, enterprise managers were frequently tainted by close association with the old regime, or even the State Security apparatus (the infamous *Stasi*).

Enterprise organization in the GDR fostered such a skewing of the labor force that severe structural problems continued to confront the eastern German economy through the 1990s. For example, the Halle Institute for Economic Research, in analyzing eastern Germany's service sector in 1997, found a crying want of production-oriented service professionals.[43] Eastern Germany had but 830 such workers for every 10,000 people, whereas western Germany had nearly 1,200. Only 34 of every 10,000 eastern Germans worked in banking, as compared to 76 in the West. Eastern Germany had but 14 auditors per 10,000 of population, compared to 27 in the West.

Sudden exposure to market forces brought an enfeebled economy to the point of collapse in 1990. During the first year of unification, industrial output in the new German states fell by over 65 percent, with the subsequent loss of nearly three million jobs.[44] Industrial employment, at 3.2 million in 1989, plummeted to around one million in 1994. The decline in agricultural employment was even more precipitous. Of the nearly one million jobs in agriculture in 1989, fewer than 200,000 were left by 1993.[45] In the state of Brandenburg alone, the agricultural workforce dwindled from 180,000 in 1989 to around 30,000 in 1992. Official unemployment in the eastern states has hovered around 20 percent in the 1990s, with hidden unemployment, including the underemployed, the temporarily employed, or those in public retraining and work creation programs, remaining above 30 percent.

Unemployment has disproportionately affected older workers, women and young people. Those most beset by job loss have been in the fifty-two- to sixty-three-year age group: of those working in 1989, nearly 90 percent became unemployed.[46] Many of these worked in bankrupt or significantly downsized "smokestack" or bulk chemical industries, and few have much prospect of again finding work. Overall, seven of ten men have managed to remain employed; yet only six of ten women. One youth in three is effectively unemployed, and of those who were under twenty-three and working in 1989, unemployment has hovered around 30 percent.[47] In the autumn of 1997, overall eastern unemployment stood at 18.3 percent; western at 9.7 percent.[48] The overall unemployment rate for eastern women was nearly 20 percent, whereas for eastern men it was 14 percent, and for western women, just under 10 percent.

Clearly, the promises of "blossoming economic landscapes," conjured up by well-meaning or vote-seeking leaders during the euphoria of 1989-90, are far from realization. But shocking as the employment statistics are, the eastern states have been spared mass poverty or social unrest. Sizable financial transfers from west to east since 1990 have seen to this. In the first year of unification, public transfers to the eastern states amounted to nearly DM 100 billion, much of this going for unemployment assistance. The amount would increase to DM 180 billion in 1993, and has since averaged around DM 150 billion annually.[49] Public transfer payments continue to account for approximately two-thirds of eastern Germany's GNP, on a per capita basis, nearly DM 10,000 a year. Before the 1990s draw to a close, financial transfers will have exceeded one trillion DM. Two-thirds of the public transfers are nondiscretionary entitlements, and thus largely beyond legislative control.

Public spending in eastern Germany has focused on two areas: income maintenance and infrastructure improvement. Regarding the former, Germany's generous social welfare net provides ample pensions, and has largely safeguarded the unemployed. As to the latter, the eastern states have made substantial progress in overhauling the infrastructure that is key to economic development. Much-needed roads have been built, and battered highways, many of pre-World War II vintage, reconstructed. Tumble-down railway lines have been replaced with world-standard track. Drab, ramshackle city centers, much the worse for the burning of lignite, and still showing the destruction of World War II, are being reconditioned. Electricity grids have been modernized. Residential natural gas pipelines, a rarity in the former GDR, have been installed throughout the country. Areas that short years ago had seen no modernization of their telephones for a half century, now have some of the most modern communications systems in the world. In November 1997, *Telekom* announced the completion of eastern Germany's fully digital telephone and data network. At a cost of over DM 50 billion over a seven-year period, *Telekom* installed what it claims is the world's most modern telecommunications network in the eastern German states.[50] Primitive atomic power stations were decommissioned, and use of lignite as a primary energy source phased out. But while much has been accomplished in refurbishing infrastructure, even large investment in this area offers gainful employment to relatively few. Thus public spending has done little to alleviate prolonged joblessness.

Price and Wage Adjustment

Lack of competitiveness in the industrial sphere stemmed from the rapid rise in eastern prices and wages engendered by MESU. The 1:1 conversion of virtually worthless GDR currency into rock-ribbed deutsche marks, combined with the wage demands of Germany's national trade unions, swiftly priced much eastern labor out of all markets. By 1991, eastern wages were only 20 percent lower than in Japan, and in consequence, the new states had no opportunity to avail themselves of any comparative wage advantage.[51] Trade unions, wary of an influx of inexpensive labor into western regions and apprehensive about rising eastern living costs, sought hefty wage hikes, vowing initially to equalize eastern and western wages within five years. Although equalization of wage levels would prove unsustainable, the conjunction of low eastern labor productivity and relatively high labor costs induced many firms to expand production in western German facilities to serve the new eastern markets. Such expansion came at the expense of a region in critical need of private investment to jump-start its economy.

Not only were firms obliged to meet their payrolls in DM at the 1:1 ratio following MESU, but most debts were denominated at the same rate. Costs and debts thus skyrocketed several hundred percent in real terms. Managers, accustomed to easy credit in "soft," i.e., nonconvertible, currency, from the State Bank of the GDR suddenly faced unserviceable debt burdens. Large, private West German banks, taking control of the assets of the State Bank of the GDR, procured the loans of surviving eastern firms. Linear conversion of enterprise liability into hard currency debt entailed somewhat improbable financial logic, though, because such liability bore no relation to the value of assets.

Banking under central planning had little connection with credit operations in market economies, where risk is assessed by the creditor and assumed by the debtor. Extension of credit in the GDR was primarily a means to target and subsidize particular sectors of the economy. As a facet of state planning policy, central bank credit was a routine procedure. Avoiding any monitoring of enterprise performance or production costs, financial officials readily bankrolled planning projects. Central planners, focusing upon industries geared up for export, bestowed plentiful credit. This in turn encouraged managers to engage increasing amounts of relatively inexpensive labor. The incentive on the part of enterprises to hoard labor was accordingly high, and growth rates in the GDR owed far more to greater labor input than to increased productivity. Only later would the resultant overstaffing create downsizing dilemmas. Little enterprise attention was accorded to such matters as debt-equity ratios, financial objectives or budget limitations. Currency inconvertibility encouraged inattention to foreign debt until the amount became exorbitant. Broader financial markets, such as a stock market, which is instrumental to raising enterprise capital in many economies, did not even exist.

Devoid of proper credit arrangements, markets cannot function, and thus financial cleansing is a necessary part of the transition to a market economy.[52] Banks must enforce debt contracts and allocate credit according to careful risk assessment. That said, a vicious circle ensued in eastern Germany when debts suddenly became denominated in DM. The easy credit and payments that were implicit subsidies in "real existing socialism" ceased. Lagging productivity, caused mainly by a dilapidated plant and equipment, translated into low enterprise asset values that prevented credit extension. Without adequate credit lines, producers had no opportunity to modernize their capital assets to allow them at least a chance to survive fierce domestic and international competition. Then, the overhang of enterprise debt brought on waves of bankruptcy declarations, leaving the *Treuhand* to implement liquidation in many instances. Bank credits doled out at the behest of central planning authorities were transferred to the *Treuhand,* as firms went into receivership.

With productivity in the GDR at less than 40 percent that of the FRG, the playing field was hardly level, and economic disruption ensured that labor in the new Länder would not quickly narrow the gap. In consequence, eastern labor has remained comparatively expensive even in a country where wage costs are among the world's highest. In 1992, with productivity continuing to lag, average unit wage costs in the eastern states exceeded those in the western states by a factor of two. By 1998, eastern productivity had not yet reached 60 percent of that in the western states. Labor is thus nearly 65 percent more expensive in private services; in commerce and transport 50 percent; in manufacturing 30 percent.[53] Unemployment in the eastern Länder cannot be expected to decline until these numbers change significantly, and wage policies cannot alter the hard realities. High wage levels will, in all likelihood, cause the eastern export sector to remain a laggard for another decade.

Nor is this all. People in the eastern states, deprived of Western-quality consumer goods for decades, initially shunned indigenous products in favor of Western varieties. Sometimes the difference was only one of brand and packaging; sometimes the difference material. The upshot, though, was largely the same. Aggregate demand for local goods, especially agricultural products, plunged in the first years of unification, with the foreordained consequence for producers. Although the domestic demand situation has shifted over in recent years, the initial downturn impacted many firms, driving some out of business altogether.

Loss of Export Markets

The shocks to the economy of eastern Germany had concurrent internal and external dimensions. Exact measures of the size of the GDR's export sector are subject to data problems, but with certainty, it generated over 20 percent of GNP directly, and as much as 35 percent with all economic linkages included.[54] Adoption of the DM decimated the GDR's export sector, when products designed for shipment to countries belonging to the Council for Mutual Economic Assistance (CMEA), the Soviet bloc trade organization, became uncompetitive and, on a large scale, unaffordable. CMEA provided a network of trade and supply functions, and intra-CMEA relations were as much political as economic.

The high percentage of export-produced GNP in the former GDR suggests an economic paradox. Statistically, the share of exports in national production reflected a degree of openness, comparable with Western European countries. Yet, CMEA markets were not open; the multilateral exchange of goods was circumscribed. Bilateralism and currency inconvertibility remained hallmarks of intra-CMEA trade, despite the creation of the "transferable ruble" (TR) in the 1960s as the "international socialist collective currency." Intra-CMEA trade transactions were denominated in TRs after world market prices were converted into TRs at the official ruble/dollar exchange rate, as determined by Soviet planning authorities.[55] This rate was set arbitrarily high in favor of the Soviet currency and bore little relation to market prices. TRs were not convertible into Western currencies, gold, or even other Soviet bloc currencies. Currency inconvertibility prevented an adequate settling of trade imbalances between countries. Nor did there exist any sort of "commodity convertibility," whereby a state with a trade surplus requests conversion into goods. As a rule, intra-CMEA trade was bilateral in that transactions were to "balance" bilaterally, effectively precluding states from running surpluses. Credit balances in CMEA's International Bank for Economic Cooperation (IBEC) were not transferable, and states with account surpluses were required to arrange an offsetting deficit individually with trading partners. Total volume of CMEA trade was curtailed by the need constantly to discharge transactions on such a bilateral basis. Because currency inconvertibility inhibited the movement of capital, commercial exchange was limited to traditional commodity trade. Thus CMEA members were insulated from the world economy, and respective national export sectors accordingly shielded from international market forces.

The paradox of "openness" confronted the GDR with an acute dilemma. "Openness," or, as the SED described it, "socialist economic interpenetration" entailed a heavy orientation of GDR production toward commodity delivery to the Soviet Union. The latter, in turn, was the GDR's primary supplier of oil, natural gas, and uranium. Achievement of the GDR's economic planning targets presupposed considerable dovetailing of the two economies. And the GDR was usually the first of the bloc states to be asked to accord financial sacrifices whenever the Soviet Union required.

Havoc in the GDR's export sector coincided with, and was exacerbated by, the disintegration of CMEA. As the Soviet Union's largest trading partner, the GDR was particularly hard hit; more than 65 percent of its trade was with CMEA countries, and over 40 percent of its product exports went to the Soviet Union.[56] Another 5 percent of trade was with developing countries, for the most part those friendly to the Soviet bloc, and accordingly granted concessionary trading terms. With the sudden changes in payment conditions brought on by MESU, aggregate demand tumbled. Product prices invoiced in DM brought on rapid forfeiture of market share, prevented orchestration of exchange rates to improve competitiveness, and complicated trade reorientation. Nor was the GDR afforded the luxury of replacing a large part of its exports to the CMEA markets by expansion in other markets. Economic growth in the GDR was predicated largely upon untroubled and increasing trade with the West, meaning the FRG, through which the GDR gained sectional access to the European Community (EC), now the European Union.

With the deterioration of CMEA, trade patterns began to shift noticeably. In the first five years of the 1990s, western German states' share of exports as a percentage of total German exports to East-Central Europe increased by more than a fourth, while their respective share of imports as a percentage of total German imports from this area nearly doubled. Western Germany's expanded trade figures reflect to a considerable degree the supplanting of former GDR market share: western Germany has taken over many of the former GDR's markets in the CEECs. In 1996, eastern Germany's share of total German exports was just over 2 percent.[57] In 1998, it was still only 5.4 percent.

Although export sales of electrical products, machines, and motor vehicles increased over 20 percent between 1996 and 1998, eastern Germany is still far from achieving self-sustaining growth. It will continue to require transfers from western Germany, according to nearly all assessments. Exporting is still a critical weakness of eastern German small- and medium-sized firms. The east's export ratio, the percentage of goods produced for export, was 15.6 percent in 1998, whereas in the west it was 33.4 percent.[58] Poor countries remain poor largely because of low productivity, and eastern Germany's development will depend critically upon the export sector.

In hindsight, GDR industrial indicators strongly suggest that subsidized production in targeted sectors adversely affected other areas. Export of industrial machinery to Western countries, for instance, declined by more than a fourth in the two decades prior to the GDR's collapse.[59] Manufacture of basic industrial machinery was the GDR's economic strong suit and was an important component of eastern Germany's economy long before the establishment of the GDR. Furthermore, CMEA members appeared to harbor growing doubts in the 1980s about the dependability of GDR products, and, more broadly, about the longer-term reliability of this leading supplier and trading partner. The Soviet Union, in particular, increasingly grumbled that it was receiving lower prices for its fuels and raw materials than could be obtained on world markets, while paying above-market prices for imported finished products. Even so, by 1982, the GDR was reported to be paying more than ten times what it was paying in 1973 for Soviet crude oil. In hindsight, such undercurrents were symptoms of very deep-seated problems.

Conclusion

The extension into the GDR of West Germany's economic system without prior reform encumbered the conversion from communism to capitalism. Present economic difficulties stem in part from systemic weaknesses whose roots reach back to the era of national division, but the costs of unification by themselves would have compelled reform of the social market economy. Reconstruction of the former GDR will involve a transitory, albeit heavy, burden if sweeping reform is realized. Short of this, the burden could persist, and the eventual self-sustaining recovery of the eastern economy will be imperiled.

The political leadership has vacillated and appears unsure which way to turn. United Germany has difficulties contending with current challenges to the system. Dissimilarites between eastern and western Germany, exacerbated by complex social changes, have engendered a mental division of the country, a sort of wall in people's minds. Resentments on both sides of the old divide have deepened in the last years. Many people are perplexed; some profoundly disappointed by a country laden with perceived social and economic distress. Germany's problems are greater than most people bargained for during the euphoria of unification. Since Germany is finding its domestic problems so onerous, one wonders how it will manage to redefine its proper European and international roles. As is the case with a number of EU countries, Germany will be absorbed for some time in reconfiguring its social contract.

To say that the unification process has been more expensive, time-consuming, and perplexing than most anticipated, borders on the banal. The travails of unification have become woefully commonplace. The economy of eastern Germany proved feeble, unable to withstand the piercing winds of market competition. Within a year of unification, eastern industrial production declined by nearly two-thirds. Fears persist that parts of eastern Germany will degenerate into the country's "mezzogiorno," an allusion to Italy's impoverished southern region, afflicted by unemployment and dependent on public transfer payments. However, current economic difficulties reflect not only this legacy but also the structural problems of an overregulated system. Unification has brought underlying problems to a head. Now longer-term economic recovery requires getting to work on a number of supply-side issues, including tax and social security reform, and cutting public subsidies. In effect, Germany's economic restructuring and transition have become fused in complex ways.

Germany can no longer afford choosing not to choose. The economy has been undergoing a structural crisis for some years, reflected by the waning viability of *Modell Deutschland*. Policy muddles could jeopardize the country's economic great power status, and even foster social disorder in the eastern Länder. To create conditions for better economic performance, and, above all, to modernize these new states, Chancellor Schröder's new coalition government must develop and implement fundamental reform. This will require leadership able to mobilize broad support countrywide. It also will necessitate considerable elite cooperation and agreement between Bundestag and Bundesrat. Successful policymaking must be effected within a new political-economic consensus at both the mass and elite levels. That also means that the Berlin Republic's "red-green" government will have to convince both itself and many of its own supporters of the need for more market-oriented reforms.

The crucial first step, and perhaps the acid test for Chancellor Schröder's leadership, will be comprehensive tax reform. Significant additional steps to make the labor market more flexible seem inevitable, although they are likely to encounter resistance from organized labor. Eventually, Germany will probably also have to find a way to restructure its national revenue-sharing arrangements. This could turn out to be the most difficult reform of all, but it is sorely needed. At present, less-than-affluent western Länder subsidize even poorer eastern ones. Ideally, the restructuring would ultimately result in a consolidation of several Länder, and produce a more balanced federal union of perhaps seven largish states. Such a consolidation would initially discomfit many people, East and West. Yet some of the Länder, particularly the eastern ones, need to develop new and more efficient configurations in conjunction with a renovation of their economies.

As the new government embarks on its first year in office, Germany's structural and post-communist dilemmas endure, and doubts increase whether these are going to be alleviated anytime soon. Europe's largest economy will continue making heavy weather streamlining its social welfare state, while encouraging greater personal initiative to deal with the competitive challenges associated with modern communications and global markets. Any German government must endeavor to infuse more flexibility into ponderous political institutions designed primarily to prevent the abuse of power. Indeed, some observers see the country's institutions as unwieldy and even ossified. They view the system of pervasive checks and balances as a substantial hindrance to the resolution of Germany's most pressing difficulties.

Confronted with a major unemployment problem and facing persistent structural issues, federal and state governments quarrel about responsibility, with finger-pointing all around. For its part, the SPD-led coalition shows little sense of direction, raising the specter of continued financial and economic policy muddle. In one early and widely noticed gesture, however, Finance Minister Oskar Lafontaine flung down the gauntlet before the Bundesbank, the designated model for the new European Central Bank (ECB). Scorning the principle of cenral bank independence, Lafontaine advocated a "target zone" for the exchange rate of Europe's new currency, the Euro, against the dollar. He also remains attached to low interest rates as a means of economic stimulus. The coalition's apparent inability to agree about Bundesbank policy could spell trouble for the smooth functioning of the supranational ECB.

Notwithstanding the public sector's achievements in the Herculean adjustment process in the eastern region, economic progress and development are likely to depend largely on the private sector. The new government's "Alliance for Jobs" program (a framework for seeking consensus among unions, employers, and government) is little more than old wine in new bottles. It seems as likely to inhibit as to foster employment growth. The program offers few incentives to augment innovation within established firms, much less outside them. Altogether, entrepreneurship seems to warrant little consideration in the government's economic strategy. Yet only through innovation in the private sector will Germany's economy be enabled to produce high wages along with low unemployment. Innovation in turn will entail a substantial shift away from mature industries, such as steel and bulk chemicals, and into more knowledge-based enterprises.

Notes

1. Peter Norman, "Gerhard Schröder: Germany's Moderniser," *Financial Times*, 11 May 1998, 1.

2. Kurt J. Lauk, "Germany at the Crossroads: On the Efficiency of the German Economy," *Daedalus* 123, no. 1 (Winter 1994): 58.

3. Peter J. Katzenstein, *Policy and Politics in West Germany* (Philadelphia: Temple University Press, 1987), 131-32.

4. Patrick Minford, "Europe and the Supply Side," in *A Supply-Side Agenda for Germany*, Gerhard Fels and George M. von Fürstenberg, eds. (Berlin: Springer, 1989), 68-9.

5. Quoted in M. Donald Hancock, *West Germany: The Politics of Democratic Corporatism* (Chatham, N.J.: Chatham House, 1989), 139.

6. W. R. Smyser, *The German Economy: Colossus at the Crossroads*, 2nd ed. (New York: St. Martin's Press, 1992), 84-5.

7. David Marsh, *The Germans: A People at the Crossroads* (New York: St. Martin's Press, 1989), 144-46.

8. "Model Vision: A Survey of Germany," *The Economist*, 21 May 1994, 8.

9. Werner Tegtmeier, "Challenges to Germany's Labor Market Policy: A View from Government," The 1994 Dieter zur Loye Lecture Series No. 12 (Washington, D.C.: American Institute for Contemporary German Studies, 1995), 23.

10. Rüdiger Soltwedel, "Supply-Side Policies Since 1982? The Lessons Are Still to be Learned," in *Supply-Side Agenda*, 94-5.

11. *The Week in Germany*, 4 April 1997, 4.

12. Tegtmeier, "Challenges to Germany's Labor Market Policy," 23.

13. *The Week in Germany*, 23 January 1998, 1.

14. "A Survey of Agriculture," *The Economist*, 12 December 1992, 5.

15. *The Week in Germany*, 9 January 1998, 6.

16. *The Week in Germany*, 21 November 1997, 4.

17. *The Week in Germany*, 28 November 1997, 4.

18. Hans-Peter Fröhlich, "Supply-Side Policies in Germany: Economics versus Politics," in *Supply-Side Agenda*, 39-40.

19. Soltwedel, "Supply-Side Policies Since 1982?," 83.

20. "Model Vision," 5-6.

21. *The Week in Germany*, 3 October 1997, 5.

22. *Deutschland Nachrichten*, 17 April 1998, 4.

23. *The Week in Germany*, 21 February 1997, 4.

24. Fröhlich, "Supply-Side Policies in Germany," 29.

25. Klaus Murmann, "Management's View: Structural Problems of the German Economy and the Challenge of Remaining Competitive in the Global Market," The 1994 Dieter zur Loye Lecture Series, 6.

26. *The Week in Germany*, 11 April 1997, 5.

27. *The Week in Germany,* 20 February 1998, 5.

28. *The Week in Germany,* 5 December 1997, 5.

29. *The Week in Germany,* 25 April 1997, 5.

30. *Statistical Pocket Book of the German Democratic Republic* (East Berlin: Staatsverlag der DDR), various years.

31. Hartmut Zimmermann, "The GDR in the 1970's," *Problems of Communism* 27, no. 2 (March-April 1978): 18.

32. *GDR: 100 Questions 100 Answers* (East Berlin: Zeit im Bild, 1978), 98.

33. David M. Keithly, "Agricultural Policies and Markets in the New Germany," *Global Economic Review* 26, no. 2 (Summer 1997): 5.

34. Daniel S. Fogel and Suzanne Etcheverry, "Reforming the Economies of Central and Eastern Europe," in *Managing in Emerging Market Economies,* Daniel S. Fogel, ed. (Boulder, Colo.: Westview Press, 1994), 9-10.

35. *DDR Handbuch,* vol. 1 (Bonn: Bundesministerium für innerdeutsche Beziehungen, 1985), 16-22.

36. Manfred Wilke, "Die Kritiker der ökonomischen Entscheidungen im Prozeß der Wiedervereinigung übersehen oft die katastrophale Ausgangslage," *Politische Meinung* 41, no. 315 (February 1996): 23-9.

37. Ullrich Heilemann and Reimut Jochimsen, *Christmas in July? The Political Economy of German Unification Reconsidered* (Washington, D.C.: Brookings Institution, 1993), 18.

38. *Die Tätigkeit der Treuhandanstalt* (Bonn: Bundesministerium der Finanzen, 1991), 8-13; "Germany," *The Economist,* 14 September 1991, 24.

39. "Model Vision," 27.

40. Kazimierz Z. Poznanski, "Property Rights Perspective on Evolution of Communist-Type Economies," in *Constructing Capitalism,* Kazimierz Z. Poznanski, ed. (Boulder, Colo.: Westview Press, 1992), 87-88.

41. Fogel and Etcheverry, "Reforming the Economies," 15.

42. Heilemann and Jochimsen, *Christmas in July?,* 10.

43. *The Week in Germany,* 28 February 1997, 5.

44. "Model Vision," 10.

45. *Unsere Landwirtschaft im Wandel* (Bonn: Bundesministerium für Ernährung, Landwirtschaft und Forsten, 1994), 28.

46. David Schoenbaum and Elizabeth Pond, *The German Question and Other German Questions* (New York: St. Martin's Press, 1996), 111.

47. "Model Vision," 10.

48. *The Week in Germany,* 3 October 1997, 2.

49. *The Economist,* "Divided Still: A Survey of Germany," 9 November 1996, 9.

50. *The Week in Germany,* 28 November 1997, 5.

51. Heilemann and Jochimsen, *Christmas in July?,* 31.

52. Domenico Mario Nuti and Richard Portes, "Central Europe: The Way Forward," in *Economic Transformation in Central Europe,* Richard Portes, ed. (London: Centre for Economic Policy Research, 1994), 16.

53. "Divided Still," 4-5.

54. *DDR Handbuch*, vol. 1, 122-130.

55. Morris Bornstein, "East-West Economic Relations," in *The Soviet Economy: Continuity and Change*, Morris Bornstein, ed. (Boulder, Colo.: Westview Press, 1981), 208

56. *GDR: 100 Questions 100 Answers*, 97-99.

57. "Divided Still," 9.

58. *The Week in Germany*, 27 February 1998, 5.

59. *DDR Handbuch*, vol. 1, 126-28.

10

Welfare State Reform:
The Gridlock of Social Entitlements

Irwin Collier

Over the past half century the social market economy of the Federal Republic of Germany has evolved into a vast and dense net of social entitlements that not only protects individuals and their dependants from the classic threats of premature death, disability, sickness, poverty in old age and unemployment, but is also intended to promote a greater equality of income along with a socially guaranteed minimum standard of living for the economically weak. In addition to this latter redistributive function, the institutions of the German welfare state have also been expected to support such social institutions as the family and to equalize educational opportunities. From slightly over one-fifth of the gross domestic product in 1960, the official social budget for Germany has grown to about one-third of GDP, of which two-thirds flows through the statutory systems of social insurance (pensions, health, unemployment, long-term care) with the remaining third representing tax-financed transfers of one form or other.

Social entitlement spending on this scale requires an equally massive scale of taxation and social insurance contributions. Both social entitlements and ways to fund them can significantly affect economic decisions of labor force participation, hiring, production, and spending. Social policy makers, like doctors prescribing medicine, need to be aware of adverse side effects and treatment interaction problems, especially where heavy dosage is involved. Furthermore there is no guarantee that the value of entitlements and the sources of their finance will automatically remain in balance with each other. The fiscal crisis of the welfare state is not a mere figment of reactionary imaginations. It is here, it will not go away by itself and, making matters more complicated, it is not Germany's sole economic problem.

High unemployment, the economic consequences of German unification and the aging of the German population would each by itself constitute an extreme test of the capacity of the German social safety net and the strength of the economy that supports it. Together these circumstances will force significant changes in the German welfare state that will dominate policy debate for this and the coming legislative periods in Germany.

A Chronic Condition, a Severe Shock, and a Bleak Future

The present German unemployment problem has been a long time in coming. Figure 10.1 displays the eerie upward trend of measured unemployment in West Germany from the early 1960s to the present. The four vertical shaded columns mark recession years when real GDP actually fell in West Germany. One sees that starting with the OPEC induced slowdown in economic activity in the first half of the 1970s, each successive recession managed to ratchet the unemployment rate up to a higher level. While each of the first three recessions displayed in figure 10.1 was followed by a slight and gradual reduction in the unemployment rate, the post-unification recession was followed by a significant period of further rising unemployment rates. Long gone is the confidence that the German social market economy would deliver low unemployment rates. Instead we observe a blame game between employers, unions and government on the one hand, and between governing coalition and parliamentary opposition on the other hand. This fundamental trend of rising unemployment is the chronic problem in German labor markets, and one that long predates German unification. An important consequence of unemployment at this scale is that the financial health of all the systems of social insurance become threatened as increases in unemployment lead to increases in certain kinds of social spending (early retirement pensions as well as unemployment benefits) and a drop in the social insurance contributions (payroll taxes). The reemphasis on demand-side economics (i.e., the use of discretionary fiscal and/or monetary policy for macroeconomic stabilization) by Federal Finance Minister Oskar Lafontaine and his advisers is entirely legitimate for the top several percent of unemployment. However figure 10.1 does indicate that below the surface of "business cycle unemployment" lurks a far deeper supply-side problem in German labor markets.

Turning to figure 10.2 one can see how the collapse of economic activity in the new federal states has contributed to the now chronic imbalance between social insurance contributions and social entitlements. The German Council of Economic Advisers in their annual reports have calculated a more accurate measure of actual unemployment, especially in the new states, consistent with the classic definition of unemployment: including all those persons able and willing to work at existing wages but who do not have jobs. The official measure of unemployment excludes

Figure 10.1. Unemployment rates in West Germany, 1961-1998
(Columns show years of negative real GDP growth)

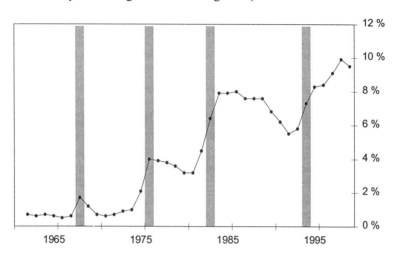

Figure 10.2. Hidden and open unemployment in Germany, 1980-1998
(Percentage)

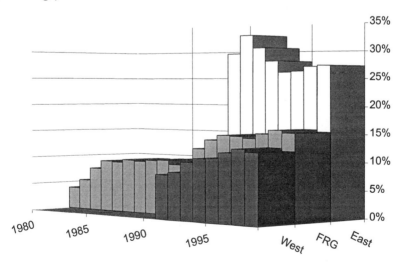

Source for both figures: *Annual Reports* of the Council of Economic Experts.

workers receiving early retirement pensions and those in retraining or requalification programs that were introduced on a massive scale in the new states to catch many of those without jobs. While the peak of unemployment in the new states was passed several years ago, the enormous difference with respect to the western levels remains one of the striking legacies of the postunification crash in production in the East.

When ones adds together all the different kinds of social spending on pensions, health, labor market policies, child benefits, and so forth one obtains the so-called social budget that can be divided by the level of gross domestic product to provide a rough measure of the relative importance of social spending in German economic activity. This proportion is plotted in figure 10.3. Besides the marked difference between the proportions in East and West that mirrors the difference in unemployment experienced in the two regions, one can see that the years of the Kohl government were ones essentially of stability in the share of social spending, with an ever so slight downward tendency from the high level that had been achieved by the end of the earlier period of SPD government. However, once the massive transfers from West to East became necessary, the share of social spending in Germany as a whole began to climb again.

The lion's share of social spending in Germany is gathered through payroll taxes split evenly between employers and employees. In contrast to the relatively slow growth in the share of social spending seen in figure 10.3, the steady increase in the four social insurance payroll taxes seen in figure 10.4 is quite dramatic, almost doubling over the period. An important issue for the impact of these taxes on labor supply is the extent to which such contributions are seen as equivalent to the present value of expected future entitlements. Even if the link between contribution and entitlement is tight in that sense, there can still be an efficiency loss if people are constrained to buy either more or less social protection that they would actually demand at such a "price." However when the link between contributions and expected benefits is weak, social insurance contributions take on the character of a tax, that is, the amount of entitlement is hardly changed by changes in social insurance contributions so there is an incentive to avoid the payment altogether. Evasion takes the form of shifts into types of employment not subject to these taxes or into self-employment.

The shift in the burden of the sum of social insurance payroll taxes and all other taxes expressed as a proportion of GDP shows that both the share of taxes as well as the share of social contributions have risen, though the rise in the social insurance taxes has been definitely the larger of the two (figure 10.5).

Up to this point we have been looking at the world through a rearview mirror. Policy makers of course should really keep their eyes on the road ahead. You do not have to be a trained actuary to see that the German pay-as-you-go (unfunded) system of old age pensions is about to drive into a demographic wall of old people. There are many ways of expressing the economic impact of this unfavorable demo-

Figure 10.3. Social expenditure quotient in Germany, 1960-1997
(Percentage of GDP)

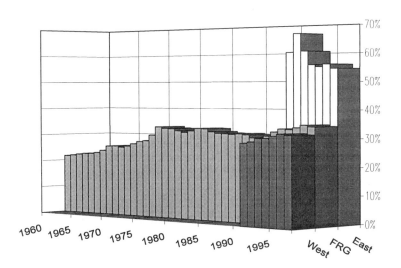

Source: *Annual Reports* of the Council of Economic Experts.

Figure 10.4. Social insurance contribution rates 1960-1997
(Western Länder only, end of year, in percentage)

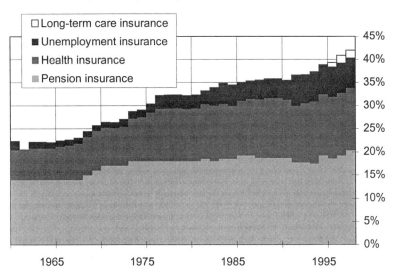

Source: *Sozialbericht 1998.*

graphic trend. One way combines demographic projections with economic forecasts to calculate what the projected payroll tax rate would have to be for a working population in a country with low birth rates (currently ten Germans only leave seven offspring) and where life expectancies have grown seven years over the previous quarter of a century. Even allowing for an average of 250,000 immigrants annually until the middle of the next century, under the benefit structure of the reforms passed by the Kohl government (but suspended for the next two years or until the red-green coalition puts into place its own pension reform), there would have to be an increase in the combined employer-employee contribution of about half: from about 20 percent to somewhere near 30 percent. The projection displayed in figure 10.6 is taken from the special report written by the scientific advisory council of the Economics Ministry and submitted in March 1998.

A slightly different light is cast on the matter when one estimates the implicit rates of return to public pension contributions for individual birth cohorts. These are displayed in figure 10.7 and compared with two other rates of return. The upper line offers as a benchmark the expected real rate of return were people to place their contributions into a fund that held ten-year German government bonds instead of paying for pensions of the currently retired to acquire an entitlement drawn from a pool filled with contributions from workers in the future. As can be seen from figure 10.7, this implicit real rate of return on pension contributions has steadily dropped, essentially following the path of the rate of real growth of payroll (which may be regarded as the sum of the growth rate of covered employment times the growth rate of the average real wage of covered employment). The downward path reflects the forecasted rising ratio of retirees to people in covered employment. The meaning of the growing difference between the real market rate of interest and the implicit real return on pension contributions is that the pension contribution will be perceived to an ever increasing degree as a tax. The "return" on one's current contributions into the public retirement scheme will be a pension that a funded retirement account would provide at only *half the cost* in contributions. The next two decades provide an opportunity to smooth some of the burden of the disproportionate growth of the elderly population across several generations. This was essentially the motivation of the Kohl government's start of a gradual reduction in the ratio of average retirement benefits to average net wages.

Keeping in mind both the current problem of high unemployment (with genuinely pathological levels throughout the new states of Germany) and the long-term structural problems of the retirement and long-term care insurance systems, we consider next what will be the likely course of social policy reform under the Schröder government.

Figure 10.5. Taxes and social insurance contributions 1960-1998
(Percentage of GDP)

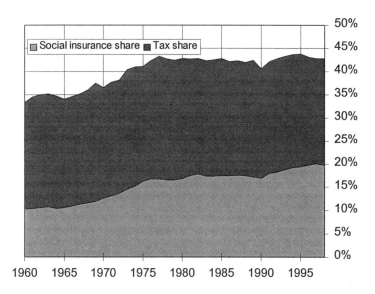

Source: *Annual Reports* of the Council of Economic Experts.

Figure 10.6. Projected payroll tax rates for the German public pension system

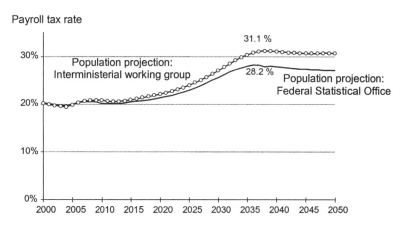

Source: March 1998 report of the academic advisory council to the Federal Ministry of Economics.

Figure 10.7. Comparisons of projected rates of return

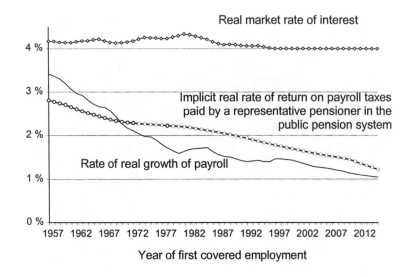

Source: March 1998 report of the academic advisory council to the Federal Ministry of Economics.

The Red-Green Coalition Agreement:
Stop or Go for Welfare State Reform?

Compared to the promises of campaign platforms, coalition agreements of a new government are at least a marginally better indicator for the drift of future policy. The stability of this coalition for a given legislative period will depend upon the terms of the coalition agreement being respected. Nonetheless down the electoral road voters will almost certainly judge this government according to the same standard as they did the last—whether a significant improvement in employment is delivered after four years in power. The outline of future red-green social policy can be found somewhere between the mutual statements of intent found in the coalition agreement and the electoral necessity of reversing the upward ratchet of unemployment seen in figure 10.1. In this section I offer the reader an interpretative summary of those sections of the red-green coalition agreement that discuss German social policy in light of this important electoral constraint. Italics will designate text taken directly from the red-green coalition agreement.

The coalition agreement pledges *to protect the individual against life's major risks*, meaning both premature death and long life, sickness, unemployment and need for long-term care. There is no indication that the list of "major" risks will become longer, but one big question begs resolution: how are we to draw the line between major risks (i.e., those that it makes sense to share) and minor risks (i.e., those that it makes better sense for each of us to deal with on our own)? Much of the controversy about health care (e.g., the use of co-payments and deductibles) is concerned precisely with where to draw this line.

The welfare state is seen to work best when it is built upon the foundation of *the solidarity of all members of society*. Because of the historical origin of the grand institutions of social insurance as employment-related schemes, participation in the public pension system or unemployment insurance system has not been required of the self-employed, nor have contributions been collected from the so-called negligibly employed (West 620/East 580 DM per month). Also outside these systems are certain occupational groups, in particular the career civil service who, because of lifetime job tenure, are not subject to the risk of unemployment and because employer-provided health benefits are free from contribution to both the unemployment insurance as well as the statutory health insurance systems. The general unwillingness to consider social entitlement cuts as anything but a step in the direction of Manchester capitalism is often masked by a declaration that German social policy does not have an "expenditure problem" but that it has a "revenue problem." Hence, the search for ways to broaden the social insurance revenue base is regarded by many in the government coalition as the only legitimate fix for the financial crisis of the German welfare state.[1] The problem with this view is that it ignores the fact that the people who are brought into the system today will have new entitlements tomorrow as a result. Whatever budgetary relief is gained in the short-run (essentially by bringing in contributors and not beneficiaries) can only come at the cost of a larger scale imbalance between social expenditures and revenues in the future, as long as the underlying structural imbalance is not corrected.

The expressed intent of including *all retirement systems* in the pension reform intended by this coalition appears to be just a populist appeal to get career civil servants pensions on a comparable footing with employees generally. But given the fact that the writing of legislation is firmly in the hands of career civil servants and the judges who will interpret and apply the law are all locked in as well, it is hard to imagine a turn other than a symbolic sacrifice to the public pension system of schoolteachers and university professors. To the extent that existing pension and health entitlements of such groups are respected, there is a mere gain in fiscal transparency without any genuine budgetary gain over the long run. To the extent that a real budgetary gain is achieved, such reform is a targeted tax increase.

In addition to protecting individuals from the major risks of life through universal solidarity, the Schröder government pledges itself to *expanding equality of opportunity*, implicitly seen as a necessary condition for a greater role for individual responsibility and self-reliance in dealing with life's risks. The dogmatic insistence on zero-tuition for German universities is typically justified as a necessary condition for equal opportunity to higher education. An aggressive affirmative action program from occupational training programs, through higher education and private employment practices will be discussed below.

When the coalition agreement speaks of modernizing and further developing the systems that provide social security, the issue of the *accuracy of targeting* benefits with its emphasis on the goal of poverty prevention receives a prominent role. Oskar Lafontaine's early trial balloon regarding means-testing for unemployment benefits or long-term care benefits has met a barrage of opposition polemics to the effect that his proposals if implemented would mean the replacement of the German *Sozialstaat* with a (gasp) welfare state.[2] This is an area (much as his willingness to consider demand-side macroeconomic policy) where Lafontaine appears to be much nearer a sensible policy than the Bundestag opposition.

Actually no different than anyone else in Germany, the red-green coalition wants an *affordable public pension system that guarantees an appropriate living standard.* The important question is what do we expect this government to do when the twin targets of lower contribution rates and higher pensions come into conflict with each other. Will the public pension system cut future pension entitlements to stabilize the contributions or will it increase future contributions, or more likely subsidies from outside the system, to maintain future entitlements? There is more or less a consensus in German politics (except for the years immediately preceding and following a Bundestag election) that the future entitlement will have to adjust, should demographic trends go as expected.

However, the logic of electoral politics is not the same as that governing the long-run feasibility of a pay-as-you-go financed public pension system. Thus the first thing on the red-green agenda was to postpone the introduction of planned reductions in the relationship between average pensions and average covered labor earnings introduced by the previous government (more below). A cynic could regard this as nothing more than a post-electoral sleight of hand until the red-green coalition can put together its own promised major pension reform in 1999.

The decision to suspend the slowdown in pension increases does mean an increase in pension expenditures above original projections, so that additional revenues are needed to fill the gap. This is where the tapping of the so-called "negligible jobs" as sources of revenue was to fit in, as well as a dramatic tightening of the definition of self-employment in order to obtain contributions from the "pseudo-self-employed," characterized as consultants who work essentially for only one contractor.

According to the red-green coalition agreement the pension reform will take the three existing "pension pillars": the public pension system, company pension systems, and private saving and life insurance and augment them with far greater employee ownership of corporate equity and stronger elements of profit sharing in labor compensation. Unfortunately the most innovative aspect is also the most ambiguous at the present time, so that the reader is simply well-advised to monitor the employee ownership and profit sharing elements as red-green pension reform begins to take concrete form.

While the public pension system will remain the mainstay of old-age income maintenance, there is very serious consideration of using some of the contributions collected to build a reserve fund from which pensions can be paid during the second quarter of the next century to avoid a sharp increase in contribution rates. Those pension entitlements that result from time being credited for raising children in the home will be tax financed (i.e., all forms of income to form the tax base) rather than contribution financed where only covered employment income forms the tax base.

Besides the introduction of greater elements of employee ownership and profit sharing into old-age income maintenance, the second major area of reform would transform the public pension system to a general principle of independent individual pensions, in the first instance the creation of independent old age pensions for women whose market work histories have left them dependent on their husbands' pensions and/or survivors' benefits. Such a transformation would involve a complex interaction between the issues of minimum income, survivors' pension rights, and pension rights from part-time work.

The next big-ticket item in German social spending is the system of health insurance. Throughout the red-green coalition, but especially within the SPD, one encounters a belief that it is morally objectionable to have different standards of medical care for different segments of the population, especially with respect to the "haves-more" versus the "haves-less." The fact that the former drive nicer cars and take nicer vacations than the latter only offends a mere preference for equality of outcomes, other things being held equal. In contrast differences in medical treatment are regarded as offensive as, say, a different right to vote for people who are married than for those who are single. This means that the scope for experimentation with the use of deductibles and co-payments (understood broadly to include the use of fractions of days of paid vacation to maintain 100 percent replacement levels of sick pay) has become much more limited.

Section VIII of the coalition agreement discusses women's employment issues, an area where we are likely to see radical deviation from existing social and labor policy over the coming months and years. During the next legislative period the German federal government can be expected to become very active in promoting the professional integration as well as the advancement of women at all levels of business and government administration. The red-green coalition promises increased support for women going into business for themselves, but one would be surprised if much action follows in light of the mixed signals the red-green coalition has given those who would set up businesses for themselves (it seems that self-employment is regarded as honorable only when social-insurance covered jobs are generated *for others*). The explicit statement of intent to introduce binding rules that would regulate the promotion of women that "must be applied in the private sector" as well as in the public sector should be regarded as much more serious. The promise to implement the European legal mandate against wage discrimination according to the principle "equal wages for work of comparable worth" is a fairly clear indicator that German labor courts will soon play a major role in deciding the issue of comparable worth in wage/salary discrimination cases.

No discussion of the red-green coalition would be complete without some mention of the ecological tax reform that will increase energy taxes and earmark the new tax revenue to help reduce payroll fringe costs. This is one of few supply-side measures seriously being proposed by the Schröder government to address Germany's employment problem. It is certainly a less objectionable way of promoting energy conservation than the suggestion by a prominent Green politician before the election that people should really only fly to their vacation destinations every other year (a reminder of the time in the GDR when every other street light was turned off for the same reason). Nonetheless, this is merely a green pill with a social coating to help the senior coalition partner swallow it. Social-ecological tax reform is unlikely to make much of a difference for the financial sustainability of the German welfare state.

First Stop

On December 10, 1998, the Law to Rectify Social Insurance and Protect Employees' Rights together with the Law to Strengthen Solidarity in the Statutory Health Insurance System of the red-green coalition passed the Bundestag. This legislation for the most part represents a clear reversal of several of the modest social policy reforms that had been introduced at the end of the Kohl era, which were nothing if not timid to a fault. Their undoing was declared to be the down payment on red-green campaign promises. While the re-implementation of the social status quo ex ante does not necessarily constitute a deathblow to the sort of serious reform ultimately required for the long-term sustainability of the social market economy in Germany, it does appear that social sacred cows will slow down reform traffic for the time being. *Der Reformstau geht weiter!*

Pending a promised red-green pension reform law that is to take shape by the end of 1999, the so-called *Korrekturgesetz* suspended the planned slow-down in the growth of pensions in 1999 and 2000 that would have resulted from the introduction of a so-called demographic factor in the formula used to index pensions. This planned slow-down was part of a gradual adjustment of the relationship between average pensions and average net labor earnings from the present level of 70 percent to 64 percent in the middle third of the next century that was needed to avoid even greater increases in future contribution rates than currently forecast. A leading U.S. economist, Martin Feldstein, once commented on the subject of re-forming the U.S. social security system that if one wants to get out of the hole one is stuck in, then the very first principle is to stop digging deeper. The Schröder government apparently believes it needs to dig for a couple years before *it* decides to stop digging. Similar reversals were the fate of the Kohl government's tightening of eligibility requirements for disability pensions and measures that would have increased the age of retirement for the severely handicapped.

In an attempt to provide small businesses greater flexibility in hiring and dis-missal, the Kohl government had raised the threshold for companies falling un-der the law covering employee dismissals to ten employees. With the first major red-green social legislation, this threshold is once again six employees and above. Reinstatement of "social-criteria" (e.g., married or single) to be employed in deter-mining dismissals in the event of required job cuts takes away some of the adjust-ment room for companies forced to deal with large unexpected drops in demand. Finally, one of the most holy of the sacred social cows has been restored in German labor law: all employees are to be paid *by law* 100 percent of their normal labor earnings for sick leave (though forgone overtime not included), as opposed to a formula that would have given employees a choice between accepting employer provided 80 percent sick pay or trading five sick days at full pay for one day of paid vacation *unless otherwise negotiated in a collective bargaining agreement.*

In order to "reestablish order" in German labor markets, the new coalition has empowered the federal minister of labor to set standards for wage rates in con-struction, even for businesses and workers not participating in the collective bar-gaining process. General contractors are directly liable for the violations of their contractors, for example, for violations of minimum wages and contributions to the vacation fund of the construction industry. Violations of the principle of the same wage for the same job at the same location as well as the undermining of the principle of social insurance coverage for paid regular dependent employment are seen as the result of the "wage-dumping" of foreign firms and domestic firms hiring foreign workers.

The other labor market threat is the conversion of social-insurance-covered jobs into noncovered "pseudo-self-employment." The new legislation provides a formal definition: Pseudo-self-employment is presumed when two of the fol-lowing four indicators are observed:

- when a self-employed person has no employees (other than family relations) in social-insurance-covered jobs;
- when the activity in question is performed for a single contracting party;
- when, the activity is carried out as it would be by a paid employee, for example, the contractor is included in the formal organization plan of work, or the contractor is subject to close supervision and direction; and/or
- when the person in question is not active on the market, for example, actively searching for new clients/customers.

If the "contractor" is not able to meet the burden of proof that there is genuine self-employment, then normal social insurance contributions by both parties will be required.[3]

As a first red-green step to transfer some of the pension burden to the broader shoulders of the federal tax system, pension insurance contributions during leave time to raise children will be paid by the federal government as will the costs of topping up pensions in the new states starting in 1999 (such topping up is required whenever the existing pension entitlement from earlier rules exceeds the pension entitlement under current rules). From earmarked proceeds from the planned eco-tax, there will be a reduction of the contribution rate to pension insurance beginning in the second quarter of 1999 of .8 percent, for a rate of 19.5 percent.

The attempt by the previous federal government to clear a path between the significant health risks that are appropriate for health insurance and the small risks that could be acceptably and effectively born, at least in part, by each household has been suspiciously regarded as an attempt to put a private foot in a social door. Compared to the militant tone of the anti-copayment rhetoric regarding payment for prescription drugs, the actual changes from the proposed increases by the old government appear more like token changes, for example, a 1 DM reduction in co-payments for a prescription.

Remember the GDR?

In the last years of the old German Democratic Republic every minor change in economic policy was declared a part of the perfection of that real and existing economic system. The policy chatter heard today in Germany about improving the social market economy to meet the challenges of globalization or to address the problems on the rapidly approaching demographic horizon sounds about as convincing. There is still insufficient awareness that the good fortune (strong productivity growth and nonfalling population) that made an unfunded system of old-age pensions work so well in the past has in fact run out, little sense that perhaps policymakers of the past and present do bear responsibility for current dilemmas of social policy. Instead parties in power try to paint those who stand in opposition to their "improvements" as those who would block genuine social progress. Parties out of power are quick to point to particular entitlement cuts suggested by the government as threatening the destruction of the German social way of life.

Behind the rhetorical facades of parliamentary democracy is a difficult reality that all serious contenders for power who would do good must ultimately deal with. Interlocking systems of social entitlements in Germany hinder the transfer of both human and nonhuman resources from relatively low productivity uses (of which unemployment represents the polar case of an absolutely no-productivity use) to relatively high productivity uses. These systems have weakened the capacity of the economy to innovate and to respond to ever changing challenges, the ultimate source of rising living standards. The strains from the disproportionate expansion of social entitlements relative to economic potential through German unification, the integration of product markets especially within Europe but also in general across the globe, and the unavoidable shift of the structure of the German population have forced major rethinking in Germany and elsewhere. Yet social policy reform essentially remains a political game where winning depends on the skillful application of the so-called Saint Florian's principle, inspired by the following short prayer to the patron saint of firefighters: Oh Lord, please spare my house from lightning . . . let it strike somebody else's house! In the mad scramble of special interest pleading it is sometimes difficult to keep one's attention on genuine problems and to avoid the political sideshows for a rise or fall of any particular social insurance contribution rate of a few tenths of a percentage point in a given year.[4] And it will take considerably more than legal walls against "pseudo-self-employment" and "social dumping" on construction sites in Berlin to take the German social market economy safely through the next century.

Notes

1. If any significant cuts take place on the entitlement side, these will be reductions in social entitlements for the "better-off."

2. The distinction is essentially between a social insurance system in which the expected value of benefits from participation is mostly determined by an individual's contribution history versus schemes relying on tax-based redistribution to the poor.

3. There is yet a further distinction: the "as-if-employed" self-employed. These are people who themselves do not have employees in the social insurance system and who generally have a single source of work contracts. Even if the presumption of pseudo-self-employment is overruled, these people must participate in the public pension system, with a few exceptions.

4. One need only recall the political posturing about the "importance" of the 3 percent of GDP government budget deficit for allowing a country to participate in the European Monetary Union to begin to suspect that the function of such statistical fetishes is precisely to block the discussion of substantive issues.

11

Germany and European Integration: Bonn between Berlin and Brussels

Michael G. Huelshoff

The end of the Cold War and the unification of Germany have thrust the Germans onto the centerstage of European and world politics. Germany has the largest and strongest economy among the West European states, overshadowed globally only by the United States and Japan. Germany also has significantly strengthened its position within the European Union (EU), the largest economic bloc in the world. As memories of past German aggression fade, and as the stability of democratic norms in the new Germany is reaffirmed, it is asserted that the Germans are for the first time since 1945 ready to become a "normal" participant in European and world politics.

In this chapter, I examine one dimension of Germany's new position in world politics, its relations with the EU. I argue that the traditional integrative role that the Germans have played in Europe—an argument that has been overstated—is under pressure. The financial and political costs of unifying Germany, the domestic political costs of pushing European Monetary Union (EMU), and clashes over basic notions of the government's role in addressing Europe's key economic problem, unemployment, all have contributed to a degree of drift in German EU policy. This drift is more than a simple tactical hold until EMU is completed, or a reflection of the German government's domestic political weakness. The growing disparity between the definition and realization of German and non-German goals and interests, heightened domestic dissatisfaction with European integration, and growing financial pressure on Germany are encouraging Bonn to resist, at least in the near term, broadening European cooperation. While it is too early to determine how the new German government will differ from the old regime, initial signs point to little more than a change in emphasis. Without a focused Germany, therefore, we can expect that the EU will continue in its current period of relative stagnation.

The chapter begins with an exploration of the conventional wisdom about Germany in Europe—the argument that the Germans are "good Europeans." I note at the end of this section that the argument has been over-drawn—there are numerous instances where German preferences have been in sharp contrast to those of other EU members and EU institutions. The second section turns to current problems in German EU policy preferences. I examine German policy on three important issues facing Germany and Europe: fighting unemployment, managing the internal market, and completing economic and monetary union. Here I argue that, much as in the early 1980s, the Germans are moving into a period where internal debates and uncertainty are resulting in a loss of German focus upon European integration. Finally, I conclude with a brief discussion of the implications of this for German foreign policy and the development of the EU.

Germany in Europe

At the level of political rhetoric, German politicians, like many politicians in most of the countries in the EU, express almost uniform belief in the wisdom and importance of European integration. Only in some—and not all—of the political fringes is it possible to find elites who do not chant the mantra of European cooperation, integration, and good neighborliness. In Germany, for example, opponents of the EU are found only in some (and currently the politically weak) elements of the Greens, some members of the PDS, and in some leaders of the far-right parties. Even the few dissidents often support the ideal of cooperation, if opposing its current institutional form. Elite-level commitment is not just political rhetoric: there are good reasons for this. When asked, well over half of the populations in almost all the member countries of the EU (the exceptions are, not surprisingly, the United Kingdom and Denmark) express the belief that European integration is a "good thing."[1] While it might be expected that politicians have helped to create this public climate, it is still true today that any politician in any democracy who ignores such sentiments runs real political risks.[2]

There are good historical reasons for such strong mass and elite support for European integration. When the EEC (later the EC, and now the EU) was founded in 1958, Franco-German rivalry had resulted in three major wars in less than a century. The EU contributed to ending this rivalry. Further, the last round of Franco-German rivalry, World War II, unleashed unprecedented barbarity in Europe—the Holocaust. As Markovits and Reich have argued, the "historical memory" of German savagery has scarred not only the Germans, but also many of their neighbors, both in and outside the EU, who were the targets of Nazism.[3] The impact of history can be seen in the deeply personal commitment to European integration of many German politicians who experienced the war. Chancellor Kohl was indicative of this point. The EU has contributed to the clean break with history that the Germans have striven to achieve in the past few decades.

It is therefore not surprising that at the core of the German position on the EU is a very high level of elite and public commitment to European integration.[4] If public opinion and history help to explain this commitment, so too do economics and politics. The German economy has long been relatively resource-poor, requiring the export of finished goods to pay for imports of raw materials and food. In 1996, 57 percent of German exports went to EU members, and 57 percent of their imports came from other EU members. German foreign investment is also heavily skewed toward the EU. Thus, the Germans have a real economic interest in European integration.

Yet Germany's preferences in the negotiations leading to the Treaties of Rome in the late 1950s were more than an assertion of traditional German pursuit of access to markets and investment opportunities. Indeed, some German business people in the mid-1950s feared that French dominance of the EU would unleash a wave of dirigisme, or state management of the economy, that would engender protectionism on the part of Europe's trading partners. This could hardly have been good for German economic interests outside the EU.[5] There was also opposition from other social actors, including the trade unions and the SPD. Why, then, did the Germans sign the Treaties of Rome?

Konrad Adenauer, Germany's first post-war chancellor, had much more than economic growth in mind when he committed Germany to European integration. Adenauer hoped that the EEC might become a means to reacquire German sovereignty. In the rather counterintuitive and ultimately brilliant logic of Adenauer's analysis, the only way the Germans could become truly independent and sovereign was to demonstrate that the Bonn Republic was willing to sacrifice its independence and sovereignty to collective management. Adenauer's personal dominance of post-war German foreign policymaking meant that there were few effective domestic opponents to the linking of Germany to Europe, whether political or institutional, in Germany. One of Adenauer's lasting impacts on German politics was that this value-based commitment to Europe disseminated throughout society, especially in the mass political parties, the CDU and the SPD.

Are, then, the Germans "good Europeans"? As Adenauer's example suggests, it is very difficult to disentangle German interests from European interests—by tying Germany to European integration in this fashion, Adenauer clearly saw little or no difference between his perception of German interests and European integration. What was good for Europe was good for Germany; what was good for Germany was also (presumably) good for Europe. This example demonstrates a very basic point about European integration. Just as it is notoriously difficult to define a nation's national interest, it is also difficult to define what is Europe's interest. Interests, be they national or regional, are inherently contested concepts. The Single European Act (SEA), for example, can be conceived as a project that is inherently collective. Even though some national economies may benefit more than others, all have access, and all define the internal market. Yet plans for monetary union, beginning with the Werner Report in 1970 and through the Maastricht criterion for EMU membership, all carry the stamp of German conceptions of how a common currency should be created and managed. Is EMU a German interest, or a European interest? Simply put, it is logically impossible, and empirically very difficult, to separate individual (national) interests from collective (European) interests.

Regardless, at a very general level, one can argue that German and European interests coincide in significant ways. The original Treaties of Rome were, fundamentally, about creating an internal market in Europe, and most sectors of the German economy have grown in its aftermath. The logic of the internal market has also disciplined the German economy, forced open otherwise protected sectors such as foods, transport, and energy. EMU can be conceived of as a Europeanization of German monetary interests. The same is true of the so-called "flanking" policy areas, social and environmental policy. Broad swaths of European-level policy initiatives seem largely consistent with German economic and social interests. These Europeanized policy areas are also more than just an example of the ability of the Germans to dominate agenda-setting in Europe. German interests coincide on many major points with collective interests in Europe. If this were not so, then it would be hard to imagine how all the other EU members could have allowed themselves to be so dominated by the Germans so soon after the end of World War II.

The combination of history, economics, and politics has also contributed to the ideological orientation in Germany that favors European integration. This is seen formally in the German Basic Law, or Constitution. Article 24 of the original draft of the Basic Law allowed German governments to transfer sovereignty to international institutions. Article 23 of the amended Basic Law specifies that German politicians must pursue European integration. It is rare that a constitution is so specific as to the foreign policy goals of the state. Further, the rather weak basis for German democracy after World War II was strengthened by, among other factors, German commitment to European integration. As Anderson and Goodman put it, after 1945 Germany chose to define its self-identity in Europe.[6] If, as Markovits and Reich suggest, ideology and self-identity define interests, then German support for the ideal of European integration has been fused with the economic and political benefits that Germany expects to receive from European integration.

This fusing of ideological preferences and material interests has also helped to institutionalize German commitment to European integration. German policy-makers routinely include consideration of European-wide issues when making domestic policy, leading some to argue that Germany has become a "Europeanized" state.[7] Yet the German state is also institutionally decentralized, meaning that governmental authority is divided between the federal and the state governments, and that the federal government itself is divided.[8] What makes the German state "European," though, is the impact of the aforementioned factors: history, economics, politics, and ideology. Even if decision-making authority in German is fractured, the context within which these institutions operate biases them toward European ways of thinking, arguably to a greater extent than other EU member governments.

This is the argument for the Germans as good Europeans. One should be careful, however, not to over-emphasize the positive role of Germany in Europe. In fact, there have been a number of times when German analysis of the utility of further European integration was negative. German Chancellor Schmidt, for example, was noted for taking a rather national view of European politics during a time when cooperation in Europe seemed especially fragile.[9] Further, there have been a number of times when Germany failed to support key European initiatives. While, or perhaps because, Germany is the largest net contributor to the EU budget, successive German governments have opposed open-ended commitments of funds (except the Common Agricultural Policy, where German governments have long worked to enhance the welfare of farmers, despite the cost). Additionally, after the collapse of the stable exchange rate regime in the spring of 1973, and the oil shocks later the same year, the Germans resisted attempts by their EU partners to stimulate the European economy by stimulating the German economy.[10] Much the same was true during the French franc crisis in the summer of 1993, when the German central bank, the Bundesbank, refused to support the franc. The result was a significant weakening of the European Monetary System, the precursor to monetary union.

German reticence toward European initiatives is not limited to major fiscal and financial issues. German governments have fought hard to weaken Commission policy proposals to create open and subsidy-free markets for coal, electric power, transport, insurance, shipbuilding, aircraft, food, public procurement, and investment in insurance and pension funds.[11] It is also quite ironic that many of the landmark European Court of Justice (ECJ) rulings that underpin the internal market—long a German policy goal—have come at the expense of the Germans, including the Creme de Cassis, and beer and sausage purity rulings. This is a long list of exceptions to the "Germany as good European" conventional wisdom.

Furthermore, there are good reasons for believing that the Germans are moving into another period of pessimism about European integration. In the next section, I examine German positions on EU issues in three policy fields: social policy, the regulation of the internal market, and monetary union. In these areas, I find that German positions are changing. In the first case, the Kohl government found itself increasingly unwilling to support the Commission's agenda on social policy making, even the rather limited goals of the Santer Commission. The likely preferences of the new government are uncertain, but there are likely to be elements of both continuity and change. Growing skepticism about the utility of more social policy is increasingly coupled with impatience regarding limitations that EU law places on national flexibility. The question of the functioning of the internal market raises a different set of problems for the Germans. Here the main question facing Germany and Europe is the regulation of subsidies, especially subsidies granted to firms in the troubled eastern states in united Germany. Finally, in the case of monetary union, the problem is not that the Germans are unwilling to support monetary union. Indeed, the government has been very successful in fighting off efforts to either place political constraints on the future European Central Bank (ECB) or to be overly strict in interpreting the convergence criteria. Rather, the problem that monetary union poses for the Germans is its domestic political implications—in short, the political costs of implementing a vastly unpopular policy in Germany.

Despite these problems, it is not the case that Germany is becoming disengaged from the EU. Germany will not leave the EU, or allow it to fall back into a period of morbidity. Rather, I assert that German support is more contingent, limited, and means-tested than it has been in the past. The implications of this argument are explored in the conclusions.

Changing German Preferences:
Social, Internal Market, and Monetary Policy

The Treaties of Rome, via their revision in the Single European Act, and the Maastricht and Amsterdam treaties, have greatly expanded the role of the European Union since its founding in 1958.[12] The original conception was primarily economic in scope: Europe was to be an economic space. Many of the proponents of the Treaties, however, expected that the process of economic cooperation would spill over into noneconomic policy areas. The argument, known as functionalism, has largely been discredited in studies of the EU, although the notion of spillover or momentum remains a central element in many analyses of the EU's development. Indeed, while the core of the EU agenda remains economic, later treaty revisions, especially the Maastricht treaty, have vindicated the belief that the EU would grow into something more than the common market envisioned in 1958.

As might be expected, the EU has expanded its competence first and most fully in those policy areas that have relatively close links to its core goal, the common market. Social policy, for example, can be seen as having a natural link to an open and free internal market in the EU. That is, once the more obvious impediments to trade are eliminated—tariffs, quotas, and the like—high and expensive social standards might be expected to continue to distort trade. At worst, "social dumping" might occur, where firms use lower social standards elsewhere in the internal market to drive standards down at home, threatening to shift investment to where the social costs of business are low. Accusations of social dumping have grown of late. The most notable cases were the Hoover Corporation's decision to relocate plants from France to Scotland in 1993, and the 1997 dispute over the closing of a Renault plant in Belgium.

An active social agenda was debated when the Rome Treaties were being negotiated, but the final draft offered only limited room for developing European-level social policy. The European Council expanded the room for maneuver in the early 1970s. Yet the several Action Programs initiated in the 1970s and 1980s proved capable of generating only a limited number of new EU social laws, and major issues like representation and wage bargaining failed to win support from member governments. Social policy received renewed attention in the SEA, even more so in the Maastricht treaty. The Amsterdam treaty in 1997 increased attention on social issues even further by giving employment its own title in the revised treaty.

If social policy focuses upon the expansion of EU competence, problems remain with the core of the EU agenda, the internal market. While the SEA, aided by key ECJ rulings, made heroic (if still unfinished) strides toward completing the internal market, management of that market remains troubled. A key problem is the regulation of subsidies. By providing subsidies to firms, governments artificially strengthen the competitiveness of firms, and defeat the intent of the internal market. The most common subsidy is cash transfers, normally going to firms facing financial difficulties, but there are many other ways that governments can financially underwrite firms. The Treaties of Rome specify that subsidies over a given size are illegal, if their purpose is to protect firms from competition. Yet governments have regularly flaunted EU rules. Action to force member compliance has been among the most controversial issues pitting member governments against the Commission.

Finally, the key issue on the EU agenda today is monetary union. The EU has tried since the late 1960s to fashion monetary union. The reasons are similar to those argued for social policy: monetary union is necessary to complete the internal market. Even a fully free market in Europe can be distorted when fluctuations in exchange rates affect the relative price of goods. Additionally, the cost of transferring money across borders raises business costs. The Maastricht treaty takes the boldest steps yet to realize monetary union. It specifies both a set of requirements for membership in the EMU and a tight timetable for imposing a single currency in Europe.

In each of these three policy areas—social policy, controlling subsidies, and monetary union—the German government has strongly supported common action. In the case of social policy, German governments have been caught between conflicting pressures. On the one hand, high German social standards add to the costs of doing business in Germany. On the other hand, those standards are the result of long and bitter conflict among capital, labor, and the state. Much of the social peace that marks post-war Germany has been attributed to the development of a highly regulated relationship among these actors. The government's solution to this paradox has been to attempt to expand German social protections throughout Europe. This is not to say that German policy makers always support Commission social policy proposals, or that the political makeup of the German government does not influence its support for Commission proposals. Rather, for much of the Commission's social agenda, German interests and European interests mesh closely, and German governments have striven to enhance the similarities in preferences.

The German position on subsidies is similar. In principle, German governments have opposed the use of subsidies to prop up ailing firms. In practice, the German government has granted subsidies to ailing firms and subsidized sectors deemed necessary to protect in order to meet social goals. Indeed, three major exceptions to this rule have caused the Germans considerable grief in Europe—subsidies for rail transport, subsidies for the production and consumption of coal, and subsidies for regional banks. In the first two cases, German governments have argued that over-riding social needs warrant subsidization, but have been forced—if slowly—to back down by the Commission and Germany's partners in Europe. In the case of regional banks, the German government argued that these banks are key elements of German federalism and successfully defended its preferences for the regional banks at the Amsterdam summit in June 1997. Regardless, direct operating subsidies to otherwise private firms have been comparatively rare in Germany, and the German government has long opposed EU policies that lean toward dirigiste tendencies in Europe.

The German position on EMU is much the same. Since the Hague Summit in 1969, the German government has insisted that any scheme of monetary union in Europe follow the German monetary model closely. This model is simple in its form, but radical in its implications for other members. The Germans have insisted that monetary union only take place once economic union and economic convergence have (largely) been achieved, that the resulting European Central Bank be designed to fight inflation, and that the Bank be independent of political influence. These were not, at least until recently, the preferences of Germany's partners in Europe.

As the following sub-sections will show, in each case German policy preferences are shifting. In the cases of social and subsidy policy, financial constraints are at the core of German reticence to support EU initiatives. In the case of monetary union, the problem is more a function of second-order effects. Monetary union is immensely unpopular in Germany, and the political costs of selling monetary union to a public accustomed to a stable currency may influence what are even more basic adjustments that Germany must withstand as the EU budget is reformed and the EU expands into central and eastern Europe.

Social Policy

As stated above, in social policy the Germans might be expected to support an active EU agenda. The high social standards found in Germany today are the result of historical compromises among capital, labor, and the state, compromises that are popular among the public and receive strong rhetorical support from politicians. For example, Chancellor Kohl rejected a draft EU company statute (after decades of debate in the EU) in the fall of 1997 because it failed to incorporate important elements of the German model, including worker representation in management (codetermination). Even the business sector's view of the current debate about "Standort Deutschland" (in short, about the competitiveness of the German economy) focuses upon issues like the length of the workweek (substantially below forty hours), and not upon codetermination. Further, the Germans have strong economic interests in seeing European social standards rise to German levels and in seeing the social market economy vindicated in Europe. In short, it is not surprising that the Germans have been consistent supporters of most of the EU social agenda.

The current issue at the top of the social agenda in Europe is unemployment. Unemployment in Europe now averages about 10 percent, and is even higher in Germany. Further, there are signs that much of this unemployment is structural in character, meaning that unemployment will not drop to more acceptable levels even if the current recovery in Europe continues through 1998 and 1999. While the reasons for this "sticky" unemployment are beyond the concern of this chapter, the implications are not. One implication is the growing linkage between unemployment and other EU issues, including between unemployment and monetary union. Faced with strict budgetary discipline needed to qualify for EMU, many governments in Europe have found it difficult to fund expanding unemployment programs. Quite naturally, then, most European states, including the newly elected Socialist French government that campaigned on a platform emphasizing jobs, have turned to Europe to answer the unemployment problem, especially since unemployment is linked to EMU. The EU treaties did not give the Union specific powers to address unemployment, but many EU governments pushed for a European-wide program to address unemployment in Maastricht II, the treaty renegotiation, mandated by Maastricht I, which began in 1996 and culminated in the Amsterdam Summit in June 1997.

Only the Germans, with indirect support from the Spanish, opposed developing stronger EU unemployment competence. Indeed, the Germans agreed to consider the issue only after virtually every other EU member government aggressively lobbied Bonn, and then only in the last few days before the summit was to start. At the summit, Chancellor Kohl was able to block any but the most symbolic support for EU unemployment policy. As a result, the Amsterdam treaty accomplished only three significant goals. First, unemployment was formally included under its own Title in the treaty (a small if important step, guaranteeing that the issue might continue on the EU agenda). Second, some of the European Investment Bank (EIB) funding rules were re-tooled to provide more funds for small and medium-sized firms, which are the main generators of new jobs. Finally, a follow-on jobs summit was planned for November 1997. This summit also resulted in few significant new programs to fight unemployment. Again, Helmut Kohl led the charge against wider EU competence on jobs.

The German federal government's position on EU unemployment policy was based on a number of factors, including the definition of the problem and its solution, financing of EU programs, and, more fundamentally, the desirability of giving more legal authority to the EU.[13] First, the Kohl government did not believe that the unemployment plaguing Europe could be addressed with more public spending. In the minds of German policy makers, European unemployment is largely a function of overly rigid labor markets. The proper way to address unemployment, then, was not to create new publicly funded jobs, which would be financially unsustainable in the long run (an important concern if the unemployment is indeed structural). Rather, the liberalization of labor markets was viewed in Bonn as the key step in addressing the long-term, structural unemployment that plagues virtually every EU member. For Bonn, unemployment was a national, not a European, problem, requiring national solutions.

German policy makers also argued that the proper level at which to address unemployment is the local level. Hence, unemployment programs are decentralized in Germany in two ways. First, the Federal Employment Office is charged with administering unemployment policy. This office is "para-public," meaning that the federal government exercises only indirect control over its daily operations. Further, the provision of employment services is left to local employment offices. Hence, in the German conceptualization, unemployment is an issue whose solution is best found at the local level. This argues against EU-level policies of much significance in fighting unemployment.

The third concern expressed by the German government was financing. In the negotiations leading to the Amsterdam summit, the proposals tabled to fund EU-level unemployment policy were unacceptable to the Germans. One idea was to pool national unemployment budgets. Since German programs are relatively well funded, this would mean two things. The Germans would face a net decrease in funds for the unemployed, as German monies were drained off to fight unemployment elsewhere. Alternatively, if the German government insisted that its contributions be returned in full (as do the British on their total EU budgetary contribution), then an unnecessary and resource-absorbing level of administration would have been created. Hence, pooling of funds was unacceptable for Bonn.

An alternative was to shift funds around within the existing budget. This was accomplished by requiring the EIB to give preference to lending to small and medium-sized firms. While shifting funds within a given budget line proved politically acceptable, there was no specific EU budget line for employment (some provisions of the Social Fund and sector-specific policies, such as coal and steel, address unemployment). Shifting funds from other budget lines into a new unemployment budget line would naturally generate opposition from the vested interests benefiting from the old distribution of funds. Shifting funds from the Common Agricultural Policy (CAP) to fight unemployment—a natural target, given its size (half the total EU budget) and perceived wastefulness—would likely generate a violent reaction from European farmers. The same holds, if less intensely, for other vested interests benefiting from EU spending. Hence, proposals to shift funds to finance EU-level unemployment policies were also controversial.

It was also impossible to imagine that the members could come up with new funding, while many were trying to cut spending to join EMU. This is especially true in Germany, where the public and elites are convinced that the Germans can no longer afford to be Europe's "paymaster" (*Zahlmeister*).[14] Overall Germany receives only about 40-45 cents in return for each Mark it pays into the EU budget.[15]

As pre-negotiations have begun for the next round of EU budgeting in 1999, the Germans made it clear, from Chancellor Kohl on down, that this could not continue. Not only must Germany receive a higher percentage of what they put in, but also their total contribution should fall. In this political context, finding new funds for the EU was a nonstarter.

Finally, there was a growing perception in Bonn that EU social policy had gone too far. In particular, German policy makers expressed concern for the loss of flexibility that occurs when new EU competencies result in new EU law. In other words, some policy makers have learned that generating EU social law unduly limits their ability to make policy. While this clearly has affected the government's interest in EU employment policy, its effect is not limited to this debate. Policy makers expressed general disinterest in codifying most of the EU social agenda, preferring to keep social issues at the intergovernmental level where EU law cannot restrict their flexibility.

On the surface, the election of an SPD-Green government in Germany indicates a new approach in European social policy. The campaign was fought and won largely on the unemployment issue. The newly elected government shares many of the ideological values of those in Europe pushing for a more active European-level unemployment policy. The Commission's first Amsterdam Summit-mandated review found the outgoing government's unemployment policies inadequate. Yet the new government is unlikely to find itself radically departing from the views of the former government. First, the SPD is likely to be even more unwilling to embrace the Commission's views of social reform, such as weakening German codetermination. Second, the new government faces the same financial and institutional constraints as did the former government, and the SPD led the criticism of the German budgetary contribution before September 1998. Changes in the willingness of the Germans to use active policy tools can be expected, but the new government still faces institutional constraints in moving unemployment policy up to the EU level. While it is too early to determine the precise nature of SPD social policy, initial signs indicate that the new government will place greater emphasis on European-level coordination of policies to fight unemployment. In all likelihood the SPD-Green government will support the shift of more EU funds into fighting unemployment without increasing German budget contributions.

The Internal Market

German unification has presented Bonn with five new Länder that are economically backward, environmentally devastated, and socially troubled. Correcting these problems is taking much more time and money than was initially estimated. The unanticipated high costs of unification have put Bonn on a crash course with the Commission and Directorate General (DG) IV, the European agency responsible for vetting subsidies in Europe.

In principle, the use of subsidies in troubled sectors or regions is highly restricted in the EU. In practice, not only is it difficult to ascertain the fairness of subsidies, but also the member governments face incentives to over-subsidize and hide their behavior. As noted above, the German position on subsidies has been inconsistent—while railing against the behavior of others, German governments have been caught subsidizing. If the Germans have often expressed fears that the EU might develop along dirigiste lines, they have also supported key sectors and ailing firms.[16]

Two related factors have complicated German policy vis-à-vis subsidies. The first is the policy independence of German Länder. As a federal political system, the central government in Bonn has only limited influence over the Länder. Land governments have often subsidized firms. The classic case is the Bavarian government in the late 1970s, which subsidized the steel firm Maxhütte while Bonn was aggressively trying to end subsidies to steel firms elsewhere in Europe. Second, the unification of Germany in 1990 put Bonn and the state governments at odds with DG IV. The unanticipated high costs of unification have led to more and more requests for approval of subsidies for firms operating in the new Länder. Commissioner Van Miert, who in responsible for competition policy, has complained about the proliferation of German requests for subsidies.[17]

Article 92, section 2c of the original EEC Treaty extended special treatment to the border regions of Germany whose natural and historical markets were disrupted by the Cold War. These special provisions were extended to the whole of eastern Germany in the Maastricht Treaty, and steps were taken to facilitate the speedy transfer of funds to the east. All these provisions were predicated on Bonn's (wildly mistaken) expectation that reconstruction of the new Länder would quickly become self-supporting. Hence, the Maastricht provision for vetting of subsidies in large bloc grants ended in 1995, and was replaced with a special task force in DGIV to oversee German transfers only. As the reality of the problems in the new states became clear to Bonn, the government asked for extension of EU programs such as structural fund eligibility after their negotiated cutoff date, the end of 1999.[18] It is expected that the German position on the next budget will include continued EU financial support for the new Länder.

A result of the continued financial demands of unification is growing conflict between Bonn and Brussels. An example is the dispute among DG IV, Bonn, and the state government of Saxony over subsidies for Volkswagen investments in Mosel, Chemnitz, and Zwickau. In June 1996, DGIV argued that DM 240 million of a DM 800 million aid package granted by the Saxon government was illegal. When the Land government ignored the DGIV ruling and began to dispense funds to Volkswagen, DGIV declared that DM 90.7 million of the initial aid tranche must be repaid, and threatened to take the government to the ECJ. Saxony Premier Kurt Biedenkopf refused, and began his own suit in the ECJ.[19] The exchanges between Santer and Van Miert, on the one side, and Biedenkopf on the other were especially acrimonious.

The federal government weighed in between the two, arguing that while the aid was legal, granting it in the face of a Commission ban was illegal. A temporary compromise between Bonn and Brussels resulted in the federal government freezing an equivalent amount of its own tax credits to Volkswagen in order to create time for further (at this writing) negotiation, but the Commission also blocked other aid to the firm.[20] Similar controversies between the Germans and the EU have arisen over subsidies paid to Bremer Vulkan to rebuild two east German shipyards, and subsidies paid to Leuna, the French-owned east German petrochemicals firm.[21]

In sum, the VW case, one of the most bitter subsidy cases in Europe in the last few years, is indicative of growing problems between Bonn and Brussels over subsidies, especially subsidies for eastern Germany. Even the OECD has warned Germany of a growing "subsidy culture," and the annual German "Subsidy Report" indicates that subsidies reached a post-war high in 1996. As the Germans increasingly argue for cutbacks in their EU budget contribution, and as the demand for subsidies continues beyond original expectations, conflicts between Bonn and Brussels are likely to continue. The new government committed itself to a more aggressive program to help the new states, but the financial constraints remain. Its general ideological orientation would suggest that the new government will find itself in conflict at least as often as did the outgoing government.

Monetary Union

German policy on monetary union remained firm and was largely successful before the election. As noted above, the Bundesbank and German government played key roles in the Maastricht negotiations over EMU.[22] Price stability was to be the primary aim of the ECB, and successive attempts by the French to place political controls over the ECB were resisted by the Kohl government. Despite the success of the former government in shaping EMU, the policy was very unpopular at home. A stable Mark is a key element of post-war German politics. While the poll data suggested that, over time, Germans resigned themselves to the replacement of the Mark with the Euro, it was never popular.

Ex-Chancellor Kohl, who publicly linked his career to monetary union, suggested that support for monetary union would determine the outcome of the 1998 federal election. Kohl was wrong. Most election analyses indicate that public unease with replacing the Mark with the Euro played a minor role in the voters' rejection of the former coalition. There are a variety of explanations for why this was so, including elite support for EMU, the length of time before the Euro becomes legal tender (2002), and the technical nature of the issues and debates about the Euro. Yet EMU remains a key theme in German politics. There are at least two ways through which public antipathy toward the Euro might affect German and EU politics. The first involves the new government's approach to monetary policy generally, and its orientation toward the ECB. The second involves the interaction of

EMU with the rest of the current EU agenda, especially fighting unemployment, negotiating the next budget, and expanding into central and eastern Europe.

The politics of implementing and moving beyond EMU must be seen in light of the German debate about EMU. At a political level, the general elite support for the *principle* of EMU should not be confused with support for the former government's *approach* to EMU. If there was general faith in the former, there was seldom commitment to the latter. In opposition, SPD chancellor candidate Gerhard Schröder and SPD party chief Oskar Lafontaine linked EMU to job creation.[23] The most prominent Green politician, Joschka Fischer, held similar views. Opposition to Kohl's approach to EMU was also found in his party and coalition. Kurt Biedenkopf, a longtime Kohl adversary in the CDU, questioned the wisdom of monetary union in the face of large-scale, structural unemployment. The poll data also fueled dissent to early EMU within the CDU Bundestag *Fraktion* (the parliamentary delegation).[24] Edmund Stoiber, minister-president in Bavaria and a key figure in the CDU's sister party, the CSU, criticized Kohl whenever he seemed to stray from a strict interpretation of the Maastricht criteria.[25] Thus, with Kohl's defeat, the political space has been opened for modification, but not rejection, of the German position on EMU.

The first possible modification of EMU involves the new government's view of the proper role of Euro-11, the coordinating committee created in the Amsterdam Treaty. Led by the French, a number of governments tried to create a political counterweight to the ECB. The ECB's responsibilities, according to the Maastricht Treaty, were to mimic the political independence and anti-inflation orientation of the Bundesbank.[26] Yet the Amsterdam Treaty and subsequent negotiations failed to fully clarify the relationship between Euro-11 and the ECB, primarily because the Germans resisted giving Euro-11 any significant powers.

The new government, and especially Finance Minister Lafontaine, have not yet clarified their position on the relationship between Euro-11 and the ECB. Early signs suggest that the new government does not support the former government's views on the separation between monetary policy and politics. Lafontaine has called for the Bundesbank to lower its interest rates to stimulate economic and thus job growth. Opposition politicians seized upon this to criticize the government's commitment to a stable Euro. Almost all German governments, including the most recent CDU/CSU-FDP coalition, tried to influence the Bundesbank at one time or another. Yet the new government has linked monetary policy generally, and EMU specifically, more closely to job creation than did the Kohl government. While it remains to be seen if the red-green coalition will be willing to support an active role for Euro-11, it is clear that the new government has a different view of the proper relationship between politics and monetary policy than the old government. Red-green support for Euro-11 would constitute a significant change in German preferences in the EU.

Another possible change in focus derives from the impact of EMU on the German economy. Most analyses of the economic impact of EMU indicate that it will not positively affect the most pressing German problem, unemployment. Some analyses even suggest that EMU will actually worsen unemployment. The problem is not among large firms, but among small and medium-sized firms, which generate most jobs in a modern economy. A Deutsche Bank survey in 1996 found over a quarter of respondents from small and medium-sized firms expected negative effects from EMU, around half expected no effects, and only 22 percent expected positive effects. Additionally, polls of these firms show that, as of the spring of 1997, they were poorly prepared for the introduction of the Euro.[27] If bankruptcies grow in the aftermath of EMU, it is argued, and if unemployment does not significantly decline, the new German government may find that the public will be hostile to further integration. Given the new government's commitment to fighting unemployment, it might be expected that any new EU policies that have impacts upon employment in Germany would receive particular attention from the government.

This discussion includes a lot of ifs, and requires a lot of issue connectivity, which is not a common phenomenon in studies of voting behavior. Yet the issues that follow on the EU agenda make it arguable that the debate about European integration in Germany started by EMU will not end with EMU. Two issues are key. The first is the budget. As has already been noted, the large German net contribution to the EU budget is unpopular in Germany, and German policy makers at all levels and in all parties were making it quite clear that Germany must receive fairer treatment. This position will be difficult to maintain through the budget debate, especially as there is no candidate country or group of countries willing or able to take on Germany's "Zahlmeister" role, nor willing to accept cutbacks in order to balance more fairly the German contribution.

The second issue, enlargement, is directly related to the budget, in that the first round of potential new members will require substantial financial support from the EU (and these five, Poland, the Czech Republic, Hungary, Estonia, and Slovenia, are among the most advanced of the current EU aspirants). The former (Kohl) government strongly pushed quick EU enlargement, but also wanted to pay less to the EU, get more back from the EU, and continue EU funding for the five new Länder. The new government's priorities are similar. How all this can be financed is less than clear. On top of all this, the potential new members are all likely to be most competitive in those sectors of the economy that are among the most sensitive in Germany and elsewhere in the EU: steel, textiles, shipbuilding, agriculture, and so forth.

My point here is not that EMU, the budget debate, or enlargement are, in and of themselves, issues that cannot be sold to the German public. Rather, these issues are evolving so close to each other, and are so inter-related, that selling one is likely to so exhaust any German government that it will find it hard to muster the political will and public goodwill to sell the rest. If Germany were facing a period of low unemployment, strong growth, and financial stability, then this agenda might be manageable on its current time schedule. Germany no longer enjoys any of these strengths. The public may prove unwilling to accept the continued cutbacks that EMU, budget reform, and expansion will require, especially if there is little substantial improvement on unemployment.

Conclusion

Germany no longer has the resources it enjoyed in the past. Its limited resources suggest a period of political retrenching. In the three cases examined here, some initial evidence is found of this "step back from Europe." In the case of unemployment, German governments have traditionally defined the issue as a national problem with local solutions. The new government may be willing to push more for European solutions, but it will be limited by the shortage of financial resources and domestic institutions. While it is clear that the new government is ideologically more suited than its predecessor to European-level policy solutions, in the case of subsidies, the financial demands of unification are still generating regular friction with the Commission. Finally, while monetary union remains on schedule, the new government is likely to be more willing to exercise political influence over the project than was Chancellor Kohl. EMU's domestic political costs have also been underestimated and may affect the willingness of the German public to bear budgetary and financial costs. While only three cases offer limited room for generalization, the significance of these cases constitute in and of themselves important data points in our understanding of Germany in Europe.

Yet in change there is also continuity. As I have argued elsewhere, there are strong institutional constraints on German foreign policy independence.[28] Markovits and Reich as well as Katzenstein argue that there are ideological reasons for believing that the Germans will remain tied closely to Europe, if coming to dominate the region.[29] Bulmer and Paterson examine many of these perspectives and argue that, for the near term, Germany is likely to remain a "gentle giant" in the EU, gentle in terms of the character of its diplomacy but not necessarily its determination to pursue its own interests.[30] As in the past, a re-definition of German interests means different strategies and goals. In other words, the *content* of German policy preferences in the EU is changing, if not the forms via which German preferences are expressed.

Notes

1. Note the very general wording of this question. When asked in reference to specific EU policies, public support often drops significantly. These data can be found in the regular Eurobarometers, the public opinion surveys conducted by the European Commission.

2. The German Social Democratic Party, for example, experimented with anti-EU platforms in several state elections in 1996 and 1997, and fared very poorly. It has been argued that part of the reason for their losses was the anti-EU portions of their message. This theme proved difficult to sell to voters accustomed to regular SPD support for European integration.

3. Andrei S. Markovits and Simon Reich, *The German Predicament: Memory and Power in the New Europe* (Ithaca: Cornell University Press, 1997).

4. Neil Nugent, *The Government and Politics of the European Union*, 3rd ed. (Durham, N.C.: Duke University Press, 1994); Simon Bulmer, "Germany and European Integration: Toward Economic and Political Dominance?," in *Germany and the European Community: Beyond Hegemony and Containment?*, Carl Lankowski, ed. (New York: St. Martin's, 1993), 73-100; Simon Bulmer and William E. Paterson, "Germany in the European Union: Gentle Giant or Emergent Leader?," *International Affairs* 72, no. 1 (1996): 9-32.

5. Other business leaders saw the opportunities that a common market might generate. Yet at the time, Germany exported many more goods outside the original six members of the EEC than inside the original EEC. This relationship has reversed, not just because the EU has expanded, but also because of the re-orientation of German exports toward the increasingly free internal market in Europe.

6. J. Anderson, and J. Goodman, "Mars or Minerva: A United Germany in a Post-Cold War Europe," in *After the Cold War: International Institutions and State Strategies in Europe, 1989-1991,* Robert Keohane, Joseph Nye, and Stanley Hoffmann, eds. (Cambridge, Mass.: Harvard University Press, 1993).

7. Bulmer, "Germany and European Integration"; Klaus H. Goetz, "Integration Policy in a Europeanized State: Germany and the Intergovernmental Conference," *Journal of European Public Policy* 3, no. 1, (1996): 23-44.

8. The institutional weaknesses often attributed to the German state include the independence and activism of the German Constitutional Court, the prevalence of coalition governments in Bonn, the relative independence of cabinet ministers, and the power of para-public institutions that move some important policymaking authority into the hands of bureaucratic agencies where the central government has only limited influence. Katzenstein argues that these factors make the German state only "semi-sovereign." See Peter Katzenstein, *Policy and Politics in West Germany* (Philadelphia: Temple University Press, 1987). Bulmer and Patterson find that these factors have made it hard for the German head of government, the chancellor, to control German EU policy preferences. See Simon Bulmer and William E. Paterson, *The Federal Republic of Germany and the European Community.* (London: Allen and Unwin, 1987).

9. William E. Paterson and David Southern, *Governing Germany* (New York: W. W. Norton, 1991), 263-64.

10. William Wallace, "Germany's Unavoidable Central Role: Beyond Myths and Traumas," in *The Federal Republic of Germany and the European Community: The Presidency and Beyond,* Wolfgang Wessels and E. Regelsberger, eds. (Bonn: Europa Union Verlag, 1988), 276-85; Stephen George, *Politics and Policy in the European Community*, 2nd ed. (Oxford: Oxford University Press, 1991).

11. Hans-Eckart Scharrer, "The Internal Market," in *The Federal Republic of Germany and EC Membership Evaluated,* Carl-Christoph Schweitzer and Detlev Karsten, eds. (New York: St. Martin's, 1990), 8-9.

12. The Treaties of Rome, signed in 1957, are the legal groundwork of the EU. Over the years, the treaties have been integrated and revised regularly, usually at summit meetings of the heads of government of the member countries. These summits, known as the meetings of the European Council, have no formal link to the institutions of the EU. Yet when the heads of government rewrite the treaties, as they did most notably in the SEA and the Maastricht revisions, the rules of the game in the EU can fundamentally change.

13. This section is based on the author's interviews in Bonn, Germany, June 1997.

14. Klaus Otto Nass, "Der 'Zahlmeister' als Schrittmacher?" *Europa Archiv*, no. 10 (1976): 325-36.

15. These are the figures widely quoted in the German press today. The actual figures might well be much lower, around 19-20 cents, due to CAP corruption and the "Rotterdam Effect," or problems with proper accounting of the calculation of tariffs of goods entering one state but intended for consumption in other states. See "Bonn Trägt 80 Prozent der EU-Nettobeiträge," *Handelsblatt*, 24 July 1997.

16. The SEA, for example, generated strong expressions of concern for foreign subsidization from German business, much as did the internal debate at the founding of the EU in the late 1950s. Yet the Germans negotiated special treatment for markets disrupted by the division of Germany, the "Kohlepfennig" has long subsidized uncompetitive coal mining in Germany, and the French often complain about German subsidies for rail transport. There are numerous other cases of inconsistencies in German policy toward the use of subsidies.

17. Entre Nous, *European Voice*, 28 November-4 December 1996.

18. "German Plea Over Eastern States Aid," *Financial Times*, 21 May 1996.

19. "EU Plan to Trim Car Aid Hits Snag", *Financial Times*, 19 June 1996; "German State Defies Brussels With Grant Aid to VW,", *Financial Times*, 30 July 1996; "Brussels Fury Over Cash for VW," *Financial Times*, 31 July 1996; "Brussels Stance on VW Grant Attacked," *Financial Times,* 5 August 1996; "Saxony Appeals on VW Ruling," *Financial Times,* 26 August 1996.

20. "German State Defies Brussels With Grant Aid to VW," *Financial Times*; "Bonn Stays its Hand Over Aid," *Financial Times*, 28 August 1996, "Bonn and Brussels in Deal Over Aid for VW," *Financial Times,* 5 September 1996; "VW: Im Streit mit EU keine Lösung Absehbar," *Reuters WWW Edition*, 8 April 1997; "Brüssel Will bei VW Hart Bleiben," *Handelsblatt*, 2/3 August 1997.

21. "Brüssel genehmigt Beihilfe für Ostwerfen," *Handelsblatt*, 24 April 1997; "EU Wittert Tricks bei Leuna-Privatisierung," *Handelsblatt*, 12/13 July1997.

22. Wayne Sandholtz, "Choosing Union: Monetary Politics and Maastricht," *International Organization* 47, no. 1 (1993): 1-39; David R. Cameron, "Transnational Relations and the Development of European Economic and Monetary Union," in *Bringing Transnational Relations Back In: Non-State Actors, Domestic Structures and International Institutions,* Thomas Risse-Kappen, ed. (New York: Cambridge University Press, 1995), 37-78.

23. "SPD Refuses to Pay High Price for EMU," *Financial Times*, 13 December 1995; "Monetary Union must be Postponed," *Süddeutsche Zeitung*, 11 January 1996, reprinted in Inter Nationes Special Topic—In Press, "European Monetary Union," ST 5-1996, 760 QS 2316; "Voschherau: Bei Euro Noch Nicht Festgelegt," *Reuters WWW Edition*, 27 June 1997; "Pressure Mounts on Bonn to Delay EMU," *Financial Times*, 7 July 1997; "Mover and Shaker," *Financial Times*, 17 March 1997; "SPD Plädiert für eine Europäische Sozialunion," *Süddeutsche Zeitung*, 15 May 1997.

24. Author's interviews, Bonn, June 1997.

25. "Aus dem Stabilbaukasten," *Frankfurter Allgemeine Zeitung*, 28 February 1997; "Biedenkopf Will Euro Fünf Jahre Später," *Handelsblatt*, 26/27 July 1997; "CSU-Kritik an Kinkel wegen Euro," *Handelsblatt*, 9 April 1997; Bayerische Staatskanzlei, "Regierungskonferenz 1996/1997: Wirtschafts- und Währungsunion," *Pressemitteilungen*, 4 April 1997; "Stoiber Will die Währungsunion Notfalls Lieber Verschieben," *Frankfurter Allgemeine Zeitung*, 9 June 1997; "Germans Clash Over EMU," *Financial Times*, 26 June 1997; "Kohl Backs Down Over EMU Criteria," *Financial Times*, 2 July 1997; "Kohl's Hard Line on EMU," *Financial Times*, 3 July 1997; "Defender of a Decimal Point," *Financial Times*, 7 July 1997.

26. In fact, the ECB is even more immune to political influence than is the Bundesbank.

27. "In der Euro-Falle," *Die Woche*, 14 March 1997; "Mittelstand auf Euro Schlecht Vorbereitet," *Handelsblatt*, 15 April 1997.

28. "Germany and European Integration: Understanding the Relationship," in *From Bundesrepublik to Deutschland: German Politics After Unification*, Michael G. Huelshoff, Andrei S. Markovits, and Simon Reich, eds. (Ann Arbor: University of Michigan Press, 1993), 301-20.

29. Markovits and Reich, *The German Predicament*; Peter Katzenstein, "Tamed Power: United Germany in an Integrating Europe," paper prepared for delivery at the Annual Meeting of the American Political Science Association, San Francisco, CA 29 August-1 September 1996.

30. Bulmer and Paterson, "Germany in the European Union," 32.

12

German Security at the Crossroads: Mixed Signals Still Point to NATO

Mary N. Hampton

Not long ago, there was much debate about NATO's future in the post cold war Europe. The discussion was especially intense in Germany, where uncertainty about German security interests in Europe and the world was spawned by unification and the collapse of the cold war. The demise of the Soviet threat and the enhancement of Germany's potential influence in Europe led to a plethora of forecasts and prescriptions concerning Germany's new role in Europe and its relationships to erstwhile allies and adversaries. Some projected that NATO would simply wither away with the disappearance of the Soviet Union. In this scenario, NATO represented an outmoded defense alliance. Others argued that the alliance should be replaced by a more inclusive organization like the OSCE, where the military superiority of the United States would be deemphasized and the pan European nature of a new security order enhanced. Still others sought an ascendant role for the West European Union (WEU) in Europe, promoting the Franco-German axis as its core.

These views are still held by some in Germany. Today, however, the talk about superseding, replacing, or challenging NATO has largely dissipated. The alliance's future is largely taken for granted, and debate concerning the desirability of its continued existence is minimal. The purpose of this chapter is to examine why German support of NATO has become more robust than ever, despite the serious discussions after unification that sought to recast German security interests and policy, and the window of opportunity that opened for achieving such revisions. Particularly pronounced is a seeming complacency about NATO in Germany; it stands virtually without peers as the institution which is currently perceived to best meet Germany's security needs. Both among the majority of German elites and in the general public, NATO is accepted without much question. The most recent example was that continued German participation in NATO essentially played no role in the national election of September 1998. How much impact the recent change of government might have on continued German support for NATO will be discussed.

It should be understood, however, that the NATO supported by German elites and the German public is perceived as a new NATO; a more German NATO. The second purpose of this chapter, therefore, is to analyze why NATO is increasingly imprinted by German interests and influence. The Germans are very successful in molding the alliance to their needs. The German blueprint for maintaining NATO envisions adapting the trans-Atlantic security relationship to fit the geo-political realities spawned by unification and to suit Germany's European integration objectives. Despite the fact that those goals may not be complementary, German policy has been to bind the United States and Europe through NATO while attempting to integrate the continent through the Franco-German axis.

However, the German post-unification embrace of NATO is also partly a function of German uncertainty regarding the objective of creating and maintaining intensified European integration under the aegis of Franco-German cooperation. The third objective of this chapter is therefore to analyze the inertia in European security integration that accompanies Germany's heightened influence in NATO. Because of Germany's doubts regarding European security policy integration, the U.S.-German axis in NATO has dominated, perhaps even undermined further progress in European security integration efforts.

I focus on two issues that directly reflect German influence on NATO policy and uncertainty regarding European integration objectives that result in fortifying the Washington-Berlin NATO axis. First is the NATO enlargement issue. The eastward enlargement of NATO, although promoted and led by the United States, is at its core a policy that clearly has been pursued by and benefits Germany, at least in the short run. Likewise, the possible reentry of France into the military structure of the alliance is viewed as a winning outcome for Germany. While France's potential reentry is not usually included as part of the enlargement debate, it is in fact a critical aspect of the NATO enlargement process promoted by the Germans and one that would directly affect future NATO internal reforms.

The second issue is the stalled European security integration project that at once affirms German interest in and reveals deep-going German uncertainty about the development of a European security identity separate from NATO and the trans-Atlantic relationship. While German influence has been pronounced in the area of European security cooperation, it is also clear that the integration movement, particularly Franco-German cooperation, continues to falter on two critical points: the French persistence in defining security in terms of its sovereignty, and the concomitant German mistrust of France as a security partner. The result of these tensions is that Germany has sought to bring France into NATO, an institution with which Germany is secure, and France has continued to spurn full NATO integration because it is perceived to undermine French sovereignty while enhancing the power of the United States in Europe.

Before turning to the two above mentioned issues in order to analyze German influence and uncertainty in the security area, I examine why NATO has won the domestic political debate in Germany in terms of which security organization best suits German needs in the post cold war period.

The German Debate on NATO

In the aftermath of German unification, debate among German elites emerged regarding the future of German security. For the first time in the postwar period, Germany was now a completely sovereign state. Therefore, new possibilities arose for the articulation and formulation of German security policy. On the right and left of the German political spectrum, NATO's role as the cornerstone of German security was challenged. This phenomenon opened the door to renewed debate concerning the "German question" among German observers and analysts. Was the united Germany emerging as the European hegemon?[1] Would enhanced German power lead to the creation and pursuit of new security frameworks in Europe, and possibly to the dissolution of NATO?

By 1995, however, NATO had reemerged as the widely accepted anchor for German security. The main focus of the security debate in Germany now shifted to enlarging the alliance, negotiating German military intervention in Bosnia through NATO under the Dayton Accords, and pursuing internal reform of NATO to accommodate a post cold war European identity. While contrarian voices continued to challenge NATO as the key security institution, widespread elite and public consensus supportive of NATO was stronger in 1995 than it had been in decades. This ebb and flow of German support for the alliance deserves to be more closely examined.

The German Left and NATO

As the main opposition party in Germany until their electoral victory in September 1998, the SPD had been unable since unification to find its own voice on foreign policy matters. The party's position on security issues reflected this tendency. While originally positioning itself against the possibility of German military intervention abroad, the party ended up endorsing the Kohl government's policy of German military intervention in Bosnia under NATO auspices. The SPD went from a position of near silence on the NATO enlargement discussion to one of tepid endorsement at the leadership level. Why, then, did the SPD, and to a lesser extent the leadership of the Greens, end up largely in lockstep with the Kohl government on NATO questions? Moreover, in view of this development, does Gerhard Schröder's new "red-green" government portend possible changes in German security policy?

A large segment of the German left over time promoted the evolution of the Organization for Security and Cooperation in Europe (OSCE) framework as an alternative to NATO in meeting German and European security needs. For advocates of the OSCE alternative, NATO represented a traditional alliance through which the United States projected its military dominance in cold war Europe as it balanced against the Soviet threat. The OSCE, on the other hand, was promoted as the foundation for a new collective security system in Europe, one that was inclusive of the United States, Russia, and most of Europe, and one that did not allow for the military domination of any state.

For many on the left, the alternative OSCE model further reflected the continuing and deep-going aversion of the left to the prospect of German military interventionism and to NATO's preeminence as a cold war military structure. The emerging alternative OSCE model would allow Germany to promote a new peaceful, demilitarized, and inclusive European order, with Germany playing a pivotal role at its center as a civilian power. In calling for the demilitarization of Europe, Russia would be given a voice in determining the parameters of European security on an even playing field.

The immediate post cold war, post unification period, therefore, represented a watershed opportunity to realize this security blueprint in earnest. The end of the cold war meant that the need for opposing military alliances in Europe was gone. Therefore, in its antiquated form, NATO would wither away in the not too distant future. The OSCE counter-model would replace the American-dominated military alliance structure that now appeared as a remnant of the cold war. Accordingly, the time was ripe for constructing a post cold war security structure that rejected both Soviet and American military dominance in Europe. A collective security structure could now be constructed wherein the military power of both superpowers played diminished roles.

Former West European NATO members and their counterparts in former Warsaw Pact Europe would work together to create this new structure. East European states should therefore be discouraged from seeking entry into NATO as it existed, and commit their security futures to the pan-European structure that was being built. When the OSCE was granted new powers as a crisis management organization at the 1990 Paris summit, this development was seen a major step in realizing the goal of a new European and German security future. However, as I will discuss below, a major setback for those that promoted the OSCE alternative collective security future was that they quickly faced the resistance of the democratizing East European states whose support they sought; states who preferred to cast their fate with NATO.

While much of the SPD rank and file, and the Green Party, still hold to the OSCE blueprint for Europe, most of the SPD leadership and some of the Green's leaders joined the CDU coalition government in endorsing NATO as the preferred anchor for German security interests into the foreseeable future. Recently, for example, the SPD and many Greens endorsed German military intervention in Bosnia under NATO auspices. Further, after much internal debate, the SPD leadership endorsed NATO's eastward expansion. While the Green Party rejected the policy, its leadership remained divided. Both the Bosnian intervention and NATO enlargement bolster NATO as the key framework for German security interests, and clearly undermine the basis upon which the OSCE alternative security model was built.

The demise of the alternative security model for a large segment of the German left leaning elite was critical to explaining NATO's current success, and it is therefore important to understand the change in thinking that went on among the elites. First, the public consensus against German military intervention in any form has been eroding since unification and the debate directly afterwards in 1991 spawned by German inaction in the Persian Gulf War. The subsequent debate regarding intervention in Bosnia focused on the German obligation to act as a partner of the Western community of democracies. In sending German troops into a potential combat situation for the first time since World War II, the German government had the support of a number of SPD and Green parliamentarians.

As observed by the Greens' Joschka Fischer, now the foreign minister in Chancellor Gerhard Schröder's government, Germany crossed its Rubicon with the Bosnian intervention. In this process, the decades-long public consensus against German military interventionism was beginning to be replaced by the view that Germany should act in concert with its Western allies in situations where Western interests and values are threatened. Not only did German presence in Bosnia receive a majority vote in the Bundestag, a majority of Germans in public opinion polls also expressed their support for the policy. Since then, the taboo against German military intervention has weakened, as recent approval for NATO operations in Kosovo revealed. As the consensus against intervention erodes, Germany becomes increasingly "normal" in the conduct of its foreign policy, and the alternative OSCE security model loses much of its attractiveness.

Second, and extremely important, the SPD has been gradually confronting and shedding the cold war underpinnings of its policy toward Eastern Europe and Russia.[2] At the center of its Ostpolitik, a policy implemented by SPD Chancellor Willy Brandt in the late 1960s was the critical role of Russia. Because of its eastern policy, the SPD was long faulted by some for overlooking or actually harming the nascent reformist movements in East and Central Europe.[3] Therefore, while offering Russia an equal voice in Europe is critical in the OSCE model of European security, leaders of the SPD have been increasingly convinced by the arguments put forward by East and Central Europeans that their security and their aspirations to join the democratic West get marginalized by the too prominent focus given Russia. Since 1990, but especially since 1994, when enlargement really became a dominant NATO issue, key members of the SPD leadership and a few pivotal Green

leaders gradually moved toward their current position of endorsing NATO enlargement and emphasizing the German relationship with East European states.

A third related point has to do with the democratization process in Europe.
Again, East European leaders, especially the Polish, have emphasized that their
dedication to democratization needs to be rewarded and strengthened by their
admittance to Western institutions. While EU enlargement is part of that process,
it has become clear that entry into the Union can not be achieved immediately, and
that a European security guarantee for the Eastern democracies is years away from
realization. Entry into NATO is therefore promoted as the Western institution best
suited for the current mission of stabilizing and democratizing the eastern and
central European countries.[4] The OSCE alternative meets neither criteria: it is at this
point not strong enough to play a convincing stabilizing role, nor is it constructed
to promote and enhance democracy. To undermine the democratic reform movements in Eastern Europe now by focusing on Russian sensitivities is therefore
perceived by many inside the SPD as an increasingly untenable position.

In sum, most SPD leaders and some Green leaders have aided the revitalization
of NATO through their support of the NATO intervention in Bosnia and by signing
on to the alliance's eastward expansion. While the OSCE alternative security model
still remains the choice of some left leaning elites, it has been significantly marginalized
in practice over the past few years. Most revealing, for example, was the Green
Party's decision in the spring of 1998 to revise their party platform, which called for
the dissolution of NATO. The revised document ended up accepting the continuation of the alliance. That being said, with the SPD now in the German leadership
position, and with the Greens occupying the foreign office, it is quite possible that
a shift back towards invigoration of the OSCE will occur.

The German Center Right Parties and NATO

While the CDU/CSU-FDP coalition government remained a staunch supporter
of NATO before and after German unification and played an activist role in shaping
the "new" NATO, there was a period of time after unification when NATO's central-
ity for German security was at least open to debate on the right and in the center
right coalition parties. Proponents of invigorating the WEU through greater Franco-
German cooperation became vocal. Still other members of the center-right constellation spoke increasingly openly for a more assertive German foreign policy. CDU
Minister Wolfgang Schäuble, but especially the CSU's Alfred Dregger, beckoned
Germany to fill its rightful power position in Europe. These views were taken much
further by the so-called "new right," whose spokespeople proposed a reassess-
ment of German ties to the West, and a freer hand in German foreign policymaking.
The voices of the far and new right were particularly audible in the 1990-1994
period. Far right parties made some electoral gains at the local and state levels. A
number of publications from the right emerged prescribing the articulation of a

German foreign policy that followed more narrowly conceived German interests, unshackled by the cold war Western transnational institutions to which Germany was member. The perceived subservience of West Germany to the United States was a particularly annoying thorn in the sides of many of the new right.[5]

Since 1994, however, the center right coalition parties essentially rerallied around NATO as the cornerstone of German security, and the rising star of the new right imploded. The Kohl coalition government opted to revitalize the alliance by attempting through NATO enlargement and internal reform to mold the alliance into the post cold war security structure that best met German security interests. As I argue below, the center-right coalition government took a leading role in steering the course for NATO enlargement.

I do not argue that the revitalization of NATO replaced the quest among the center-right parties to create a real European security identity through the WEU and eventually through the EU. Instead, an unintended consequence of Germany's focus on NATO was more inertia in developing an independent European security identity. German uncertainty about its European security partners, in conjunction with a series of on-the-ground policy decisions regarding the alliance's enlargement, led the German government to breathe new life into NATO and resulted in the "NATOization" of the WEU.

NATO Enlargement and the Role of Germany

While the United States is seen today as the main mover behind NATO's eastward expansion, the policy was promoted by prominent German policymakers well before the Clinton administration actually endorsed it. During his tenure as NATO's secretary general, for example, Manfred Woerner spoke of the alliance's obligation to remain open to potential new members in the democratizing states of East and Central Europe. His arguments were echoed by then Secretary of Defense Volker Rühe before the Clinton administration signed on wholeheartedly in 1994. Once President Clinton adopted the policy of pursuing enlargement, Chancellor Helmut Kohl's coalition government endorsed the policy and played an activist role vis-à-vis the admittance of new members.

The objectives behind the German support for NATO enlargement were several. The first clusters of goals are geopolitical and -strategic in nature. For example, it is critical for German security that stability be created in Central and Eastern Europe. It is to Germany after all that the various migration waves of discontented and disempowered refugees from the east have come since the collapse of the cold war order. Because of Germany's adjacency to these countries, an important element of NATO enlargement is the diminution of the chances for further destabilization or renationalization of national security policies in the region. A component of this reasoning includes a normative element as well: the lessons of the past learned by many German elites include the conviction that the two class security system that dominated Europe for centuries, where the great power center states ended up petitioning or colonizing the second-class periphery states, was a process that inevitably led to instability and crisis. Only by eradicating the two tier system and bringing full status to democratizing countries such as Poland and Hungary can real stability be achieved in Europe's center.[6]

Equally important are three other geopolitical considerations. First, by incorporating Poland into NATO, the alliance's eastern front moves farther east and away from the German border. While this reason is not discussed much publicly, it is a fact of NATO expansion that clearly serves German geopolitical and -strategic interests and is one that was acknowledged and supported by Rühe. Second, by admitting Poland, Hungary, the Czech Republic, and at some point Austria, and through potential full French reintegration into the alliance, Germany is for the first time in its history surrounded by allies. The historic German fear of being isolated and surrounded by adversaries, a fear expressed by German leaders from Bismarck to contemporary elites, is thus attenuated. This development offers Germany security in a very distinct and crucial way not shared by other NATO members. Finally, by moving NATO farther east, Germany becomes the literal center of the alliance. As Bonn moves to Berlin, the symbolism and reality of a more eastern Germany will be embedded in and secured by an eastward moving NATO.

While Germany stands to gain much in the short term, the enlargement of NATO eastward also reflects German uncertainty concerning its political role at the heart of the new Europe. By continuing to embed its security identity in the NATO relationship and encouraging that institution to embrace Eastern democracies, Germany saves itself from making choices about an uncertain future from its new post in the East. The debate over whether or not to admit Romania into the NATO fold during the summer of 1997 was revealing of both German influence and uncertainty. While there were indications that the Kohl government did not support Romania's entry in the first wave of new members, Bonn allowed Washington to take the lead and the heat for publicly declaring its resistance to Romanian membership. Standing in the shadows of Washington granted Bonn a win-win outcome. The Kohl government got the outcome it may have wanted, but was not forced to publicly reject the French and Romanian policies of pushing openly for Romania's admittance.

The center right and left parties in Germany also promoted the eastward expansion of NATO for some very specific political reasons. The sense of historical obligation to Eastern countries like Poland has led German leaders to see and portray themselves as the champions of eastern and central European Western integration hopes. Placing themselves in that role enables German leaders to continue the process of reconciliation with former adversaries in Europe, a process that started with French-German reconciliation through West European and trans-Atlantic integration. It also increases German influence in the enlargement process, although the focus on Germany's historical obligation to the East, especially to

Poland, is a two-way street. As mentioned above, the Poles encouraged such thinking in Bonn precisely because it enhanced their chances of being admitted to Western institutions.[7]

Presenting themselves as the advocates for eastern European integration naturally put German policymakers side by side with American leaders. The United States sees itself not only as the power that enabled the democratization of eastern Europe through its role as leader of the Western cold war alliance, it sees itself as the base of international democratic "soft power" as well as the only credible security guarantor of Europe through its superior "hard power" capabilities. Berlin, however, will have a couple of advantages over Washington in terms of soft and hard power. First, German economic presence in eastern Europe accedes that of the United States or any other Western power, a factor that adds to German influence in the region. Germany is now the leading Western trading partner with many of the central and east European states, a situation that again requires stability in the region and increases German influence. Poland, for example, has overtaken Russia as Germany's largest trading partner in the East. Second, and related, most east European states see Germany as the key to eventual membership in the EU, an influence that the United States obviously lacks. Opinion polls in Poland show that while the United States wins as the country found most sympathetic in Polish eyes, it is Germany that most Polish respondents believe to be their most important partner in terms of economic and security cooperation.

Finally, the assumption of the advocacy mantle also increases the prestige of Germany inside the alliance and is one clear response to former President George Bush's summoning of the Germans as America's "partners in leadership." An important caveat to add, however, is that once states like Poland enter NATO, the dynamics of internal alliance politics may not necessarily work to German advantage, as discussed in the final section.

In the enlargement debate, the role of Russia is critical. The charter signed between NATO and Russia in May 1997 was a crucial element in the new relationship between the two players, and a good part of the charter's evolutionary text was written by the Germans.[8] Similar to the role the Germans play vis-à-vis the central and east Europeans, Berlin will be the most important European actor concerning Russia. German elites are more comfortable with their newfound economic power with Russia, and they are able to transfer that power into political influence in the enlargement process. The German bilateral relationship with Russia was critical at the early stages of the enlargement process and remains so today. Again, then, when it comes to negotiating the terms of the future NATO-Russia relationship, the Germans have taken their place next to the United States as the crafters of the new NATO policy.

France and NATO Enlargement

As stated at the outset, an important ingredient in the enlargement of NATO is the possible reentry of France into the military structure of the alliance. Should France reenter the military structure of the alliance, which momentarily looks doubtful, the outcome would be clearly welcomed by most members of the German political elites. The Germans have been pressing for a French return for good reason. Having France back in the NATO fold would reduce the pressure Germany has felt in constantly having to choose between Washington and Paris on vital security and political questions. This tension is not new, but has dogged German policymakers since the 1950s. When asked whether Germany would someday have to choose between France and the United States, Franz Josef Strauss once responded: "Do you choose between your shirt and your underpants?"[9]

An example of the German predicament in having to choose between Paris and Washington was reflected in the debate spawned by the founding of the Euro-corps in 1991 between France and Germany. The corps was envisioned by both as setting up a cornerstone for future European, especially Franco-German, military cooperation. The question was whether to place the new corps under WEU or NATO auspices. France clearly preferred the former option, and French policymakers at the time were already promoting the revitalization of European security identity through the WEU and the OSCE, and concomitantly, more independence from the United States and NATO.

The Bush administration reacted generally negatively to the development of the Euro-corps, fearing its impact on the effectiveness of the alliance and questioning the consequences on Germany's NATO focus. There ensued over the next year much debate about how to institutionalize the corps, with the Germans prodding the French to bring it under NATO auspices for the time being. By 1993, the Euro-corps was effectively integrated into the NATO framework.

With France fully integrated inside the alliance, Germany could then deal with potential cleavages between the United States and France as domestic alliance politics. While the Germans have learned over time to trust the NATO relationship, and how to influence Western security policy from within, they remain ever skeptical of a European security alternative led by France. Indicative of the German position was a comment made by Rühe in early 1997 describing the newly negotiated "joint French-German security and defense concept": he spoke of the "Natoization of France," a comment that set off much criticism in the French press and among French elites.[10] Therefore, full French membership in NATO would both maintain the secure the NATO bond, and Germany's influence therein, but would give the Europeans added political clout from inside the alliance to develop a European identity.

In fact, having France in NATO would potentially enhance Germany's political position more on issues concerning the construction of a European pillar in the alliance, a development that remains elusive as long as France remains outside. Many of the structural reforms of the alliance that France demands before it fully reenters would indeed increase the political influence of the Europeans by reducing the role of American military authority. As followed from the Harmel reforms of 1967, which were advocated by the West Europeans, and especially the West German SPD, enshrining the political objective of detente into the alliance enhanced the political maneuverability of the West Europeans, the West Germans in particular. Future internal NATO reforms could have equally profound consequences.

The Certain Ally: Keeping the United States in Europe

Finally, expanding NATO revitalizes the alliance, at least in the short run, and thereby preempts both the retreat of the United States from Europe and the pursuit of a military security structure alternative to NATO. To most German elites in the center-right parties and to many in the SPD, these are crucial security objectives. The devolution of American power on the continent could have the consequence of rekindling suspicions of an overbearing Germany, which given the underdeveloped nature of real European security integration, could lead to the renationalization of European security, rather than to closer cooperation. Behind Germany's overall continued support of NATO is therefore the goal of averting the renationalization of European defenses, a development that would put the powerful united Germany in a very vulnerable political and geostrategic position. Thus, pursuing alternative European security structures through the WEU or the EU is not in the interests of Bonn if such pursuits weaken NATO in the short run. As I will discuss below, the move toward closer European security integration, therefore, remains more in the realm of declaration than implementation.

Further, the retreat of the United States from Europe and the demise of NATO would open a German Pandora's box. German security identity has become embedded in the NATO relationship and dependent on the presence of the United States as the ultimate security guarantor for Germany, especially in nuclear matters. This position has allowed Germany to project its international influence through a domestic self-image where it is portrayed as being nonaggressive and nonthreatening. One could argue that German democratic identity has therefore been intimately linked to the continuation of NATO and the American presence.[11]

In sum, leaders of the mainstream parties in Germany have been out front as advocates of NATO enlargement for reasons that clearly promote and protect German interests, but that also reveal German uncertainty in the post cold war period.

The Underdevelopment of European Security Cooperation

There is much talk among the German political class of spending more time, energy, and resources to join France, Great Britain, and others in building a separate and viable European security identity through the WEU and the EU. The WEU and the development of a common European security and foreign policy are still important German policy objectives. However, real cooperation and the development of a unified European security identity remain far off, as the disunited European response to the crises in the Balkans revealed. The reasons for the continued delay are many.[12] One is obvious: so long as NATO continues to thrive, there is little incentive for the Europeans to develop their own military capabilities. That Germany has decided to maintain NATO as its security anchor means that other alternatives have been weakened in the short run. Rather than being torn between Paris and Washington over competing strategic visions for Europe, conflicting loyalty claims, and contested security structures, the Germans have helped encourage France to reconcile with NATO, possibly to the point of rejoining the alliance. Thus, an important unintended consequence of Germany deciding to breathe new life into NATO is the continued inertia in efforts to forge closer European security cooperation.

German hesitance vis-à-vis closer cooperation with France dampens chances for real progress in developing an independent European security identity that is anchored in the French-German relationship. Will the emphasis on Franco-German cooperation falter further given the change in the German coalition government? While it is too early to forecast the Schröder/Fischer effect on this critical dyad, fears have already been raised in Paris that the new SPD-led coalition may bring more focus to the triangular relationship of Germany, Britain, and France. When asked about a possible triangle emerging between German, France, and Britain, Foreign Minister Fischer recently responded, "I don't believe in axis' or triangles. . . . If the British want to play a stronger role, or the Italians, or whoever else, then that is good and not bad."[13] Interestingly, British Prime Minister Tony Blair in fact recently called for greater European security cooperation through the EU, reinforcing the triangular concept of European defense cooperation.[14]

However, there have been other important reasons for the faltering European program of developing a European security identity that again point to German uncertainty. A fact of life in the search for German security in the post unification period is the financial crunch that has dramatically reduced the German defense budget. The defense budget has been cut in the years since unification. Further, the percentage of the German defense budget going to research and development has also been reduced. From a high of over 30 percent in the early 1980s, recent statistics on the percentage spent for research and development in the German defense budget showed about 18 percent, well below the 30 percent hurdle needed to innovate. Today, the United States outspends all West European NATO allies together in research and development spending by a three to one margin. The German armaments industry has lost nearly 100,000 jobs in recent years and is forfeiting through reductions important competencies needed for armaments innovation.[15] The downward trend of German defense spending is further fortified by a public that is disinclined to support an enhanced German military profile.

Likewise, France has recently been forced to cut its defense spending as well. Much of the reduction is related to the domestic austerity programs being forced through to enable France to achieve competency for entering the Euro on schedule. Through cutting the French defense budget, however, important joint military and armaments industry cooperation between France and Germany was put on ice. Not only does the military technology gap between the United States and Europe continue to grow, the weakened commitment to defense spending in Europe makes a reversal of the trend unlikely in the near future.

This factor is reinforced by the traditional French inclination to focus on its independent military security needs first, thereby assuring its sovereignty in the area of high national security interests. This consideration brings me to a basic cause of German uncertainty and the current inertia in European security cooperation. Alongside the current economic limitations to closer European security cooperation is the continued lack of political will to forge ahead with an independent, or at least a parallel, European security capability. While France has always promoted a more independent European security identity vis-à-vis the United States, it has always done so with two major caveats. First, France does not want to see the United States presence disappear completely from the continent for the reason that the American presence contains German power to some extent. Second, and most important, France has not been, nor does it appear now, ready to surrender enough of its own sovereignty to create effective European security structures.

Gaullism, which is at heart a permanent claim to French sovereignty in matters of national security, has been revised and reformed, but not toppled from its place at the center of French politics. Thus, it is easier to comprehend the statement made by then President François Mitterrand in 1990 regarding the impact of international changes like the unification of Germany on French policy: "It is clear that France's independent defense policy and its nuclear deterrence doctrine will not be altered even in the long run." France's position has been consistent: counter without erasing the American influence on the continent through a European security structure that does not dilute French sovereignty, but rather enhances French influence.

In sum, France's continued claim to sovereignty reinforced Berlin's political determination to ensure the survival of NATO. The political will to develop an independent European security identity thereby remained stalled and was further stymied by the economic limitations in defense spending. The result is that the Europeans lack the communications infrastructure, the transport capacity and the military hardware, alone and collectively, to project military power abroad in an effective manner. One recent example was the fact that of the forty-six surveillance satellite channels being used in the NATO Bosnian operation, forty-three of them were American.[16] The lack of political will and military capability thereby leaves Europe dependent on NATO.

Are Changes in Store Under Chancellor Schröder?

Continuity in German foreign and security policy has been the mantra of the Schröder government. The promise and intention of continuity have been repeated over and over again. For example, when asked what he wants to change in German foreign policy, Fischer reiterated: "The most important change is that nothing changes in the fundamentals of German foreign policy."[17] Yet, a number of factors could undermine the bedrock certainty of Germany's current policy to NATO, and there are already signs that the promise of continuity may be fleeting. Because the coalition remains largely untested on foreign policy matters, this section remains necessarily speculative.

Sixteen years of Kohl leadership established a pattern in German security policy that in a sense allowed Bonn to have its cake and eat it too. Kohl, in a way analogous to Bismarck's dexterity in foreign policy, was able to maintain Germany's loyalty to the trans-Atlantic security relationship through NATO, to maintain Germany's commitment to the French-German axis by supporting the Europeanization of Germany's security through continued declaratory support for the WEU, to present Germany as a supporter for Polish and other East/Central European state membership in NATO and the EU, and to placate Russia through bilateral relations and through German influence on the NATO-Russian charter. Such dexterity, or what some called indecision,[18] meant that Germany under Kohl's leadership upset none of the important institutional apple carts in which German security was placed. However, as I have argued, the Kohl government's resolute loyalty to NATO and its influence on the NATO enlargement policy had the unintended consequence of causing more inertia in the European security integration efforts.

How will the Schröder/Fischer coalition pursue the fine balancing act of addressing the crosscutting, but not necessarily complementary institutional demands placed on Germany security policy without upsetting the apple cart? Both the SPD and the Greens are internally divided over the juxtaposition and importance of what Egon Bahr calls the "alphabet salad of UNEUNATOWEUOSZEKSEPfP."[19] As discussed earlier, the SPD and the Greens have historically manifested open skepticism regarding NATO, particularly of the preeminent role played by the United States.[20] For example, only with their party platform revision in the spring of 1998 did the Greens expunge their long-held position of calling for the dissolution of NATO. A large number of the party's rank and file continues to call for the superseding of NATO by an all-European security framework, like the OSCE. Likewise, important voices on the left of the SPD have long argued for the gradual dissolution of NATO.

Whether Chancellor Schröder and Foreign Minister Fischer can keep these potentially divisive factions at bay is not yet clear. Relative to the previous government of Chancellor Kohl, Schröder's coalition undoubtedly contains more voices that would challenge the policy of continuity toward NATO. Even subtle changes to the institutional brew Germany now mixes in its security policy could have a dramatic impact on the stability of the NATO relationship.

First, as stated earlier, a renewed commitment by the left of center to empower the OSCE could subtly affect Germany's NATO policy. For example, the SPD/ Green coalition agreement, written in October 1998 as an overview of the coalition's policies, gave scant attention to NATO. While the document endorsed continuity in Germany's NATO policy, it also highlighted the importance of the OSCE in the NATO enlargement policy.

Second, and related, the Schröder government must confront issues regarding German military intervention under the auspices of NATO. The coalition agreement specifically ties German participation to actions that have a UN mandate. As discussed earlier in the chapter, the question of German military intervention was an issue that wrought tremendous debate in the left of center parties in recent years. A recent example regarding German military intervention under NATO was instructive in revealing both continuity in German security policy and a potential for change. In November 1998, the German coalition leadership and the Bundestag passed a resolution supporting German participation in the OSCE and NATO interventions in Kosovo. The policy thereby revealed continuity with past German policy. However, it is also noteworthy that the OSCE observer mission was given more support by many members of the Greens and SPD than was the decision to support the NATO emergency force. In the end, some Green members voted against the rescue mission and others were brought along on the NATO question only because the NATO role was in aid of the OSCE.[21] Further, it was noted by an SPD member that the OSCE engagement in Kosovo was historic, and reflected the "old dream of realizing a 'European civilian community.'"[22] Thus, while continuity with past German policy could be claimed, nuanced differences by the left of center approach to military interventionism was already in evidence.

Third, the SPD's unresolved revision of its former *Ostpolitik* leaves open the question of how the new German government will respond to future Russian resistance regarding NATO intervention and enlargement policies. In choosing to endorse NATO enlargement, for example, the Kohl government reflected the significant voice given to East and Central European states' desire to join NATO. To diminish the fallout that the policy had on Russia, the Kohl government also played a critical role in bringing about the NATO-Russia charter. The Kohl government made clear, however, that the agreement did not give Russia a veto on NATO policy. Especially outspoken in this regard, for example, were Rühe and CDU parliamentarian Friedbert Pflüger. How the Schröder government will deal with Russia's role and influence regarding future enlargement questions, or internal NATO decision-making, remains untested. Its approach to Russia will necessarily impact the relationship with East and Central European states. The fact that the coalition has already emphasized the connection of further NATO enlargement to the OSCE decision-making process portends a potentially larger role for Russia in NATO business, and a shrunken role for the hopes of democratizing East and Central European states who seek entry into NATO.

Fourth, the seriousness with which the new government pursues NATO internal reform, and the consequent impact such reform would have on the American role, remains to be seen. Many on the left advocate the full reentry of France into NATO in order to enhance the European identity inside NATO. While this position was also supported by many in the former right of center coalition government, the issue is again one of emphasis. What would be the objectives of a greater European identity inside the alliance? In the case of the Kohl government, internal changes were indeed sought to bolster a European identity, but one that was projected to be complementary to the trans-Atlantic relationship. British Prime Minister Tony Blair recently reiterated the call for developing a European security identity that would complement NATO. At the other end of the spectrum is the vision articulated by the SPD strategist Bahr, where "(t)he 'European peace' is the European assignment, not without America, but emancipated from it."[23] In Bahr's version, German-French security integration is envisioned as the core of a Europe capable of projecting its own security interests in a multipolar world. It also raises the possibility of greater competition with the United States. While the differentiation between the two approaches may be subtle, it is potentially dramatic in terms of the future direction of trans-Atlantic security relations and could have an important impact on the internal political dynamics of NATO.

How the Schröder coalition government defines the objectives of internal reform will therefore be critical. A recent signal was sent that Berlin and Washington could well clash over reform issues. When Fischer announced in November of 1998 that NATO's long-standing policy regarding nuclear weapons policy was antiquated, immediate trans-Atlantic friction ensued. Fischer, reflecting the position of the Greens and many in the SPD, argued that NATO should adopt a policy of no-first use, a policy proposal that set Berlin not only at odds with the United States, but also with France and Britain. As of this writing, the Schröder government had backed away from Fischer's comments, but then retracted the retraction.[24] The example makes clear that uncertainty regarding current German intentions for NATO reform will continue.

Finally, and significant, the change of government from the Kohl coalition to the Schröder coalition represents a watershed generational change in German politics, comparable to the ones that have taken place in the United States and Britain. Gone are the public reminiscences of Kohl that dwelled on the positive role the United States played at the end of World War II in helping to rebuild a war-ravaged Germany. Instead, the youthful memories of current leaders like Schröder and Fischer include demonstrating against the American involvement in Vietnam. The so-called "68ers" have come of age and now inhabit the highest offices of power.

With their ascension comes the possibility of a less inhibited, more independent German foreign policy. While this process is in no way a direct threat to the resilience of NATO, it is at least a cautionary note to assuming a continuation of the underlying relationships of trust, loyalty and positive identity that evolved over a half century of trans-Atlantic history.

In sum, the new government has promised continuity in its security policy. Yet, as I have discussed, continuity in general does not tell us enough. Nuances are important. The specific emphasis the government gives to each institutional ingredient of German security policy will reverberate throughout the institutional network, thereby having an impact on NATO.

Conclusions

NATO received a new lease on life over the past five years. Critical to its success was the German decision under Kohl's leadership to continue anchoring its own security identity and interests inside the alliance. As I have argued, that decision reflected a heightened German influence on alliance policy but also an uncertainty that produced more inertia in the efforts to move forward with the development of an independent European security identity.

The new NATO ensures that allies exist on all German borders; it gives new stability to the lands east of Germany and helps ensure that the renationalization of European security policy does not occur; it is enhancing the status of German influence inside the alliance without invoking fears of a too powerful unified Germany; it is positioning the development of certain European security structures inside the alliance, thus simplifying the trade-offs Bonn has to face in choosing between Paris and Washington on important security matters; it is maintaining the American commitment to Europe. All of these potential outcomes of NATO western and eastern enlargement benefit Germany and ensure the continuity of German foreign and security policy and the preservation of the German self-image through NATO.

The potential downside to NATO enlargement speaks to German uncertainty in its current security position. First, it is not certain that France's reintegration into NATO will be successful, leaving Berlin once again stuck between Washington and Paris. Second, equally unforeseeable is the effect that adding new members from the East will have on alliance dynamics. While Germany was indeed the critical European player in helping Poland and others in eastern and central Europe gain entry to Western institutions, it is not clear that Poland, for example, will align itself with Germany politically once inside NATO. Adding new members like Poland opens the door to a plethora of coalition possibilities in domestic alliance politics on a host of issue areas. Regarding policies such as future NATO relations with Russia, for example, it is imaginable that Germany and Poland could find themselves in contrary positions. That possibility looms larger with the change of government in Germany.

It is also conceivable that NATO western and eastern enlargement could effectively undermine organizational coherence and thereby threaten the credibility of Article 5 guarantees. That outcome combined with an increasingly "emancipatory" European effort at alliance reform could well lead to a reduced American willingness to continue actively engaging the alliance. Should any of these possible scenarios be realized in the short to medium term, and in the face of continued slow progress toward European security integration, Germany could end up being the net loser in the quest for security.

Finally, the future of German policy toward NATO will be greatly affected by the SPD-Green coalition government. While continuity has been promised and delivered, the potential for drift in Germany's policy toward NATO has increased. That being said, the political capital that Germany has sunk into its security relationship to NATO will likely outweigh any benefits that intense change could bring. Particularly now, with the German political class so focused on the multitude of domestic and European political and economic issues that demand attention, a radical alteration in German security policy is unlikely. The stability of the NATO anchor is therefore, at least in the short run, likely to remain intact.

Notes

1. For an in-depth discussion of the hegemony debate, see James Sperling's chapter in this volume. Also see Andrei S. Markovits and Simon Reich, *The German Predicament: Memory and Power in the New Germany* (Ithaca: Cornell University Press, 1997).

2. See my discussion in "'Borne Ceaselessly Into the Past?' Poland, Germany and NATO Enlargement Policy," *German Comments* (January 1998): 85-94.

3. Mary Hampton, "Borne Ceaselessly Into the Past?," 92.

4. See the discussion of promoting stability to Central and Eastern Europe through NATO enlargement in Ronald Asmus, "NATO Enlargement: A Framework for Analysis," in *NATO's Transformation*, Philip H. Gordon, ed. (Boulder: Rowman and Littlefield, 1997), 93-120.

5. For example, Rainer Zitelmann, a member of the new right, was one of the editors of a book called *Westbindung: Chancen und Risiken für Deutschland* (Frankfurt am Main and Berlin: Ullstein, 1993). In the introduction, the co-editors characterize German identity with "the west" as a "new political religion." For a general discussion of the intellectual new right in this period, see Jacob Heilbrunn, "Germany's New Right," *Foreign Affairs* 75 (November/December 1996): 80-98. See also the discussion in one section of Gerard Braunthal's chapter in this volume.

6. I thank Roland Freudenstein for his helpful insights on this matter.

7. Hampton, "Borne Ceaselessly Into the Past?"

8. Lothar Rühl, "Die Funktion der NATO als Bündnis muss erhalten werden," *Die Welt*, 29 April 1997.

9. Anthony Sampson, *Anatomy of Europe* (New York: Harper and Row, 1968), 22. I thank Wolf Gruner for pointing me to this quotation.

10. Jan Bielicki and Franz Josef Hutsch, "Weltmacht Europa?," *Die Woche*, 7 February 1997.

11. See Mary Hampton, "NATO, Germany, and the United States: Creating Positive Identity in Trans-Atlantia," *Security Studies* (Winter 1998/1999).

12. On the continued problems of and opportunities for European security integration, see Wolfgang Proissl, "Europas Gesicht in der Welt," *Die Zeit*, 26 November 1998.

13. Joschka Fischer, "Realo Sieht die Welt," interview in *Die Zeit*, 19 November 1998. My translation. I thank Christian Kunst for calling my attention to the interview.

14. Tony Blair, "It's Time to Repay America," *New York Times*, 13 November 1998. See also "Blair's Defence Offensive," *The Economist*, 14 November 1998.

15. I thank Holger Mey for his helpful points on this matter.

16. Bielicki and Hutsch, "Weltmacht Europa?"

17. Fischer, "Realo sieht die Welt."

18. On the view that Kohl's policy was one of indecision, see Egon Bahr, *Deutsche Interessen* (Munich: Karl Blessing, 1998).

19. Bahr, *Deutsche Interessen*, 142.

20. See the chapters by Gene Frankland and Andrew Denison in this volume.

21. Richard Meng, "Bundestag Votes to Support Kosovo Action," *Frankfurter Rundschau*, 14 November 1998.

22. "Grosse Mehrheit für Beteiligung der Bundeswehr an Schutztruppe," *DPA*, 13 November 1998.

23. Bahr, *Deutsche Interessen*, 152.

24. See the discussion in "Germany Drops Call to NATO on Nuclear Use," *New York Times*, 25 November 1998.

13

Less than Meets the Eye:
A Reconsideration of German Hegemony

James Sperling

The German Question—whether Germany could be peacefully and successfully integrated into the European state system on terms acceptable to both Germany and its neighbors—was temporarily put aside with the truncation and division of Germany at the end of World War II. This quandary has reemerged with the end of the cold war and the unification of Germany, two events that reconfigured the European security space. Today Germany is increasingly perceived as a latent European hegemon. The German Question can now be posed in an alternative form: Will Germany prove too large even for an institutionalized Europe?

In this chapter, I address the issue of whether Germany in fact is capable of achieving hegemony in Europe. Toward that objective, I examine recent analyses that predict the emergence of a dominant or hegemonic Germany based on German structural power; and address three questions: Why should we anticipate a German hegemony? What kind of structural power does Germany actually possess? Did Germany function as a reluctant actor in Europe owing to the constraints of the cold war?

In the conclusion, I focus on a critical issue generated by the ongoing debate about German power: What role does historical memory play in understanding German foreign policy in post cold war Europe? I argue that the metaphor of Auschwitz is best understood as a system level constraint on the exercise of German power. In short, Germany's past serves as an external constraint on its ability to project power in Europe.

Germany's Role in Europe

The second unification of Germany in 1990, the reconstruction of central and eastern Europe, the Maastricht Treaty, a renewed German confidence in its European role, and the end of the formal occupation reinvigorated the debate over what constituted German "normalcy" in the post cold war order.[1] It also raised the specter of a fourth Reich and a new bid for European hegemony.[2] Simon Bulmer and William Paterson, for example, reached the guarded conclusion that German hegemony was a potential outcome of German unification and the relaxation of tensions in the European security area.[3] They heavily discount the emergence of a conscious German bid for hegemony owing to Germany's vulnerability to the adverse macroeconomic fortunes and protectionist commercial policies of its partner countries; to nagging questions over Germany's continued competitiveness captured by the most recent debate over *Standort Deutschland*; to the continued embrace of multilateralization that had served German foreign policy and economic interests so well in the postwar period; and most importantly to domestic and external institutional constraints on German policy options and freedom of movement, particularly those imposed by the European Union (EU). Rather than a fourth Reich, Germany would emerge as a "gentle Giant" reluctant to press its claims in the new Europe.

Andrei Markovits and Simon Reich have provided two sequential interpretations of German hegemony in post cold war Europe, which can be called the strong and weak versions. In the strong version,[4] they focus on the underlying structural economic power of Germany in western and central Europe complemented and activated by the willing emulation of the German model by its central and eastern European neighbors. At the core of their argument is the notion that Germany exerts a cultural hegemony in Europe largely independent of German agency and, more interestingly, intention. In the second weaker version,[5] the German question is wrapped in the puzzle of structural power constrained by an "ideology of reluctance." This version of the argument combines structure—defined largely in terms of the distribution of material capabilities in Europe—and human agency in a compelling manner. But it privileges agency and locates the ideology of reluctance in the lesson of and continuing contrition for Auschwitz. The combination of structure and agency is implicitly or explicitly endorsed by any number of authors: Bulmer and Paterson speak of a "leadership avoidance reflex,"[6] Franz-Josef Meiers speaks of Germany as a "reluctant power,"[7] Gunter Hellman invokes Bismarck's doctrine of self-limitation,[8] and even former Foreign Minister Klaus Kinkel spoke of the German "culture of restraint."[9]

Privileging agency and the employment of powerful and seductive metaphors to capture the constraints on German power have deflected attention away from third image explanations of Germany's role in Europe and the evolution of the European state system itself. The treatment of Germany as a Gulliver constrained

by its Lilliputian neighbors closes debate over the actual extent of German structural power in Europe and steers the debate towards the dynamic of
multilateralization, or the self-containment of Germany.[10] The Gulliver metaphor
misleads on a number of levels. First, Germany's neighbors were not and are not
Lilliputians; rather Germany has had a leading edge (in terms of GDP) that falls
nonetheless far short of dominance. Second, Germany was willingly constrained
by integrative institutions in the immediate postwar period. What is often forgot-
ten is that Germany, in the early 1950s, surrendered sovereignty that it did not
possess and in exchange gained a symmetrical loss of sovereignty by its partners,
formal equality within multilateral institutions, a leveled diplomatic playing field,
and multilateral cover for the pursuit of narrow German interests. Third, these
analyses "forget" the second third of Swift's classic: Gulliver also visited
Brobdingnag where he was dwarfed just as Germany was dwarfed (and occupied)
by the United States and the Soviet Union. Consequently, Germany as Gulliver
provides an unwarranted exaggeration of German power and an unwarranted diminution of the power of Germany's neighbors.

The reordering of the European state system in 1989 generated fears, concerns,
and hopes that Germany will (or will not) act in a manner commensurate with its
power in post cold war Europe. Regardless of the disposition of the analyst toward
the exercise of German power or the uses to which it should be put, the disjunction
between German capability and German action is located either in agency defined
as self-containment or in structure largely defined in terms of institutional
embeddedness. Moreover, the attendant debate on the normalization of German
power, which is seen as the mechanism relieving the tension between structure and
agency, misses the point about the nature of power and German interests in the
contemporary international system. A consensus would appear to exist that German normalization would be demonstrated by a reversion to the (failed) policy of
exploiting power asymmetries for short-term gains rather than seeking longer-term
contextual or systemic goals; or by German bargaining strategies that leave its
partners unnecessarily aggrieved. Another potential signifier of German normalization is the remilitarization of German foreign policy. The deployment of military
power "out of area" becomes the litmus test of normality, and there is a tendency to
equate Germany's status as a civilian power with the status of an incomplete power.[11]
Some suggest that the transition to a normal power would only be signaled by the
possession of nuclear weapons;[12] and others believe that the changed context of
the European security order has already ended the viability of Germany's role as a
civilian power and demands an adjustment to the new geopolitical context.[13] No
one has yet demonstrated that the deployment of German forces "out of area"
would in fact leverage German power or serve German interests. Arguably, the
changed sources of power and changing nature of the threats to European security
imply that the military instrument has become a second best solution to the challenges facing the European security space.[14]

Structural Power in the Contemporary European System:
Trade, Capital, and Macroeconomic Policy

The role ascribed to Germany by virtue of its power resources usually occupies the ground between dominance and hegemony. François Perroux, for example, generated a theory of the domination effect, which postulates that interstate economic relationships are mediated by a market conditioned by power.[15] The domination effect, which draws on the insights of oligopoly theory, requires an exploitable asymmetry of power that enables the dominant state to exercise "in a dominant field ... an irreversible or partially irreversible influence."[16] Although Perroux generally limits the cases where the domination effect is most likely to emerge to instances of formal occupation, colonialization and totalitarian political organization paralleling the German role in the Danube basin in the 1930s, he allows that the domination effect may also exist in a liberal international economic order. However, in a liberal international economic order, the dominant economy has an interest in and the ability to compel or persuade other states to conform to its economic value system.

This last point focuses attention on the self-interest of a dominant state in creating an economic order that services its interests disproportionately well.[17] The exercise of a Gramscian cultural hegemony legitimates and lowers the costs of hegemonic rule. The successful exercise of cultural hegemony requires a hegemonic state to "develop a world view that appeals to a wide range of other groups within the society, and they must be able to claim with at least some plausibility that their particular interests are those of society at large."[18] The components of the dominant culture that require the consent of the subordinated include the belief, normative, and ideational system that will support and define the existing distribution of goods within the geopolitical space; a legitimate set of institutions that determine how the distribution of goods will occur; and one that demarcates the range of disagreement over the distribution of goods. Key to the exercise of cultural hegemony is the presence of structural power and the threat of coercion.[19] Without structural power neither the domination effect nor cultural hegemony will exist. Does Germany possess the structural power necessary for presence of the one or the exercise of the other? An affirmative or negative response to this question depends upon whether Germany possesses the ability to manipulate meaningfully the channels of economic influence—trade, capital, and money—to construct a more favorable external environment.

National Power and the Structure of Trade

Albert Hirschman's *National Power and the Structure of Trade* is approvingly invoked in many studies of German structural power.[20] This study not only provides a benchmark for comparing the Schachtian system of commerce in the 1930s with Germany's role in central and eastern Europe today, but investigates a chapter of economic history acknowledged by Perroux as illustrative of the domination effect. Hirschman focuses on three measures of power derived from the structure of trade: the trade preference of the dominant country; the trade concentration of the subordinate country; and the commodity composition of trade. Although each measure highlights a different dimension of a bilateral trade relationship and indicates potential levels of dominance and dependence, the most telling is the trade concentration ratios of the subordinate countries.

The trade concentration index, or the Herfindahl-Hirschman index, is designed to capture the extent to which a group of large states achieves oligopolistic or a single large state achieves a monopolistic position in the trading structure of a smaller state.[21] The Herfindahl-Hirschman index has a value that ranges to 100, which would indicate a trade monopoly, and approaches zero with n countries with an equal trade share. The index has three ranges of values that are significant for our purposes. The first range of value is an index less than 34.64. A trade concentration ratio of this magnitude indicates a lack of market concentration and therefore the inability of any state to exercise market power. Likewise, if the index exceeds 42.43 it suggests a structure of trade that is concentrated and provides an opportunity for a state or group of states to exercise market power. And the third range comprises values falling between 34.64 and 42.43. This range of value is considered a gray zone and may or may not provide the potential for the exercise of market power.

In his consideration of trade concentration, Hirschman had two sets of findings.[22] First, he found that in only five of the forty-four countries studied did the concentration of imports exceed the concentration of exports. Since it can be assumed that it is easier for a small country to switch suppliers of goods in the international market than to find alternative markets for home country goods, the interwar experience suggested that Germany (and to a lesser extent the United Kingdom) possessed the market power to affect the terms of trade of central and eastern European (CEE) states with the equivalent of an optimal tariff. Second, he found that there were three categories of small countries in interwar Europe: those countries where Germany was the dominant market for goods (Bulgaria, Hungary, Romania, Yugoslavia, Greece, and Turkey), those countries with dispersed trade (Poland and Czechoslovakia), and those countries facing an Anglo-German duopoly (the Baltic and Scandinavian countries).

Post cold war Europe has a markedly different profile of trade concentration. First, in 1993 75 percent of the nations of central and eastern Europe had an import concentration of trade that exceeded the level of export concentration (nine countries to three), although by 1995 that figure fell to 50 percent (six countries in each category). While it remains true that the economically more significant CEE states now have trade export concentration profiles that make the exercise of oligopsonist power possible, central and eastern Europe as a region remains less susceptible today than in 1938 to the exercise of power or the threat of an optimal tariff by its larger and wealthier western European partners.

This interpretation of the data is supported by a consideration of the export concentration ratios of specific countries. While the exercise of power derived from an oligopoly or monopoly is possible, particularly with respect to a single commodity for which there is no ready alternative producer, it is a remote consideration for the CEE states. There is nothing produced in central and eastern Europe that can not be readily obtained elsewhere; and there are few goods that lack multiple sources of supply in the OECD. What is more relevant in a power political sense is the export dependence of the nations of central and eastern Europe and the ability of Germany to act as a monopsonist or as an oligopsonist with others. The greater a state's dependence upon any single state as a market, the more difficult it would be to break relations with that state or, particularly if the dominant state can easily afford to break those ties, the greater will be the potential for the exercise of structural power.

A state's vulnerability to structural power is dependent upon two variables: a high ratio of exports to GDP, which indicates the vulnerability of the national economy to trade; and a high export concentration ratio. The former measure is not easily summarized across central and eastern Europe. The share of exports in GDP ranges from a low of 12.35 percent (Romania) to a high of 50.97 percent (Estonia). The export to GDP ratios for Hungary and Poland are similar to that of France; while that of the Czech Republic is similar to that of the Netherlands. The export dependence ratios of the other CEE states, excluding the Baltics, do not differ significantly from the range of rates found in the small member-states of the EU. The export-to-GDP ratios suggest some vulnerability to the exploitation of trade asymmetries. Yet there is a marked decline in the level of export concentration of these nations in 1995 as compared to 1938 (see table 13.1).

In 1938, five of eight countries had export concentration ratios that fell either in the gray zone or exceeded the level indicating a high concentration of trade. In 1995, only Slovakia and Ukraine had high export concentration ratios; only the Czech Republic, Poland, and Slovakia fell in the gray zone; and the remainder faced a dispersed export structure. More importantly, Germany was only the primary trading partner for Poland (38.3 percent share), Hungary (28.6 percent share) and Slovenia (30 percent share); Russia was the largest for Latvia (25 percent share) and Ukraine (46 percent share); a duopoly only existed for the Czech Republic (a 35 percent and a 16 percent share for Germany and Slovakia, respectively) and Slovakia (a 35.5 percent and 25 percent share for the Czech Republic and Germany, respectively). The other states—Estonia, Belarus, Bulgaria, Russia, Lithuania—had dispersed structures of trade. Perhaps more telling than a comparison of the trade concentration ratios for 1938 and 1995 is a comparison of export concentration ratios for Canada and Mexico. In 1995, the export concentration ratios for Mexico and Canada were 83.70 and 80.57, respectively. The United States was the primary market for each with a share of 83.63 percent and 80.39 percent, respectively.

Table 13.1. Export Concentration Ratios, 1938 and 1995

<34.64		34.64-42.43	>42.43
		1938	
Romania		Lithuania	Bulgaria
Czechoslovakia			Hungary
Poland			Estonia
			Latvia
		1995	
Bulgaria	Hungary	Poland	Slovakia
Romania	Estonia	Czech Republic	Ukraine
Latvia	Lithuania		
Belarus	Russia		

Sources for 1938: Albert Hirschman, *National Power and the Structure of Trade* (Berkeley and Los Angeles: University of California Press, 1969), 102-03; for 1995: IMF, *Direction of Trade Statistics Yearbook* (Washington, D.C.: International Monetary Fund, 1996), author's own calculations.

While the concentration ratios of Mexico and Canada are not replicated in central and eastern Europe, either in 1995 or 1938, it suggests that some caution should be exercised in speaking of German hegemony exercised through a set of asymmetrical trading relationships in that part of the world

National Power and the Structure of Investment

A second element of power may be located in the structure of direct foreign investment (DFI). The role of capital (and capital flows) is increasingly treated as a structural element of the international system, either as a constraint on state economic policy or as a channel for the discrete exercise of power.[23] The importance of DFI to a national economy varies, and the ability to exploit an asymmetry in an investment position is a function of the depth of national capital markets, the relative scarcity of capital in the target economy, and the ratio of DFI to gross fixed capital formation (GFCF) or to GDP. Markovits and Reich, in particular, suggest that one of the more effective instruments of German influence and proto-hegemony in

Europe is derived from the dominant investment position of German firms in central and eastern Europe. This particular line of argument is potentially attractive owing to shallow financial markets in central and eastern Europe, underdeveloped equity markets, the slow process toward the reform of the banking system, and the absence of an institutional framework facilitating the transformation of savings into investment.[24]

While the structural opportunities exist for exploiting a potential dependence upon DFI in central and eastern Europe, the role of DFI as a share of GDP or GFCF and the subsequent level of external vulnerability varies considerably.[25] Nonetheless, the direct foreign investment ratios for the Czech Republic, Hungary, and Slovenia suggest the potential for a structural asymmetry derived from the role of DFI in the national economy; and the absence of such a potential in Bulgaria, Poland, Romania, and Slovakia. The DFI concentration ratios for direct foreign investment in these and other central and eastern European countries also provide some support for the potential exercise of power in central Europe (see table 13.2).

The DFI concentration ratios for the central and eastern European states generally demonstrate a high level of concentration: the concentration ratio exceeds 40 for the Czech Republic, Slovenia, Bulgaria, and Hungary; and only three states have a relatively low level of concentration (Poland, Romania, and Ukraine). Only four states face a DFI duopoly—Russia, Bulgaria, Slovenia, and Hungary. And of those four states, Germany serves as one-half of the duopoly in only Hungary and Bulgaria. Germany functions as the most important source of capital for Belarus (20 percent share), Bulgaria (38 percent share), the Czech Republic (30 percent share), Hungary (29 percent share), and Slovakia (22 percent share), but its potential market power is neutralized by the countervailing market power of the second most important source of DFI: in Hungary, the United States holds a 24 percent share; in Slovenia, Austria holds a 22 percent share; and in Belarus, Poland holds a 19 percent share. Moreover, the United States is the primary supplier of capital to Poland and Ukraine, the United Kingdom the primary supplier to Latvia, Switzerland the primary supplier to Russia, South Korea the primary supplier to Romania, and Sweden the primary supplier to Lithuania. Only in the Czech Republic and Bulgaria does German capital enjoy a clear margin of dominance. Germany, therefore, while clearly the most important source of DFI for a number of CEE states, only gains a potential source of political leverage in the case of the Czech Republic where foreign capital has an important share of GDP.

National Power and the Macroeconomy

One of the least controversial manifestations of German hegemony in Europe is the success that the German government and Bundesbank have had in exporting German macroeconomic precepts and practices to its European neighbors; and the German ability to set the European interest rate structure.[26] While some skepticism

Table 13.2. DFI Concentration Ratios, 1996

<34.64	34.64-43.43		>43.43
Poland	Czech Republic	Slovakia	Slovenia
Romania	Estonia	Russia	Bulgaria
Ukraine	Hungary	Belarus	

Sources: Urszula Kopec, "Foreign Capital in Central and Eastern Europe," in *Foreign Investments in Poland*, Barbara Durka, ed. (Warsaw: Foreign Trade Research Institute, 1996), 129-49; Dorothy M. Sobol, "Central and Eastern Europe: Financial Markets and Private Capital Flows," *Research Paper #9626* (New York: Federal Reserve Bank of New York, 1996); author's own calculations.

is deserved for arguments that German power in the area of macroeconomic policy has been unwanted[27] or unintended,[28] there is support for the position that German dominance in the European macroeconomy is systemic and linked to the fixing of European exchange rates, the advent of capital mobility in the majority of the EU states, and the anti-inflationary credibility of the Bundesbank.[29] Yet even this modest argument, which is consistent with the expectations of a simple model of the small open economy, is empirically contested.

German macroeconomic power has been classified as ranging from simple predominance to asymmetry to dominance.[30] Some empirical studies support German predominance by detecting a bilateral causality in the structure of EMS interest rates, although interest rate innovations in Germany have a larger impact than do interest innovations undertaken by its partner states.[31] Other empirical studies support German asymmetry. These studies find unilateral causality in the structure of European Monetary System (EMS) interest rates, where causality is located in German interest rate innovations that affect the structure of EMS country interest rates.[32] And some studies support a qualified German dominance where Germany acts as a Stackelberg leader: the unilateral causality characterizing German asymmetry is augmented by the independence of the European interest rate structure from global (specifically American) conditions.[33]

German macroeconomic dominance faces troubling empirical bad news. First, there is evidence of American macroeconomic dominance: American short- and long-interest rates are independent of European or Japanese interest rates; and the structure of American interest rates exerts influence on the structure of European interest rates.[34] This position is joined by another body of literature that finds that German short-term interest rates are determined jointly by the structure of U.S. interest rates, the DM-$ exchange rate, and German domestic variables, including its payment position and foreign reserves.[35]   Second, questions remain about the direction and influence of interest rate innovations, which suggests a fragility in German monetary influence. Edward Gardner and William Perraudin found that in early 1990 France seized a short-lived leadership role in Europe; and Jürgen von Hagen and Michele Fratianni found, more importantly, evidence of a symmetrical causality in the structure of the Dutch-German interest rate structure.[36] The ability of France to seize a leadership role in Europe, albeit for a relatively brief moment in an extraordinary set of circumstances, and the potential for portfolio shifting as other currencies like the Guilder achieve a reputational "hardness" on a par with the DM, suggest a deterioration in the asymmetry of monetary relations within Europe paralleling the deterioration of the asymmetry in monetary relations within the Atlantic economy.

The hegemony thesis in the context of German macroeconomic influence none-theless finds support in two areas: first, the ability of the Germans to write the rules of the monetary game for post-Maastricht Europe; and second, the German suc-cess in convincing its European partners that the independence of central banks from political accountability is a virtue rather than a vice, that price stability is to be prized above any other macroeconomic policy target, and that following German economic precepts will guarantee long-term economic success and societal stabil-ity. The second element supporting German hegemony, however, can be read alter-natively as a response to the seeming failure of Keynesian demand management policies in the postwar period and the economic success of Germany and the United States, countries that both have independent central banking systems.

Unraveling the Paradox of German "Structural Power" and German "Reluctance"

Much of the debate surrounding German power invokes a confrontational logic. The postwar hesitancy to employ German military power outside the narrow com-pass of NATO Europe is interpreted as a political failing rather than as an appropri-ate response to an external environment where a German military contribution would neither yield an improvement in Germany's material interest nor lend a marked advantage or political cover to an American-led coalition. The German reluctance to become party to militarized conflicts should be viewed as a "normal" case of free-riding in an alliance dominated by a benevolent hegemon. More misleading, how-ever, is the conception of Germany as a political dwarf and economic giant, neither of which is completely supported by the empirical or historical record. In other words, Germany does not face the option of either seeking its rightful place as a *Weltmacht* or being consigned to economic wealth conjoined to political dwarfism. Germany, to draw on an indigenous literary metaphor, is neither Alberich nor Siegfried. The debate has largely excluded the middle ground occupied by a conceptualization of Germany as a middle power with a legitimately narrow set of regionally defined interests. There is no compelling reason why any state or Germany in particular should possess the ability to project military power or seek military power in the contemporary European security order. Peace and stability in post cold war Europe are best secured by the economic instruments of statecraft; solutions to the challenges presented by the post cold war order resist a military solution, Bosnia notwithstanding.

The puzzle of German structural power and the "ideology of reluctance" exists only if it can be demonstrated that Germany does in fact possess structural power and that there has been a pattern of reluctance in the exercise of that power. The "ideology of reluctance" rests on at least two assumptions. First, Germany's objective power should have produced a foreign policy agenda—and outcomes—that produced a more favorable external context for German interests and preferences. And second, that Germany has not pressed its interests in key areas of international politics and has abandoned sovereignty to multilateral institutions in the pursuit of what Arnold Wolfers called policies of self-abnegation. Put differently, those who favor the argument that Germany has been a reluctant power must demonstrate that there has been a gap between German power capabilities and German policy objectives. These two assumptions, and the argument suggesting an ideology of reluctance to explain the real and imagined constraints on Germany, face three separate objections.

First, German power and the (in)ability of Germany to achieve its internal or external policy objectives is not adequately captured by recourse to suspect indicators of German power, particularly the German share of European GDP. Rather, what is important is the countervailing power posed against Germany during the postwar period and into the post cold war period. The exercise of German power was curtailed by the presence of Allied troops in Germany, the dependence of Germany upon those troops for its security, and Allied prerogatives attending the postwar occupation. Allied goodwill and a certain subservience to Allied interests was the price to be paid for diplomatic support of German unification. The decontextualization of German power—of treating the European state system as independent from and unencumbered by an international system dominated by the United States and populated by Japan and others—generates an unwarranted gap between German power and expected German ambition and influence.

Second, Germany has not been a reluctant actor in international politics. To argue that Germany has practiced a policy of self-abnegation in the conduct of its foreign policy over the course of the postwar period violates the historical record.[37] While it would be foolish to argue that Germany did not face formidable constraints in the conduct of its foreign policy, particularly in the early postwar years, it is also remarkable how consistently Germany pressed its interests in two of the most important domains of foreign policy: nuclear weapons and macroeconomic policy. Both of these issue areas were core elements of the German foreign policy agenda and for good reason: the disposition and use of nuclear weapons threatened the very existence of Germany; and a stable macroeconomy was viewed as the bedrock of a successful and stable democracy.

The third argument to be marshaled against a German foreign policy dominated by an ideology of reluctance may be located in what Emer Martin called in a different context the lesson of the blind midget: the choice of the yardstick employed for comparison speaks volumes about the expectations held for the subject measured.[38] Nazi Germany is all too often the unspoken yardstick against which postwar Germany is measured. While Germany fares well in comparison to Nazi Germany, the comparison carries with it an expectation that Germany could suddenly go over the edge in its foreign policy ambitions or actions. A more appropriate and demanding yardstick would treat Germany as a status quo power aligned with a global hegemon, rather than as a revisionist power opposed to it. Arguably, the German elite belatedly drew the appropriate lesson from the twin defeats of World Wars I and II. Rather than speaking, therefore, of a reluctant Germany constrained only by an act of will, we should speak of a modified return to Bismarck's "doctrine of self-limitation" which carries with it an implicit understanding and acceptance of the limits of German power.

The countervailing power of the United States and the Soviet Union, the membership in integrative international institutions and the multilateralization of the German foreign policy rhetoric, the constancy of effort in securing German interests in the areas of nuclear command and control as well as in defending the internal and external value of the DM, and the treatment of Germany as a state that has belatedly accepted the limits of its power: these factors portray a Germany that has behaved as something more assertive than a reluctant power and yet more responsible than the antecedent regimes of the Federal Republic.

The convergence of many authors around a domestic explanation of German foreign policy in the post (cold) war period is located in the common assumption that Germany dominates the European economic and political space. While it would be unconstructive to argue that Germany is not an important, or even the most important European state, that rank does not provide Germany with a fungible and exploitable source of structural power, particularly in its relations with France, the United Kingdom, or Italy. Second, neither the structure of trade nor direct foreign investment supports a position of German dominance in Europe. A third problem exists with German dominance of Europe even if there were structural dominance derived from the structure of German trade and financial flows: it is difficult to understand how a German trade and financial monopoly in central and eastern Europe could be translated into tangible power that a German government could exploit. The structure of trade and finance in Europe is derived by a felicitous combination of liberal trade policies and the individual decisions of economic agents independent of government coercion, at least in Germany. If German corporations, traders, and bankers make their decisions to lend, buy, sell or invest based on calculations of profit and loss rather than national prestige or jockeying for geoeconomic or geostrategic position, it is hard to argue convincingly that the

German government derives any fungible power from the decisions of autonomous actors in the economy. Put simply, it is difficult to understand how the state can wield power derived from trade and financial relationships that reflect the decisions of autonomous decision-makers responding to the twin impulses of profit and loss as well as the pressures attending the globalization of the German economy.

In the area of the macroeconomy and exchange rates, however, a case can be made for asymmetrical German influence within Europe. This power is derived from three conditions that are currently met: first, money remains the one commodity that the government can plausibly claim to control; second, the attractiveness of the DM as an alternative to the dollar and yen is derived from the credibility of the Bundesbank for preserving the internal and external value of the mark and the sustained economic performance of the German economy; and third, the continued quasi-fixing of many European currencies to the DM within the exchange rate mechanism of the European Monetary System. But even in this policy domain, German dominance remains problematic. First, the semi-sovereignty of the Federal Republic is derived in part from the political independence of the Bundesbank and its single-minded devotion to price stability.[39] The Bundesbank, while it can wield influence in the pursuit of stable prices, is ill-positioned and disinclined to employ that power for cross-issue linkages; and the federal government cannot credibly offer to do so. All the German government can do is offer to exchange German (pre)dominance in economic policy making in exchange for German subordination in military affairs, a pattern of behavior that emerged in the offset agreements with the United States and has been institutionalized more recently between France and Germany with the establishment of the joint defense and monetary policy councils. Second, German power and influence in this domain will evaporate once its partner states achieve a similar level of stability and economic performance; and Germany itself may be hoisted on its own anti-inflationary petard—the recent decision to increase the repo rate in October 1997 was seen as a step in the realignment of German interest rates with those of its European partners.[40] A third problem confronting German monetary power is located in the necessary collusion of the other European central banks and treasuries required for it to occur. Without relatively fixed rates of exchange and integrated European capital markets, the German ability to act as a Stackelberg leader is short-circuited. And finally, German autonomy and power in Europe depends upon a stable and benign American macroeconomy. Without that external environment, Germany becomes the "antipolar" currency of the dollar, and domestic monetary policy must be conducted to compensate for American mismanagement and the gyrations of the dollar.

Conclusion

As I have shown, the structure-agency problem is particularly acute in any discussion of Germany's role in Europe. It is critical when assessing the impact of Auschwitz

on German foreign policy calculations. The argument has so far privileged structure over agency.

This emphasis on system structure denies agency anything other than a limited
role in explaining the evolution and content of German foreign policy over the
postwar and post cold war period. It would suggest that Auschwitz has played no
appreciable role in the evolution of the European state system or German foreign
policy. While this line of argumentation possesses the virtue of analytical consis-
tency, it is troubling empirically and normatively. While Markovits and Reich draw
attention away from structural and institutional explanations or interpretations of
German foreign policy with their emphasis on the collective historical memory of
Auschwitz, they only capture conceptually half the collective memory relevant to
an analysis of Germany's postwar past and its post cold war future. There are two
historical memories that are relevant to this analysis: the historical memory shared
within a national society that contributes to national identity and the definition of
interest; and the historical memory shared by a society of states that contributes to
collective identity formation and definition of interest.[41] The German collective
memory, particularly as it is relevant to foreign policy ambitions and intentions, is
better captured by the broader metaphor of Weimar.[42] The failure of Weimar is
causally attributed to hyperinflation, political chaos, war, defeat, division,
immiseration, and occupation. Much of German foreign (and domestic) policy may
be read as a preoccupation with avoiding any domestic or international development that could unleash in the Federal Republic the forces that aborted democratic
Weimar and midwifed National Socialist Germany. Auschwitz is certainly the most
shameful chapter in that larger story, but its prominence and emplacement along the
hierarchy of trauma in the German collective memory is dominated by the failure of
Weimar.

The placement of Auschwitz in that same story for Germany's partners and
neighbors is weighted much differently and figures more prominently.[43] Auschwitz
is more than a historical event; it is the metaphor that represents not only the
industrial genocide of European Jewry, Gypsies and others, but the slaughter of
World War II on and off the battlefield. This collective historical memory plays an
important system level role in any assessment of Germany because Auschwitz
forms an important part of the historical context within which we frame our assessments and judgments of German power. Many authors draw what I believe to be the
incorrect inference about the role of Auschwitz in their explanation of the German
"culture of reticence." Some draw attention to former Chancellor Helmut Schmidt's
quip, for example, that the selling of Leopard II tanks to Saudi Arabia (and Germany's
foreign policy in general) should no longer "be held hostage to Auschwitz."[44]
Rather than supporting the metaphor of Auschwitz as a source of reticence, it
suggests instead an external constraint placed on German statecraft that is located
in the historical memory of its neighbors.

Historical context as a variable in our understanding of (German) foreign policy,
identified by Gary Goertz as one of the three substantive contexts relevant to the

study of international relations, simply underlines the importance of history in understanding how states interact.[45] While Goertz focuses on the notion of path dependency to explain how history matters, in the German case Auschwitz represents a case where the past functions as a powerful prism through which we interpret German intentions, ambitions, and capabilities. Only recourse to a common historical memory (and identity in opposition to Germany) can explain for example the differentiated treatment of France and Britain as compared to Germany on the nuclear question: while many dismiss the British and French nuclear deterrents as the unnecessary, bothersome, and generally harmless accoutrements of fading European powers, a German nuclear deterrent is treated by most as a potential threat to European stability and a harbinger of the apocalypse. Thus Auschwitz as a system level context contributes to the oftentimes unwarranted exaggeration of German power in the contemporary international system.

German policy options are constrained by the common historical memory of Auschwitz and the war. The weight and meaning given to the various elements of German power are filtered through that historical prism; and perhaps more importantly it provides the frame of reference employed to assess (or attribute) German intentions and ambitions associated with the exercise of German power in the new Europe. A focus on collective historical memory at the system level better explains the containment of Germany in the postwar and post cold war period than a second-image emphasis on self-restraint. The limitations on the exercise of German power reflect the twin external constraints of countervailing power and the collective memories of Auschwitz. The Berlin Republic will remain constrained not only by the structure of material power in the international system, but by the unwillingness and inability of its European partner states to forget the past harvests of German power.

Notes

I would like to thank Mary Hampton, Michael Huelshoff, Peter Katzenstein, Emil Kirchner, Andy Markovits, and Christian Søe for generous and constructive comments on an earlier version of this chapter. The usual disclaimers apply.

1. Gunther Hellman, "Goodbye Bismarck? The Foreign Policy of Contemporary Germany," *Mershon International Studies Review* 40, supplement 1 (April 1996): 1-39. See also John S. Duffield, *World Power Forsaken: Political Culture, International Institutions, and German Security Policy after Unification* (Stanford: Stanford University Press, 1998).

2. Christopher Coker, "At the Birth of the Fourth Reich? The British Reaction," *The Political Quarterly* 61, no. 3 (July-September 1990): 278-84.

3. Simon Bulmer, "Germany and European Integration," in *Germany and the European Community: Beyond Hegemony and Containment?*, Carl F. Lankowski,

ed. (New York: St. Martin's Press, 1993), 73-100; and Simon Bulmer and William E. Paterson, "Germany in the European Union: gentle giant or emergent leader?" *International Affairs* 72, no. 1 (January 1996): 9-32.

4. Andrei S. Markovits and Simon Reich, "Should Europe Fear the Germans?" in *From Bundesrepublik to Deutschland: German Politics after Unification*, Michael Huelshoff, Andrei S. Markovits, and Simon Reich, eds. (Ann Arbor: Michigan University Press, 1983), 271-90.

5. Andrei S. Markovits and Simon Reich, *The German Predicament: Memory and Power in the New Europe* (Ithaca: Cornell University Press, 1997).

6. Bulmer and Paterson, "Germany in the European Union."

7. Franz Josef-Meiers, "Germany: The Reluctant Power," *Survival* 37, no. 3 (Autumn 1995): 82-103.

8. Hellman, "Goodbye Bismarck?"

9. Foreign Minister Klaus Kinkel cited in Meiers, "Germany: The Reluctant Power," 85.

10. Simon Bulmer and William E. Paterson, "West Germany's Role in Europe: 'Man Mountain' or 'Semi-Gulliver'," *Journal of Common Market Studies* 28, no. 2 (December 1989): 95-117.

11. For a specific equation of the two, see Meiers, "Germany: The Reluctant Power," 84.

12. See David Garnham, "Extending Deterrence with German Nuclear Weapons," *International Security* 10, no. 1 (Summer 1985): 96-110; and John Mearsheimer, "Back to the Future: Instability in Europe After the Cold War," *International Security* 15, no. 1 (Summer 1990): 5-56.

13. See Mary McKenzie, "Competing Conceptions of Normality in the Post-Cold War Era: Germany, Europe, and Foreign Policy Change," *German Politics and Society* 14, no. 2 (Summer 1996): 12.

14. See James Sperling and Emil Kirchner, *Recasting the European Order: Security Architectures and Economic Cooperation* (Manchester: Manchester University Press 1997); and "The Security Architectures and Institutional Futures of Post-1989 Europe," *Journal of European Public Policy* 4, no. 2 (June 1997): 155-70.

15. François Perroux, "The Domination Effect and Modern Economic Theory," *Social Research* 17, no. 1 (June 1950): 188-206.

16. The domination effect itself is a function of three elements: the relative power position of the state, defined in terms of market power; the bargaining power possessed by the state that allows it to fix the conditions of exchange; and the strategic placement of the state enabling it to exploit the existing asymmetries of power, a function that is intended to capture advantages accruing to the state owing to the character of its domestic political-economic organization. See Perroux, "The Domination Effect," 189. In this chapter, I will only focus on the first element, which bears directly on the potential for the exercise of dominant power by Germany.

17. See Robert Gilpin, *War and Change in World Politics* (Princeton: Princeton

University Press, 1981).

18. T. J. Jackson Lears, "The Concept of Cultural Hegemony: Problems and Possibilities," *American Historical Review* 90, no. 3 (June 1985): 571.

19. Lears, "Cultural Hegemony," 568.

20. Albert Hirschman, *National Power and the Structure of Foreign Trade* (Berkeley and Los Angeles: University of California Press, 1969).

21. Hirschman, *National Power*, 98-101.

22. Hirschman, *National Power*, 101-11

23. On capital mobility forming a structural constraint on state autonomy, see David Andrews, "Capital Mobility and State Autonomy: Toward a Structural Theory of International Monetary Relations," *International Studies Quarterly* 38, no. 2 (June 1994): 193-218; and on the discrete use of monetary power, see Jonathan Kirshner, *Currency and Coercion: The Political Economy of International Monetary Power* (Princeton: Princeton University Press, 1995), 115-70.

24. See Ronald W. Anderson, Erik Berglöf, and Kálmán Mizsei, *Banking Sector Development in Central and Eastern Europe*, Forum Report of the Economic Policy Initiative no. 1 (London: Centre for Economic Policy Research, 1996), 28-30 and 34-9; and Michael Huelshoff, "CEE Financial Reform, European Monetary Union, and Eastern Enlargement," in *Two Tiers or Two Speeds? The European Security Order and the Enlargement of the European Union and NATO,* James Sperling, ed. (Manchester: Manchester University Press, forthcoming).

25. The ratio of GDP:DFI presented in the text may exaggerate the role of DFI in the national economies of these states. The ratios for the CEE states range from a high of 4.5 percent in Hungary to a low of .05 percent in Romania according to European Bank for Reconstruction and Development statistics cited in the *Economist* (1 November 1997, 108). This lower range would simply qualify further the leverage that Germany could possibly derive from its investment position in those states.

26. See Jérôme Henry and Jens Weidmann, "German Unification and Asymmetry in the ERM: Comment on Gardner and Perraudin," *IMF Staff Papers* 42, no. 4 (December 1995): 894-902.

27. Norbert Kloten cited in Jürgen von Hagen and Michele Fratianni, "German Dominance in the EMS: Evidence from Interest Rates," *Journal of International Money and Finance* 9, no. 4 (December 1990): 361.

28. Bulmer and Paterson, "Germany in the European Union," 31.

29. See Francesco Giavazzi and Marco Pagano, "The Advantage of Tying One's Hands: EMS Discipline and Central Bank Credibility," *European Economic Review* 32, no. 5 (June 1988): 1055-82; Charles Wyplosz, "Asymmetry in the EMS: Intentional or Systemic?" *European Economic Review* 33, no. 2/3 (March 1989): 310-20; Bernard Herz and Werner Röger, "The EMS Is a Greater Deutschmark Area," *European Economic Review* 36, no. 7 (October 1992): 1413-25; and David Currie, Paul Levine, and Joseph Pearlman, "European Monetary Union or Hard EMS?," *European Economic Review* 36, no. 6 (August 1992): 1185-204.

30. Henry and Weidman, "Comment on Gardner and Perraudin," 894-95, fn. 1.

31. See Edward H. Gardner and William R. M. Perraudin, "Asymmetry in the ERM: A Case Study of French and German Interest Rates before and after German Unification," *IMF Staff Papers* 40, no. 2 (June 1993): 427-50; von Hagen and Fratianni, "German Dominance."

32. Henry and Weidman, "Comments on Gardner and Perraudin"; Michael J. Artus and Dilip Nachane, "Wages and Prices in Europe: A Test of the German Leadership Thesis," *Weltwirtschaftliches Archiv* 126, no. 1 (1990): 59-77; and Hans-Dieter Smeets, "Does Germany Dominate the EMS?," *Journal of Common Market Studies* 29, no. 1 (September 1990): 37-52.

33. Henry and Weidmann, in "Comments on Gardner and Perraudin" find such a relationship only for the period 1991-93; and Herz and Röger, in "The EMS in the Greater Deutschmark Area," find such a relationship only for Denmark, France, Ireland and the Netherlands.

34. See Deutsche Bundesbank, "Die Bedeutung inernationaler Einflüsse für die Zinsentwicklung am Kapitalmarkt," *Monatsbericht* 49, no. 7 (July 1997): 34; and Deutsche Bundesbank, "Capital Market Rate Movements since the Beginning of the Nineties," *Monthly Report* 48, no. 11 (November 1996): 25.

35. See Bundesbank, "Die Bedeutung internationaler Einflüsse"; Bundesbank "Capital Market Rate Movements"; Michael J. Artus, S. Avouyi-Dovi, E. Bleuze and F. Lecointe, "Transmission of US Monetary Policy to Europe and Asymmetry in the European Monetary System," *European Economic Review* 35, no. 7 (October 1991):1369-84; Smeets, "Does Germany Dominate"; and Gardner and Perraudin, "Asymmetry in the ERM."

36. Gardner and Perraudin,"Asymmetry in the ERM," 446; von Hagen and Fratianni, "German Dominance in the EMS," 374 fn.

37. See Mary Hampton, *The Wilsonian Impulse: U.S. Foreign Policy, the Alliance, and German Unification* (New York: Praeger, 1996); and Wolfram F. Hanrieder, *Deutschland, Europa, Amerika: Die Außenpolitik der Bundesrepublik Deutschland, 1949-1994* (Paderborn: Ferdinand Schöningh, 1995).

38. Emer Martin, *Breakfast in Babylon* (New York: Houghton and Mifflin, 1995), 196.

39. On Germany as a semi-sovereign state, see Peter Katzenstein, *Policy and Politics in Germany: The Growth of a Semi-Sovereign State* (Philadelphia: Temple University Press, 1987).

40. *New York Times,* 10 October 1997, 1. The Central Bank Council of the Bundesbank explained the rise in the repo rate in terms of the weakening of the external value of the DM, the historically low levels of interest rates since the summer of 1996, and the need to "prevent the build-up of inflation potential in the run-up to European monetary union." Deutsche Bundesbank, "Decision on Interest Rate Rise of October 9, 1997," *Monthly Report* 49, no. 10 (October 1997): 17.

41. On the interaction between the definitions of interest and of identity, see Alexander Wendt, "Collective Identity Formation and the International State," *American Political Science Review* 88, no. 2 (June 1994): 384-96.

42. Weimar overshadows Auschwitz, for example, in Barthold Witte, "Two Catastrophes, Two Causes, and How the Germans Dealt with Them," *Daedalus* 123, no. 1 (Winter 1994): 235-49.

43. See the contributions to Dirk Verheyen and Christian Søe, eds, *The Germans and Their Neighbors* (Boulder, Colo.: Westview Press, 1993).

44. Cited in Jeffrey K. Olick, "What Does It Mean to Normalize the Past? Official Memory in German Politics since 1989," *Social Science History* 22, no. 4 (Winter 1998): 570.

45. Gary Goertz, *Contexts of International Politics* (Cambridge: Cambridge University Press, 1994).

Index

About the Editors and Contributors

Gerard Braunthal is professor emeritus of political science at the University of Massachusetts, Amherst. He has written extensively on German political parties, interest groups, and civil liberties. His latest books include *Political Loyalty and Public Service in West Germany* (1990), *The German Social Democrats Since 1969* (1994), and *Parties and Politics in Modern Germany* (1996).

Clay Clemens teaches government at the College of William and Mary. He is co-editor, with William Paterson, of *The Kohl Chancellorship* (1998) and author of *Reluctant Realists: The CDU/CSU and West German Ostpolitik* (1989). His articles have appeared in *West European Politics*, *German Politics*, *German Politics and Society*, and *International Affairs*.

Irwin Collier is professor of economics in the Faculty of Business and Economics of the *Freie Universität Berlin*, where he teaches the economics of social policy. In addition to his interests in the issues of welfare state reform, he has followed closely the economic reconstruction of the new states of Germany. He is co-editor of the recently published book, *Welfare States in Transition: East and West* (1999).

Andrew B. Denison has lived in Bonn, Germany, since 1991. His Ph.D. dissertation dealt with the SPD and European security (SAIS, Johns Hopkins University, 1995). He has worked as an independent political consultant and with the Institute for Strategic Analyses and the Marshall Center (Garmisch). He is a faculty associate in political science at the University of Bonn.

E. Gene Frankland is professor of political science at Ball State University. His primary teaching and research interests are comparative politics and environmental law and policy. He has written scholarly articles on parliamentary recruitment, political socialization, and the green parties of Germany, Britain and Austria. He co-authored with Donald Schoonmaker *Between Protest and Power: The Green Party in Germany* (1992). He is currently co-editing with John Barry *The International Encyclopedia of Environmental Politics* (forthcoming 2001).

Mary N. Hampton is associate professor of political science at the University of Utah. Her research interests include international security and German and American foreign policy. She is author of *The Wilsonian Impulse* (1996). Her recent articles include "NATO, Germany, and the United States: Creating Positive Identity in Trans-Atlantia."

Christoph Hanterman completed his Ph.D. in political science with a dissertation on the FDP and German foreign policy (the University of California at Santa Barbara, 1996). He teaches at Ventura College and is research director at the Nuclear Age Peace Foundation in Santa Barbara.

Michael G. Huelshoff is associate professor in political science at the University of New Orleans. He does research and has published extensively on German political economy topics as well as EU policy making. He is co-editor of the book, *From Bundesrepublik to Deutschland: German Politics After Unification* (1993).

David M. Keithly teaches at National Defense University. He has twice been a Fullbright Fellow and now serves on the executive board of the Fullbright Association. His several books and more than fifty articles in professional journals include studies that deal with economic and security aspects of German politics.

Gerald R. Kleinfeld is professor of history at Arizona State University and Executive Director of the German Studies Association. His research and publications include many articles on German-American relations as well as on German political and social developments, among them studies of the PDS. He is one of the editors and authors of the *Yearbook on German-American Relations, Germany's New Politics* (1995), and the forthcoming *Power Shift in Germany (1999)*.

Dieter Roth is co-director of the Mannheim Electoral Research Group (*Forschungsgruppe Wahlen*), co-host of the monthly *Politbarometer* on the Second German Television Channel (ZDF), and professor at the University of Heidelberg. He has written extensively on German electoral and party developments, based on the Mannheim institute's extensive public opinion surveys. His publications include *Empirische Wahlforschung* (1998), and he is co-editor with Wilhelm Bürklin of *Das Superwahljahr* (1994).

Christian Søe is professor of political science at California State University in Long Beach. He is editor of the annually revised *Comparative Politics* (seventeen editions) and writes on German party politics, with special attention to the FDP. He is one of the editors and authors of *The Germans and Their Neighbors* (1993), *Germany's New Politics* (1995), and the forthcoming *Power Shift in Germany* (1999).

James Sperling is professor of political science at the University of Akron. He is editor of *Two Tiers or Two Speeds? The European Security Order and the Enlargement of EU and NATO* (1999) and co-author of *Recasting the European Order: Security Architectures and Economic Cooperation* (1997).

Andreas Wüst is lecturer in political science at the University of Heidelberg and works as a scientific freelancer on projects for the Mannheim Electoral Research Group (*Forrschungsgruppe Wahlen*). He is author of articles, chapters and reports on survey methodology, electoral research and voting behavior.